LETTERS FROM RING

EDITED BY CLIFFORD M. CARUTHERS

© 1979 by Walden Press
ISBN 0-91193-808-7 (Cloth) $10.95s
ISBN 0-91193-809-5 (Paper) $6.95s

Printed in the United States of America

FOREWORD

My father was not a frugal man but he must have saved a few thousand dollars on carbon paper during his professional career. The story has been told many times of how the first collection of his short stories had to be assembled by copying them from old magazines in a library. It would have been even more out of character for him to keep copies of his own letters. Prudent people generally make carbons or photocopies nowadays, of at least their important business letters, filing them away against tax audits and other contingencies. There were no files in my father's workroom.

He received a good deal of mail every day and he read it all except the junk mail. Some of it gave him material for his daily column in the Chicago TRIBUNE and later his weekly nationally syndicated feature. He tried to answer most of the requests for advice from aspiring writers, even the most pathetic ones; only after illness made sitting at the typewriter an ordeal did he begin to delegate some of these chores to my brother John when John was around to perform them. Always a family man, he kept in close touch with his relatives in the Middle West, especially his sister Anne Tobin and her family. He wrote separate letters to as many as three sons away at school at the same time; only in the last couple of years when he was addressing four of them plus a nephew did he resort to a "round robin" to cover us all with the same effort.

He also wrote letters to and in behalf of a number of comparatively obscure friends from his home town and the early Chicago years. And he carried on intermittent correspondence with some of the most famous names in literary and theatrical circles of his day. The mail from both these groups suffered the same fate. Letters from Mencken and Nathan, Kaufman and Woollcott, Laurette Taylor and Claudette Colbert, all went as inexorably into the wastebasket as those with no autograph value. Not one letter was saved from Scott Fitzgerald's side of the most prolific and sustained correspondence Ring Lardner ever conducted outside the family.

Most of the recipients of his letters, including his sons, were not much better than he was about keeping them. His publishers kept theirs, of course, in designated file folders, and so did a critic and literary historian, Burton Rascoe. Scott, who preserved report cards and prom programs, held on to all of his. My mother didn't quite match that percentage, especially during the first couple of years, but she saved so many that in number and length they formed the overwhelming bulk of the material available to Dr. Caruthers.

Thus a comprehensive or even a truly representative collection of Lardner letters could not be achieved. On the other hand, that's a practical goal only with a man who made and kept copies of all his personal letters. When a writer does that you have to suspect that he wrote them with posterity as well as the recipient in his mind. One thing you can be sure of in my father's case is that he didn't dream you or any other third party would ever read these words of his. It never even occurred to him, when he started selling short stories, that they would survive their issues of the SATURDAY EVENING POST.

                                        - Ring Lardner, Jr.

INTRODUCTION

Ring Lardner first emerged from the obscurity of ordinary
journalism through his witty, incisive analyses of Chicago White
Sox and Cubs baseball. Through this involvement with the game
and its players he developed his "philological" ear for American
dialects which resulted in his unique "Pullman Pastimes" and "In
the Wake of the News" columns, and by 1914 in the immortal
"busher" stories of that period. All together, he did not write
much fiction--only a little over a hundred stories--but they are
enough to establish him as a major author of this period, along
with Fitzgerald, Hemingway, Anderson, Lewis, and Wolfe. As a
maker of plots he was the least innovative of this group, but in
the best of his narratives he created characters with more
accuracy and vividness than any of them. No dialogue of any
other 20th century American fictionist, even Hemingway, has been
so widely imitated as has that of Ring Lardner's fictional world.
But it was not primarily his fiction that made him
famous--though his largest collection of short stories, ROUND UP,
sold over eighty thousand copies in 1929. By 1923, when Ring was
in his fourth year of writing a nationwide weekly column of humor
and satire for the Bell Syndicate, the name of Lardner was a
household word, one of the ten best known names in the country.
And though he played the role of the half-educated midwestern
provincial, to the extent that even his close friend Scott
Fitzgerald believed that the scope of his world was limited to
the confines of the baseball diamond, he saw with intense, often
depressing accuracy the foibles and limitations of the
middle-class American lowbrow. In most of his writing, however,
both fictional and journalistic, Ring either used a persona or he
wrote with such dispassionate objectivity that he managed to
reveal less of himself in his work than did any other major
American writer of the 1920's.
Thus the publication of his major correspondence is
especially significant in providing us with considerable insight
into his sensibilities, and, incidentally, in correcting Clifton
Fadiman's frequently echoed assessment that Lardner's fiction was
the expression of a burning misanthropy which eventually
destroyed him. Ring's letters reveal, among other things, that
while he deplored the egotism, greed, and dishonesty which he
depicted in his fiction as widespread and frequently pervasive,
he was never, ever, a misanthrope.
The letters, written over a period from 1907, when he was 22,
up to his death at the age of 48 in 1933, reveal Ring first as a
devoted suitor for a woman he always felt was above him; then as
a young sports writer, covering primarily the Chicago baseball

world; then as a columnist accepting the challenge of writing a daily article of mainly sport-oriented humor for the Chicago TRIBUNE at a little less than three thousand dollars a year; next, after a move to New York, as a nationally syndicated columnist whose work appeared in over 150 newspapers across the country from 1919 through part of 1927 (during which time he earned up to $30,000 a year from the column alone); secondarily from 1914 on as a short story writer (he appears never to have considered himself primarily a writer of fiction); and finally as a playwright and lyricist of popular songs (always one of his first loves). Lardner's record is one of amazing versatility.

It is of course his close relationships with other people, revealed in some depth in these letters, through which we learn more about Ring's values. Nearly half the letters contained in this volume are courtship letters written to his future wife Ellis Abbott over a four year period before they were married in 1911. Their correspondence provides a nostalgic insight into the manners and conventions of a time quite different from 1976. The courtship is nearly unique in the degree to which it is literary; only once during the entire four years were Ring and Ellis in close proximity for any sustained length of time--and then only for a few weeks. But he did court her, with an eloquence far beyond that of the ordinary love letter, while Ellis played the roles required of a beautiful, intelligent young woman of considerable social and economic standing in Goshen, Indiana, in the first decade of the 20th century. Taken together, these courtship letters also depict for us the initial saga of a young man, who in 1907 had already been dismissed from five of the thirteen positions he had held since high school, discovering himself by 1911 as a newspaper writer who had begun to see his world with considerable distance and increasing clarity, while he remained morally and philosophically a person of his own time and place.

Relationships with publishers are also exhibited in a number of letters to Hewitt H. Howland of Bobbs-Merrill and, later, to Maxwell Perkins of Scribners. They form an excellent contrast, for Lardner's relationship with Bobbs-Merrill was moderately profitable but, though professional, not particularly stimulating, while Perkins' praise probably did evoke more fiction from Ring than he might otherwise have written. Ring had a special respect for the judgment of the man who shepherded Scribner's coterie of such famous writers as Fitzgerald, Hemingway, Wolfe, Stark Young, Struthers Burt, James Boyd, S. S. Van Dine, Marjorie Rawlings, Conrad Aiken, Christine Weston, Will James, and Arthur Train. It was Perkins, at Fitzgerald's urging, who convinced Charles Scribner that a "slangy sports writer" ought to be included among Scribner's authors. The correspondence with both editors also reveals the problems which arose in a time when fiction customarily was published in magazines before it was collected in book form. Though Lardner did unquestionably set high standards of accuracy and technical perfection for whatever he wrote, he seems to have cared little

about his material once it was sold to a publisher. He rarely
kept copies of his manuscripts (Perkins had to obtain back copies
or photostats of the magazines in which Ring's stories had
appeared in order to put together HOW TO WRITE SHORT STORIES) or
even his books, though magazines paid him as much as $4500 a
story, a top price in those days. Clearly Ring wrote for money
(and he was highly successful at it), but both the fiction and
the newspaper pieces which he wrote under the pressure of
deadlines regularly achieve a high level of quality.

Perhaps the most fascinating letters in this collection are
the ones written to Scott and Zelda Fitzgerald, mostly while the
Fitzgeralds were in France. From October 1922, when the
Fitzgeralds became the Lardners' neighbors in Great Neck, Long
Island, Scott and Ring were close friends and heavy drinking
companions, and it was Fitzgerald who brought Ring to the
attention of Scribner's, much as he later did Ernest Hemingway.
Fitzgerald was probably Ring's greatest admirer, though he always
felt, erroneously, that Ring limited himself in focusing in his
fiction on the semi-literate American middle-class "boob." Ring's
letters to Fitzgerald are fascinating not only because of the
intimate glimpses they provide of famous literary people but also
because Ring continually attempted to provide Scott with all the
gossip, some of it rather sensational, about happenings in the
New York social world of the mid-twenties.

Among other famous people to whom Lardner wrote were H. L.
Mencken, Burton Rascoe, Theodore Dreiser, George S. Kaufman, and
Grantland Rice. Unfortunately, all the letters to Kaufman, with
whom Ring collaborated so effectively on JUNE MOON, are now lost.
But there is substantial extant correspondence with the others.
Mencken was one of the first to praise Ring's fiction, and the
two thought alike on many issues. Rascoe was a good friend from
Ring's early days on the TRIBUNE. On the other hand, Ring could
not have thought highly of Dreiser's writing because of the
imprecision of Dreiser's diction. The brief exchange of
correspondence in early 1932 between the two resulted from Ring's
reportedly having termed Dreiser "the prince of bad writers,"
though Ring vigorously denied having used the phrase. Grantland
Rice, whom Ring had known since Ring's earliest days as a Chicago
sports reporter, was probably Ring's closest friend. They were
contrasts in temperament, since Rice was ebullient and positive
about the sports world while Ring was an analytical critic, but
they shared the same interests, took family vacations together,
and eventually became next-door neighbors in East Hampton.
Ring's letters to him are family letters, because he and Ellis
were also devoted to Kate Rice, to her mother and sisters, and to
the Rices' daughter Florence.

The portrait we develop from these letters is neither that of
a "half-educated midwestern sportswriter" nor of a bitter hater
of mankind. Yet Ring was to a significant degree a disillusioned
man. Though he was always devoted to Ellis and his children, his
marriage could not possibly have measured up to the idyllic
proportions he imagined repeatedly in his love letters, and he

must have blamed himself for the disparity. He had believed
totally the myth that marriage to the right woman guaranteed
complete reformation, but though he did marry her, he was never
able to stop smoking or drinking, and those habits did eventually
contribute heavily to his ill health after 1926, and to a
relatively early death. His later letters to Ellis and to his
four sons are letters of absolute devotion; yet he must have
felt--in the light of those irrational early ideals--that he was
at least a partial failure as a husband and a father. Still, he
took much satisfaction from his family, and from his work, for he
was highly successful in three different professions--as a
journalist, as a fictionist, and, with JUNE MOON, as a
playwright. And he had always loved to write song lyrics--even
for Florenz Ziegfeld (whom he disliked)--though he once wrote
that membership in the Lyric Writers Union was "limited to boys
and girls who graduated from school at the age of three." He had
no faith that virtue and human sympathy would be rewarded in
kind. In his fiction generally they are not, and Stephen Gale,
the frustrated versifier and gas company bookkeeper of "The
Maysville Minstrel" speaks for Ring when he realizes after the
cruelty of Charley Roberts' deception that "there was nothing he
could do about it." But Ring never gave up. In the months
preceding his death, on 25 September 1933, he was working at his
home, and he had written an act and a scene of a play on which he
hoped to collaborate again with Kaufman. He had spent time in
the West on his doctors' advice, in attempts to regain his
health, but he was growing weaker, and when he returned to East
Hampton for the last summer, he must have known that he would
never write the longer fictional work which Perkins had urged.
Yet he faced death courageously, by going on with his life and
his work as long as he could.

Ultimately, what this correspondence achieves is the
reinforcement of what many have felt was true of Ring
Lardner--that in addition to being a great writer he was
essentially a "healthy" person, who deplored dishonesty and
self-deception, and who responded warmly to others who struggled
to see clearly amid a world of hostile or indifferent values.

- C. M. C.

EDITORIAL PREFACE

In selecting and editing the major correspondence of Ring Lardner, primary objectives have been to include letters of informational value and to achieve as much continuity and balance in the correspondence as possible. Since the number of extant courtship letters is much greater (and the content more repetitious) than the number of surviving later letters, many more of the early letters have been omitted. Faithful transcription of the letters has been a goal insofar as it was practicable, but in order to provide for greater readability, the author's directions have been silently followed by omitting words crossed out, by inserting without notation words marked for insertion, and by following superimposed corrections without note. Spelling and punctuation have been reproduced with two exceptions: Lardner's placing of commas and periods either inside or outside quotation marks has been rendered consistent to minimize distraction from content. His irregular spacing between words (most of his letters, except for the courtship letters and other early letters to Ellis Abbott's family, are typed) has necessarily been altered to achieve regular page margins for the printed text. Ring's signatures have been included (in type), because frequently they indicate the degree of intimacy with the recipient. Printed stationery headings, or portions of them, have been included where they seemed to be of interest. In instances where letters were not fully dated, postmark dates on envelopes or dates derived from the content have been provided in brackets. Substantial interstitial commentary has been provided for needed transitions or to amplify the subjects at hand. Such commentary appears in 55-character lines; letters to Ring and other lengthy quotations appear in 51-character lines; and the letters by Ring are printed in full 65-character lines. Explanatory footnotes appear at the bottoms of pages.

For continuity and balance, a few of the more important letters to Maxwell Perkins which appeared in RING AROUND MAX have also been included in this volume.

ACKNOWLEDGEMENTS

I wish to thank Ring Lardner, Jr. not only for permission to edit the Lardner letters for publication but also for invaluable information and other assistance. I am also especially grateful to Diane Haskell of the Newberry Library for her efficient cooperation in making available and copying needed manuscripts. Other helpful sources have included Mrs. Montgomery Ostrander; Richard Lardner Tobin; Mrs. Scottie Smith; the New York Public Library (H. L. Mencken Papers, R. H. Davis Papers, Manuscripts and Archives Division, Astor, Lenox and Tilden Foundations); the Lilly Library of Indiana University at Bloomington; Princeton University Library; the Enoch Pratt Free Library of Baltimore, Maryland; the Historical Society of Pennsylvania; the William R. Perkins Library at Duke University; Charles Scribner's Sons; Bobbs-Merrill Company; Doubleday and Company; the Purdue University Libraries; the Academic Center Library of the University of Texas at Austin; the University of Washington Library at Seattle; the Charles Patterson Van Pelt Library at the University of Pennsylvania; Mrs. John N. Wheeler; the Chicago Historical Society; Matthew Bruccoli; and Bert Luth. Gay Davidson assisted ably in library research, and Dorothea Center accomplished much of the early computer typing with admirable speed and accuracy.

Finally, I wish to acknowledge my wife Linda's invaluable assistance in the selection of these letters and the compilation of the index.

CONTENTS

1907-1911:

THE COURTSHIP YEARS

Most of the surviving letters Ring Lardner wrote prior to 1911 are courtship letters to his future wife, Ellis Abbott. The two met in July, 1907, during a marshmallow roast at the home of Ring's friend Billy Beeson on the St. Joseph River in Niles, Michigan, Ring's home town. They were probably introduced by Wilma Johnson, a friend of Ellis's whom Ellis was visiting (and Ring was dating) at the time. Ring was so impressed that he appears to have devoted a good deal of time to her that summer, and then initiated a correspondence that fall which continued until their marriage nearly four years later. At the time of this first meeting Ring was still working on his first newspaper job, as a reporter for the South Bend TIMES. Ellis, the daughter of a wealthy lumber merchant in nearby Goshen, Indiana, was at the time enjoying a summer vacation from Smith College, located in Northampton, Massachusetts, before beginning her junior year that fall. From the first she obviously enjoyed Ring's attention and found him a witty if somewhat daunting correspondent.

In 1907 Ring was twenty-two, six feet two inches tall and somewhat self-consciously stoop-shouldered because of his (for that time) exceptional height, lean and rather dark-complexioned, with black hair and brown eyes (noting the prominence of his eyes, some of his baseball friends later nicknamed him "Old Owl Eyes"). In his recent book THE LARDNERS: MY FAMILY REMEMBERED, Ring, Jr. (Ring's only surviving son) also describes Ring's eyes as "gentle and unusually large, with heavy dark brows, his nose so impressively aquiline that when Bob Davis, a well-known columnist and photographer of the twenties did a portrait of him, he captioned it 'the look of eagles.' Most descriptions of him emphasize that he was never seen to laugh; what is literally true is that he never laughed at his own jokes and he applied high standards to other people's comedy. But he did laugh at people who amused him." Ring, Jr. describes Ellis, on the other hand, as "a full foot shorter, small-waisted, wide-hipped, medium-breasted. Her hair was brown, her eyes blue, her complexion light. She had a small, straight nose and a full mouth . . . . She laughed easily and her voice had a vibrant quality that added interest to whatever she said. Intended or not, she had a smile and a way of walking that men found provocative."[1]

Their correspondence which follows is truly remarkable not only for what it reveals about Ring (and Ellis) Lardner but for its reflection of the conventions of a departed era. Ring was attracted to Ellis at first sight, and wrote to her frequently thereafter (nearly every day for the last year and a half before the marriage), usually managing some element of wit which elevates his letters considerably above those of the ordinary courtship. These letters reflect roles which young lovers felt compelled to play in the first decade of the twentieth century that were far more demanding and restrictive than those required of the nineteen-seventies.

After indulging in some humorous puns on two postcards to Ellis earlier that fall, Ring wrote the following letter to her in Northampton, recalling in poetry their meetings during the previous July and August. Significantly, Ring refers to her in this first letter as "my affinity." The nickname "Rabbits" by which he addresses her is of course a pun upon her name, as his frequent signature "Ringlets" is a pun upon his own. Ring, Jr. suggests that "Ringlets" may also have "an ironic quality in view of the fact that he started to lose his hair early--to a considerable extent by the time of his marriage at twenty-six."[2]

South Bend, Third Thursday
[3 October 1907]

Dear Rabbits, listen carefully to what I say to you:
Now, postal cards are all too brief from Ringling's
    point of view;
I met young Ellis Abbott on a warm night in July,
'Twas at a fine marshmallow roast, the St. Joe river by,
The first time that I cast my eyes upon young Ellis fair,
I thought: "It's my affinity who's seated over there
But she and I exchanged few words 'til the next
    Saturday
When she arrived in old South Bend, to see Grand
    Rapids play.

----

[1]Ring Lardner, Jr., THE LARDNERS: MY FAMILY REMEMBERED (New York: Harper and Row, 1976), pp. 38-39.

[2]Ring Lardner, Jr., p. 37.

Next evening, it was Sunday, Sabbath calm was over all,
My brother Rex and I at Johnson's paid a friendly call,
But Billy B., right there was he, and I regret to tell
I didn't get a chance to know young Ellis very well.
A few weeks passed and then, at last, at the M. C.
   day-poe
I saw her jump from off a train, which Eastward then
   would go.
On my way home I purposely walked slowly and with ease
In hopes that I might get a chance to chat with Eloise.
The chance, it came, and that same eve I bore her
   gripsack down
Until we reached the Ginseng house - they live quite
   close to town.
At Beeson's house again that night, we had a quiet
   chat;
Her manner dazzled me 'til I knew not where I was at
And then, next night, Sunday again, we took a quiet
   roam
And on our way, we burglarized the Trammel Tremble
   home
A few days later, years it seemed, to Goshen traveled I,
A picnic fair to witness there a pretty dam site by,
And Ellis once again I saw and said goodbye, alas,
For she was just about to go to that Northampton, Mass.,
And now I pray that she'll address a letter long to me
To 225 Piquette Av-nue, care M. Y. Bertole,
Detroit, for on next Sunday night, vacation does begin,
And I am going to the largest town in Michigin.

        During his vacation from the South Bend TIMES, Ring
had attended the World Series in Chicago, between the
Cubs and the Detroit Tigers, where he had met Hugh
Fullerton, the popular sportswriter of the Chicago
EXAMINER. The meeting was arranged at Ring's urging by
a mutual friend, Arthur Jacks. Ring had just
experienced the end of a first romance (of dubious
intensity, since Ring had met Ellis and was writing to
her two months prior to his vacation) with Ethel
Witkowsky (Pick),[1] a Jewish girl from Chicago whose
family vacationed during the summers at Barren Lake, as
did the Lardner family. In any case, Ring wanted to
move on to Chicago and big-time journalism.[2] The

_____

[1]See letter of 11 February 1931 to H. L. Mencken.

[2]Ring's peerless newspaper career was to consist of the
following associations: Fall 1905-November 1907 with the South
Bend TIMES; December 1907-December 1908 with the Chicago
INTER-OCEAN; February 1908-November 1908 with the Chicago
EXAMINER: November 1908-November 1910 with the Chicago TRIBUNE;

meeting developed into a test by Fullerton of Ring's drinking capabilities as well as his baseball expertise, after which Ring was recommended to and hired by Duke Hutchinson, sports editor of the Chicago INTER-OCEAN.[1]

In addition to Ethel Witkowsky and Ellis, Ring was popular with other women. The following verse epistle is one of approximately forty existing letters to Wilma Johnson, the Niles friend who had introduced Ring and Ellis. She had known Ellis when her family earlier lived in Goshen, and had become acquainted with Ring after the Johnsons moved to Niles. It is probable that Ring was attracted romantically to Wilma, as he must also have been to Helen Hawks of Goshen (to whom he also apparently wrote letters during his period, though none have survived). Helen was a close friend of Ruby Abbott, Ellis's older sister, who of course knew them all well and who testified, many years later, to Ring, Jr., "that each of the others, Wilma and Helen, privately hoped Ring's affections would turn to her."[2] In any case, the friendship between Ring and Wilma, whom he nicknamed "the Ginseng girl" and addressed frequently as "Ginnie," involved at least a close and witty camaraderie at the time, causing occasional jealousy on Ellis's part.

In any case he often wrote poetry as well as prose to "Ginnie," of which the following, in the style of Longfellow's "Hiawatha," is an example. This and other imitative verse by Ring demonstrate both his interest in poems popular in this period and his sensitivity to poetic forms.

December 1910-February 1911 with THE SPORTING NEWS; February 1911-October 1911 with the Boston AMERICAN; December 1911-January 1912 with the Chicago AMERICAN (as copyreader only); February 1912-May 1913 with the Chicago EXAMINER; June 1913-June 1919 with the Chicago TRIBUNE; November 1919-March 1927 for the Bell Syndicate; December 1928-February 1929 with the New York MORNING TELEGRAPH; and February-April 1931 for the Bell Syndicate. See Matthew J. Bruccoli and Richard Layman, RING W. LARDNER: A DESCRIPTIVE BIBLIOGRAPHY (University of Pittsburgh Press, 1976) for listings of Ring's newspaper pieces.

[1]Ring described the meeting with Fullerton in "Caught in the Draft," in the 9 January 1932 SATURDAY EVENING POST; the piece has recently been reprinted in Matthew J. Bruccoli and Richard Layman, eds., SOME CHAMPIONS (New York: Charles Scribner's Sons, 1976).

[2]Ring Lardner, Jr., p. 33.

Saturday.
[30 November 1907]

Dear Ginnie,-
   To continue in the same strain:

Walter tells me he has written
To my friend, Miss Wilma Ginseng,
Asking said Miss Wilma Ginseng
If her friends at old Lake Forest,
Who attend the Ferry Hall school,
Uttered compliments about us
After we had left the chapel
Where dramatic reads were given
By our old pal, Kuntzey-Baker;
Let me say to Wilma Ginseng:
Nought care I for those unknowns
Or for their opinions of us
Which my friend so boldly asks for--
Only care I what our hostess,
Gracious Peter Wilma Ginseng,
Thinks of me, who all unworthy,
Profited by her great kindness
And was entertained so highly,
Not by sight of unknown maidens,
But by her own gracious presence--
Therefore, do not bother, Ginnie,
To inform Old Boy Ringlets
Whether they have cursed or blessed us;
Walter, as is usual with him,
Has to Miss Maud Rogers written
What he wrote he will not tell me,
But I'm betting him the seegars
That she will not deign to answer.
Not a word I've had from Rabbits;
P'rhaps she's angered at what we thought
Was the best one ever dreamed of;
Probably the very best one
That a human ever thought of.
Lonely is the Old Boy Ringlets,
Now deprived of daily journeys
To and from the place Lake Forest
And the pleasant moments spent there
'Mong the Indians and Miss Ginseng.
Indians made me heap big happy
When they lifted Midway's scale
And rolled little Walter Steffen
All around the grassy meadow,
Till he got himself mixed up with
Loaves of bread, still in their childhood.
Answer Walter if you care to.

Answer me whate'er befalls you.
I'm important--he is nothing.
Anyway, you now are owing
Me two large and full-grown missives.
They will reach their destination
At 4-3-8 North State street, or
At the Inter Ocean office.
I will eagerly await them.
--Yours, half-wittedly, Old Ringlets.

Unfortunately, Ring's propensity for poetry
resulted in the first crisis in his courtship of Ellis.
Apparently during a date with Wilma Johnson at Ferry
Hall (a girls preparatory school and junior college
affiliated with Lake Forest College, located about
twenty miles north of Chicago), which Wilma was then
attending, the two composed together a piece of
humorous doggerel which Ring polished and then sent to
Wilma with the comment: "You are supposed to copy the
enclosed and mail it. Your version will require one or
two slight changes." Then they both sent separately the
poem, referred to above as "the best one ever dreamed
of," to Ellis in Northampton. The following piece, of
which only Wilma's copy has survived, in her
handwriting, was probably her version of this offensive
"Lake Forest piece" to which Ellis did not immediately
reply:

In the wildness of Lac Forest
Far from Knolls and far from kindred
Far from Goshen, Indiana,
But yet not so far from South Bend-
Mid the millionaires and Indians,
Savage Indians from Carlisle,
Training here for bitter warfare,
Warfare with the Midway army;
'Mid the millionaires and Indians
'Biding here along the North shore
Of Lac Michigan's wet waters;
Here I met fair Wilma Ginsing,
Wilma Ginsing, late of Goshen,
Goshen where the wild young rabbits
Chase about in mad carousal
Where the rabbits and the wild hawks
Chase about in mad carousal,
Where the warlike, mammoth rockwells
Cast young rocks down in the oil wells,
Where young R. B. Kelly[1] hailed from,
Who, while fighting for the South Bends,

---

[1] See letters of 29 July 1909.

Tried in vain to boost them upward
From the downmost depths of baseball;
Wilma Ginsing, late of Goshen,
Which young burg was really never
Quite the same when she had left it.
Late of Goshen, which is over ,
Thirty miles from Kneels, Mich-a-gan,
Kneels, where roasts of marshy mallows
Constantly delight papooses,
On the bank of laughing water,
Namely, the St. Joseph river,
On the bank owned by the Beesons,
William Beeson, of whom when he
Tried to put some good one over,
Some young witty Lardner shouted:
"Who let in the grewsome greyhound?"
Knolls, where all the Trommels tremble
When young ruffians knock upon their
Front doors, after Walt has left them.
In Lac Forest, met I Wilma,
Vividly we strolled together,
Yesterday, today, forever,
Up and down the winding roadways,
On the beech and past the beach trees,
Where the airy Ferry Hallers
Ferry Hallers holler "Hawl her!"
To the skippers trying hard to
Sail their skiffs with too full tops'ls.
There met I fair Wilma Ginsing,
And we sobbed our very hearts out
That the Rabbits could not be there;
Absolutely, positively,
Sobbed our hearts and sobbed our souls out,
Till police gents hollered to us:
"Sobber up, you rascal Knollsites."

One may surmise why Ellis found this poetry
offensive: some of her earlier comments suggest that
she had felt uneasy at the necessity of responding in
kind to Ring's witty poetry--e.g. "You may have a
fertile enough brain to think of a wonderful new poem
each time but believe me mine is not fertile enough to
coin a new adjective to fit each new one so don't
expect it" (8 November 1907). And in a January 1908
letter, she writes: "I think you suffer from Chronic
Imagination." Further, she was clearly conscious of
Wilma as a rival. In a letter dated 31 October 1907
she says:

Your poem, as usual, was the best ever--and
the sentiment beautiful. Do you do them
extemporanously or are they studied productions?

Did you meet your fate on Hallow'een? Perhaps you did not know that Halloween had been but it has and I would advise you to examine your past of the last few days.

My fair sister and the Miss Hawks have gone away on a visit so Goshen sees their beaming faces no more--Also Miss Ginseng has gone to Lake Forest, so Niles is doubly bereaved--Perhaps you will meet her in the busy Metropolis, even, it might happen, on Halloween.

Thus Ellis did not receive kindly two copies, one from Ring, one from Wilma, of a poem which celebrated an evening with Wilma. She responded:

When I received on the same mail twin epistulas I was tempted to wire two telegrams of congratulations, but refrained. Don't do it again and if you write me any more poetry I am going to rebel and never answer your letters as long as I live. SO the very next poetry I receive from you I shall understand as a tactful suggestion to whoa Elizabeth--in other words stop.

Ring seems to have been genuinely, if somewhat naively, puzzled and responded with the following:

[5 December 1907]
Thursday.

Dear Rabbits,
In the happy past, I often boasted to myself thus:
However harshly I may be used by others, the Rabbit is incapable of a deliberate attempt to hurt my much-abused feelings.

Vain boast--the Rabbit, with premeditated malice, ridicules my poetry to my very face and requests that I burden her with it no longer. All right, Rabbit; if you should ask me on bended knee to ship you more of my inimitable verse, I will refuse you with a curse in my throat and sneer in my ear.

You have the advantage of me in prospects. I have no "home and Christmas" to look forward to. I may jaunt to Knoles about December 25th, but, if I do, I wont have time to kiss my nearest relatives--towit, my sisters and domestic pets--both hello and goodbye. It will all be merged into one.

I want to remind you, before we go a step farther--that you hinted some time ago at a Christmas surprise for me. I can almost guess what it is--a lemon peel or an invitation not to write any more. But I want to ward this off and tell you what I really want Santa Claus to bring me from old Northampton, Mass.,--a Kodak picture (afraid to ask for a larger one) of Miss Ellis Abbott to cheer me in my hours of melancholy, anxiety and grouch. I wouldn't get very mad if Mr. Claus came in far ahead

of time with such a welcome gift. Is this too much to ask?   You
know you owe me something for slamming my poetry.
    The black snow is about five inches deep in this city of
sighs and tears.   I am looking eagerly forward to a sleighride
some of these days, as I intend to put in at least one afternoon
at catching on bobs in State street. There are about as many of
them there as there are in the Rockwell family.
    A gent who works on The Examiner hails from Goshen. His name
is "Duffy" Cornell. He asked me whom I knew in Go-shen. I named
the Rabbit girls among others and he said he remembered them as
little bunnies. He is an old pal of Bob Rockwell's.
                            Remember the address.
                                 Ringlets
You are again falling behind the regular schedule.

        Ellis replied, in part:

        I am sorry. I did not mean to hurt your poor
    abused feelings. I won't _ask_ you to write any more
    poetry, but if you _should_ I will read it--really I
    will and gladly, if I did say I wouldn't. . . .
        Wilma wrote me about your gay and happy
    meeting in Lake Forest. I envy you both and was
    that not prettily said?

        The next letter to Ellis refers to an
    after-Christmas dance in Goshen, at which Ellis was one
    of several hostesses. Ring did not attend.   It is
    unclear whether his work prevented attendance, or
    whether he declined because he did not like to dance.
    He had been born with a deformed foot, and had
    undergone a corrective operation, after which he had
    worn a brace on his leg until he was eleven. Though he
    did not limp, this medical history may have contributed
    to a distaste for dancing. The "request" which Ellis
    had ignored was for the photograph Ring had asked for
    in his letter of 5 December. Though Ellis had
    responded to the earlier queries about the
    offensiveness of the "Lake Forest piece" with "words of
    comfort," Ring cannot quite forget the matter:

                          ⌈15 December 1907⌉
                          Sunday afternoon
Dear Rabbits,-
    I have just received an invitation from you to attend a dance
in Goshen the 28th. Perhaps you didn't know you sent me one, but
you did. You have me very much fussed over the Christmas
surprise, but you paid absolutely not a bit of heed to my
request.
    I would certainly like to be in Northampton these dismal
days, that I might see and hear you perform in your plays; also
that I might hear your laugh, which I enjoy even more than Evan

Harter's. Which reminds · me that I have a trade for you--Wilma
Ginseng said you were the best screamer she ever knew. You owe
me one.

You have blighted my poetic hopes and your kind, but false
words of comfort came too late. I have eschewed poetry. Never
again will my peculiar pen burst into verse for your or others'
eyes. You may have positively, usually done the world a service.

I would like to meet your Evanston room-mate. I will see her
on the corner the day after Christmas. Mystery--why do all
Goshen girls have Evanston room-mates at college? For the same
reason that all the half-witted members of the Lardner family
have moved to Chicago.

It staggers me to think that our days of Summer frolic are at
an end. All of my vacations in this job will come in the Winter
time. While you are roasting marshmallows and others, or are
rapping on Tremble's door, or are watching the others cook supper
at the dam Goshen, I will be pining away at the near desk, the
sweat of my brow mingling with my rapid, vapid tears. Some day,
though, you will be · in our midst--perhaps even at Evanston.
Then I will come and serenade you until you scream as Miss
Ginseng says you alone can scream. And the sound of your voice
will keep me afloat for another year.

I went to Church this morning, hoping I would see an Abbott.
The collection plate cost a dime and I saw nothing.

When do you come home?

                                    R. W. L.

Ring obviously hoped to see Ellis on Christmas day,
but his plans were thwarted by an assignment to cover a
Yale University basketball game and by uncooperative
train timetables. Ring had to depart from Chicago only
fifteen minutes before Ellis arrived en route from
Northampton. Apparently Ring and Ellis saw each other
over the Christmas holidays only long enough for Ring
to give her a Christmas present (in addition to a box
of candy he had sent her earlier), after which she
departed to Northampton and he returned to his boarding
house in Chicago.

The following letter to Ginnie, written the same
day of the Goshen dance, narrates, in the style of
Longfellow's "The Midnight Ride of Paul Revere," a
calamitous horse-drawn sleigh-ride through the streets
of Niles:

                              Saturday, the 28th

1. Listen, Miss Ginseng, and you shall read
    Of a ride, which for daring and nerve-
            wracking speed,
    Makes the one once made famous by old Paul
            Revere

Resemble the price of six glasses of beer.

2. 'Twas on Christmas eve that one E. Harter,
        bold,
   Called up his familiars, the young and the
        old,
   And said, "Would ye like to go out for a
        ride?"
   And thousands accepted, their hearts thrilled
        with pride.

3. There were Edith Baumberger and Nannie Bonine,
   Of course they could not leave Bill Beeson
        behine,
   And A. Louise Woodford and Ostrander Doc[1]
   And Blanche Millard, wrapped in a fur-covered
        frock,

4. And four other persons accomp'nied they he,
   Towit, Wilma Ginseng and 3--Lardners--3
   And over the snow-covered streets did they
        glide,
   Intent on enjoying a beautiful ride.

5. But rough was the ocean and slipp'ry the
        decks
   And awful the many death-dealing wrecks,
   Aside from Rex Lardner, who acted quite dear
   And helped fix up breaks in the old speeder's
        gear.

6- Not more than 12 times did the outfit break
        down
   Before it had traversed one-third of the
        town,
   And cold were the riders, on my solemn
        word,
   When one vessel hit bottom 'way up on South
        Third.

7-. One ship was borne off to its 'Evan of rest,
   While two Lardners left for the home they
        love best,
   They dragged Doc along and thus left Billy B.
   In charge of the good ship--oh, sad day for he.

8- For down Third to Larned, then over to Fourth
   He drove the perspiring and galloping horth,
   Turned up Fourth to Larned, but turned late

---

[1]Walter Ostrander, whom Wilma Johnson married on 7 July 1912.

at Green,
There followed the worst spectacle ever seen.

9- The horsey was tired--he loved Billy B.,
And proceeded to sit in the soft lap of he.
The others were scattered, some far and some
    wide;
Oh gents, what a terrible, prodigious ride.

10- That night as upon my soft pillow I lay,
I thanked heav'n for saving me, for Christmas
    day,
One sister, one brother, a half-dozen friends
And one Wilma Ginseng, whose answer now
    pends.

Rlts.

When Ellis wrote "admonishing" Ring for having
written a bad story, and commenting: "I like to say
very mean things to you because I know they don't make
the slightest bit of difference," Ring answered
soberly:

Sunday, January 19th

Dear Bunny,-
I realized that my story was bad. You were right about that;
but you were wrong about something else--you said you knew it
didn't make the slightest bit of difference to me if you said
mean things. It does, and you really should know it if you do
not. This and another, or two other, reasons prevent me from
burdening you with more of my luscious poetry. One reason is
that I am not at all sure that you would go back on your threat,
but would refuse to answer. The other reason is that I have
sworn and hate to break my oath. On one condition will I do
so--namely, that you tell me why the Lake Forest effusion failed
to please. Both Wilma Ginseng and I thought it was probably the
most perfect epic we ever saw. I have never been able to figure
what was wrong with it and I am very curious to know.
I think The Chicago American is going to want me soon,
strange as it may seem. And if the opportunity comes, I am going
take it, because the reasons why I should outnumber and outweigh
the reasons why I should not. This latter class consists almost
entirely of my innate aversion to the sheet.
One of my reasons for accepting if I have a chance and do
accept, is that it will give me one or two journeys through the
East during the coming Spring and Summer. I should consider it
extremely fortunate if I were sent to Boston for two or three
days-- How far is Northampton from Boston? And are Smith girls
as much imprisoned as Ferry Hall students?
I am to dine today at a house on Ellis avenue. If it were on
any other avenue, I would decline. Is there a Ringlets alley in
your old town?

Do you realize that you write grievously short letters? To prove whether or not you like to read mine, I am going to count the words in yours hereafter and then answer with the same number.

We will now play truth:

Didn't you wish, just a little, that I had written more awful poetry when you told me not to, so that you really could carry out your threat?

Please don't be thoroughly disgusted with this missive. It is caused by my hunch that one Ellis Rabbit is weary of her bargain. If not, my real address is 438 North State street.

Always,
<u>Ringlets</u>

This foray into "truth" evoked the following reply from Ellis, who again explained her wrath at the "Lake Forest piece" and assured Ring that she wished to continue the correspondence. Actually, though Ring had apparently been negotiating with the Chicago AMERICAN, he was about to transfer, in February, to the EXAMINER, where he would shortly become the next of a series of reporters to write under the by-line pseudonym of James Clarkson.

⌈24 January 1908⌉
Dear Ringling

Now I wonder--if a man takes me to a dance and asks me if I am tired and want to go home, I always have a lurking suspicion that he wants to go home himself, I never do. There seems to me but one obvious conclusion. . . .

If the only condition to your writing poetry is to explain my apparent wrath I will do so gladly. I did appreciate it--really thought it wonderful--but you see I thought I was getting two, perfectly, good, nice, letters and when I found they were just the same--well you see I just got raging--nasty little spitfire that I am and there was the result. I apoligize. Am I sufficiently humbled?

The upshot of this letter was that Ring tried again to please Ellis with poetry, this time with an imitation of "The Night before Christmas":

⌈3 February 1908⌉
Sunday
Dear Rabbitt,-

If you and I went to a dance and I grew tired (as I would if you were stingy with dances) I would say: "Come, Rabbitt, I am tired; we are going home."

Therefore, enough of this folly, I will grow tired of hearing from you about the time you are a Sophomore at West Point.

Boston is quite a spell from Northampton. However, if Sunday and I ever reach Massachusetts at the same time, meet me on the corner.

It has been zero for two days and Ringlets is cold. He longs for Summer at the dam Goshen. He pines to carry pine logs for the camp fire and to consume large hunks of steak where none can see him devour them.

The explanation you offer in regard to the Lake Forest epic only convinces me that you have a terrible temper and one greatly to be feared. However, you are forgiven for attempting to blight my poetic future.

And we will join in the following:

Appropriate Song
----------//----------

1. 'Twas the night before Ground-hog, and all through the flat,
   Not a rodent was screaming--not even a rat,
   The mousees had ceased from there noisy horse-play
   For Ground-hog would look for his shadow next day

2. 'Twas the day of the ground-hog--'twas Feb-roo-air 2
   And the coldest day probably we ever knew,
   And Ringlets arose from his cradle of down
   And made preparations to hasten to town

3. The folks' cross the way from their windows did stare
   As Ringlets' small form met the chill of the air;
   They whispered together and looked at the sky
   Through which tender cloudlets in large flocks did fly.

4. "'Tis funny," said they, "that he comes out so soon;
   "Why, surely it can't be its already noon."
   Now, true as I live, ('though the joke's of a lost age)
   They thought me ground-hog 'cause I looked like a sausage.
   (Explanatory note--I am still punishing you for your criticism
   of the Lake Forest masterpiece).
                                         Ringlets.

Ring had gone to work on the Chicago EXAMINER on 1 February 1908, having been recommended for the position by his friend Hugh Fullerton. At a salary of twenty-five dollars a week he was one of several reporters struggling at the sports desk mainly with the proofreading or rearranging of stories coming off the wire, though eventually he did also write the "James Clarkson" by-line.[1]

---

[1]"Eckie," in the 20 February 1932 SATURDAY EVENING POST (reprinted in SOME CHAMPIONS), describes one of Ring's experiences with the wire service at this time.

In March, Ring was assigned to travel with the White Sox; the following "guide" was sent both to Ellis and to Wilma, and probably to other friends and relatives:

THE ROUTE OF RINGLETS.
Published as a Guide for his genial Correspondents.
(With carbon copies)

On March 18, young Lardner'll go
Down to the city of N.O.,
New Orleans is the city's name,
A city not unknown to fame.
From March 19 to March 2-2,
He'll tarry in New Orleans, Lou.
And then, on March the 23,
He'll sojourn in Montgomery.
From this cute town in Alabam
He'll travel up to Birmingham
And there remain the 24th.,
Before proceeding farther north,
To Nashville up in Tennessee,
And there the next three days he'll be.
On 28 and 29,
In burg of Evansville so fine,
On 30th and 31st/
In Terre Haute, of towns the worst.
And on fair April's first two days,
In Indianapolis he stays;
In Cincinnati 4 and 5,
And then, my goodness, sakes alive,
To old South Bend he'll go once more
Renew acquaintance made of yore,
The 6th day of the month he'll spend
Among the ruins of old South Bend.
The next three days in cute Champaign,
Eleventh, twelfth in cute Fort Wayne,
And then back to Chicago go,
To stay about ten days or so.
And through this era, do not fail
As follows to address his mail:
"For Mr. Lardner, in the care
""Of the White Sox," and b'lieve me, fair
Young correspondents, large and small,
I'm glad to hear from one and all.

That spring, having heard the rumor that Wilma Johnson had become engaged to someone else, Ring wrote to ask:

                              The Chicago Daily Examiner
                              Chicago, Ill.
                              Hell, May 7th.
                              [7 May 1908]

Dear Ginnie,-
        Heard some most distressing news
        From an old time friend of youse,
        Told me Ginnie was engaged
        To be married--much enraged
        I did shout aloud: "To whom?"
        And was answered: "You big Broom,
        "What's the difference who he is
        "Really, its none of your biz"
        "But please answer me," said I
        "If I know not, I will cry"
        Fearing to be drowned in tears,
        Gossip whispered in my ears:
        "He's a bright Lake Forest prof.
        "To him you your hat must doff"
        "Well, Miss Ginseng" now say I,
        "Why and wherefore, how and why,
        "Did it happen that Lard-nore
        "Did not hear this news before?"
        Nor congratulate you will
        I, young Mr. Lardner, 'til
        You have made plain to me
        Who he is and when 'twill be.
        Now, to change the subject, ripping
        Did I think your Niles Sun clipping.
        That's a poor excuse you wrote,
                ,ungainly,
        Large   boat.
                        fishing
        'Bout not answering my old
        Letters, glittering as gold.
        Pardon these accusing names.
        Dangerous as moths and flames
        I, of course, am somewhat peeved
        That I was so grossly leaved
        Out of your sweet confidence
        Please explain, explain at wence.
                        Ringlets.

        Ring may have been relieved to hear that the rumor
about Wilma was false, but he was about to face a
crisis of sorts in his pursuit of Ellis. In the spring
of 1908, Ellis still enjoyed Ring's attention, but she
had, of course, other suitors, and she was clearly
occupied with her life at Smith College. One of her
other admirers, a Mr. Loring Hoover, whom she had
apparently known in earlier years and who was now

attending Yale, she invited to her junior prom at
Smith. Hoover evidently had made a special impression
on Ellis, for she wrote to her mother that he was "so
much older and more self-possessed and nicer all around
than he used to be that I was very pleased with him."
The news of Loring Hoover and the junior prom obviously
made a lasting impression upon Ring also, for thirteen
years later, on Ellis's birthday in 1921, Ring amused
Ellis with a play he had written reenacting the prom
and featuring Hoover as Ellis's date.

At the time of the prom, Ring, in his new job with
the EXAMINER, was covering the White Sox through spring
training on the West Coast, during the pre-season
exhibitions through the Southeast, and on through the
regular season which began in mid-April. Thus, Ring
had few chances to see Ellis, though he probably wrote
to her as regularly as ever. If he did, she apparently
took less care to save these letters of the spring of
1908. What is clear, anyway, is that she wrote to him
less often during these months, and that it worried
him. The extant letters from her to him run about
three to four a month in the first months of 1908, but
there is only one letter in April--wishing Ring a happy
Easter. The beginning of this letter, postmarked April
19, 1908, suggests tonally that Ellis is more
preoccupied with other matters:

As you are next on my Sunday afternoon
communication list I guess you'll just have to sit
still and take all that's a'coming to you. You
don't deserve any kind of a letter at all but as I
have not a postal card to my name and as I suppose
you have been _more_ or _less_ busy, I will just make
this a little note to wish you a "Happy Easter."
The dreadful thought has just occurred to me
that I haven't the least idea where you may be.
Why don't you stay in one place? It would be more
convenient for your friends and save you a lot of
trouble.

The courtship was clearly declining. Five weeks later,
Ellis wrote:

Last week we had our wonderful Junior Prom.
And we are all still in the process of recovering.
One of the most exciting events of the weeks
festivities is to take the man (or men) out to a
tea in the orchard and eat ice cream and have a
dozen people take your picture at the same time.
You see men are such a rarity here the girls want
to keep them as long as possible even if only in a
picture.

Meanwhile, Ring described a particularly exciting eleven-inning Sox victory to Wilma. Significantly, Ring habitually wrote with ease to Wilma of his work and the fortunes of the White Sox, while in letters to Ellis he strove more self-consciously to be suitor and humorist. This fact implies much about his relationships with these two young women. It seems clear that although Ring may have felt more at ease in writing to Wilma, he did not regard her (or Helen Hawks) as romantically as he viewed Ellis.

Friday
[Chicago,
5 June 1908]

Dear Ginnie,-

Arrived on the home lot this morn, minus baggage and sleep.

Glad to hear that you are coming to our immediate vicinity, but regret to say that there are no Indians at Lake Forest now. However, if you will do some date setting, it would bring me delight to welcome you at our ball yard for the afternoon on your way hither or thither.

I would have been in Kneels yesterday and today, but for an accursed rain in blessed St. Looie on Wednesday, which caused us to spend our off-day at hard labor. But I think I would rather have missed Kneels than that second battle yesterday afternoon, which was probably and absolutely the most passionate I ever saw. Bitterly opposed, as a usual thing, to the talking of shop, yet I must needs give you a brief outline of the amazing happenings. Eleventh inning--score 1 to 1--pitchers, Rube Waddell, demon, for St. Louis; Frank Smith, hoodoo, for Sox. Hahn opened with single; Jones forced him. Davis singled, Jones taking second. Anderson flied to Stone. Two out. Donohue stung to left and Jones scored. Parent out, Waddell to first. St Looie's inning--Ferris singled; Spencer and Criss beat out bunts. Score 2 to 1, bases full of Looies, none out. Cold blast of air blows into press box, striking Ringlets in feet. Manager Jones hastens into infield for consultation. (Wilma Ginseng should know that left-handed batters are usually weak against left-handed pitchers) Situation--Stone, good left hand hitter, and Hoffman, ditto, coming up. Smith, right hand pitcher in box. Consultation ends. Exit Smith and enter White, good left hand pitcher. Stone, whiff, whiff, whiff. One out--bases still full. Foolish (like a fox) St. Looie manager withdraws Hoffman, left hander, and sends Stephens (not Plowden) right hand hitter to bat. Another consultation. Exit White and enter Walsh--right-handed spitballist. Stephens--whiff, whiff, whiff-- Two out--bases still full. But here is James Williams; he who had scored the only St. Looie run with reefo over right field wall. Williams--whiff, whiff--no whiff, no whiff, no whiff. Three balls, two strikes, bases full, two out, one run needed to

tie. Zowie--ah, but the ball is reposing in the sumptuous mitt
of Jagger Donohue and the chill blains disappear. But believe
me, Ginnie, they never got my goat that way in South Bend, Ind.
    I realize that this letter is intensely interesting and I
don't want to carry it too far.
    In regard to your reported betrothal, if I had believed it
true, I would have maintained a dignified silence. I know you
would consult me before taking so rash a step. I will tell you
of the origin of said rumor when we meet.
    New route list will be published soon.
    In Chicago until 21st of June.*
                              Ringlets.
*A couplet.

    The managerial strategy exhibited in the game
described above reflects the kind of baseball which
Ring enjoyed most, rather than the long-ball style
which emerged in the 1920's with Babe Ruth and the
"TNT" ball.[1] As early as 1911, in some of his Boston
AMERICAN pieces, Ring was deploring the use of what he
suspected was a livelier baseball.[2]

    By this time Ring had heard of Loring Hoover and
Ellis's Junior Prom. Uneasily, he wrote the following
verse letter to Ellis in mid-July, just after she had
returned home from Smith for the summer vacation.

What, Rabbits have come home to roost?
Is this what you would tell us?
A full-fledged senior now is she,
But still heart-whole and fancy free,
This girl entitled Ellis?

Why no, she brought her trunk back home,
Its each and every part,
Then what was it she left behind?
Her fertile brain, her brilliant mind?
No, just her Goshen heart.

Far East of here she left her heart;
Is that what you would tell us?
Ah, rather had she left her shoes.
Her powder rag, the gum she chews,
This most forgetful Ellis.

----

[1]See letter to John McGraw of 4 June 1932.

[2]See also Ring's letter to Ellis of 15 May 1911.

What will she do without her heart?
Why that no one can tell us,
And least of all young Ringlets tall,
Why, no, he cannot tell at all,
So peeved is he and jealous.

We've lived full twenty years and more
And nothing e'er befell us
That stung so much as this same news
That she her Goshen heart did lose;
Is't true? Come, tell us, Ellis.

    Concerned over the decline of Ellis's interest in him, Ring planned an extended telephone call to Ellis from the Goshen train depot during the team's return trip from New York. It seems likely, judging from the content of the next letter and the accompanying verse, that on that particular Friday evening Ellis was indeed in Goshen, in anticipation of talking with Ring. But because of some confusion on the telephone operator's part when Ring called, he did not speak with her and assumed that she was not at home.

                    The Chicago Daily Examiner
                    146 Franklin Street
                    Chicago, Ill.
                    Tuesday.
Dear Rabbit,-
    The enclosed tells you the truth about Friday's fiasco. Fate is certainly against me. I thought, when she told me you were not at home, that you probably were at Wawasee and, perhaps, had not yet received my former missive, or, having received it, had not been able to leave Wawasee, or had not cared to come to Goshen. I'm honestly sorry if you were inconvenienced and I guess I had better give up hope of trying it again. Aren't you coming to Chicago ever?
            Write.
                Ringlets.

    "The enclosed" was the following verse narrative:

                    Tuesday.
Dear Rabbit,-
    Where I was but grieved before,
I now am angered, peeved and wroth and sore.
On Friday night, the tears of pain did rise;
Now tears of rage fall from my lustruous eyes.
For, b'lieving then you did not care to see
Your bosom friend, I thought at Wawasee
You had remained, but now the truth is known
And realized, there issues forth a groan

Of anger, impotent, from my young throat,
As impotent as Rocky Mountain goat.
And, being now prepared, pray hear the tale
Of how, unwillingly, your friend did fail
To see you Friday night: At Buffalo,
On Friday morning, they had planned, you know,
To switch our car onto a reg'lar train
Which carries passengers out West again;
But we arrived in Buffalo too late
To catch the train with which we had a date;
We then were hooked behind the old Fast Mail,
Which ne'er to stop at Goshen town does fail.
We whizzed through Goshen shortly after five,
So fast we sped, why gracious, man alive,
We couldn't see the town, so fast we sped,
But, on attaining Elkhart, we stopped dead
And there they told us we would bide awhile,
Which news caused me to giggle and to smile,
They said that there in Elkhart town again,
They'd switch us back onto another train,
A half-hour's wait in Elkhart quaranteed,
Into the Lake Shore station I did speed,
And, gleeful, choked with gladness, and alone
I did approach the cute young telephone.
"Hello" I shouted, and the answer came,
From some young lady, heaven knows her name.
I told her then, in language plain and terse,
That I with Ellis Abbott would converse,
With young Miss Ellis Abbott would converse;
I told her this in language plain and terse.
She answered: "Well and good--please hold the phone"
I did as I was bid, though quite alone.
Eftsoons, she spoke again, "Hang up" said she,
"I'll call you when I get your fair par-tee"
I did as I was bid, though quite alone,
And eftsoons rang the cute young telephone:
I answered and the girl said, plain and terse:
"Miss Abbott's not at home, you can't converse"
Then, sadly, turned I to our train once more,
And rode to old South Bend, my home of yore,
And thence, by trolley, traveled I to Niles,
Whose distance from South Bend is 'leven miles,
And there I stayed till Saturday at noon,
And came back here, alack, alas, too soon.
That is the true tale of last Friday night.
Can you explain it? Much I wish I might.
I wish I might to Elkhart come once more
And seek the girl in that tel-e-phone store,
Who told me you were not at home and thus
Caused me to rant and tear my hair and cuss.

From Detroit, the following Tuesday, Ring sent the following note to Ellis:

                                    Hotel Cadillac
                                    Detroit, Michigan
                                    Tuesday
Dear Rabbit,-
     Realizing that you wont write until I do, and desiring greatly to hear from you once more, I now take advantage of a brief season of rest to tickle you to death with the following pensive note.
     I was in Kneels over Sunday. Wilma Ginseng informed me that you were at Wawasee (if that is close to the way it is spelled). This statement disappointed me beyond expression, because I had counted on seeing you next Sunday morn. On that day, we (the league leaders and myself) are going through Goshen on the way "home" from Cleveland. I think we pass by about 4:30 A.M. and it would be an easy matter for you to be at the daypo. But, of course, you had to go wandering off in the woods and just because you knew I was coming.
     Oh, yes, I was told by a small bug that you came home from Northampton minus a vital organ towit, your heart. So I will know what's the matter if you haven't the heart to write to me any more. But I wish you would relate every detail of the romance to me. Talk to me as you would to your attorney. I can advise you.
     You have evidently forgotten that I requested some more poetry from you. I enclose a special telegram. Please answer so I will hear the worst before leaving for the East again. At 438 North State street all next week.
                                    Ringlets
     Pardon both brands of stationery

     Clearly enjoying Ring's attention and his jealousy, Ellis wrote the following letter which both reassures and withdraws from definite commitment:

     Dear Ringer--
     I just think you must live in a dreadfully buggy place but dont you hurt those bugs -- they are not safe. You see my heart is a much traveled organ and I think it is now in Chicago. . . .
     I cant write you a poem today because it is raining and I just cant write rainy poetry. Do you know I think you and I are doomed to just miss each other through the rest of life. When I visit Johnny this summer you will come home the day I leave and when I am in Chicago you will leave the day I come. Isn't it tragic--and I long to see you so! I have a vision that when you are on your honeymoon I will dash past you in an automobile and toot my horn. Will you watch for me?

That was sufficient encouragement for Ring to renew
the courtship that summer with vigor. Early in August,
Ring, again on the road with the White Sox, also wrote
to Wilma, lamenting in detail his sufferings with the
team:

Thursday.
[Philadelphia, Pa.
20 August 1908]

Dear Ginnie,-
This stationary[1] is used, not because I am an employe of of
the Hearst papers, but because it is lemon color, my national
shade. Being well aware of your ready sympathy and standing in
need of it, I append a diary of my wretched existence in
Washington, preceding it with the assertion that I will never go
there again, except in the event that I am elected to the
president's chair.
Thursday, August 13--Arrived this afternoon, finding the
thermometer at 105 in the shade, so sat out in the sun until
supper time. Ate supper and became sick immediately afterward.
Didn't sleep at all during the night.
Friday, August 14--The Sox were beaten twice, and by
Washington at that; watched the games.
Saturday, August 15--Game was started at 3:30 o'clock, an
hour earlier than usual at Washington. Scribes were all glad, as
Saturday is a day when their first story has to be in the office
before 6 o'clock. Game went fifteen innings. My story all right
up to time and apparently being sent along by operator. Game
ended and was informed that not a line had been sent. Tempest
followed and usually sweet temper all shot to pieces. Too late
for supper, which was a lucky thing, as it would have made me
sick again.
Sunday, August 16--Wrote masterpiece for paper at 6:30 P.M.
Called Western Union boy and boy came, bearing away with him the
masterpiece. Midnight, wire came from paper, asking where my
story was. Failing to find it, wrote joke story in ten minutes,
sent it and went to W. U. office to see what had happened. W.
U. officials disclaimed all knowledge of ever having seen
masterpiece; had sent a boy to hostelry, but he had returned
masterpieceless, having been told by clerk that he was too late.
Said clerk's vacation was to begin next morning and he had gone
away for the night. No satisfaction.
Monday, August 15--Sox lost all kinds of chances to win game
and it was finally stopped in the eighth inning with score tied.
Fearful storm broke. Athletes and scribes in hurry to catch
train. Refused to ride in athletes' bus to hotel, thinking I
could beat it on a car. Cars stopped in storm on account of
trouble in the trolley wires. C. Dryden and I held up so we

_____

[1]One of Ring's rare misspellings.

couldn't make 8 o'clock train. Asked ticket office (Getting shock in the ear while telephoning) what time next train left. Was told that an express went at 10 o'clock. Boarded train with C. Dryden to find that it was called express because there were so many express cars on it. Had received your letter at hotel and settled in train to read it. Looked in pocket for it and there found score of game which should have gone with story. Hysterics. Laughter from C. Dryden. Got off train at Baltimore and ordered Washington W. U. to send C. Dryden's score also to Examiner. Colored lady got on at Elkerton and came in smoking car which C. D. and I had had to ourselves. Thinking we were near Phila., I remarked the same to C. D., namely, that we must be near Phila. Colored lady butted in and said: "The next stop is Wilmington." C.D. "Thought you got on at Wilmington" C.L.- "No, I got on at Elkerton. I have lived in Baltimore two months" C.D.- "Thank you" C.L.- "Are you traveling men?" C.D.- "Yes, woman" Arrived at Philly at 2:35, covering the 115 miles in four hours and thirty-five minutes.
                    Answer.   R. W. L.

          When Ring and Ellis were able to be together, the courtship was usually advanced considerably. On 4 September, after Ring had returned from an eastern road trip with the White Sox, he met Ellis by prearrangement at Marshall Field's downtown; they attended a White Sox game and saw a show. The evening was a great success, and Ellis wrote afterward: "Even if you are a bold wicked man you were very, very nice to me in Chicago."

                              The Chicago Daily Examiner
                              146 Franklin Street
                              Chicago, Ill.
                              ⌈13 October 1908⌉
                              Wednesday.
     Dear Rabbit,-
          Instead of enclosing my usual cute little poetical work, I am this time sending you, u.s.c. (under separate cover) "The Sentimental Song Book" by the Michigan song-bird. Mrs. Moore,[1] who is the authoress, has long been my ideal and I have emulated her style repeatedly, as you, who have seen so much of my work, can easily discern. I have added explanatory notes in the early pages for the purpose of helping you to get into the spirit of the poems. I want you to read every one and to write me your honest opinion of them and their composer.
          Thank you very much for admitting that you are afraid of

----

[1]Julia A. Moore was a poet of the late nineteenth and early twentieth centuries whose first book, THE SWEET SINGER OF MICHIGAN SALUTES THE PUBLIC (1876; later reissued as THE SENTIMENTAL SONGBOCK) exhibited such banality and pedestrian detail that she became the object of much parody and laughter.

me. You haven't much to fear from your sister, though, for I will subsidize her when we meet again.

My poor ball team lost out on the last day of the season, when most of us expected it to cop. I am almost over the shock, but have resolved to quit the national pastime, i.e. baseball, forever.

Let me know how you get along in your political studies and remember me kindly to the Smiths.

Rodently,
Ringlets.

The following letter was written shortly after 21 October 1908, when Ring's sister Anna married Richard G. Tobin, Ring's colleague on the INTER-OCEAN. Ring was best man, and, along with his brother Rex, went to stay with the newlyweds shortly thereafter in their southside Chicago apartment. The section entitled "The Tribune" relates to the fact that Ring after the World's Series had left the EXAMINER to replace his friend Charles Dryden on the TRIBUNE. Dryden, who retired, had recommended Ring. In those days the TRIBUNE'S talented staff included Burton Rascoe as literary editor, Walter Eckersall as sports commentator, H. E. Keogh as Ring's predecessor writing "In the Wake of the News," Finley Peter Dunne as author of the Mr. Dooley pieces, Harriet Monroe as a commentator on art, Lillian Russell as commentator on beauty hints, and John T. McCutcheon as a topical cartoonist. It was clearly one of the better newspapers in the country.

The Chicago Examiner
146 Franklin Street
Chicago
Friday.

Dear Rabbit,-
Here is a bunch of short ones:

Representative is the first stanza of "Little Andrew":

Andrew was a little infant,
And his life was two years old;
He was his parents' eldest boy,
And he was drowned, I was told.
His parents never more can see him
In this world of grief and pain,
And Oh! they will not forget him
While on earth they do remain.

The most famous parody of Moore's poetry appeared in HUCKLEBERRY FINN, as the morbid poetic effusions of Emmeline Grangerford.

Going South.

The winter blasts are coming on, and Ringlets is a'cold,
No more he stands them as he did before he grew so old.
To warmer clime he must depart, to sunny, sunny South,
Before icicles close his eyes and freeze up tight his mouth.
Next Monday, he will Southward fly, 'bout sixty blocks or more,
To stay at least until the winter's worstest chills are o'er.
Therefore, when you do write him next, his address it will be
At 468 West Forty-eighth street, care of R.G.T.,
In care of Mr. R. G. Tobin, his young sister's spouse;
O, yes, please write him after this at Mr. Tobin's house.

The Tribune.

And what is it, pray, this Chicago Tribune?
Which Ringlets is gone to work on so soon?
'Tis a paper that's gen'rally rated the best
In North, or in South, or in East, or in West.
And better than best it is quite sure to be
When it has the services of Bright young Me.
I can't just yet tell you what I am to write,
Whether checkers, or football, or racing or fight.
The chances are, Rabbit, I'll write not a thing
Till winter has yielded once more to the spring.
There'll be headlines, of course, and I'll send you a sheet
With each little task marked in pencil so neat;
I know this will please you, my innocent dove,
In return for which act, as a proof of your love
Devoted and grand, you must send out to me
Whatever that day's lesson happens to be,
And thus I can judge which is working the harder,
Miss Ellis, the Rabbit, or Ringlets, the Larder.

Consolation.

I used to come to this large town
Thanksgiving day of ev'ry year,
When Michigan's great football team
　　Played over here.

I was a football bug for fair,
But now I honestly don't care
What happens, since Chicago can
　　No more play Michigan.[1]

It's really an outrageous shame
That I must go to ev'ry game
When I would rather be in bed
　　Pounding my head.

----

[1]Because of intense crowd reaction at previous games, the Universities of Chicago and Michigan had discontinued their annual football game.

And still, a game I would not miss,
And the reason's, Rabbit, this:
(But, p'rhaps, quite probably you may
    Not know where they play)

Well, then, they play on Marshall field
A field which Marshall Field did yield
For just that purpose; well, and where
    Is this field, fair?

Now to the reason we have got:
This Marshall field's a favored spot
With me; because it does remind
    Me of you, Rabbit, kind

At Marshall Field's one time we met;
That meeting I will not forget,
Nor joyous time that followed, at
    The ball combat.

And furthermore, I must tell you
The field's on _Ellis_ avenue
So can't you see there are two things
That serve to counteract young Ring's
Dislike to going thither? Yes,
      I guess.
                Write.
                 B.W.L.[1]

                     The Chicago Daily Examiner
                     146 Franklin Street
                     Chicago, Ill.
                     [26 October 1908]
                     Sunday.
Dear Rabbit,-
    I don't believe you are thoroughly subsidized yet. It
should take a lot of nerve to call me both a liar and stupid in
the same missive; it would not happen if your spirit was
completely crushed (or were completely crushed) as I hope soon to
have it.
    Now I will take the two accusations separately and offer
testimony in rebuttal. You charge me with lying when I asserted
that I had something on Miss Florence Abbott of Goshen, Ind. I
have something, but I have forgotten exactly what it is. That
proves the falsity of your first accusation. As for being
stupid, I will say that I am not; so you lose both arguments.
    Furthermore, it was a very delicate sentiment that prevented
me from writing and telling you that I was going to switch to the

---

[1] Probably an imitation of Bert Leston Taylor, who signed his
TRIBUNE column ("A Line o' Type or Two") "B.L.T."

Furthermore, it was a very delicate sentiment that prevented me from writing and telling you that I was going to switch to the Tribune. Knowing that you are looking forward with rapturous longing to my was-to-have-been Christmas vacation, I didn't want to dishearten you by saying that I am to be robbed of another well-earned rest by making the change just at this time. Four straight times have I changed jobs before I had a vacation coming. But if Miss Ellis Abbott of Goshen, Ind., is in Niles, Mich, during the Holidays, Ringlets will try his worst to get over to that fair city for one day.

Certainly glad for your sake that part of the story of your future is true--also glad for other sakes that it isn't all positively true. When you do go abroad, I want you to promise me to visit Wales and the Whales; also France and the ants; also Italy and the Kittens, and Armenia and the Hyenas. As for the Prince, I have this to say:

    (After Julia A. Moore)
    Put not your trust in princes,
    They may be just plain quinces.
    A title won't buy meat and bread,
    And other luxuries, it has been said.

    Marry for love and love alone,
    'Twill make you a queen in your own home,
    Marry not wealth if it comes not with love,
    'Tis a dangerous practice I've been told.

    I knowed a maiden, hair of gold,
    Who lived in our town years ago,
    She was her mother's joy and pride,
    This pretty little bit of child.

    When she growed up, to her mother said:
    "Ma, I think's its time that I should wed:
    Her mother answered: "Wait awhile,
    "Until He comes along, my child"
    But, oh, she waited not at all,
    One night she met a prince at the ball,
    She married him without delay
    I've heard that these two ran away.

    It nearly broke her mother's heart
    That she from her daughter had to part;
    It nearly made her mother wild
    To get along without her little child.

    The pair were married, I believe,
    In April, 1893,
    They separated, I've been told,
    In August, 1894.

From sorrow broke the poor girl's heart,
They laid her body in a cart
They shoved it to the cemetery,
Where she was afterwards dead and buried.

Her mother sat in her lonely home
And for her daughter she did mourn,
She doesn't know for sure her daughter's in the grave,
For they haven't dug her up since the grave was made.

This tale is true, as true as steel,
How bad that mother, dear, did feel;
I hope a similar fate won't overtake Ellis,
You probably think I wrote this because of the Prince
    I was jealous.
                        Can you call me stupid, now?
                        B.W.L

    The salutation of the following letter communicates
a further advancement of the courtship. It is also
clear from the content of the letter that Ring was
thinking seriously about marriage.

                        [18 November 1908]
                        Wednesday
Love of my Life,-
    No sooner had I mailed you the note regarding the
peculiarities of addresses than your missive reached me in a
dazed condition. The envelope told of visits to all parts of
Chicago. I can't imagine what led me to say 468 West 48TH street
when the real one is 868 East 48TH. Please remember the
latter--868 East 48TH. You are now at liberty to omit the "c/o
R.G. Tobin," for I have already become notorious on the south
side. (Since joining the Tribune forces, I have learned to spell
south with a small s.
    Helena Hawks of Goshen, Ind., came over to our city a
week ago Sabbath. Her and Me went slumming. In the course of a
pretty nice conversation, Helen said: "Ellis is really the
Brightest Girl. She writes the cutest and most interesting
letters. You would enjoy hearing from her."
    R-"Yes, indeed I would; continuing, to myself, "and I
does."
    Sister Anne wrote home to my mother, Mrs. H. Lardner
of Niles, Mich., and a very merry soul, telling her, for lack of
something more interesting, of the aforesaid slumming expedition.
Mrs. Lardner told Sister Fatima, sometimes called Lena, of the
awful affair. Said Fatima, the only member of the family for
whom you ever admitted your love, then wrote to Ringlets, saying
she was very jealous of Helena Hawks, as she herself had always
wanted to go slumming, but had been afraid to ask Brother to take
her--knowing his rude habit of laughing at girls' ridiculous
notions. All of which is relevant and appealed to me at the time

as a strange coincidence, as follows: Ellis Rabbit likes Fatima and is jealous of Ringlets because he is her brother; Fatima likes Ringlets because he is her brother and is jealous of Helena Hawks because Ringlets didn't laugh at her when she wanted to go slumming; Helena Hawks likes slumming and is jealous of Ringlets because he can go every day if he wants to; Ringlets likes Fatima and is jealous of her because Ellis R. likes her too; he likes Helena and is jealous of her because she lives in Goshen, where Ellis R. sometimes lives; he likes Ellis R. and is jealous of slumming because she has never slummed with he.

This is the most funniest farce comedy plot I ever will hear of and if I had the time, the space and the inclination, I would write the most Comical Farce Comedy you ever read.

In your letter, you said nothing about my offer to exchange a page of the Tribune for a list of the tasks given you by Mrs. Smith for a day. Unless I hear from you at once on this subject, I will consider the proposition declined.

Having nothing to do last night, I happened to pick up a Girls' Basketball guide. Therein I discovered several views of games at Mr. Smith's house, but I looked in vain for a long time, among the athletes and spectators for a sight of thy dear face.

Finding it not, I said to myself: "What's this old guide good for anyway?" And I cast it into the debris. (Debris being a French word derived from de Brie, or Fromage de Brie, meaning Cream of Wheat Cheese. De Brie means, or suggests, Cheese. Debris means rubbish, the equivalent--rather, a synonym for all kinds of cheese.)

Example--"He ate a debris last night."

This means, "He ate a heap of rubbish, or cheese."

We (used editorially) are hoping that your mother, yourself, the weather and Ginnie Ginseng will act harmoniously in bringing you to Niles Christmas week. Better still, your mother, yourself and the weather will bring you to Chicago. See that they do.

And remember, Rabbit, leap year is drawing to a close. Remember, I am as shy as a kitten, but ready and eager to jump at an opportunity when it is presented in the right spirit.

Here is a trade Last, as my father says:

Sister Anne (looking at pictures of Rabbit) "Who is this?"

Ring, with funny lights; "Ellis Abbott."

S. A.--Well, these don't flatter her at all. I think She is an Awfully Pretty Girl."

In giving Me a Trade in Return, please don't say Anything about My Hand-writing. A new picture will be gladly accepted in payment.

Write.   R. W. Tobin, nee Lardner
868 East 48th

Wilma had now returned to Niles and had taken a job as bookkeeper with the gas company. Ring, who had worked at the same position in 1904 and 1905, counselled her humorously in the light of his own experience:

[Chicago, Ill.]
Saturday
[6 December 1908]

Dear Ginnie,-

The beauty of this ink more than makes up for the rather faded condition of the paper.

I knew of your promotion long before you told me of it. I want to congratulate you, also to make a few suggestions. If you desire instruction in keeping books, I refer you to Harry Walker, who has kept a book of mine for six years.

Don'ts

Don't argue with Mrs. Steinman about the post office bill. She will talk a long time tearfully--then she will pay.

When W. H. Bullard comes in, smile pleasantly and say: "Well, Mr. Bullard, this weather is just about like (or very different from) the kind you brave men had to endure in '63." This will make him forget all about the 12 cents increase over last month. Don't sneer and say! "Hello, Billy."

3- Mr. K. W. Nobles will want discount on the 11th., because he, she or it was sick on the 10th and couldn't strut across the street. Don't give her to it, or he will want it on the 12th of next month.

4- When Charley (alias Tod) Montague comes in, pretend you Don't recognize him, else he will pretend he doesn't recognize you. Beat him to it.

5- Stay back of the cage when Miss C. Southworth wants to look at lamps. Supply yourself with a magazine and make believe she isn't there. Don't try to answer any questions.

6- Always joke pleasantly with Fred Eisner, and Dr. Toefry. Don't joke with W. E. Platt.

7- Don't trifle with Clayton Seely. He lost his sense of humor when he married Mrs. Clayton Seely.

8- Tommy Freeze will say:"You ought to make it pretty cheap to me. Look at the mail I bring you." This is a good joke - laugh. Don't ignore him.

You may be able to struggle along with the help I have given you.

The Daily Sun didn't give you much space, did it? When I have more time - I mean it - I will write you up, send you the stuff and you can submit it either of the papers.

Sorry you got Genevieve's letter instead of your own. You couldn't expect her to admit it was her'n, as our love is a secret (from both of us, too).

Your father goes to New York and other points in the East tomorrow, and will be gone two weeks.

I have become almost acclimated. Bet you $.15 you don't pronounce that word correctly. Even I didn't until yesterday.

Write.

L. F. Brown

In 1928, when Ring wrote "The Maysville Minstrel," he also obviously drew in part on his own experience in describing Stephen Gale's problems as a gas company bookkeeper.

On Christmas day, Ring wrote from Niles to Ellis in Goshen:

                                         Krismus.
Dear Rabbit,-
Mutter wants me to go to bed, a thing I had no time to do last night. She isn't very nice to seek to be rid of the company of her youngest child when he is at home on so brief a visit. I am anxious to tell her so, but wouldn't hurt Mutter's feelings just for spite.
Therefore, as a subtle reprimand to (or for) her, I move to the next room and start out blithely on said twelve page letter, which was not due until Tuesday.
First and foremost, this will be my first twelve page letter. Never before has man, woman or beast enticed me into spilling so much ink. Please bear in mind the fact that I am not doing this because you have me subsidized or because your will is the stronger. I am doing it from a sense of shame. I heartily am ashamed of the booklet[1] and shipped it only because it was too late to do otherwise.

As a partial reparation I intend writing a melodrama for your perusal at an early date.
As predicted in these columns exclusively, you were the loser in the exchange of works. Of course, I am not forgetting that you cheated in leading me to believe the album would contain many views of the same Rabbit, instead of many views of many rabbits. Nevertheless, your gift was and is a masterstroke. I will never allow it to wander far from me. In passing, let me not forget to mention the strangeness of the coincidence of the numerous rabbits portrayed in both volumes.
Twice have I called up the residence of Miss W. J. for the purpose of extending to myself an invitation to her festivities. Twice have I failed to get a response. But before this is finished, I will have consulted her, if it takes all summer.
Don't forget to give yourself ample preparation for the contest of wills which is to be one of the features of our next session.

One ought to train for these events as for basketball games. In all fairness to you, I will say my training starts tomorrow morning. I will board an M. C. train (always train on a train)

_____

[1]The booklet is his Christmas gift to Ellis. He had proposed the exchange--he to write and illustrate a booklet of poems for her and she to have a new picture taken for him.

and will refuse absolutely to discuss the question of tickets with the conductor. If I get his mind on something else by sheer force of will, I'll know I am in fairly good shape. If, on the other hand, I am struck or put off the car, it will prove I am not at my best and I will have to work hard to recover my form. You, of course, have the privilege of making similar tests. You know, plain obstinacy will not count as will power. I have planned part of the events in which we will compete:

1. You will say: "Please take me out for a stroll or ride." I will refuse in so many words. Then we shall see which rules on this proposition.

2. I'll say: "I'm going home at once." You'll coax me to stay just a little while longer (personal feelings are not considered)

④

I'll persist in my statement that I must set out immediately and you'll continue to coax until one of us has acknowledged defeat.

I have other events in mind which I'll name later.

Nor must we overlook our determination to have a serious discussion on topics of the day.

Page 5

Just now I located Miss W. J. She was docile and even gave me the privilege of making out the program for her party on the evening of January 4th. She was mystified regarding my quick cognizance of the fact that a party was scheduled for that date. She informed me you were to attend a meeting of the Supuwa Club in the afternoon. In the evening, you are to tell me, among other things all you learned at that meeting.

Page 6.

Miss W. J. was hurried away from the phone,

⑤--Page 7. 7 + 5 is (or are) 12)

leaving me to suspect either that she had an honored guest or that parental objections cut off her edifying conversation with me.

Never mind, Ringlets, some day you'll find parents far-seeing enough to overlook your partial insanity.

If this function of January 4th is not pulled off according to schedule, I shall cease to be a man and become a vicious beast.

You owe me.

Really Ringlets

The following letter narrates another thwarted effort to meet Ellis, this time at Goshen during a trip to a baseball meeting in Cincinnati.

[10 January 1909]
868 East Forty-eighth street
Sunday

Dear Rabbit,-

Your letter wasn't awaiting me when I came back nor has it appeared yet. I'm afraid the wrong address got on again.

You must have thought I had gone crazy the other night.   The history of the affair follows:

You remember I was expecting to see you in Niles last Monday. During all the week previous I had no word from you or from Miss Ginseng regarding her "party." On Saturday, it was decided to send me to Cincinnati for a baseball meeting. As I had to see some South Bend people and wanted to see one Goshen person, I decided to go early Sunday morning by way of Niles. I called up Miss W. J. about 11 o'clock to ascertain when you were coming. She said the "party" had come off the night before and that you had started home half an hour before I phoned. My intention had been to go to Goshen Sunday night to see you and then to leave there for Indianapolis early Monday morning. But on receiving Miss W. J's. information, I thought to myself thus: "She "(meaning you)" didn't care whether or not she saw me, for she didn't tell me the new arrangement, and I might have gone to Niles Monday night and have seen nothing but dogs, horses and cows before she would have stopped me."

Thus thought I and it was rather discouraging thinking. Then when I reached South Bend my wishes overcame my pardonable pride and I called you up. About an hour afterward I found out I would have to be in Cincinnati before noon Monday. I couldn't make it if I went to Goshen first, so back I had to go to Chicago and thence to Cincinnati. The before noon business is the practical and most conven-[1] reason for my not coming to Goshen. There was another, less practical but just as important, which I'll tell you when I know you better, if the Lord ever relents and allows me to. Not that you want to know any reason at all, but that I want to try to convince you I'm not entirely insane.   The attendant disappointment and other uninteresting features need not be touched on in this extremely serious missive.

When you write, which you soon will do unless you care to be morally guilty of manslaughter, tell me what you said in the letter that I longed for,--and some more.
                                        Ringlets
868 East 48th Street

            This epistle evoked the following answer:

                                    Friday
Dear Ring-
            I did send my letter to the right address! Your postman must walk in his sleep. Please wake him up in time to get this letter. Besides Johnny has never told me why she changed the party. Your explanation is complicated but lucid and I have everything carefully assorted and put in its proper

---

[1]The word is obviously "convenient," but it appears at the end of a line, and though Ring uses a hyphen, he does not complete the word on the next line.

place in my mind. I was, really and truly, very
sorry not to see you and please dont say you dont
know whether I mean it or not because I always mean
what I say.

I suppose you think you are dreadfully
mysterious with your "other less practical reason"
but you neednt because I know what it was. This
was it: You didnt come because you didnt want to
and the reason you wouldnt tell me was because you
thought it would hurt my feelings. Therefore you
wait till you know me better to tell me. You
neednt deny it because I intend to beleive it
unless you tell me some other reason.

I cant tell you what I said in the missing
letter because I didn't say anything, as usual.
You might have known that without asking.

I could tell you about the bridge party I went
to and the prize I didn't win or the coasting party
I went to and the spill we did get or many other
equally exciting events. I think, however, on
deliberation, that I wont tell you about anything
but will write to my mother instead.

This is a very long letter and I am a very
busy person. Moreover I know that you are busy
too. That has a familiar sound, has'nt it? Anyway
I am going to stop before I forget to.

                    Ever
                        the Rabbit
I forgot to tell you that I put on my very
prettiest new dress Sunday after you telephoned.
And then -- I had to take it off again.

                    [16 January 1909]
                        Saturday
Dear Rabbit,-
Your logic is great. A person is working in Chicago. He is
told to go to Cincinnati on a certain date. In order to do this,
he might start from Chicago the evening before after having
enjoyed his full quota of sleep the night before that. Instead
of acting in this normal manner however, he sets out in the
middle of said night before that, sleeps not at all, goes a
roundabout way in order that he may stop at Goshen, gets almost
there, calls up a Rabbit to apprise her of his advent, then,
later, finding he can't come after all his well-laid plans, he
calls up again-----Because He Doesn't Want To See Her. Then he
prepares to tell her this reason when he is better acquainted
with her, because he would prefer hurting the feelings of his
oldest acquaintances to those of persons he has not known as
long. That "hurting the feelings" part was kind of you, but you
don't believe it.
No, small Rabbit of the Indiana prairie, I wasn't trying to
be mysterious and you are hereby forbidden to do any more

guessing unless you admit the folly of your former attempt.

Your mention of the new dress (or gown) only added to my misery—not that I would like you in said new dress (or gown) any better than in a purple calico ulster.

In the last year or two, after resolving to use my head, think twice etc., I have done the wrong thing nine times out of nine chances. If there had been ten chances, my average of mistakes undoubtedly would have remained 100.

Now we have talked long enough about the tragedy of Ringlet's existence. One of his New Years resolutions is: Next time he thinks he has a chance of seeing certain desirable people, he is going to say to himself, "You will not see them, you really haven't a chance, something will butt in and break it up." Then he is going on his way without making any preparations and, perchance, things may break in his favor for once.

Where did the coasting party come off? On Sycamore street hill, Niles, Mich?

Your old friend, Duffy Cornell, is to wed a week from Sunday. Peculiar day to select, but you and I can't help that. This is a secret, so please don't tell anyone in Massachusetts, Indiana or Michigan.

As soon as I can get to it, I will write a long epic for your private eyes. I mention this to keep you on the qui vive.

Your letter came two hours ago. Remember that when you get this one. Also remember you are to admit you see several flaws in your reasoning.

Lithely,
R--ts.

That might mean three things--Ringlets, Rats or Rabbit's 868 East 48th Street

When Ring's travels, this time with the Cubs, prevented his seeing Ellis during her college spring vacation, which she spent at Goshen, Ellis penned a warning to Ring: "You know, you cant expect one to keep up a _very_ exciteing correspondence on one conversation a year - and _that_ over the telephone." Ring reacted early in May during the Cubs' road trip by taking a side trip to Northampton to see Ellis at Smith College during the team's transition from Boston to Brooklyn. It was apparently during this hard-won Sunday afternoon together that Ring first asked Ellis to marry him. The parlance about ballplayer-type contracts in the following letter alludes to the proposal:

[26 May 1909]

Dear Ellis,-

You see I know you well enough now to call you by your first name.

I enclose the contracts, both copies, which you are to fix up to suit yourself. You are to sign and date them both and the one

I have not signed you are to return to me to keep. You may add
anything I have overlooked. Please be lenient.

Your F. and F.

R.

Route--May 29--Fort Pitt hotel, Pittsburg
May 30--Home, Chicago
May 31 to June 2--Havlin hotel, Cincinnati
June 3+ Home, Chicago.

Please excuse the alleged Pome.[1] I think it will be the last
inasmuch as they get worse all the time.

Saturday.
[29 May 1909]

Dear Ellis,-

Your letters pursue me even if you do not. The last one
greeted me in Pittsburg this morning, so you see there has been
no delay in this case either.

I'm afraid you don't understand the contract business. I
quote you the following, which is part of Rule 33 of the National
Commission:

"Each manager must send each player a contract before May 27.
Said player must sign said contract or agree to the terms thereof
on or before June 1. If said player refuses to sign said
contract or to agree on terms thereof, his (or her) case shall be
brought before the Commission for a trial. Said player, for
failure to sign or to agree on terms, may be asessed a fine or
suspended and blacklisted for five years."

You know very well I will not ask for your suspension or
blacklisting, but I WILL fine you and you have no idea how heavy
the fine will be. You still have time to fix up before June 1.
Think it over carefully.

Why do the collegians so furiously chase me around? Arriving
here this morning, the Yale club greeted me at the hotel
mentioned above. Later, President Taft puffed in and the
collegians had to quit me to entertain him. He is going to the
ball game this afternoon and, afterward, we are to be presented
to him at the clubhouse. Glad to know you, Judge. Oh, Mr.
Lardner? From Niles? That's near Goshen, isn't it? How do you
do?

Tomorrow morning we shall pass through Goshen on the way
home. I shall wake up. I shall be sorry not to see you, but I
shall be properly grateful you are not there, as it might cause
me to leave the train ("it" meaning your presence in Goshen) and
leaving the train might be synonymous with losing the job, which,
by the way, is still with me despite my flight to Northampton.

Something you thought (you didn't say it) when we were in

----

[1] Accompanying this letter was an undistinguished 83-line
doggerel poem narrating the events of that Northampton Sunday
afternoon--a day of "rabbit hunting / In the valleys of
Mass'chusetts."

Mrs. W. H's.[1] reception room (?) just before Mrs. W. H.
introduced me to my rhyme, has been cutting ever since. At the
next meeting, an explanation will be asked and the matter
discussed thoroughly, for I want to know why. In order that you
may prepare the explanation, I'll state the case:
I said, "I'm going to be a promoter next fall."
You thought I said, "I'm going to be promoted."
My own limitations, not those of the subject, made the pome
bad. As for the term "chatter," it had no double significance.
Once, years ago, we agreed to talk seriously for an entire
conversation, at least, I did. But I forgot it before I saw you,
which, I think, was some years later. But I've remembered it
again now and propose to go through with it at the next meeting.
Quotation from your letter: (1)"I am very humiliated to think
what you must think of me." Further quotation (2) "Please, this
is not fishing." Remark (1) What I think probably won't do me
any good, but I can't help it. Remark (2) The fish already has
been hooked. It never can swim again, so why don't you take it
home or else put it out of its misery? Remark (2) is rather
deep, but there is no double significance about Remark (1). I
thought I knew exactly what (2) meant when I was writing it, but
I know only vaguely now.
                    *Good Poem

          Them pictures that I have of you,
          Them pictures, miss, is mine.
          I'll send them to you, will I not?
          Yes, I will not. Behüt Dich Gott!
          Es hat nicht sollen sein.
              *Good because short
Havlin hotel, Cincinnati--Monday, Tuesday and Wednesday. After
that, home.
                    R. W L.

        The following letter, written to Ellis after she
        had returned home from her graduation from Smith
        College, reveals that she has given Ring no definite
        answer to his proposal:

                    Sunday.
                    [4 July, 1909]
Dear Ellis,-
    Please, how could I send you a pretty picture post card when
I had no idea where you were? As for your letter, it came to me
at Pittsburg last week, my brother having forwarded it, special
delivery. The brothers of some people use good sense. As for
your failure to find a Tribune, I can't understand it, as I
procure the great paper daily while in eastern cities. And
please cease reminding me that I am an unaccepted suitor for your

---

[1]Washburn House, Ellis's residence in Northampton.

hand--I keep remembering it all the time and will keep on suing
until you accept me from sheer desperation or kill me with a
cruel look.

The suggestion that I come to Lake Wawasee was another bit of
cruelty. I am going east Tuesday night to remain until the
twenty-first of August. I will go with the Cubs, try to clinch
another championship for them and then change allegiance and see
what I can do for the poor, misguided White Sox. You say no one
here would miss me--you are wrong, Mr. and Mrs. Tribune would
both miss me and dismiss me and then how could I pay your bills?
But I desire to and will say this: If I were given my choices of
a place to spend a day off, including Niles, Rome, South Bend,
Paris etc., I would select the lake mentioned above, provided a
certain Miss Ellis Abbott, A. B., were there.

One thing have I resolved on--I am going to see the party
named before this summer is over. If she wants to look on a game
of baseball as it sometimes is played, surely she can come to
Chicago after the twenty-first of August--soon after it.

Yes, I had seen that number of the Philadelphia North
American[1] before, but was not so much interested in it until I
found out, through your labors, whence my most wonderful
characteristics were derived. As for my being married, that part
came as a complete surprise to me and I don't think it was nice
of the paper to hook me up without my knowledge or consent. I
would have told you long ago if I thought it could have made any
difference. My wife--that is, my former wife, was divorced from
me ten years ago, so you see I am free to do the suing referred
to in the previous column. The grounds for divorce were
prohibition and madness. I don't think you knew the woman in the
case. It makes no difference anyhow. I've forgotten her name
myself.

Please don't wait so long before answering. And if you have
a picture of yourself to spare, please ship it along--I need more
than I have. Following is long route:

    July 7--Fort Pitt hotel, Pittsburg
    July 8-12--Majestic hotel, Philadelphia
    July 13-16--Copley Square hotel, Boston
    July 17-24--Colonial hotel, New York
    July 24-28--Doubtful
    July 29-31--Washington, Arlington hotel.
    July 31-August 5--Majestic hotel, Philadelphia
    Aug. 6-Aug. 10--Copley Square hotel, Boston
    Aug. 11-Aug. 14--Somerset hotel, New York
    Aug. 15-Aug. 19--Cadillac hotel, Detroit
    Aug. 21--Home if still alive.
                        Yours,
                        R. Wilmer
P. S. I saw Goshen at 4:30 this morning.

---

[1]The 31 January 1909 Philadelphia NORTH AMERICAN contained an
article on the Lardner family which listed Ring as being married.

The letter below to Wilma should be compared with
the following one to Ellis written on the same date.

The Arlington
Washington, D.C.
[29 July 1909]

Dear Ginnie,-
I haven't written to you for quite a spell. I'm telling you
this because the chances are you haven't noticed it.
I was astonished to see R. B. Kelly[1] sitting on the
Washington bench today. I had noticed the name in the paper
while I was with the Cubs, but I didn't know what Kelly it was.
They say he was throwing them around a little whimsically while
they were trying him out. All they did today for him was to let
him carry a sponge up to the plate when the catcher was injured.
After this city had been enjoying a period of comparative
coolness, we ran into it just as the change came. No one can eat
or sleep. The thought of the St. Joe river drives me wild, for
between the heat and the athletes, I want either to swim or
drown. Never travel with a ball team, Ginnie, for it means
suicide if you stick at it long enough.
The Niles Daily Star told me you had moved from north to
south. I don't know whether I am glad or sorry. You are nearer
Lardner's, but you are fu'ther from the station. You are nearer
church, but you are fu'ther from Montague's. You are next to
Carmi, but you are no longer next to Harriet and Jean and Ed and
Jennie.
I presume you did your share toward marrying off Miss Rogers.
I sent you an S. P. C.[2] while you were out in Linoleum, Kas, but
no answering S. P. C. came to me.
On Saturday night last, the Cubs tearfully left me at New
York and Mr. and Mrs. Tribune said I could do whatever I pleased
until today. I pleased to go swimming, so I asked New Yorkers to
point out a quiet spot. They evidently never heard of one so I
had to go to Atlantic City. After swimming there all through
Sunday, I met some one I didn't want to meet and as said some one
was going to stick around, I had to get out. In the meantime,
Mrs. Carroll Hamill, nee Pauline Micks, invited me to come to
Parkesburg, Pa., so thither I hastened. It is a town of 3,000
inhabitants and I had one grand time there. If ever you hear of
a town of that size that wants me, let me know please.
Helena Hawks dropped a line off the Cretis[3] the other day.

----

[1] Robert Brown "Speed" Kelly was a resident of Goshen and, for
the 1909 season only, a major league infielder-outfielder with
the Washington Senators. He played in seventeen games.

[2] Perhaps "Special Post Card."

[3] The ship on which Helen Hawks traveled to Europe.

According to her account, the travelers divide their time between sleeping and reading. It will not be thus when you and I go abroad.

The fact that I lapsed a little as regards my correspondence does not excuse you from writing as soon as you are in receipt of this. Moreover, if you had been as true a friend of mine as I had been led to believe, you would have written without waiting for an answer. There is an opening for a quarrel, a thing which you refused to start in your last, after promising you would.

You will find me as follows:

      Aug. 2-5, Aldine hotel, Philadelphia
      Aug. 6-10, Copley Square hotel, Boston
      Aug. 11-13, Somerset hotel, New York
      Aug. 15-18, Cadillac hotel, Detroit.
              R. W. L.

Thursday

Ring's allusion above to travelling abroad with Wilma is of course a joke, but it is still surprising because of his pending proposal and because Ring rarely indulged in jokes with sexual implications.

At the same time he expressed a concern in the following letter which is understandable but seems excessive since Ellis's letters reveal no current serious interest in anyone else.

                    Thursday.
                    [29 July 1909]

Dear Ellis,-

I certainly was glad to hear that one of my rivals had become ineligible. Why should you say I ought to be careful or you will accept me? Don't you know I have been waiting years for your yes? I'm afraid you don't appreciate the value of my offer even yet. To make it stronger, I will add some special inducements:

1. If you tire of my companionship, I will leave home and stay away until you recall me.

2. If you don't want to hear me talk, I'll remain absolutely silent for days at a time.

3. If you cease to care for me as you do now, I will leave the premises, not to return until the old fire is kindled anew.

I wish you were here in Washington, taking your share of the heat. Among the impossibilities are sleeping, eating and walking. If I were the Senate and Mr. Taft, I would pass any tariff measures they offered and go home.

I was vacationing from Saturday night until yesterday. One day was spent in the ocean and the rest at Parkesburg, Pa. Mrs. A. C. Hamill, nee Pauline Micks of Elkhart, who lives there, said she would find me a soul mate among her new friends. She did, but I am holding out pending word from you. The S. M. is six feet, two inches tall, has a nose as long as the baseball season, is as pretty as the Carnegie library in Niles and a Roman Catholic. Please save me from this fate.

R. B. Kelly was seen on the Washington bench at the ball yard
today. I shut my eyes, pretended I was at South Bend and that
you were nearby, but the heat beat down just the same.

Regarding the pictures referred to, I don't think you are
crazy and I only know that I still have some of my wits about me.
But you evidently misunderstood some remark of mine. I <u>never</u>
promised to send them back to you and I <u>never</u> will send them
unless I receive something of equal value in exchange--equal
value meaning more pictures. Why do you persist in talking about
them?--you can't have them. And why should you want pictures of
yourself when you have yourself? If I were as blessed, I'd never
look at a picture.

Did you make the weekend visit to Chicago? You know right
well it is possible and plausible to visit that city more than
once in a season and there is lots of time after the twenty-
first of old Augie. I don't blame you, though, for staying away
when you have a lake.

Oh, yes, another thing--Do you mind telling me where you are
going to be this fall?

There is one switch in the schedule I sent you. We are going
to stay at the Aldine instead of the Majestic in Philadelphia.
Write.

R. W. L.

Thursday

     Late in August Ellis visited Ring in Chicago, they
attended a ballgame, and she stayed overnight at the
Tobin apartment. Since the proposal, Ring had begun
his letters with "Dear Ellis." When she chided him,
probably during her visit, for his formality, he
responded with the following:

Hotel Euclid
Cleveland, Ohio
[6 September 1909]

Dear E_____e,-
You can't tell what I am calling you now. The fear that you
would hurt those B. Eyes looking so hard for the postman is one
of the reasons I have answered promptly. The other is that I
wanted another letter <u>right away</u>.

Two gents from South Bend came that far on our train last
night and the result was I didn't retire until we had passed
Goshen. I looked for you, hoping you had broken your other
engagement, but evidently you had not. Why?

I thought for just a minute I would be in Goshen. The team
is going back to Chicago tonight and tomorrow is an off day, them
Sox going to St. Louis late in the evening. Said I to me: "I'll
get off at 5 A.M. at Goshen and remain till 6 P.M." Then again
said I: "I can't see E____s, for she thinks more of her
certificate than she does of me." So I'm going right on through
to St. Louis, wishing it were October and vacation time.

We were trimmed again this morning. Why didn't you stay with us? Because of your certificate?

My boon companion and old familiar friend is impatient. He wants me to start immediately for the ball orchard, but I won't until I want to.

Important query: "Do prospective brothers-in-law have the kissing privilege, too?" I thought of that the other day and it's been worrying me, for what privileges do I have, who am neither b. in l. or h. Please appoint me to some office--I'm tired of being in the ranks.

I'm glad you are considering seriously the offer of hand and heart. The family is after me, which fact would cause me to balk under other circumstances. Don't let them persecute me.

We will be at the Planters hotel in St. Louis until Saturday night and I will expect a letter there.

                    Yours,
                        Ringlets

In the meantime, Ellis had decided to attend normal school in Goshen briefly in order to obtain a teaching certificate. Clearly she was not yet committed to marriage.

Ring did visit Ellis at Goshen on a weekend in October. A week after that visit, Ellis went at Ring's invitation to the Lardner home in Niles. What happened there is described by Ellis in a 27 October letter to her sister Florence:

Their house is a great big tumbled down old fashioned one. Mr. & Mrs. Lardner, Anna & Dick--that is Mr. Tobin--and Lena and Ring were the only ones there. We really had a good dinner. I am crazy about the whole family. Mrs. Lardner is enormous and queer but very bright & a great talker. Mr. Lardner is an old dear. We spent the evening playing and singing. Ring plays awfully well and played an hour or more. We tried to play authors but he cheated so that we had to stop. I am crazy about Anna. She is great and was too nice to me for words.

After Ring had returned to Chicago from having accompanied Ellis back to Goshen, he wrote the following letter:

                            [Chicago, 27 October 1909]

Dear Ellis,-

I was accompanied from Goshen to Elkhart by Jud Micks, who teaches in your very good college Tuesday and Friday mornings. Being greatly interested in my large affairs, he wanted to know what I was doing in Goshen, but was afraid to ask. He hinted around, and I led him to believe there was a great deal of mystery surrounding my visit. The chances are he thinks I am trying to buy the News-Times. I wish I could. I would engage you at once as a copy reader, regardless of Grace Schwendler's judgment.

Mr. Boss relieved my mind last night by assigning me to the Wisconsin-Northwestern game at Evanston next Saturday. The best thing about Evanston is that you don't have to use a sleeping car to get there. Brother Rex has agreed to go along to keep me company.

Part of last evening was spent in figuring up how much vacation was coming to me. Answer--thirty-three days. I was told it was possible, but not probable that I would get it all at once right after the football season's close. Some of it is coming then anyway. Don't you dare to leave Goshen, that is, unless you leave it for Niles.

Also, don't forget you have a diamond ring coming. I would send it at once if I knew where to get it, but such a thing and at such a price is hard to find even here in Chicago. I also must find a bank in which to plant my safety razor savings. Remember, at the end of ten months you will have not only a fortune of thirty dollars, but also a better looking husband. This isn't a hint. I already have an unsafety razor, which serves its purpose fairly well although it fails to improve the husband's looks. Nevertheless, your investment would be a profitable one, paying you sixty per cent interest a month on your money, whether or not the looks were improved.

I am writing a letter I don't owe. But that is only one of the hardships I am willing to endure rather than be cast off entirely by you. I am hoping you will be kind enough to let me win just one argument from you some time. I mean I hope you will be gracious enough to acknowledge defeat, for I already have some victories to my credit which you will not admit.

Heres a new bargain offer, another of the kind by which I alone profit. You are to write me twice a week as long as I write you that many times. Answer.

On the train yesterday were two alumni of Dartmouth. They never had seen Chicago and they took pains to knock it all the way over. Although neither was much bigger than B. Rockwell, I never opened my clam, knowing full well that both of them would be run over and killed by real street cars in a real city before they had been here long.

Will you write immediately, partner? I prithee, do.

Gaffer

P. S. How many people came to take you to the ball?
Wednesday.

[Chicago, Ill.]
Friday
[29 October 1909]

[To Wilma]
Dear Sir,-
If, in the sorrow attending our disagreement, there is room

for a laugh, it is on me. The other day, while you were in Lake
Forrest (Daily Sun spelling), I was up in Niles. I didn't know
you were away. Walking up Fourth street, I hesitated in front of
your former residence, at the corner of Cedar, and said: "I
wonder if Wilma is at home." My sister then replied: "If she
is, she isn't in this house." Further inquiry revealed to me the
fact that you don't live where I thought you did and where I
stood most of one recent afternoon, trying to gain admittance. I
told said sister about it and she said Grace Bunbury probably
would have come to welcome me if I had stayed around long enough.
Then she showed me your true abode.
     Why don't you write and beg my pardon?
     I prithee do.
                         R. Wilmer

     At this time Ring sent Ellis the
previously-mentioned engagement ring, though it was by
agreement not to be publicly acknowledged as such.
Ellis responded:

     The ring fits, thank you, and I wear it
     constantly to the unlimited amazement of my family
     who are all unsatisfied curiosity. Your savings
     bank will be shipped this evening. Just what sort
     of a quitter do you think I am? Also - the ring
     still continues to sparkle. It seems to be a
     characteristic of Rings.

     Late in November Ellis, in response to Anne's
invitation, visited Ring and the Tobins at the Chicago
apartment. Afterward, she wrote:

     In the first place I have so many things to
     thank you for that I dont know where to begin so
     I'll begin at the wrong end and go backwards. I
     certainly was glad to see Blanch Ring and like
     DeWolf Hopper I am "delightfully grateful" for the
     music. When I attempted to pay for my seat in the
     Pullman the gentleman said "Arent you the young
     lady the man brought down to the train? Well
     that's all right mam." Once more I am grateful.
     That I enjoyed my visit in Chicago goes without
     saying and for the third time I am grateful.

     The next letter, to Wilma (and his last to her--at
least the last which Wilma saved), illustrates again
the marked contrast in personalities which Ring
exhibited in his correspondence with these two young
women:

Chicago, Ill.
⌈29 November 1909⌉

Dear Ginnie,-
    This is called local stationery and can be procured at almost any downtown store.
    Sister Anne has deserted us again. Rex, not knowing whence his next meal is coming, refuses to get up. Ringgold wouldn't be up either if he had not remembered to procure the local stationery last night.
    I hope Mrs Miley hasn't sold all the pie. I'm coming, but no one knows when.
    Did you read in the Chicago or Niles papers about the marital troubles of Attorney Louis J. Fletcher, former coach of my high school football team? I ran into him while I was buying stationery. He has lost fifty pounds of flesh and a wife since last I saw (or seen) him. But the point of the story is this--Before we got through talking, he began to cry. You can't imagine my feelings unless you have been standing at some time in the midst of a Buck and Rayner drug store and the gentleman with you has started to cry--not just to sniffle, but to sob with loud sobs. I won't tell you what I did prior to my hasty exit.
    Just when football season was over and vacation was due, a large and perfectly senseless baseball war[1] had to break out. So the dandy little war correspondent had to stick around awhile regardless of his desire to hurry to Niles and to the M. C. dining hall.
    Mother hasn't been very regular about sending the papers lately, so I don't know what is going on in society. When you write, tell me all about your club life and affairs of the heart--I would have used the French term for that if I had knew it.
    Rex is stirring about, so I may be asked out to breakfast--lunch--dinner.
    Did you ever see such fall weather? Be sure to answer "Yes" or "No."
                                        Ringgold.
Sabbath.

        The following letter to Ellis is particularly
    interesting because it exhibits the athlete's dialect

———————————————————

    [1]The baseball war had developed as a result of American League President Ban Johnson's opposition to John Ward, a New York lawyer who was then a leading candidate for the vacant National League Presidency. Johnson had accused Ward of unethical contract negotiations as a player's attorney, and had threatened to pull the American League out of its partnership with the National League if Ward were chosen. The war was averted when Thomas J. Lynch, chief umpire of the National League, was elected as a compromise move.

with which Ring had already been experimenting for
several years, which he would continue to develop in
the "Wake of the News" and other TRIBUNE pieces in
1913, and which he perfected in the SATURDAY EVENING
POST "busher" stories of 1914.

Thursday
[Chicago, 16 December 1909]

Friend Ellis,-
Well, Ellis, I was glad to hear from you. How have you been?
I have been so busy making Exmas presents that I haven't had
time to write to you before now. Well, Ellis, you know how it
is. I don't have much time to get out let alone write letters
any time of the year, but of course this time of the year, just
before the holidays is the busiest time of the year for me, as I
suppose it is the busiest time of the year for you, in fact for
all.
Say Ellis, I must insist that you come to Niles before Jan.
6. I know Ellis you must be busy at this time of year, so near
the holidays, but say Ellis you certunly will have one evening to
spare before then. Why, Ellis, I intended to show you a good
time some evening before then; we could go to South Bend to some
show. I don't suppose we could see anything there as fine as we
seen in Chicago.
Ellis, I wish you lived in Chicago. Sometimes on my nights
off I could take you out and we could have great times. I don't
know many people here, that is girls, none that I care anything
about and of course you can't real enjoy yourself with someone
who you don't care for, at least I can't. I never was one of
those pretenders. I always show my feelings and I can't pretend
to not care for anyone when I don't. I don't suppose it's a very
good way to be, but Ellis, you know it's my Nature and I can't
help that, can I? If people don't like me for what I am they
don't half to like me, that's all.
Well, Ellis, I suppose I am tireing you with all this talk
about myself. But, Ellis, you have knew me a long time and if
you hadn't of liked me you would of told me so a long time ago.
You see I know you got a frank disposin, to.
My married sister and myself are going home to Niles next
Friday morning that is a week from tomorrow (Friday) morning. My
sister isn't going to stay but till the following Wednesday
morning. So you see you must come over to Niles before then.
I hope you'll anser real soon, dear, (you don't mind if I
call you dear, do you dear?)
Yours with love,
Ringgold Lardner
P. S. I don't think none of us can come to your party. My
married sister and her husband will be back from Niles and so
will Rex.

The opening lines of the following letter are written between the lines of a letter from Ring's sister Anna Lardner Tobin to Ellis. Apparently Ring appropriated a note Anna had penned to Ellis inviting Ellis to visit, and wrote his own letter between the lines and following Anna's note:

Thursday.
meaning Tuesday
But really it's Monday
[Chicago, 20 December 1909]

Dear Ellis-
Dear Pearl,-
    You have nothing to
As set forth by my sister
do Monday night, at least
so aptly, you haven't made any
you mentioned nothing--
excuses about Monday night.
why can't you come to
As for my demands, I'm not
see us that night, like
going to wait until Saturday
you did before? Say you
after Christmas, which you give
can--and write to
as your first idle moment.
me when you say it--
                A. L. T.
The Tuesday afternoon stunt you mention isn't going to last all night, is it? If you refuse to come to Niles Monday, I shall insist on Tuesday evening as mine, to do with as I please. As for the rest, I am not engaged at all and do not expect to be, so I just speak for all the idle time you have. I know you will do whatever you please and I must be satisfied with the remnants. As for the party, I will admit I'm a first class decorator, but my work would be spoiled by fear. And I want to see only one pretty girl and her name is Ellis Abbott.
    How often good resolutions go for naught. I was off last night and had made preparations to spend a quiet evening at home with my sister. A bride of one month called up and said her husband, a former pal of mine (excuse the slang expression) had been missing since Saturday noon. "Oh, Mr. Lardner, won't you see what you can do?" What Mr. Lardner could do, he did. He went to a billiard room down town and found the groom in an interesting pool game which had kept him busy for thirty two hours. Then I sent him home after denying his request to make up a suitable story. But, remember, Ellis, when you and I are married, I will eschew pool.
                Write.
                C. and J.

Please don't mind the peculiar odor of this paper. I don't know how, when or why.

There are fewer letters to Ellis from this point through mid-February because she was in Goshen during most of that time and Ring, having finally obtained some vacation time, was in Niles from Christmas Eve to 8 January and, after returning to work for approximately three weeks, took more time off early in February. This period was the only extended time Ring and Ellis experienced together during the entire courtship. Ring, Jr. says that during this time Ring "renewed his proposal impressively enough so that in my mother's recollection this was the real one. The event took place on a sleigh ride--one of the few means at their disposal to achieve the necessary privacy. The problem at the Abbott house, especially during vacations, was that they had five daughters and only three parlors."[1] Ellis's admission of her love, and probably her acceptance of Ring's proposal, took place on 26 January, while Ring was back in Chicago and Ellis was visiting him at the Tobin apartment. This moment is recalled by Ring in his letter of 26 January 1911, on the anniversary of the event.

However, it is clear that no date was then set for the wedding, since Ellis wished to teach for awhile and since, it seems, her father, Frank Abbott, was dubious about the respectability of Ring's position as a sports reporter and about Ring's ability to support Ellis adequately.

The Same Day
[Chicago, 11 February 1910]

Dear,-
Mr. L. S. Limited was only an hour late at Elkhart and the next interurban car beat it there. All of which left me in a que-e-r state of distemper.

Rex, one of my brothers, was alone at home when I arrived. Our conversation was such that it became necessary for me to divulge a certain pleasant secret. So I divulged, and I will quote you his comment, trusting you to come back with a trade in payment.

"That's the best piece of news I've heard yet. You will be the first of the family to get anyone near his own class."

Doesn't it make you feel q---r to know you're almost good enough for me?

Rex and Ring are the only ones of the tribe who have proven able to keep a secret. Don't laugh in scorn at this statement,

___

[1]Ring Lardner, Jr., p. 49.

for I told him because it really was necessary.

Nor did I see Mr. and Mrs. Frank P. Abbott and Miss Ruby Abbott.

After I depart from your presence I always think of something I wanted to say and didn't. This time, it will keep I guess.

Please remember I love you and shall keep on in that occupation for all time, whether you want me to or not.

I flattered myself when I said letters would be awaiting me.--There was one letter. The writer wanted to know if the pitcher should be given credit for a strike-out when the catcher let the third strike get away. But, instead of being sore about the scarcity of correspondence, I was glad, and I'll tell you why when I see you.

This town's a lonesome one tonight, dear. It's going to be worse than that. Please try to abide by the terms of your agreement. You know that doesn't mean you are to refrain from writing more than twice per week if you can. Nor does it mean you are not to answer right away.

Goodnight, dear, small girl.

Mr. Lardner

From this point to the marriage Ring's letters are even more frequent, they are more intense expressions of love, loneliness, and fear of losing Ellis, and they contain less Lardnerian wit. Clearly Ring was trying to handle the frustration of what promised to be a very lengthy engagement. One letter from Ellis at this time appeared to confirm his fear:

But, honestly Ring, you know there is something the matter with us. I wouldnt have the courage to say it at all but I know that you know it, too. You know that neither of us feels very much at ease when we are together and I know that I always have a feeling of restraint. I never can say any thing I want to or be the least bit natural. I dont know whether it is because you dont really love me or because I dont love you. Sometimes I think it is one and sometimes the other. You spoke of that evening in the 'piano-room'. Do you know its queer but I was thinking just then that perhaps I didnt love you after all and I was trying to make up my mind. And yet with my head on your shoulder and your arms around me I was perfectly sure the next minute that I did. But listen, dear, I'll never marry you until I am absolutely sure. I have wanted to say all this before but couldnt, and it is awfully hard to say it now but I just cant go on this way. If you will only tell me the real truth, if you really do care for me enough to want me forever and ever--it is a long time you know and I am a foolish

thing. I have always loved to go and to have lots
of attention and just have a good time. I dont
know how to do any useful or sensible things. But
the real me you dont know at all and I want you to.
I want you to help me to be that and I cant be true
to you or myself until I chase all these doubts out
of my mind. I think perhaps half the trouble is
that I am not sure of you and that I am makeing a
great deal out of nothing. I have given you so
much, Ring, I have let you kiss me so often and I
have given myself to you so much that I have got to
be sure that I am giving you my whole self. You
wont misunderstand me, dear, will you and you will
try to understand as much of this wandering as you
can, and see that I am trying to be true to both of
us. It is all so new to me for, though, I have had
more or less attention and people have said they
cared for me - it was always in just a childish
foolish sort of a way.

Ring received this letter on the morning of his
arrival with the Cubs at West Baden Springs, Indiana,
for spring training. The lover's agony in his response
below is painfully obvious:

Sunday.
[West Baden Springs
27 February 1910]

Dear,-
No one had enough sleep on the train and almost everyone went
to bed after breakfast this morning. I was going too, but your
letter came and changed my schedule. Do you know, before I
opened the envelope, I began to feel blue, for I knew, somehow,
that there would be "bad news."
I have been thinking about the letter and you for two hours
and wondering how to answer. I feel as if I were writing my own
death sentence and that's not a pleasant task. I feel as if you
were slipping away from me. I don't know how to prevent it and I
don't think I ought to try. You ought to know just what I
believe and feel about both of us and I'm going to try to tell
you. In the first place, there is no doubt at all in my mind
about my love for you. You have all of it--to keep and keep
forever. I'm simply sick when I'm away from you and I have no
real interest in anything but you. You are just everything to
me. Please don't think this is an appeal for sympathy--I'm just
trying to let you know the truth. When you consider my
"circumstances," the fact that I told you I wanted you may seem
strange proof of love, but I offer it in evidence anyway. I
would be less worthy than I am now if I had told you without
meaning it and had asked you to share a lot anything but enviable
if I hadn't cared so much that I couldn't help it. I don't
believe I made that very clear, but I hope you'll understand it.

What I think is the "matter with us" is just this--I don't
honestly believe you care as much about me as you sometimes think
you do--and you don't know all the time whether you do or not.
And in that connection, I have another truth--I think it's a
truth--in my mind that it's just impossible to tell you, because
you wouldn't understand it, and wouldn't believe it if you did.
You can't know how it hurts me to look at these things squarely
and to come to the summing up. If I were a "good catch" instead
of a bad muff, I could talk differently. As it is, I can say
just this--If you don't know that you love me, you don't love me
enough. I'm not fishing. Ever since that night at Anne's I have
felt that it was only a question of time before hell would follow
heaven. I believe people get out of life just what they earn. I
have not earned such happiness as life with you would be. I
don't deserve you. I don't think you want to be bound to me now,
and I know you don't want to say so, so I am saying it for you.
You are to consider yourself free unless you are sure and until
you are sure. And if, as I think, you realize it was a mistake
and that you never can care, please tell me so. And never
reproach yourself for anything, dear. There is no one to blame
except me. And you have given me a taste of more happiness than
I ever thought of. I'm not trying to pose as a martyr. This all
seems, natural, as if it couldn't have happened any other way.
But if I am wrong--I know I ought not to hope I am, but I
do--or if you ever do love me truly, so that you feel you can't
get along without me--that sounds funny and impossible, I
know--don't hesitate about telling me, if it's tomorrow or five
years from now, because there'll never be "another girl." I think
I do know you as you are, Ellis, but anyway I know I love you as
you are.
You can pretend you are keeping that ring for me, if you want
to. But please don't hurt my feelings by giving it back to me.
That's a favor I'm asking you.
I know this must be tiring you. Write to me--once at least.
I still know enough to realize I mustn't ask too much of you.
Dear, the very fact that you didn't want to write every other day
hurt me and made me see you didn't feel as I did. This has been
an awfully hard letter to write and it sounds like a funeral. I
know you'll think it is an appeal for sympathy and all I can do
is ask you not to think so.
I will try to wind up cheerfully. I don't know whether or
not you saw this cartoon. It was a delicate way of telling me I
was supposed to "buy." I couldn't see why I should, but I fixed
up something for them. The waiter pretended to be taking their
orders, which were very elaborate. Then he brought them a ham
sandwich, a cup of coffee and a cigar apiece. My guests were
very much put out. The paragraph about the feed was written by
the boss for their benefit and not for the paper.
Mr. Schulte[1] is with us. Last night, he and I made an

----

[1]In the letters of this period there are several references

agreement to speak to each other only once a week and to try to
be "decent" all season.

Ring.

The next day Ellis responded:

Cant the judge reconsider the death sentence
and make it a life sentence or make the punishment
just to take me back and keep me forever. I do
know now, dear, and I will tell you how I know - it
is just because I cant give you up. If you want me
you can have me and I will be just the best kind of
a wife I can to you my big boy--but you know I
haven't had much experience and I may not succeed -
just at first because I cant cook anything but cake
and salad dressing. And will you please forgive me
for all the dreadful time I must have caused you
and try to love me more than ever. But Ring, I
have been worried nearly frantic. Now I am never
going to think of it again and I am just going to
keep on learning to love you more and trying to be
more worthy of your love. It is always hard for me
to keep from adding - "if you really love me.' But
I am not going to say it but try to belive that you
do love me just as you say you do. You will tell
me it often, though, wont you so that I'll know it
every minute and and I'll try never to doubt you
again, never.

Do you know I cried and cried when I got your
letter and I dont know why because it made me feel
so sure. But, oh, I am glad I wrote you that
letter because I couldnt have stood it any longer
and now I am so much happier.

You know that I have never thought once in all
this time of what you call your circumstances. I
dont care and never will. I dont even know what
father has or whether he can ever do anything for
me when there are all the rest of the children, but
I dont care and I know you dont.

And now, dear, will you write to me and tell me
that you forgive me and love me. I want you to
tell me everything you think and do always. If if

---

to Frank "Wildfire" Schulte, the Cub rightfielder from 1905
through 1915, who compiled a batting average of .270 over fifteen
major league seasons. One of Ring's preferred companions on the
club, he was noted for his intelligence and wit, and for a
variety of interests, of which baseball was only one. His
nickname had developed from the fact that he owned trotting
horses, one of which he named "Wildfire" after the popular play
in which Lillian Russell, a personal friend, had starred.

could see you now I would kiss you and say I love
you and you would put your arms around me and say
that everything was all right now, wouldnt you?
                                        Ellis
        P.S. I will write to you every other day and is it
still hell?

                                Friday night.
                                [West Baden Springs
                                1 March 1910]
Dear Girl,-
        It's heaven again now and it makes up for the two long days
of hell, which was hell in its worst form and all its branches.
I don't think you are at all sensible, but you have no idea how
glad I am that you aren't. I am selfish now and I refuse to
think of giving you up, but before I forget to say it, remember
you always have the privilege of telling me when you don't want
me any more. Only, please want me.
        Besides, you make the best salad dressing I ever tasted,
although I don't love you for your cooking and absolutely don't
care what you can or can't do as long as you are you.
        Now I'm going to tell you about hell, admitting that it is a
play for your sympathy to do so Sunday night, after I had mailed
the letter to you, I went out on the porch and ran into Mr.
Schulte. He said: "How do you feel by this time?" and when I
asked him about what, he said "about our agreement." I told him I
thought we had better call it off awhile and he acted as if the
suggestion pleased him. He was lonesome and I was worse than
that. I think if he had proposed that we fight a duel, I would
have done it. It wouldn't have been any more foolish than, or
half as unpleasantly expensive as what we did do. I'm afraid he
is one athlete who hasn't profited much by his "training trip" to
West Baden. After your dear letter came this afternoon, I told
him the agreement was on again. He said "all right" without a
question.
        Poor girl, I didn't mean to make her cry and honestly thought
my letter would relieve her from a lot of worry. I won't forgive
you, though, because I don't know why I should.
        The world looks different tonight, sweetheart, even brighter
than it did before, when I was so horribly uncertain about your
feeling for me. It's hard to believe you do care when I was so
sure I was right and that you didn't. If you want me, there's
nothing on earth that can prevent your having me to keep. I
would give anything to have you with me tonight, so I could kiss
you and tell you again that I love you and want you forever.
When I thought I had lost you, I didn't care what happened. I
have been just crazy for two days, dear, and I guess I'm even
crazier now, but this form of insanity is pleasant to suffer,
while the other was like dying.
        I don't suppose I ought to, but I can't help wishing you had
been used to nothing and that marrying me would be a sensible

thing for you to do. I hate to think I can't give you anything
and that you will almost be throwing yourself away. You are such
a prize, dear, that it seems unbelievable I should have won you.
But you are foolish and you can't deny it.
I love you.
                                    Ring.
We are going away from here Thursday afternoon. Will there
be a letter awaiting me at New Orleans Friday night?

                                    Thursday.
                                    [West Baden Springs
                                    3 March 1910]
Dear,-
    I know I won't have another chance to write to you until
tomorrow night or Saturday morning, so I'll steal a little time
now while one of the afternoon paper guys is using the only
typewriter in captivity here. In West Baden I have been working
for the Examiner and Inter Ocean besides my own paper and it has
been rather difficult to send in three different stories a day
about absolutely nothing. The Examiner is off my hands after
tomorrow and I will be glad to get rid of it.
    This paper seems to have the leprosy, but I am told it isn't
really contagious, so don't you mind.
    This is a peach of a day and if you were, here, we'd go for a
long walk. You think I don't like to walk and I don't--except
with you. Every time you and I walk together after this--if we
ever get a chance--I will be reminded of our seeing Northampton
trip. I woke up on that walk, or just before it. I think it was
when you first came into the room at "Hotel Washburn" that I
fell. Then, all the rest of that afternoon and evening, I was
just thinking about "it" and about what a fine chance I had. Do
you know you always seemed unattainable--like a million
dollars--I thought of you then as something I would give anything
for, but something I couldn't have. I'm afraid you weren't very
good for me then, because you seemed so far away that I was
discouraged and discouragement always had a bad effect on me. I
know you will think I can't be "much" to let things run away with
me as they do, but, in self defense I will say that it's only the
big things that bother me and you are one of the big ones--in
fact the biggest one--despite the fact that you are really just a
little bit of a thing.
    Every change of season--since last May--has reminded me of
you in different surroundings and at different places. In the
fall I thought of you as you were at the dam Goshen--I don't know
why, because that was almost summer, wasn't it?--and in the
summer, as you were the first night I saw you. Now, just because
it's like spring, I guess, I can't put you anywhere but at
Northampton.
    Dear, do you realize you were to send me five pictures? I
can't very well get along without them and I don't think you
ought to keep me waiting.
    Yesterday and today I have felt as if I were walking up above

the buildings, although I have been horribly lonesome.
               OOOOOOOO ---just as many as you will take.
                    Yours always,
                         Ring

     The following letter exhibits significantly the
rapport Ring enjoyed with the with the Cub ballplayers
and their playing manager, Frank Chance:

                         Monday.
                    [New Orleans, 7 March 1910]

Dearest,-
     But I'm not enjoying the trip. I'm lonesome and I wish we
were training in Goshen.
     Last night I told Manager Chance it was my birthday and when
he asked me what one and I answered him truthfully, he said: "Do
you expect anyone to believe that? You are the oldest looking
guy for twenty five that I ever saw." I wish I were about
nineteen once more--I mean if you cared for me just the same, for
I was very beautiful at that age and I'm not no more. Also, I'm
getting to be a worse hand-writer the older I grow.
     You know I would go walking with you if I were there and I
wouldn't care about wet feet. I'm afraid, Miss Abbott, that you
don't take enough precautions about your health. I know I
wouldn't make much of a hit lecturing on the subject, but I don't
want you to take any chances. If you should be sick, I would be
too, so you see you have two people to take care of.
     You ought to hear the athletes discuss the relative merits of
their babies. There was an argument in my room last night that
was the funniest I ever heard. Mr. Hofman's Mary Jane has two
teeth and two others just breaking through. She weighs
twenty-five pounds. Mr. Reulbach's Edward has four whole teeth
and weighs twenty-six. But Mary Jane can pound her fist on the
arm of a chair and laugh at the noise. Yes, but Edward is a boy.
Whereupon I told them that my four months old nephew--there isn't
any such--could dive from a tower ninety feet high into a dishpan
full of salt water without making a splash. I wanted to get out
of the room so I could go to sleep. One of them left a five
o'clock call for my room by way of revenge. Whenever they start
their debates in Schulte's presence, he quiets them by saying:
"Wait till you hear what my dog can do." They don't want to hear
so they disperse.
     I'm glad you do think of me once in awhile. I think of you
all the time and spend my "spare" moments reading your letters.
You may tell your grandmother that I don't care whether or not
you can keep house. It will be enough to have you there. I know
I'll get along all right and I'll be perfectly happy and
contented as long as I have you. It's awfully hard to wait for
the time, though, especially when I don't know just when the time
will be. I'm horribly afraid of losing you, dear, and I won't be
really "at peace" until I have you all for my own. Did you ever

consider the foolishness of quarrels between husbands and wives over practical things and details? There isn't a chance of our quarreling, because I love you too much and because you are too nice.
Isn't it too much to ask you to write every day?
Yours.
Ring

The closing comments above demonstrate again the unrealistic way in which Ring idealized their future marriage. Ring naively believed that afterwards he would be able immediately to eliminate such habits as his drinking and smoking. In retrospect it is obvious that no man or woman, however gifted, could have lived up to Ring's ideals. This fact may explain why Ring's marriage, though loving, does not appear to have provided him with the solace he needed in those last years when he undoubtedly viewed himself partially as a failure as a husband, and looked out on a world he depicted in his fiction as bleak, mostly insensitive, and largely unsatisfying.

The following response is to a letter Ellis had written about teaching Sunday School, saying she sometimes felt she should not be doing it because she was "such a little heathen." This admission led Ring to state openly his own liberal interpretation of the scriptures:

Wednesday
[New Orleans, 16 March 1910]

Dear Girl,-
Even if you are a heathen, I think you would be shocked by some of my beliefs, or unbeliefs, so I won't tell you what they are. I do think, though, the people that wrote the bible never intended to be taken as literally as they have been. If I were in your Sunday school class, I would shock everyone still more by getting up and kissing you every little while.
My twin brother, Napoleon Lajoie, is here now with the Cleveland team. His mouth is wider than mine and his nose longer and he isn't quite so good-looking. Do you remember him?
They are making such awful mistakes with Mr. Schulte's poetry[1] up in The Tribune office that I am almost discouraged by

---

[1]Frank Schulte frequently entertained his teammates with dead-pan humor and satire similar to Ring's own, and Ring drew upon Schulte's extemporaneous "monologues" and "poetry" for some of his columns (see letter to Ellis of 16 March 1910). It is impossible at this time to discern how much Ring embellished them, but it seems likely that Schulte was a significant

it, or with it, and will pass it up entirely unless they leave it
alone. It is bad enough to start with, without their ruining it.
    My mutter tells me that Anne has a new piano. That's good
news, but the old one sometimes served as an excuse for not
playing well. You must come over and try it.
    We had quartet practice up in my room last night. "The Old
Gray Bonnet" and "Roses Bring Dreams of You" were sung more
effectively than any others. The Cleveland quartet will rehearse
with us tonight and I feel sorry for the guests at this hotel.
    And here is one for you:
    Miss Ellis Abbott? She knows that I do;
    That's only her name, but it's awfully true.
    I miss Ellis Abbott, I miss Ellis Abbott;
    Addressing her "Miss" is not merely a habit,
    It's true what I write on the envelope, dear,
    "Miss Ellis Abbott"--I wish she were here.

    But she owes me five pictures of herself. You wouldn't
believe she was the kind of a girl that would forget her promises
or refuse to pay her debts.
                         But I love her.
                              Ring

    The reference to the quartet made up of Ring and
    ballplayers recalls the short story "Harmony," which he
    wrote in 1915. Focusing on a ballplayer who loves to
    harmonize more than he values holding his starting
    position on the field, this story may well have been
    inspired by experiences such as the one Ring mentions
    above.

                              Sunday.
                         [New Orleans, 20 March 1910]

Dear,-
    The young man got up early and went to church this morning in
order to uphold his record of never having missed a Palm Sunday.
Then he wrote and told his mother about his good deed and sent
her a program as evidence.
    Then he still had time for the almost daily pleasure of
writing to his girl who happened to be the nicest girl in the
world, even if she didn't write to him as often as he did to her.
    Are you still nursing Florence? I wonder if you would come
and take care of me if I should get sick. I believe I'll try
it--but I guess I won't, because you wouldn't believe I was sick.

influence on the realistic dugout dialogue which Ring developed a
few years later in his short stories, and that Schulte's satiric
representations especially of the dumb ballplayer type
contributed to Ring's delineation of Jack Keefe in the "busher"
stories.

In this number, a serial, entitled "Why I am not good enough for You, or why I am not a good person to marry," begins. It is like the history of the Medes and Persians, uninteresting, but something you ought to study.

Chapter I.

I don't know the first principles of the saving of money. I never have refrained from doing anything I couldn't afford to do if I wanted to do it. I have been associated with a lot of people who had all the money they needed and spent it crazily, and I, who didn't have any, spent mine just as crazily. I am not a safe and sane person financially.

(To be continued)

But I don't know whether it will be continued or not, for some of the truths might make you see too clearly how foolish you are to care for me. Still speaking practically, though, I am positive I can be safe and sane with you, because, when I have you, the temptation to be otherwise will be gone. I will be perfectly content, just to be with you, and the things that have attracted me will have lost their power to attract. Why weren't we all born temperate? If I were as sane and reliable in all my habits as some people--Tobe, for example--I would marry you tomorrow, (if you would have me) for I would know that I could get along all right. In one of his frequent bursts of confidence, my roommate, McDonald, told me that he and his wife, before she was his wife, had thought it wise to wait until he had saved two thousand dollars. They waited two years and he hadn't saved anything; so they were married and he had a receipt for the first month's rent, and thirty-five dollars "in cash," and was three hundred in debt. After the marriage, he got out of debt and started to save and now he is talking about buying property. Query, how do some people get away with it?

If things don't break right for me and I find I can't save fast enough, I may go crazy some night and come and carry you off. Then we might fall together, but, at least, it would be together. But don't you think you had better see that the windows are locked tight?

Ball game time, honey.

Your own
Ring.

Monday night.
[Mobile, 21 March 1910]

Dear,-

I have waited in vain all day for a letter from you and I'm beginning to think you have decided to pass me up. The one you wrote last Thursday is the last one I got.. Don't you know that I'm starving for another?

We have been worrying about the critical illness of Billy Sullivan, one of the White Sox. He is out in California. He stepped on a rusty nail and got blood-poisoning and a telegram

today said he wasn't expected to live.[1] He is one of the nicest
ball players I ever met and, if he does die, I won't want to
travel with the White Sox. There are some drawbacks to this
business. People you like to be around with aren't good enough
for the team and are let out, or else they die.

You are much too good for my team, so there's no danger of my
releasing you. And please don't die.

I am still pulling desperately for rain on the twelfth of
April and I also am pulling for you to come to Chicago about the
twenty-first. There are very few inducements to offer. I can
take you to a ball game--yes, you must go with me to that, for I
couldn't bear to think you were in the same town and not with me.
I am jealous of Chicago if it can have you this week and I can't.

The farther it goes, the more I care for you, honey, and if
no letter comes tomorrow, I don't believe I can bear to look at
the ball game or do my work.

Don't you think this is a long enough note for a one-sided
correspondence.

Help.

                              R.

                              Saturday
                              [Columbus, Ohio
                              9 April 1910]

Honey,
       Your letter made me feel much better than I felt before.
I'll believe you love me till I see you and then you must tell me
so two or three times. I agree with your mother that you must
come to Chicago to have the pictures taken that you owe me and I
know Julia wants you to be there for the closing week of grand
opera. I will be home from the twenty-first to the twenty-ninth
at least. It may be longer than that, depending on when they
switch me to the White Sox. I'll be horribly disappointed if we
don't agree on dates. You know mine are fixed, so please try to
a fixer yourself.

There was much excitement last night in the station at
Dayton. The manager, Mr. Chance, heard that the Record-Herald
correspondent had sworn to "get" the job of Sheckard, one of the
players. So the scribe was given an awful bawling out and two
light punches in the nose in front of us all. When we got on the
train Chance sat down beside me and I jumped up and ran to the
other end of the car. He asked me what was the matter and I told
him I was afraid he might have heard I was going to get somebody.

Tobe and family have moved and, so far, have refused to tell
me their address, so I am now writing the following pretty cute

----

[1]Sullivan, the White Sox catcher, was out for most of the
1910 season, but recovered to play until a shoulder separation
suffered during the 1912 season eventually forced his retirement
as a player in 1916. He died in 1965.

parody on Miss Victoria's song:

> Taint all honey and it ain't all cream
> Riding 'round the country with a baseball team
> Watching the pastime, making up the score,
> Nothing in sight but a few games more.
> My dear girl, if I could see you,
> A fortune I would give.
> Poor old me, I haven't got no key
> And I don't know where I live.

Mother wants me to look up some old friends of hers here and I don't want to, but I must.
Write to me, dear.

Ring

Hotel Havlin
Cincinnati
Wednesday night.
[13 April 1910]

Dear,-
There is time for a note after all. My loving friends all have deserted me and there is nothing to do until the manager comes back.

I fully intended to write you a long letter this afternoon and was just getting ready to do it when five people came into my room and started a poker game. I was ordered to play and I lost. After the game had broken up, Mr. Tinker, Mr. Evers[1] and I made an agreement not to play poker again this season. Any one of us violating the agreement must give fifty dollars to each of the other two. There's not much danger of my playing under those conditions, but I sincerely hope the other two are unable to resist temptation. Manager Chance bought a pipe for Mr. Hofman[2] and one for me, to make our anti-cigarette resolution easier to keep. Oh, yes, the reform movement is strong in our midst.

Tobe finally has consented to tell me where I live. The address is 5042 Washington Park Place, and I think you owe Anne a letter, but please don't neglect me to write to her, for she has a husband and I have not.

It's good to be back in the real circuit, where decent hotels

---

[1]Shortstop Joe Tinker and second baseman John Evers, of the famous Cubs' Tinker-to-Evers-to-Chance double play combination.

[2]Ring had the day before resolved with Artie Hofman, the Cub centerfielder, to stop smoking until New Year's Day. Whoever resumed smoking first before New Year's was to pay the other one hundred dollars (who subsequently won or lost the bet is unknown).

abound. But I never will get over my rage at Mr. Holmes[1] for
making us play at Toledo yesterday. I could have seen you,
honey, but for his obstinacy. Maybe, if I have lots of luck,
I'll see you sometime, anyway, and I'm just living for the time.
And here comes the manager.

Yours always,
Ring

The letter below responds to a query about Ring's
interest in Wilma. A day earlier, Ellis had written:

I had such a funny letter from Wilma today. I
hadnt heard from her since sometime in January or
February and was getting worried. She said she had
been hearing gossip and thought I might have told
her about it also that Tom Swain (is that his
name?) said that he thought you were going to marry
that girl in Goshen. Are you? I dont know what to
tell her because I'll get found out if I tell her a
lie and I wouldn't tell Johnny a very big lie
anyway. But I'll fix it some way or other. I have
before. You dont like Johnny very well, do you
dear? You never said so but I just know it.
Johnny has lots of faults but she is wonderfully
clever and we have been together all our lives.
She is the kind of person you like to know even if
you dont like every thing she does. She is what I
call 'live' and always braces me up like a nice
fresh breeze. This is quite a dissertation but I
do want to know whether you like her and why not?
Did you catch that?

Hotel Havlin
Cincinnati
Friday night
[15 April 1910]

Dear,-
This is the second one today, but I'm afraid there won't be
much time tomorrow and Sunday, and this is to tell you that
you're awfully wrong about the Wilma Johnson--Ring Lardner
affair. My love for Wilma always has been unrequited. Really, I
always enjoyed her thoroughly and liked her very much, but I
began steering wide of her because she started acting as if I
bored her to death. I dont know where Tom Swain got his tip. I
guess Sister Anne, who is one of his sister Bessie's bosom

_____

[1]Howard Elbert "Ducky" Holmes was, briefly, in 1906, a major
league catcher with the St. Louis Cardinals. In 1909 he was
manager of the Toledo Mudhens. Ring's news reports from Toledo
include numerous plays on the manager's nickname and his
insistence on playing the game in the rain.

friends, has been doing some guessing herself. The Great
American Tongue again. But perhaps it's just as well that the
awful truth has been hinted to her, for a sudden shock might kill
her.

If you will tell me what paper your cruel and unusual was
from, I'll send it to Mr. Taylor, for I think he ought to have
it. My mother wrote some verses and sent them in for Hek's
column and signed them L. B. L. When Hek used them he said
they were sent in by a talented young lady at Niles.

Speaking of the Great American Tongue (you know we were) I
have a stunt for you and me to do some day before long. It is a
good one, but I won't tell you till I see you, so hurry and come.

You haven't much faith in my swearing off ability, have you,
honey? I will fool you and the rest of them who think it will be
up to me to pay the fines. No, dear, the cigarette question was
not one of health. A pipe or a cigar is just as bad the way I
smoke it. It was entirely a question of money. So you were
wrong twice in the same letter, but I love you just the same.

We lost another game today and the manager is a little sore
on the world tonight. If we don't win tomorrow and Sunday, we'll
be afraid to travel to St. Louis with him. I only wish we were
going back to Chicago tonight and that you were going to be
there.

Remember, you must come.
               Ring

                     The Southern
                     St. Louis, Missouri
                     Tuesday eventide
                     [19 April 1910]

Honey,-
Three people told me tonight that Artie Hofman smoked a
cigarette in the club house this afternoon. I must see him
before I do anything about it, for it is a question of "honor"
between us. He is staying with his family, so he may be doing a
lot of things that I know nothing about. I was so crazy for a
cigarette today that I bit a piece off the stem of one of my new
pipes just thinking about it.

I told you I wouldn't let you into the Great American Tongue
secret until I saw you and I mean it so if you are curious, you
must hurry up and let me see you.

We are going to see William Collier in "A Lucky Star"
tonight. We haven't had a ball game since we got here, for which
I have been duly grateful. How nice it would have been if you
had been visiting in St Louis this week.

Please make your mother let you come to Chicago. Tell her
it's a question of life and death--with me--and I know she'll let
you come.

I won't get a chance to write you tomorrow. We are going to
depart for home soon after the game--if there is a game. I wish
you could be there Thursday morning. There's nothing I wouldn't
give to see you and, knowing this, it will be cruelty on your

part not to come.
    Goodnight, dear girl.
          Ring

      On the following Thursday Ellis visited Ring again
in Chicago, where they attended the ball game and she
stayed overnight at the Tobin apartment.

                  Hotel Schenley
                  Pittsburgh, Pa.
                  Saturday
                  [30 April 1910]
Dearest,-
    I haven't written to you for so long that I've almost
forgotten your address. But I remember your name perfectly.
    Four of us are to spend Sunday here--Brown, Dryden, Carson
and Lardner. Carson and Dryden will stay in their rooms and
read, so Brown and Lardner will have to plan an excursion.
    I have nine or ten trades for you from persons who saw
Thursday's game. I won't give you many of them without pay.
Claire Briggs, eminent cartoonist, said, "I'll have to hand it to
you; there certainly was some class to her." John DeLong,
yachting expert, "She didn't look it, but there must have been
something wrong with her mind or she never would have stood for
you." H. E. Keough, (Hek): "I don't know how you get away with
it, but she surely was a peach."
    None of which was news to me even if they are newspaper men.
But honestly, honey, I'm awfully proud of you and everything
about you. I guess my reputation for unluckiness is all shot to
pieces. If I am lucky enough to have you care for me, I surely
will be lucky enough to have you for keeps some day.
    It was great of you to stay over Thursday night and I
wouldn't have missed those few extra minutes for anything. I
hope you weren't sorry afterward that you stayed.
    If it doesn't rain here Monday, Tuesday or Wednesday, and if
I am let off, I'll get to Goshen long before you are up Thursday
morning--at three minutes before five. I never was so concerned
about the weather before. Please pray for sunshine--I know you
have a better stand-in than I.
              Yours always,
              Ring

      In accord with the customs of a more formal age,
Ring had now to ask Mr. Abbott's permission to marry
Ellis. The following letter, written nearly six months
after Ellis had first accepted his proposal, apologizes
for his inability to make the request now in person:

                  Chicago, July fifth.
                  [1910]
Dear Mr. Abbott,-
    I'm sorry not to have been able to meet you this afternoon,

for I know it would have been more satisfactory than writing. I intended leaving here last night, seeing you this morning and returning in time to attend the ball game here. The paper is very much opposed to allowing us to skip a regular game. There is some rule about not taking the signature off a baseball story during the championship season. Tonight we are going east again and, when we come back, about the first of August, I will manage to get over and see you for a few hours anyway.

Of course you have guessed by this time that I care a great deal for Ellis. I can't help it, although I realize that no one is really worthy of such a girl and do not flatter myself that I am. That she cares for me in return is my only excuse for this letter, which is a request for your consent to our marriage. I know the life she has been used to and know I am not "well off." But I do believe I can take care of her. She told me she would like to wait awhile, and, although I want her just as soon as possible, I know it will be better to wait until I have done some more saving.

My present work takes me from home too often to suit me and I intend to have another arrangement after this season ends. I can tell you more about it after this trip. I know how a father must feel about such things and all I can do is to give the assurance that I can take care of her now, and know that I will do better as time goes along.

I realize how much I am asking of you and Mrs. Abbott and Ellis' sisters and brothers. But I care so much for her I can't help asking and hoping that you will give her to me whenever she is ready.

We are going to stop for one day--tomorrow--at Cleveland, and from there will go to New York to stay from Thursday night until next Tuesday. I would like to hear from you and will be at the Somerset hotel.

Sincerely,
Ring W. Lardner

Among the Abbott family Ring had become especially close to Ruby, Ellis's older sister, whose interest in music Ring found especially congenial. When Ellis did not write as often as he wished, he wrote the following to Ruby:

Thursday
[Chicago,
4 August 1910]

Dear Ruby,-
You have a peculiar sister entitled Ellis Abbott. I write letters to her occasionally and I don't believe she reads them. At least, she pays no attention to anything in them. There's something I'd really like to know--namely, on what day in September is she coming to Chicago and about how long can she stay? You know I want to try to arrange my schedule accordingly.

If you could find out from her and tell me, I'd do almost
anything in your behalf.

Also, I ask you personally if you know a song by Robert Louis
Stevenson and Mr. Homer called "Requiem"? Please don't let
Ellis Abbott know I have communicated with you.

As a partial reward for your trouble, I send you a picture of
myself called "Complete Bewilderment."

And please don't show that to her either.

I haven't much to do this afternoon, so I think I'll go to
the ball game.

Please remember me to Dorothy, Florence and Jeannette.[1]
                                    Your affectionate aunt,
                                           Ringgold.
      5042 Washington Park Place.

                                        Tuesday night.
                                        [Chicago,
                                         9 August 1910]

Dear Girl,-
    Richard Lardner Tobin is the title of a new he brat out at
our house.   I haven't saw him yet and I'm not crazy to, for I
never did see one that wasn't a fright. I think him and me will
get along all right. I intend to show my authority right from
the start. If he gets fresh, I'll slip him some carbolic acid.
Please don't mention that to anyone. I'm going to teach him to
talk Persian exclusively. Isn't it a shame he wasn't born a week
ago yesterday so we could call him August the First?
    You seem to think it strange that Paul[2] should be interested
in me.   I think it's very natural.   I'm interested in him.
Chiefly because he is your almost brother-in-law.   I'll be in
Pittsburg just one more day this year--the eighth of October--and
I'll look him up then.
    The Lord is having lots of fun with me. At two o'clock this
afternoon it was pouring down town, but not a drop fell at the
ball park.-- You were lucky not to be in Chicago. I ran into the
parade twice and spent an hour and ten minutes getting across two
streets. After I had sworn not to come to town in the daytime,
too.   But the arrival of R. L. T. upset my plans. He may be
nice and you may like him, but I've got it on him, for I've
kissed you and he hasn't.
    I'm expecting a long letter from you tomorrow and I'm going
to be disappointed if I don't get one. But I know I will, for
you said you were going to write this morning. I haven't heard
from Philadelphia yet, but I ought to tomorrow. Then I'll know
whether I'm ever going to get the long lost letter or not.   I

_____

    [1]Ellis's younger sisters.

    [2]Paull Torrence, Florence Abbott's fiance.

want it because I hate to miss one from you.

I thought of you all day and had all kinds of trouble   trying
to pay attention to the game.

Good night, honey.

Ring

Wednesday.
[Chicago,
10 August 1910]

Honey,-

I was just introduced to R. L. T., who, for some   reason,   is
known as B. around here. Tobe says he looks like me. I know he
does not. He has the biggest nose I ever saw, just the right
size for this part of town. He makes funny noises all the   time,
something like a recently caught fish.

I have more T. L's.   for you, but you can't have them
because you cheated me. And I trusted you, too

Your letter was great and will be answered in detail.   There
is nothing new about the song. Some night this week is to be
baseball night at the American Music Hall and Miss Mayhew is   to
sing it then.

The disappearing husband finally wrote to his   wife and she
told me where he was--down in Atlanta. So I wrote to him there.
He hasn't answered and probably won't. The creditor is very nice
about it and says I can have more time.

Your explanation about Monk[1] was satisfactory, especially the
part about his being ugly. I'm glad of that.

I know I could get a day off if I asked for it, but I also
know I ought not to ask for it. It's hard to be patient but I
guess it's best. I'm going to write to my colleague tonight   and
try to arrange the switching with him. But I'm a little afraid
to ask him to change the   first of September as that would
necessitate his suffering an extra five days in St Louis, a town
he hates heartily. But I'll do the best I can and let you know.
Some day we can laugh at the weather and at the national pastime.
I wish that day would hurry up and come.

B has broken into a loud wail. One consolation--nothing like
that ever disturbs my slumbers.

It's almost game time and no sign of rain today.

I love you.

Ring

Monday, 15 August, was White Sox night at the
American Music Hall.   The song was "Little Puff of
Smoke, Good-Night" (copyrighted on 13 August 1910), one
of two songs which Ring and White Sox pitcher Guy
Harris "Doc" White collaborated on and published (the
other was "Gee! It's a Wonderful Game," copyrighted on

---

[1]One of Ellis's escorts at Lake Wawasee

13 June 1911). Miss Stella Mayhew's performance of it
was greeted with great applause, according to the
account (obviously written by Ring) the following day
on the sports page of the TRIBUNE. The fact that she
was called back for five encores is not surprising,
since the entire Sox team and the New York Highlanders
were in attendance.

Ring was even fonder of composing lyrics (and
sometimes also music) than he was of writing his
doggerel poetry, though only eight of his songs can now
be identified as having been published.[1] Perhaps the
best-known were "Prohibition Blues" (sung by Nora Bayes
in the 1919 musical LADIES FIRST, and "June Moon" (the
title song for his 1929 play in collaboration with
George S. Kaufman). Ring once estimated that if he
were to measure his time devoted to composing lyrics
against the money they earned, he would have a $10,000
deficit. But he loved to write them, and it was to a
considerable extent his interest in music which
sustained him in his last years.

The next letter is again to Ruby:

Aldine Hotel
Philadelphia, Pa.
Sunday Eve.
[22 August 1910]

Dear Rubina C.,
You are not overpaid at all; on the contrary, you are very
worthy of your hire.
I was going to delay writing you until I had saved up or
borrowed money enough to buy some stationary, but I have more
time now than I'm likely to have again for a week, so please
forgive it.
I want your peculiar sister to be in Chicago on the eleventh
day of the coming September. If she is not there on that date
and if she doesn't stay more than a week, I will seek death by
strangulation and you will be held as accessory before the fact.
And please don't think that is meant as a threat. It is merely a
friendly warning. I am rather fond of your p. s., in fact, I
care more for her than I do for my work, or the great game of
baseball, or anything to eat. And it is rather unpleasant not to
be able to see her for weeks and months at a stretch--therefore,
when there is a chance, I want her as long as I can have her,
whether she likes it or not.
Gladly will I deliver your message to my sister and nephew,

---

[1]A few other songs probably were published, but no record
survives. See Bruccoli and Layman, RING LARDNER: A DESCRIPTIVE
BIBLIOGRAPHY, for a listing of Ring's copyrighted sheet music.

or niece, or whatever it is, when I see them. But I'm afraid
IT will not be much impressed, as it has failed to show much
interest in my conversation so far. There must be something
wrong with it.
          I can't begin to pay you for all your services, but I stand
ready to obey your commands.
          Please keep this letter a dark secret from P. S., also.
                    Yours in absolute sanity,
                         Ringgold Wilmer.

          Since Ellis's father had after six weeks still not
replied to Ring's written request for Ellis's hand,
Mrs. Abbott wrote to apologize and to invite Ring to
visit as soon as he might. Ring framed the following
response with obvious care.

                         [22 August 1910]

Dear Mrs. Abbott,-
          I was awfully glad to get your letter, although I never was
guilty of imagining that I had been unjustly treated. Ellis told
me her father was sick and I was sorry to hear it. But I could
not have blamed him for delaying his answer anyway, for I can
guess how he must have felt about it--not knowing me at all. I
knew how a father or a mother must feel about giving up a
daughter and especially one like Ellis, who is really so
superior. I didn't dream she ever could care for me, and the
knowledge that she could and would made me so happy as to cause
me to forget for a time some things more important than my own
happiness, such as hers, and her separation from her family. But
I have thought of them since and can only hope that she will care
enough for me to overlook a lot. I know she will not want for
love, for she has all of mine.
          Of course I want her as soon as I can have her and I know I
will be ready to take care of her by the first of the year, but I
am TOO grateful over the prospect of having her at all to want to
take her from you before you are ready to let her go.
          I challenge and defy her ever to discourage me and I don't
believe I would care quite so much for her if she were more
practical.
          I have been trying all summer to get down to Goshen, but I
had to wait for rain, and it never came at the right time.
However, I'm sure I'll have better luck next month and I will
come the first day I can. Thank you for the invitation and also
for writing.
                    Sincerely,
                         Ring W. Lardner
August Twenty-second.

Tuesday
[Boston, Mass.
30 August 1910]

Dearest Girl,-
It's cold in Boston, Mass., and the old shivers are present with me again. I don't think I ever could hold a job as an Arctic explorer. Anyway, I wouldn't care to try.

The Boosters club of Baltimore is stopping here and affording us almost as much enjoyment as the Boys from Amherst used to. Probably we amuse it, too.

I have an unpleasant task ahead of me. Frank Schulte's brother killed himself and I suppose I must write one of those awful letters. He is having a gay life with an insane mother and a brother who must have been as bad.

There was a letter from my mother this morning which was sort of song of praise for you. I suppose it was the result of Lena's home coming and her conversation about you. You sure are "in right" with the Lardner family. But don't you believe that the rest of them are as much in love with you as I am, no matter what they say.

I won't tell you now what your mother said about you. Perhaps I can use my knowledge in making bargains when I see you. She didn't knock you **very** much. If she had, I wouldn't have answered her letter.

I presume you have heard from Anne by this time. She says B. is becoming more reasonable every day, taking after his Uncle Ringgold. Blood will tell.

Tomorrow night we will start west, stopping in Detroit for three days. Then we'll go home just for Labor Day and then to St Louis--Planters hotel--for five horribly long days. Then I will see you and that will be reward enough for recent hardships. You can't guess how I am longing for the arrival of the eleventh and for you. Don't dare to disappoint me.

Yours always,
Ring

Though Mrs. Abbott had invited Ring to Goshen, the conference with Mr. Abbott could not take place until Ring had the necessary free time, after the World Series. In the midst of this confusion, Ellis accepted a teaching position in the elementary school of the Culver (Indiana) Military Academy, which effectively postponed any possible wedding until the following June. The letter below, written to Ellis at Culver, refers to an "interview" between Ellis and her her mother which was probably an attempt by Ellis to enlist her mother's assistance in urging Mr. Abbott to consent formally to the marriage, for he had still not responded to Ring's letter of 5 July.

Sunday night
⌈Chicago,
11 September 1910⌉

My Honey,-
I don't know Mrs. Crandall[1] or whether or not she is to be
trusted with anything so precious. Please don't let anything
happen to you.
I mailed a letter to Goshen late Saturday night because I
didn't know where else to send it. Perhaps it arrived too late.
You can bet I'm anxiously awaiting news of the result of your
interview with your mother. It means more to me than anything
ever did, and to you, too, poor girl. I will give you two T.
L's. in exchange for your two very nice ones, but I'm ashamed of
John for wishing Ruby such hard luck. Mr. Eckersall said "You'd
better hurry up and grab her before she wises up and quits you.
She looks good to me." And Mr. Briggs: "Yes, because anyone is
likely to try to steal her and you wouldn't have much chance in a
real contest." When I pointed out the fact that I had won against
a large field, they suggested the field was made up of Hoosiers,
and that even I might look classy in such a race. While it isn't
right for them to roast me--who really am or is a nice person--I
forgive them because they speak well of you. I also have T. L's
from my mother, but I'm not doing any credit business.
Perhaps we are going to have next Thursday off. If we do,
I'll go home, I guess for I promised to do so some time this
month. When that engagement is kept, I'll be free to see you
some day next week, on my way to Cincinnati to join the Cubs.
When you write, tell me all about Culver. Also, that you
love me.
Good-night, dear girl.
Always yours,
Ring.

On the 15th, Ellis was especially expressive of her
love:

My Sweetheart
I want you so! I want you so! I want you! I
came home and did a few errands and went right out
to the Fair. It was fun seeing the crowds and the
races and all the people we knew. But now the
excitement is over and I am just beginning to
realize how hard it was to leave you. And isn't it
dreadful? I might have stayed until the next train
and been with you three hours longer. I'm so
lonesome and blue. No one else helps at all. I
need just you and next September does seem a long

---

[1]The wife of Captain Crandall, commandant at Culver, with
whose family Ellis lived while teaching there.

way off. I cant tell you about that definitely now
but I will in a day or two.

I had such a nice time every minute I was in
Chicago and I love you twice as much or a hundred
times as much as I did before. If you think theres
any chance of your ever not loving me <u>please</u> tell
me now before it gets any worse. I'm thinking of
you every minute and I need you.

Give my love to Anna and the baby and dont
forget that I love you. love you, love you
Your own girl
I want to kiss you goodnight and I cant.

Monday
[Chicago,
19 September 1910]

Dearest Girl,-
I suppose you are in Mrs. Crandall's clutches by this time.
I'd consent even to be a professor at Culver to be near you, but
I don't suppose I will be offered the job. I don't see why, if
you were determined to teach, you didn't come to Chicago to do
it. I guess you don't like me.

Can you tell me what time trains go to and come from Culver,
in case I should be able to get away for a day next week? But
you haven't told me yet that you want me. If you don't, I think
I'll go to St Louis with the Sox and save my off-days till later,
for off days I can't spend with you are almost worse than none.

James J. Corbett was out at the game yesterday and was
telling us further details of the downfall of the white man's
hope.[1] I wish you could have heard them.

I guess you'd better keep sending my letters to the office,
for I can get them there at any hour of any day and sometimes
they are slow about reaching this place. Did you know there was
a new rule regarding letters? They are to be written <u>every</u> <u>day</u>
from <u>now</u> <u>on</u> if <u>possible</u>. And, in accordance with my promise:
Ode to Ellis

Before you came, I lived for something--
what, I never knew
Until the day arrived when first I gave my
heart to you;
Then living was a constant pain, a poignant
misery,

---

[1]James J. Corbett had been heavyweight boxing champion
prior to Bob Fitzsimmons. The fight reference is to the Jack
Johnson versus James J. Jeffries title bout of 4 July 1910, won
on a 15th round TKO by Johnson. Jeffries had come out of
retirement as the "white man's hope" to defeat Johnson.

Until the glorious day when first you gave
    your heart to me.
Now vainly fights the pain of knowing that
    we're far apart.
To overcome the joy of knowing that I
    have your heart.

I don't believe that's exactly an ode, and I know it's
conceited and not very fine, but please forgive it and give me
credit for keeping my promise.
And I've got to go to the ball game.
                    Always,
                        Ring

    Finally Ellis did report the substance of her
interview with her mother:

    I dont remember 'just exactly what my mother
said.' I know that she said she didnt blame
me--that of course she didnt want me to go but it
had to come sooner or later and that she would talk
to father about it. Ruby is the one that scares me
to death. Every time I say that I think I'd tell
people that I think I am engaged she says, 'No,
dont.' and then freezes up just like any old ice
berg and when I told her I might be married in June
she simply wouldnt say a word. Finally I told her
that I thought she couldnt like you or she would be
a little more enthusiastic, but she insisted that
she was crazy about you and thought you couldnt be
nicer--it was only that she didnt want me to go.
Why dont you write to her again? Its like bumping
up against a stone wall every time I try to make
any plans. She simply wont listen to them.

                    [Chicago,
                    27 September 1910]

Dear Ruby,
    Ellis said she didn't believe you liked me "any more,"
because when she mentioned the word "June" to you, you wouldn't
talk to her. Please don't dislike me because I want her, and
want her as soon as possible. I know how you feel about it--that
you girls won't be together much longer and that you naturally
want to keep her as long as you can. Also, I know you must think
me ungrateful and selfish. I am selfish, but not ungrateful. I
know how lucky I am to have her care for me at all, and I'm
living in constant fear that something will come between us. I
never can get over this fear until she is mine for keeps, and it
honestly is torture to think that we'll have to wait until June.
Also, you can guess that it's torture just to be away from her.
I have only one argument to offer--you have had her all these

years and I haven't had her at all. So please don't make me wait
longer than is absolutely necessary. And please don't think
Ellis' coming to me means her separation from you. I know she
cares a great deal for you; if the truth must be known, I do,
too. So, you see if you don't spend a very great deal of your
time with us, you will disappoint us awfully. It would be the
easiest task in the world for me to like people Ellis liked just
because she liked them, but in this case, it's twice as easy
because the people are so likable in themselves. I'll be awfully
happy and relieved if you can like me a little again and try to
forgive my nerve.

                              Sincerely,
                                 Ring
       Monday.
       5042 Washington Park Place

        The following letter was written after Ring had
     managed to see Ellis on two successive evenings. He
     had taken a train to Culver on a Thursday evening,
     stayed overnight at a hotel, and then, on Friday
     evening after Ellis had finished teaching, the two had
     gone to Niles and to Goshen to visit their parents.

                              Hotel Havlin
                              Cincinnati, Ohio
                              Monday morning.
                              [3 October 1910]

Honey,-
     Your small boy certainly has been making up for his days off.
That Big Four train from Goshen got to Indianapolis an hour late.
As we came into the station, the C. H. and D. was pulling out.
I didn't have time to ask where it was going, but I hopped on and
fortunately it was the right one. "Fortunately" is right, for I
don't know what would have happened if I'd been late. I do know
a lot of things did happen and have been happening ever since.
     In the game Saturday, Johnny Evers, one of the "stars," broke
his leg and put himself out of the world's series. Yesterday's
game made the Cubs champions of their own league and there sure
was a celebration last night. Mr. Chance suspended the rules
and said he would fine anyone caught drinking anything but wine
and anyone caught paying for anything at all. So we signed his
name to checks till they ran out of supplies and then we went to
bed and were glad to get there.
     There's an important meeting of the commission today, and
also a ball game, so business is still good.
     But I haven't forgotten you for a minute. You are still far
more important than baseball in all its branches and I'm going to
see you again the minute I can get away. I'm afraid that minute
isn't coming very soon.
     Please don't forget me, dear. I think I'll have time to
write the long letter when I get home Wednesday morning.

Meanwhile, I love you.
                              Ring

Ring did receive the following letter on the 5th:

Dearest
        I'm using my recess to the best advantage I
know how--writing to you. I dont dare let the
children see me or they'll say, "Miss Abbott is
writing to her beau."
        I am enclosing a picture which I know you'll
enjoy.   Do you think you can find me? George Ann
Lacy took it last Sunday morning. Ruby and Helen
Irwin (the middle one) and I stayed with her
Saturday night and we did have a circus. It was
such fun to be with girls again. There isnt a one
here. George Ann is to be married in March or
April and she wants me to play her wedding march.
Did you ever hear anything so funny?
        I got to thinking about housekeeping and
expenses and things last night. Mrs. Crandall had
been talking about her keeping house in a little
flat when she was just married. Wont we want a
little four roomed apartment and have you any idea
at all about rent? I havent. You do want to go to
housekeeping dont you?   I guess you'll have to
anyway because I just wont board. How much are you
going to allow me a week for housekeeping? Is'nt
it funny to be thinking about such things?   Its
such fun that now I'm started I cant think of
anything else. It gives me such a funny little
thrill to think of having a home of my very own and
when I think that its going to be our very own it
is a very big thrill. Do you think you'll get
tired of it, dear? There'll be times when we're
both tired and cross and everything will go wrong
and I'll be spending too much money and you'll be
discouraged with everything. But we can always
remember that we have each other, cant we? And
then things will look bright again.
        Its a wonderful thing to think that someone
will always be interested in you. We'll have some
splendid talks when we are all by ourselves in our
own little home wont we? And you'll tell me all
you ever thought or did and all you want to do.   I
always love to know just how other people look at
life, whether it means just the same thing to them
as it does to me.
        This has taken two recesses instead of one.
                    Dont forget my long letter.
                              Your own girl

Thursday
[Chicago,
6 October 1910]

Dearest Girl,-
I'm down at the office and I left your letters at home, but I can remember them I guess. First and foremost, I was awfully glad to get them because I heard from you for a long time.
I've been intending to order the paper for you, but the country circulation office manages to close before I get in from the ball game. I'll come down early tomorrow and do it.
I'm afraid, honey, I don't know any more about house-keeping expenses than you do. If this baseball season ever ends, I'll have time to talk things over with Richard and Anne, who ought to know something by this time. Encouraging to me are the thoughts that they got along all right--and he wasn't making any more than I am, although he always had more sense about his money.--and that I spent enough to take care of three people before you and the reform wave came. I know I can be as saving as Tobe because I won't want the things that cost when I have you. Don't worry, dear, you won't have to board. I'm looking forward too gladly to our own home to think of that. I think I'll be making enough by that time so that you can have some one to help you with cooking and other foolish things.
We must have five rooms in our flat. You are not to be shut off from your family and we want room for one or two or three of them whenever they want to come. I know all about rents, but that's none of your business and I don't think I ought to peddle my knowledge for nothing.
I want to be somewhere near Anne, so I can have an ally when you begin to think of leaving me.
You can't make me believe I ever will be discouraged or cross with you around. I'm afraid of one thing--you'll find out how little brains I possess in those talks of ours, and become disgusted me. I guess my best play is to keep still.
I must quit.
                              Yours always,
                                Ring

        The letter below contains Ring's first reference to Captain Willhite, who was frequently Ellis's escort to academic functions at Culver. Ellis was clearly flattered by his attention, and Ring became quite jealous.

                              Monday
                              [Chicago,
                              24 October 1910]

Dearest Girl,-
It's all over and we didn't have to go to Philadelphia.   I'm

glad it happened that way if the Cubs had to lose.[1]
The clipping is from yesterday's Examiner.[2] I was thinking of
you Saturday and sympathizing with you. But I'm glad the dark
secret is out, because it makes it more real. No longer will the
Hascall[3] clerk look at me and wonder why. He may look at you and
wonder why you have anything to do with me, but I won't mind that
as long as I have you.
The boss said last night that he supposed I would rather have
my vacation during the holidays and I said I would. Also I said
I would like to be off next Sunday and he said I could. So, if
you will, you can go to Niles Saturday, and await my arrival, or
I will meet you in South Bend Sunday morning and we can go over
from there together and I'll bring you back whenever you have to
go. Tell me what you would rather do.
Will you please answer this question, Miss Abbott? If you
can take moonlight strolls with Captain Willhite, why can't you
or won't you take them with me? You know I could borrow a
uniform somewhere if that's necessary. He is dangerous. No one
can help being so when you are around and his conversation about
his travels was just a stall. I'm still afraid of the officers
and I wish I had you under my eye. There are more reasons than
one for that wish.
Do you love me? I love you more now than I did yesterday and
I don't know how I can stand the daily increase from now till
June.
Write.   Ring

        Immediately after the Series ended, Ring found the
time at last to travel to Goshen for the interview with
Mr. Abbott. Ring, Jr. describes the situation thus:

        Ellis complained to her mother that her father
still hadn't answered Ring's letter, and Mrs.
Abbott agreed to intercede for her, with the result
that Ring was invited to pay a call on Mr. Abbott.
Ellis was away at Culver, but some of her siblings
and her mother were waiting outside the double
doors when the two men emerged from their
conference. Mrs. Abbott said she hoped Mr.
Lardner could stay for supper, and Mr. Abbott said
"Supper! He's staying all night," and everyone
knew the meeting had been a great success.[4]

----

[1]The Cubs had lost the World Series, four games to one.

[2]The EXAMINER clipping had announced their engagement.

[3]A Goshen hotel established by Ellis's maternal grandfather,
Chauncey Hascall.

[4]Ring Lardner, Jr., p. 56.

Ring, Jr. also points out that since Ellis had announced her engagement and a June wedding at a luncheon three days earlier, Mr. Abbott must simply have wished to be able to say that he had met Ring and to have adhered to the formal ritual of interviewing the man his daughter was to marry.

                              Wednesday
                              [Chicago,
                              26 October 1910]

Dearest Girl,-
     I started to write to you in Florence's room this morning, but I was called to breakfast. Your mother and Ruby, Mrs. Hawks and Helen and Carrie Thomas escorted me home this morning and I have Ruby's pocket book in my pocket right now and must deliver it at Field's this afternoon. I arrived in Goshen at 4:30 yesterday and went right to your house. Your father happened to be outside in the car. We went down town and then came back and he and I conversed at great length. He did most of the conversing. Beyond informing you that he gave his consent and shook hands, I won't tell you about our interview till I see you and perhaps not then. I staid to supper and all night and until train time this morning. I wanted you to be home, but I don't think I could have accomplished as much with you present. You have a way of distracting my thoughts. In the evening we children sat or stood in the parlor and indulged in something much like a rough-house. Then Ruby and John and I went after your mother's dress. We sent John home with it and partook of two ice cream sodas and I smoked two cigarettes. Then we came home and watched your mother play solitaire until Ruby ordered us to bed. I wasn't very sleepy so I read Florence's Evangeline for a spell.
     Now I'm going to town to get a letter or two which must be at the office. Then I'll deliver Ruby's pocket book.
     Tomorrow I'll give you orders about Sunday. I'm crazy to see you, honey.
                              Yours always,
                              Ring

                              [Chicago, 4 November 1910]

Dear Ruby,-
     You didn't owe me any thanks for delivering your purse, because it was a bone play to keep it, but you did owe me a letter and I'm glad you paid up.
     If you know where Ellis Abbott is going to spend Saturday and Sunday you have something on me. She is the most mysterious and secretive girl I ever was engaged to, and that's saying a lot.
     There isn't a great deal of news to tell you. They are putting a new pavement on Fifty-first street and the Tribune is going to press half an hour earlier than usual. I didn't learn

anything new in Culver about children's marches except what I saw
at Mrs. Crandall's. Perhaps that would help a little. You need
a girl about Ellis' size, shape and weight to be used as the
dance floor. Then you want five children, all of them cross-eyed
and generally homely, and three of them boys. They must range in
age from three to twelve. The dance floor sits in a chair. The
youngest child sits in her lap and the next oldest stands on her
feet. The other three assume careless poses on her head and neck
and shoulders. At a given signal, all the children start a
screaming contest, at the same time kicking the dance floor all
over with their heels. The floor sits quietly smiling until the
children are tired out. Then she says, 'Aren't they just too
sweet to live?" They certainly are. I think you will find this
very effective and inspiring.

I'm very grateful for your invitation and I'll come again as
soon as I can.

Yours with my happiest respects,
Ring

Friday afternoon.

Now, you're in debt again

[Culver, 4 November 1910]

Dear Mrs. Abbott,-
Because they were tired of seeing me around the office, Mr.
and Mrs. Chicago Tribune told me to disappear last Friday and
not to return until Tuesday afternoon. So I wrote my "orders" to
Ellis, met her in South Bend and took her over to Niles to spend
Saturday and part of Sunday. You almost lost a daughter then and
there, because my father and mother and sister wanted to keep her
and I wasn't at all sure they wouldn't lock her in the house. We
came back here last night and I am going to stay until tomorrow
morning--at the "Palmer House," which really is a good hotel for
a place the size of Culver. Just now I am waiting for the noon
recess.

I was glad to be able to get over to Goshen last week. I had
a nice talk with Mr. Abbott and fell in love with the whole
Abbott family, who were very nice to me. Next time the Tribune
wants to get rid of me, I will come again, if I may. Did Ruby's
purse find her?

I'm a little bit worried about Ellis, who, I'm afraid, is
working too hard. She has a bad cold--partly my fault--and her
eyes look tired. I lectured her about it, but I'm afraid it
didn't do much good. I think I'll have to threaten her with
something awful. If she would content herself with teaching it
might not be so bad, but she is employed as nurse and hired girl
as well, although she won't admit it.

Mother received your letter and wants you to come and see
her. I hope you will, for I am proud of my family-in-law and
want to show it off.

I don't know where that blot came from. Please forgive it.
                          Sincerely,
                             Ring

                                   Tuesday
                                   [Chicago,
                                   8 November 1910]

Dearest Girl,-
    I didn't stuff your honorable family with untruths and you
know it. I told some simple truths in the hope that said family
would cooperate with me in making you mend your awful ways.
    I didn't work yesterday. I staid home till after supper and
then Tobe volunteered to mind the child while Anne and I went
over to our new private theater on Fifty-first street. They had
the world's series pictures and I made up my mind that you never
would be allowed to see them. You would fall out of love with me
pretty quick if you did.
    If the dish towels are hemmed, I don't see why you can't get
ready by February.   I want you before June, and I hate to have
you wearing yourself out down there. I can't forget that you
said you didn't want to go back. Why should you want to? And
the worst of it is that you don't have to. We're going to have
another quarrel when I see you.
    I'm going downtown now to meet Doc White and be introduced to
a music publisher--why, I know not. Also, I'm going to find out
when I can get back to Indiana from Ithaca. Be sure to tell me
where you are going to be. As soon as you do, I'll write you
your orders.
                          Yours always,
                             Ring

         Ring was reluctant to leave the TRIBUNE, where he
    felt at ease and had matured as a reporter, but the new
    financial needs connected with his approaching marriage
    led him later that month to accept the managing editor-
    ship of the weekly SPORTING NEWS in St. Louis, when the
    job was offered by the owner, Charles Spink.   The new
    position was more prestigious (THE SPORTING NEWS was
    even then popularly referred to as "baseball's bible")
    and better paying, and it did not require traveling.
         However, the relationship with Spink was uneasy
    almost from the beginning. Hugh Fullerton later wrote:
    "I tried to keep Lardner from going to the SPORTING
    NEWS, because I knew him so well and because I knew and
    loved Charley Spink so well. I was certain those two
    never would understand each other, and they didn't."[1]
    Ring would stay only three months.

----

    [1]Fullerton's remark is quoted by Elder, p. 87, but Elder's
source is unknown.

Friday night.
[St. Louis,
2 December 1910]

My darling Girl,-
I'll tell you a little about St Louis, but not everything,
for if I went that far, I'm afraid you would have to change your
opinion of my cleverness. But first, please promise you will try
to love me even if I can't hold this job. It's a lot heavier
than I was led to believe and I started wrong today by heartily
hating my employers at first sight. They're as much like the
Tribune people as Mrs. Crandall is like Mrs. Frank P. Abbott.
What was it I told you about my hours? The real ones are from 8
to 5:30 except on Sunday, when there is only about an hour's
work. So your father needn't worry on that score. New jobs
always are awful, though, and I'm going to stick till I'm fired.
It isn't half as bad as your work at Culver, and I guess I'm just
so lonesome for you that I can't look at things cheerfully.
March and June are farther away now than they were two days ago.
I looked up rooms this noon and called up one that seemed
desirable. I came out to look it over tonight and got the wrong
house--next door to the one I thought I was going to. But it
didn't seem to make much difference. Both are regular boarding
houses and both have pianos. So I decided to stick to this
place. The landlady called me "dear" twice in the first five
minutes of our acquaintance. Tomorrow my trunk is coming with
its set of Balzac and from tomorrow night on, I'm going to divide
my time--evenings--between him and you, with the piano once in
awhile. I intend to retire at 9:30 every night, and arise at
6:45. Across from me there dwelleth a rather pretty young
lady--and her husband. They seem so happy that I'm mad at them.
They're the only ones I've seen of my new family except our
common mother. I live at 5087 Fairmount avenue, but I guess
you'd better send letters to the office for awhile.
Speaking of letters, honey, will you try your very hardest to
write to me every day? Your letter today was a great big help
and I don't know what would have happened to me without it. But
you must get out of your head that ridiculous idea that I love
you less than I did. I love you more, a million times more, and
it's just plain hell to be without you. If you were here now,
I'd kiss you and kiss you and make you promise never to leave me
again. And I wouldn't let you cry ever again. But don't think
I'm a beast when I say I'm glad you cried the other night. It
hurt me to have you, but it made me feel surer of your love.
Dear, you must tell me just how you feel all the time. I want to
know everything about you, for really you are part of me, the
bigger part, and I can't think of myself without thinking of you.
This is a peculiar, mixed-up letter, but nothing makes any
difference except that I love you and you love me. Sweetheart,
don't get tired of me now.
I'm glad you didn't hear my speech at the "banquet" last

night. They gave me a traveling bag and I had to thank them for
it. It was awful. But I was all swelled up on myself because
their efforts failed to knock me off the water wagon. Mr.
Eckersall had tears in his eyes when he said farewell to me--
they were extra dry tears. My boss said the Tribune job would be
held open for me till the first of February. That was very nice
of him.
         Tell me about your Niles trip. Also that you love me.
Have you given Florence permission to write?
                   Goodnight, dear girl.
                        Ring

         Ellis wrote back, reassuringly:

         I'll still love you if you get fired a hundred
times but Im dreadfully sorry you dont like the St.
Louis people. I know how it is though I dont go
quite so far as to "heartily hate" my many
employers. Perhaps the hours wont be so long when
you get things started. But, dear, dont you dare
think of staying there on my account - (because of
money or any thing else) if you dont want to. I
wont think one bit less of you and neither will
anyone else, if you give it up and come back to the
Tribune. Of course they'll keep the job for you.
Who wouldn't? I am keeping a place for you until
June so you can see that I love you better -- by
four months -- than they do. More than that I love
you a hundred million times more than anyone else
in the world.

         A week later Ring wrote to Ellis's mother:

                   [December 10, 1910]

Dear Mrs. Abbott,-
         I intended to come to Goshen for the purpose of telling you
and Mr. Abbott why I thought it best for me to make the change
from Chicago to St Louis, but, as you know, Ellis accompanied me,
and I don't believe I tried as hard as I might have to dissuade
her. The first two weeks here, I was a little doubtful of my
ability to hold the job. I always forget that a new job is lots
easier than it looks at first. I guess I'm all right now, and
I'm beginning to be glad I made the move, and will be even more
glad after June. That was my reason--so I wouldn't have to
travel or work nights. As it is, I never have to stay after half
past five, except when I want to get something out of the way.
You probably won't be able to see Ellis as often as you would
have if I had staid in Chicago, but you and everyone in the
family must come down--after June--just as often as you can, and
you must stay longer when you do come because it is farther away.
         Just now I am in mourning for my lost vacation. The days

aren't going a bit too fast and I don't know how I can wait till
June, but it isn't right for me to complain about a few months'
delay, when I am lucky enough to have Ellis to look forward to at
all.
   I know you'll have a merry Christmas with everyone at home.
If you can, I wish you'd persuade Ellis to have her picture taken
while she's in Goshen.
                              Sincerely,
                                 Ring
         Sunday afternoon.

         On the 14th Ring received a teasing letter from
Ellis which added to the frustrations he was
experiencing in St. Louis. In the social world of the
Culver Academy, where she was apparently the only
single young woman among a predominantly male faculty,
Captain Willhite was obviously devoting a good deal of
time to Ellis:

         Captain Willhite came over yesterday afternoon
   and we went for a little walk - then he came over
   again in the evening at 7.45 P.M. and stayed until
   11.15 P.M. Why he wanted to stay three hours and a
   half is more than I know unless he wanted a good
   listener. I was so sleepy I couldnt talk. More
   than that he offered to go to South Bend with me if
   I went Friday night and recheck my trunk for me --
   but I am not going Friday night.

                              Wednesday night.
                              [St. Louis,
                              14 December 1910]

Dearest Girl,-
   If it were not for my proud record, I don't think I'd write
tonight, because company has kept me up till after ten. A
prettier sister of the pretty Southern girl and a young lady
named Miss Marshmallow came to supper and I had to play
accompaniments for three hours straight. But I won one
argument--I made the sons of the house escort them home. The
pretty one reminded me of Marian Fox Wood, so I guess the other
must have been Bessie Shean. But, young lady, we were all in a
bunch in the parlor and not alone, like you and Captain
Willhite--for four hours. I guessed him right, and if he keeps
it up, I'm going to quit my job and make a quick trip to Indiana.
   I've had two pay days. Every paper pays by the week and this
one paid me a week ago last Saturday for two days' work.
   I did most of my Christmas shopping--my last Christmas
shopping--at noon today. I got through quickly by taking the
first thing shown me in every case.
   Dear, do you know, when you gave the addresses of Miss Hays

and Miss Garrett,[1] something told me you wanted me to call on them? That's a fact. If I acted in opposition to your sweet will, I'm sorry and never will do anything again until you give me positive orders.

But please love me, honey, and nothing else will make any difference.

Tomorrow night I'll write your first Goshen letter, and I'll try to write a better one than this.

Always yours,
Ring

On the subject of Captain Willhite, Ellis replied:

I guess I'll have to let you win one argument any way--the one about Captain Willhite. He came over again last night and stayed until 11.45. He brought me a beautiful little book as a 'Christmas gift' and we had lots of fun until just before he went. I think he forgot for a few minutes and said things he didn't mean to say. I am awfully sorry about it because we have had good times. But dont you think for a minute that I cant manage my own affairs. You stay right where you are. I am not telling you this because I think I ought to but because I want to and trust you. And besides a pretty girl is much more dangerous than any man and I am jealous.

Sunday afternoon
⌈St. Louis,
18 December 1910⌉

My Sweetheart,-
Right now you must sit down and write me exactly what Captain Willhite said and did, and what you said and did. I've got to know. It isn't just common curiosity--but it's just because you are concerned and I want to, and must, know all about it. I'll promise not to do anything crazy when you tell me. Dear, Ruby was right when she said I was jealous. I am, horribly so. I never was about any other girl, and its proof positive that you're the only one I ever really loved. Honestly, it's getting to be a desperate case with me. I can't give you up and if you should happen to stop loving me and care for someone else, I know my instinct would be to hurt him physically, to choke him with one hand and pound his eyes with the other. That's my instinct

---

[1]Probably two of Ellis's friends from Smith College. They are referred to by Ellis in a letter of 13 December as "Caroline and Elizabeth." Ellis had requested too late that Ring not call on them until she had written to them about him.

right now regarding Captain Willhite. You think I'm crazy--and
I know I am. But if there ever is any danger, I want you to
promise to tell me all about it, so I can come to you and make my
fight--for I'm not going to lose you without a fight. Don't
think I'm questioning your faithfulness, dearest. It isn't that
at all. But it's just lack of confidence in my own ability to
hold the love of a girl like you. If you could see things with
my eyes a minute, you wouldn't blame me. But you underestimate
yourself--Nobody could know you long without loving you. Captain
Hyney and Captain Fleet and the rest will be just like Captain
Willhite before it's over. It would be bad enough to have you in
a place full of girls but its just so much the worse that you are
the only girl in Culver. That doesn't sound very complimentary,
but I don't mean it the way it sounds. You'll understand. When
Captain Willhite asked you if I would object to his calling, I
knew just how far his case had gone. If he had wanted merely to
be "friends," he never would have thought of that. Probably, at
the start, he was just friendly, but it was impossible for him,
seeing as much of you as he did, to remain that way. I'm not
blaming him, dear, and never in the world will I object to his,
or anyone else's seeing you--first, because it wouldn't do me
any good, and second, because it's altogether your business. I'd
as soon tell you not to write to your mother. What I do ask is
that you'll keep me posted, about him, and the others, too, and
what I asked before--that you'll tell me everything that happened
Thursday night. Ellis, no matter how peculiar I may be, I do
love you and I have brains enough to appreciate you and to know
that you are one in a thousand million. If you valued something
higher than your mother or father or anything else you had,
wouldn't you be worried if you knew that one person, or more than
one, was trying to take it away from you, when you were miles
away and couldn't guard it? That's how it is with me--and if the
"thieves" grow bolder and make any progress, this job at St Louis
isn't going to hold me a minute, and I'm not going to wait to
pack up. There are other jobs and there are other towns, but
there's just one girl, and I want her, even if I don't deserve
her.

Here's my discovery--You are so much more interesting than
any book that I would rather just sit or lie and think of you,
than read. In fact, I can't get interested in a book any more,
but I do a lot of wideawake dreaming about you. I have to read
the baseball news, but there's nothing else I can keep my mind on
but the "Flats for Rent."

Speaking of them, Billy Grayson, who lives here, owns the
Louisville ball team and is a friend of mine, came for me in his
car this morning and took me for a long ride. We went the whole
length of Lindell Boulevard, which is about the prettiest one,
and he pointed out some flats which weren't so horribly
expensive. Also, he is going to introduce me to a real estate
man who will put me wise to anything desirable.

Write me a long letter, dear.

    Ring

Ellis answered:

Ring, I cant tell you about Captain Willhite. I cant tell you what he _said_ but he didn't _do_ anything but hold my hand a minute when he left. You needn't worry a bit, dear, and you mustnt. I feel awfully sorry for him but he knows perfectly well how things are and it's his own fault if he keeps on coming. There is no reason on earth for you to be jealous and Captain Willhite is a gentleman and you needn't worry. Sweetheart I _love_ _you_ and you _must_ know it and if you are going to _worry_ about such things I wont tell you any more.

Christmas afternoon.
⌈St. Louis,
25 December 1910⌋

My own Girl,-

I, too, think letters are unsatisfactory; they are like drinks of water in that respect, but I couldn't live without either. Honestly, dear, it's the mail's fault when you don't hear from me every day, for I write every week day evening and every Sunday afternoon. You know I love you, or if you don't know it, you are hopelessly "ignorant" on all subjects.

I worked for an hour and a half this morning and then I went to Church. After that, I went to Mr. Spink's house for dinner. He has a peach of a house, on Lindell Boulevard opposite Forest Park. It was a very good dinner and I was told how much everything in the house cost. Mrs. Spink asked me, in her daughters' presence, how I liked them--which was very embarassing. Mr. Blodgett, who edits another Spink paper, was there, too. His girl is in town for a short visit and I don't see how or why he spared the time away from her. He is interested in flats also, for he is going to be married in February. I wish I could have you that soon. We all were taken for a ride after dinner and went way out in the country up the river. It was a peach of a day--and there's been only one fall of snow since I've been here and that wasn't more than an inch. They just brought me home and I am to have another Christmas dinner in a little while. But it would have been so much nicer if I could have been with you tonight.

Florence has no right to call me crazy. Miss Hays is the insane one, for it is she who told me about Mrs. Bughouse. And you can bet Florence is glad it is Paul(1) who is coming and not I. When are they to be married?

You have a very dangerous rival whom you know nothing about. All I know about her is her name and that she lives in Malden, Mass., of which place I never heard before. Her Christmas greetings were forwarded to me from the Tribune. She signed her name, but it was a new one on me. I just tell you this so you'll

know Captain Willhite isn't the only one trying to tear us apart. Everybody envies me my cameo--I think that's what it is called. But no one can have it. The dearest girl in the world sent it to me. I wish she would hurry and send herself down here. Don't you think, honey, that you've seen enough of Culver. I do and I wish you wouldn't go back. I'd rather have you in Goshen, even if you won't come to me. And Captain Willhite isn't the only reason either. You aren't well and I know it. Dear, you must tell me just how you feel always. It does worry me to have you sick, but it would be a lot worse to know that you wouldn't tell me when you were. Can't you realize that you are all I have that counts and that my life depends on yours, and is so hopelessly entangled with yours that it can't be torn away? I'm sure I don't want it torn either. But it's because you're part of me that I want to know everything about you--what you do and say and think and how you feel. Also, that's why I want the whole Captain Willhite story. You don't tell me half of anything and the part you do tell me I hear because I coax it out of you. You are my girl, and my sweetheart. I love you, your niceness, your generosity, your unselfishness, your whole character, and I love your beauty. I don't deserve your love one bit, because I am awfully far below you, but I honestly believe it would kill me not to have it now. You have made me horribly dissatisfied with life apart from you; I'm sorry for Captain Willhite and the others, too. But they don't know you as I know you; don't know how perfect you are. So giving you up would hurt me more than it hurts them, and I won't do it.
 You owe me lots of long letters.
                                Ring.

                                Monday night.
                                [St. Louis,
                                26 December 1910]

Dearest Girl,-
 There were only two deliveries of mail today and neither of them brought a word from you, and my day after Christmas wasn't a bit merry. I'm glad I had to work, because the day went slowly enough as it was. Also I'm glad Christmas is over, for I'm beginning to hate all holidays, which are jokes as far as "journalists" are concerned. My poor girl will have to go back to work next Monday, I suppose, and I'm sorry for that.
 I don't think I told you about Mr. and Mrs. Pretty. The latter went shopping Saturday afternoon and, in some way, was left downtown without a nickel, and had to borrow one from a stranger. She came home with loud hysterics and he came in a little later. She said it was his fault and they called each other liars two or three times. I thought once he was going to kill her and I started to butt in, but one of the sons of the house said they fought about once every two weeks and that this was a mild scrap. He went out Saturday night and I don't know

when he came back, but they're all right now. You and I won't
board, because it will be much nicer to have a flat in which to
quarrel over nickels.
    You have nothing on me now, for my mother sent me your letter
to her. But if I don't get one of my own tomorrow, I'll never
write to you again. Yes, I will.
Goodnight, honey,
Ring

Saturday night.
[St. Louis,
31 December 1910]

My dearest Girl,-
    I hope you aren't tired of records and statistics, for I'm
going to give you some more of them.
    1. This is the last day of December. There were thirty-one
days in this month, and during it I have written you thirty-one
letters, <u>one</u> <u>every</u> <u>day</u>. I'm not boasting of their quality, but
you'll have to admit and admire the quantity.
    2. During the thirty-one days of December, I have not gone
outside the door of my boarding house once after supper. I went
to Moore's for supper one night and was back here before nine
that night. I claim this as a world's record for a single gent,
in good health, between the ages of twenty and thirty. Are you
proud of me? There's really no reason you should be, for I wrote
to you because I loved you and I staid in because I loved you and
because the outside had no attraction for me. Sometimes I'm
afraid you may grow tired of getting my letters. I'm still
remembering the words of Mildred, who said you ceased to care for
people when they cared too much for you. I don't know whether I
love you too much or not, but I do know I love you more than
anyone else ever loved anyone and that I'll die if March doesn't
hurry.
    Tomorrow, I will write you a beautiful New Year's poem if I
remember it.
Yours always,
Ring

Ellis wrote:

        I am very proud of you but I dont see why you
    feel it necessary to stay in every evening.
    However if you stop writing to me every day I'll
    <u>kill</u> you. You needn't worry about caring too much.
    The more you love me the more I'll love you. You
    are the one grand exception.

    Unfortunately Ring's records both in early evening
retirement and on the water wagon fell on New Year's
Eve, as his next letter reveals:

Tuesday night.
[3 January 1911]

My own Sweetheart,-
Your threat to kill came today. Please don't carry it out,
for I didn't know of it till after I'd missed two nights. And I
would have written tonight anyway. I won't tell you why my
beautiful record was spoiled for a minute or two, because of my
New Year's resolution not to lie, and I don't want to tell you
the truth. A piece of the truth is that I had been a little too
good and something had to break. But everything's all right
again now, and I'll try to keep it so.
You must send me not only your own picture, but the family
one as well. And I want them soon.
Awfully sorry to hear your father wasn't well and I hope he's
all right again. But I was glad you went to Niles. You weren't
greeted by one hundred people, nor fifty--there were just eight
outside the family and they were Bess and Florence and Nellie
Burns and Effie Deam and Seely and Lottie and Marjorie Deam, and
Lute Beeson. And here is some more dope from my mother's letter:
"She (Mrs. Abbott) is a lovely woman; sweet-faced and motherly.
I hope she likes me at first sight as well as I do her. She is
bright and witty, too: and Ellis looks as she used to, I'm sure.
Ellis is lovely to her (you see I use that word 'lovely' often,
but advisedly) and now I can realize that the family is loving,
well-bred and sympathetic; and I'm glad you have chosen a girl
out of it.
"We surely were delighted with her (Mrs. Abbott) and Ellis'
affectionate care of her showed the girl in a still brighter
light than ever. She is a 'peach' really. Perhaps you know
that?"
So you see, Miss Abbott, you mustn't jilt me now, for I never
could face my family if I lost you. There are three things that
could prevent the June 28th event--1. You might stop caring for
me. 2. You might die. 3. I might die. I'll promise
faithfully not to, if you'll promise not to let the other two
happen. It's awfully hard sometimes to realize I'm going to have
you and a thing like your going to Niles helps me to realize, so
I like it. If you're absolutely sure your love will increase in
direct proportion to mine, I'll tell you how much I love you--so
much that there isn't a second when you aren't monopolizing my
thoughts, nor when your face isn't between my eyes and my work,
and you are my last thought at night and my first in the morning,
and I like to go to the office better than I like to come "home"
because, generally, there's a letter waiting for me down there;
and it actually hurts me physically when there isn't and takes
all my spirit away, and it also hurts me to know always that I'm
not fit for you and that it would be the most natural thing in
the world for you to find it out. But if any of that makes you
love me less, dear, please pretend I didn't say it.
Cold weather has come at last and it isn't fooling either. I
hope you aren't cold at Culver and I hope also that your work

won't be so awfully hard.

Please tell me the C.--W-- News. Do you know I suspect the reason you won't trust me with what you wrote to him is that you believe it would make me still more jealous?

If you had more than one kind of picture taken, you must send me all to choose from.

The three scarf pins incident was funny--that's why I told Anne I love my cameo and you, but I see plainly that my family is not to be trusted.

> Yours always,
> Ring.

Please forgive my sins.

If you love me, I want to know why.

> Thursday night.
> [St. Louis,
> 5 January 1911]

Dearest,-

Don't you know that you ought to have been particularly careful not to skip writing to me yesterday, when I was thinking about your returning to Culver and wondering and worrying about C--W--? But you must have skipped for I didn't get a letter from you today and I'd be mad at you now if I were not too busy being lonesome and loving you. If I don't hear tomorrow morning I'll quit my job and pay you a visit whether you want me to or not. But perhaps you thought you were entitled to a vacation because I skipped two little days after not missing for thirty-one. Or perhaps you are ashamed of me and don't love me any more.

The proofs went to work with me this morning, staid all day, and are back here now. I'm afraid they'll be worn out before the pictures come. On my desk I had them fixed so I could just open the envelope a little and look at them without taking them out.

Sample Conversation at Our House.

I.

Mr. Wilson--"Do you know any grand opera pieces?"
Mr. Lardner--"Not decently."
Mr. W--"Do you know this one?" (Hums strain of Lohengrin Wedding March)
Mrs. W--"That isn't grand opera, silly. That's the Wedding March."

II.

Mrs. W--"Don't you just love Robert W. Chambers's works?"[1]
Mrs. Johnston (landlady) "Yes, and he must be right in the swim in society."

---

[1] An American writer especially popular in that era for his science-fiction, his historical romances, and his poetry. CARDIGAN (1901), a novel set during the American Revolutionary War, is probably his best-known work.

Mrs. W--"Yes. 'The Danger Mark' wasn't just interesting-- it taught one a lot about the lives those people lead."
Mr. W--"Well, I'd rather be right here where I am."

      I'd rather be right where Ellis is. Please love me, honey.
                                    Ring

                                    Monday night.
                                    [St. Louis,
                                     9 January 1911]

Dearest Girl,-
      For some reason this was the worst and most lonesome day of my St Louis existence. For one thing, there was no letter from you, but I didn't expect one because it was Monday. I had lots of work to do, but time dragged and I thought of you incessantly. June seemed a thousand miles away and things were just desperate. Will you answer me a truth question? Do you love me every bit as much as you said you did before I came down here? I don't know why it is, but I can't help thinking you've jumped down a little. If I had you here I'd make you tell me you loved me eight hundred times. You'd have to do it, too, or I'd punish you.
      Mr. Spink is going on his vacation next week and I hope he stays away forever. It's getting so it irritates me just to look at him. But I won't inflict him on you anymore.
      I dissipated tonight--Mr. and Mrs. Pretty and I going to a moving picture show. One of the stories was of a girl who forgot him when he went away and I didn't care for it a bit.
      Ruby said she was having lots of fun embroidering napkins for US. I think it must be lots of fun and we'd better have some unembroidered ones in the house all the time for emergency amusement. I'll work on them while you read to me.
      Tell me how school is going and how hard you are working and how you feel.
      I love you, honey, and it's a continuous series of jumps up or jump ups.
                                    Ring.

      At this time there was a good deal of news coverage of a number of demonstrations in New York City, Washington, D. C., and elsewhere, for ratification of the Women's Suffrage Amendment (the 19th Amendment to the Constitution, passed finally in 1920). In the following letter, Ring jokingly takes a cavalier male view of the situation:

                                    Tuesday night.
                                    [St. Louis,
                                     10 January 1911]

My dearest Girl,-
      The agitation about Woman's Rights is a dismal joke. All the

rights in the world are on the side of women and _girls_, which you
are. For instance--you can tell me you're not going to write
for three days and you won't tell me why. If I told you I
wouldn't write for three days, you'd probably say, "Don't bother
to write at all." But I can't say that, because if you didn't
write at all I'd die. You can tell me you won't write for a
month and I just have to bear it. But I have to write to you
because I'm so desperately afraid of losing you and because I
like to talk to you. All I can ask with about an even chance of
getting a reply is: Are you ever going to tell me the wherefore
of this neglect? and will you make up for it--partly--with a
long, long letter? The next three days are going to be hard
ones, honey. Please don't make me endure it longer than that.

Now that you can make hot rolls--which I know must be better
than anyone else's--why should you bother any more about learning
to cook? That's enough and I don't want you to work outside of
school hours.

I burned my bridges today and after the craziest change of
mind I ever suffered. I got a letter from the Tribune. It
wanted to know if I wouldn't come back, but of course couldn't
promise relief from travelling and night work. I sat down to
write and say I would come if certain concessions were made, and,
instead, I said there wasn't a chance for me to leave here and
that it might as well go ahead and get a successor. Then I
couldn't decide whether or not to mail the letter, but finally I
did it. So, now, it's St Louis for awhile at least. I think I
need a guardian. Do you want the job?
                    Goodnight, sweetheart.
                              Ring.

        Ring now wrote to Ellis's mother about her visit to
Niles nine days earlier:

                         [St. Louis,
                          11 January 1911]

Dear Mrs. Abbott,-
    I haven't a chance in the world to get even for all the nice
things you are doing and have done for me. All I can do is thank
you--and then make one more request, that you send me one of the
group pictures of "The Abbott Children" when they are
finished--the picture, not the children. I've asked Ellis for
one, but she may not think it's necessary to send it.
    I'm awfully glad you went to Niles and I hope you and Ellis
like my family half as much as it likes you.
    I hope the trip didn't tire you; also that Mr. Abbott is
feeling better.
    Ruby and Florence owe me letters; so does Ellis, but that's
usual.
                    Sincerely,
                         Ring.
Tuesday night.   5087 Fairmount Ave.

Thursday night.
[St. Louis,
19 January 1911]
[To Ruby Abbott]
Dear Miss Abbott,-

After long and careful deliberation, I've decided not to kill you, because (1) you are too nice; (2) We would have to get another bridesmaid; (3) Your family might not like it (4). We might not get any napkins. As for forgiving you, I will do so under the following conditions: That I receive a good picture of Ellis before the first day of February, and that you send me at once the proofs of those she had taken at home, which I had, and which I bone-headedly returned. And if you don't comply with these conditions, I will never speak to any one of the Abbotts except Ellis, Mr. and Mrs., Florence, Dorothy, Jeannette, William, John and Frank.

Ellis certainly has one record--No one in the world ever had so many awful pictures taken.

Will you explain something to me? Ellis says she doesn't see how she will find time enough to "get ready" What does that term mean? I've been "ready" for a great deal over a year (except financially) and I haven't exerted myself a bit. But if she really does want time, why does she stay at Culver?

Thanking you in advance for answering these queries in the next issue of your valuable paper, I am
Yours respectfully,
A Bug.

Friday night.
Night and Home Edition.
[St. Louis,
20 January 1911]

Sweetheart,-

I didn't write to you Monday night because I was called in consultation and it lasted till almost midnight. The reason for Tuesday's failure was very prosaic. Usually I do my writing just before going to bed. I was in a state of undress when I discovered I had left my pen at the office and I couldn't go downstairs after another one. We hope this explanation will prove satisfactory. I have had nothing to drink but water, tea and coffee.

I wish I could be with you in Chicago, or anywhere else.
Answers to Correspondents.

Yes, I honestly want to marry you very, very much and I think you are the nicest person that ever lived and I love you a tremendously great deal and a great deal more than you love me.
Queries.

1. Do you honestly want June to hurry up?

2. What are we going to do with all our napkins?
3. Why shouldn't I make a wonderful impression on your family?
Local News.
I love you.
I'm the only one in the house who isn't sick.   The rest of
them ate something that put them on the bum.
It's been actually hot today.
I love you.
Politics.
Please tell me just what you dreamed about me.
Weather Prophecy.
Before the tenth of February, Captain Willhite will tell you
so again.
But it won't do him a bit of good, for you are engaged to me
and I'm going to hold you to it.
Personal and society.
I love you and will be perfectly happy always in your
society.

Saturday
⌈St. Louis,
21 January 1911]

Sporting Extra
That you are a dear girl has been known for a long time.
That you really can write nice letters when you want to has been
shown during the present week. Please continue to write them,
dearest--letters that make me believe you love me and that make
life away from you more nearly endurable.
Editorial.
You know very well you can't blame me for making you love me.
I didn't make you and couldn't make you.   It's just your own
foolish nature and I'm thanking the Lord that you are foolish.
You are perfectly right when you say I can't stop loving you.
Furthermore, I don't want to as long as you remain insane. Dear,
I haven't time to say one hundred times that I love you, but I'll
say it once more, and also that I love you a million times more
than anyone ever loved anyone else. And I wish you could say the
same about me, but you can't.
 Please tell me all about your trip to Chicago and your
purchases. I'm very much interested, especially in napkins.
Classified Ads.
Help Wanted (Female)
Wanted--at once, girl for general housework. Must love me
almost as much as I love her. Her name must be Ellis Abbott and
she must be 23 years old. College graduate preferred. Knowledge
of cooking unnecessary. Knowledge of how to endure requisite.
No specified wages, but will divide my income with her as she
sees fit. Must stay in nights. No washing. Address, R.   W.
L., c/o The Sporting News.

                    Beauty Hints.
     Just   look   like   yourself,   my   dear   pretty   girl.

     The subscription price of this paper is your heart and one
(1) letter a day.

                              Tuesday night.
                              [St. Louis, Missouri
                              24 January 1911]
Dearest,-
     You aren't going to get a long letter tonight because I've
got to go to a "consultation," but if I didn't write at all,
you'd probably think I'd fallen again, and I don't want you to
think that.
     You didn't go into details about the "lovely" things you got
and you didn't tell me if you had a picture taken, which is one
of the lovely things I want.
     Today I sent you something; not much of a something and I
won't vouch for its goodness. It is sent you provisionally: It
is supposed to reach you on the 26th of January and you may keep
it provided you know what great event occurred on that date. If
you can't tell me, you must send it back (You'll probably want
to, anyway). Here's a hint--January 26th 1911 is the first
anniversary of the great event.
     Being the younger brother of a Prince doesn't get me
anything. You know the eldest is the heir to the throne.
     It's only fair that a girl should have everything she wants
when she's going to be married, for usually, she doesn't get
anything she wants afterward.
     Tobe's life insurance man came to see me today and landed me.
He knew all about my "prospects." So I asked him if I couldn't
make Mrs. R. W. my beneficiary and he said I couldn't because
she didn't exist yet. So my "estate" had to be put down instead.
You must pull for me to live till after June; you will be my
estate then, but if I should die now, you wouldn't get a penny.
     Write me a long letter, honey.
                              Ring

          In response to the reminder about the anniversary
     of the kiss on the sofa Ellis wrote:

          Indeed I do know what the twenty sixth is an
     anniversary of though I was'nt sure of the exact
     date. It was a very very happy day and a year from
     tomorrow will be even happier. Thank you in
     advance for whatever the something is and
     especially for remembering it . . . .
          I hate the word insurance. Father has spent
     most of his life paying out large sums of money for
     insurance but it is my opinion that all men are
     alike when it comes to that so have it if you want

it. What do you suppose I'll care about money if
you aren't here. I am going to die too.

                              Thursday night.
                              January 26
                              [St. Louis]
Sweetheart,-
    A year ago tonight, you and I sat on the sofa at Anne's house
and I read to you and Anne went out and while she was gone,
something happened that made me happier than anyone who ever
lived. I kissed you and, after awhile, you kissed me and told me
you cared. And Anne came back, but we staid up after she had
gone to bed. And we talked, and our conversation was the most
interesting--to me--I ever took part in. A year ago yesterday
noon you came to Chicago. A year ago last night we went to a
play. A year ago this afternoon it was a matinee. You see I was
trying to win you by showing you a good time--and a year ago
tonight you rewarded me for the enormously good time I had shown
you. In this year I've been happy most of the time (although the
happiness was mostly prospective) scared often, sure sometimes
that you didn't love me, and sure other times that you did.
    Do you know what I'm doing tonight? You know I told you
about a nurse's coming to take care of a little boy who was sick.
He died today and I am sitting up. His mother, who hasn't slept
for a week, keeps coming in all the time and looking at him. She
just stares at me and I'm afraid she's going crazy. After
awhile, when Mr. Perkins (alias Mr. Pretty) comes home, I think
I'll make him take my place for a little while so I can take a
walk over to the mail-box. I must go out for it's awfully hot in
here and generally uncomfortable.
    Here's a "New Year's" resolution. After this, my letters are
going to be different, for I don't believe you could like the
kind I usually write. And after insisting that you keep on
loving me, I'm never going to ask you another question, nor make
any request of you whatever.
                              Yours always,
                              Ring.

        Ellis answered by teasing Ring about the
    "anniversary":
        Oh I meant to tell you! I know now what
    anniversary the 26th of January is. Its Captain
    Willhite's birthday - he told me so last night - he
    was thirty one.

                              Monday night.
                              [St. Louis,
                              31 January 1911]

Dear Ruby,-
    You needn't expect those proofs back, because I never make
the same mistake twice except sometimes. Three of them I like

very much. I won't tell you which three because I want all of them. But I must have them the minute they are done.

I got a letter from Ellis last month and in it she said nothing about weddings, so honestly, I don't know whether or not there's going to be one. If there is, you'll have to be maid of honor because I used your name in bribing my best man.[1] When he was sixteen (he's twenty-nine now) he was desperately in love with a Ruby who was not half as many carats fine as you. He is fond of the name so he has consented to act as my second. If he knew you, he'd like you if your name were Bethia, but he's just depending on my promises now.

And you know it isn't absolutely necessary for the groom and the maid of honor to be on speaking terms. I may not speak to you but I'm going to kiss you. Please don't back out on that account, for it will all be over in a minute. Part of my reason for contemplating an alliance with Ellis is the privilege it will give me to kiss her sisters and mother.

This letter didn't intend to be an essay on kissing, but it seems to have developed into one, so I guess it had better stop.

I'll thank you when the pictures come. Also now.

H-pp-e-t R-sp-cts,
Peer Gynt.

You owe me

As the following letter makes clear, Ring had now decided that working for Charles Spink was intolerable.

Friday.
[St. Louis,
3 February 1911]

Dear,-

I think I would rather be kicked downstairs than write this letter, but it's got to be written. But before I forget, I've been perfectly well and I'll tell you why I haven't written before when I see you, perhaps. Also, I don't understand why you, with the prettiest and most perfect teeth in the world, should have anything to do with a dentist unless you're going to act as an advertisement for him.

Now for business--It didn't take me all this time to discover that Mr. Spink was dishonest. I knew it before I'd been here a month, but I decided to swallow it "for the good of the cause." He did something about a month ago without my knowledge that was against all newspaper rules, but I explained my innocence to the offended person and was believed. Day before yesterday he tried to put over something else, but he told me about it and I kicked. I told him I'd quit if he did it, and he was afraid to have me quit because Ban Johnson, the president of the American League,

---

[1] Arthur Jacks, Ring's close friend from childhood. They were neighbors in Niles and later in both Chicago and Great Neck.

which is responsible for his paper's success, recommended me.
But we had some warm words and I told him I would just as soon
work for Jesse James and that I was going to leave very shortly.
Yesterday he tried to square things and I just listened to him
and didn't say anything. If you care to listen to details, I'll
tell them to you when I see you again. Anyway, I was invited to
lunch yesterday by Billy Grayson of whom I have told you. He is
owner of the American Association team in Louisville. He asked
me how I'd like to be business manager of the Louisville Club. I
told him not at all because it would necessitate my travelling.
That closed the incident until today, when he took me to lunch
again. We talked for an hour and a half and he finally said he
would fix things so I would have to take only one trip after we
are married. The towns in that association are Louisville,
Indianapolis, Toledo, Columbus, Milwaukee, Minneapolis, St. Paul
and Kansas City. The trips never last more than fifteen days. I
figured I could take you along on the only one after
June--probably in August or September--and we wouldn't have to
mingle with the athletes. The salary is the same I get here. He
has promised me a bonus if he makes so much money. Here's how
the matter stands now: I'll go with him if you can stand for
Louisville. I don't know whether you know anything about the
town or not. To boost it I'll say it is just as pretty and much
cleaner than St Louis. Also, I'll say we don't have to stay
there after the middle of October if we don't want to.

If I "accept the position," I'll probably quit here a week
from next Tuesday. A week from Tuesday night, I'll start for
Chicago, spend Wednesday and part of Thursday there, come to
Culver Thursday night, take you to Niles Friday night, to Goshen
Saturday morning and back to Culver Sunday afternoon. I do want
to talk to you and convince you I'm not a grass-hopper because I
jump around so much.

Here's what I want you to do: If you aren't awfully
disappointed, if you think you can stand it, telegraph me, as
soon as you get this, in care of the Sporting News. If you don't
want to make the change, telegraph me to that effect. In either
case, send the message collect and remember I love you.

Later--I've decided to mail this special delivery to Goshen,
so you'll get it Sunday, so when you wire, address the message to
5087 Fairmont Avenue. And please don't say anything about this
to anyone for awhile.

Ring

The fact that Ring was willing to risk Ellis's--and
her father's--disapproval by changing positions three
months before the wedding indicates how desperate Ring
must have been to remove himself from a situation in
which he felt he could not get along with his employer.
From Goshen Ellis immediately wrote back reassuringly,
but with the alarming news that her father objected to
the Louisville offer:

Dearest
    I just got your letter an hour or so ago and
will do my best to answer it coherently. In the
first place and before everything I want you to
know that whatever you do will always be all right.
I didnt know what to think when you got your
letter--I am about as good at deciding things as a
hedgehog--so I told father about it in spite of
your telling me not to say anything about it.
However I dont think he will spread the
information. He quite agreed with you about
staying with Mr. Spick and Span under the
circumstances and so do I. I wonder you have'nt
murdered him before this but I am very proud of you
for having principles and sticking to them. I wish
I had them. On the other hand dad thinks a
"sporting man" is a "sporting man" and cant change
his spots--and that his daughters are delicate and
rare things and that they must not come in contact
with that "damned sporting crowd." He is in fact
quite strenuously opposed to the Louisville idea.
    As far as I am concerned it does'nt make one
bit of difference about the city we live in.
    Father wants to know whether it would be in
any way possible for you to come up here before you
decide definitely. But if it is'nt he says go
ahead and do whatever you think best--that you
know more about it than he does--which is very
strange indeed. I want to do whatever you
do--honestly!
    I've got to hurry down town with this. I am
dreadfully sorry you are having such a worrying
time and wish I could help you more. I have'nt
said much but the sum and substance of it all
is--to do whatever you think best and it will be
all right with me.
                    always
                your own girl
    There is one right thought in this business -
that I may see you soon.

    Ring wrote to Ellis's father, attempting to
convince him that the Louisville position was a
desirable one:

                        St. Louis, February 5th
                        [1911]

Dear Mr. Abbott,-
    I just heard from Ellis, who told me of her conversation with
you regarding my prospective change of cities and jobs. She told
me you were opposed to the Louisville idea and I can quite

understand your opposition. I myself am opposed to some features of it. However, it is a much different thing, in respect to my relation to the ball players, from my former job with the Tribune. Then it was up to me to mingle with them so that I might know what was going on. In the Louisville proposition, it will be to my interest and the interest of the owner, to keep away from everyone but the manager, who, in this case, is one of the most decent men I ever met. You can depend on it, Ellis won't ever have to see a ball player or a ball game. She can go to a game when she wants to, but I'm just as much opposed to her being "mixed up" in it as you are. It was impossible for me to delay my answer beyond tonight, so I told Mr. Grayson I would accept. He agreed to the conditions of my acceptance, which were that I would be allowed ten days off in June and that I wouldn't be obliged to make more than one trip after that. He also has a secretary who can do that travelling part of it a couple of times. My chief duty is to see that none of his employees, such as his ticket sellers and privilege men, are stealing from him, to oversee things in general, and have his books in such shape that he will know always how he stands. He's in a hurry to have me on the ground to prepare programs, advertising etc., for the coming season. He is in the lumber business here with his brothers and baseball is a sort of side issue with him. He wants to be able to leave Louisville any time his other business calls him.

So I will leave St. Louis about a week from Tuesday. I want to spend a couple of days in Chicago, and I probably will be in Goshen a week from Saturday. Then I will explain things to you more fully. I don't intend to spend my life as "guardian" of the Louisville club. In fact, Mr. Grayson and I plan to start a paper of our own within a year. We were going to do it this spring, but we thought we had better wait until we had thought things out and been able to go into it with more certainty of making it pay. He, of course, is to furnish the capital, if we do make the plunge before I have enough capital of my own saved up to put in with his.

As for The Sporting News part of it, it doesn't require knowledge of newspaper work to see that it's publisher is not on the square. I will tell you this side of it when I see you, but I can assure you now that it's absolutely impossible for me to stay in his employ. It's a shame, too, because I liked the work, when I was let alone in it, and I believe I could have improved the paper. The Tribune held my old place open until the first of February, but I couldn't go back there, because that would mean travelling about five months of the year, night work when I wasn't travelling, and it also would look as if I had failed to make good down here. I could have gone to work for one of the St Louis papers, but they don't pay as much and I would hate ever to work for less money than I had received before. So, as I had to have a job, I picked the Louisville one as the best, and I don't think I'll regret it. I waited for Ellis' consent, which came

tonight, and then caught Mr. Grayson just before he started for
Louisville.

You needn't be a bit afraid that she will be forced to meet
an "athlete." I won't let her, but I guess she won't be so
anxious that I'll have to "forbid" it.

Sincerely,

5087 Fairmount Ave.   Ring Lardner

This letter to Mr. Abbott must have been
especially difficult for Ring since he obviously did
not share Mr. Abbott's low opinion of ballplayers,
even during a time in which major league ballplayers
generally were not particularly well educated or
economically privileged. What is probably clearest
about the athletes of Ring's fictional world is that
though many of them are unintelligent, self-centered,
and insensitive, they are mostly represented
sympathetically, as beings no worse than other people.
Many of Ring's close friends were ballplayers.

Sunday night.
[St. Louis,
5 February 1911]

Sweetheart,-

I have just written a long letter to your father, (It was all
right for you to tell him) explaining things, and promising to
explain more fully when I saw him. I couldn't wait, because Mr.
Grayson was in a hurry. So I called him up and accepted as soon
as your letter came--taking your dear word for it that you didn't
mind. Your father was right when he he admitted I "knew more
about it" than he did, because there isn't a chance in the world
for you to mix up with the damned sporting crowd. I think I have
done the best thing for us, but if I haven't, I'll find it out
soon enough and I'm so used to jumping that it won't feaze me to
hop out of Louisville to Portland, Oregon, if it becomes
necessary. But it's done now, honey, and we'll hope we won't
starve to death. You are a dear girl even if you do send
telegrams with nothing in them and disobey orders by not sending
them collect.

Now for the "bright spot"--I will leave here a week from
Tuesday night at the latest. I want you to keep on writing--to
5087 Fairmount Avenue--until Sunday. Then I want a letter
waiting for me at Anne's--5042 Washington Park Place--on
Wednesday morning. I will reach Culver Thursday afternoon or
evening. But, listen, you know a week from Friday is Lincoln's
birthday and you may not have any school. Tell me about that
right away. If you don't have any, we can go to Niles Thursday
night; if you do, Friday night, and to Goshen next day. Anyway,
I'm going to see you just as soon as I can. I love you, but I'm

afraid you won't love me unless I improve and become reliable and
stationery.
                        Write.
                    Ring.

                            Monday night.
                            [St. Louis,
                            6 February 1911]

Dear,-
    I've decided to get some extra insurance on my life before we
go to Goshen for there's no telling what your father will do to
me, and some one may as well profit by my death. Honestly, I'm
awfully sorry about the whole business and I'd give anything if I
could undo it, but I guess there's only one way I could manage to
stay here, and that would be to have Mr. S. sell out and he
won't do that because he's making too much money. Here's a
secret--I don't think you and I will ever be rich because I don't
believe I've got good common sense.   Sister-in-law May always
said I would make more money than anyone in the family, but she's
just crazy.   Speaking of sisters-in-law, Anne said you weren't a
good one because you hadn't written to her since Merry Christmas.
    Mr. Grayson and I are to have a final conference Wednesday
noon and, if he doesn't decide he made a mistake (which he did) I
will tell Mr. Spink about it shortly afterward and that will be
a delight. However, I'm not going to tell him where I'm going.
    I've written to almost everyone I know tonight and I'm
sleepy. Please remember to tell me about Lincoln's Birthday, and
also that you forgive me for my craziness.
                        Yours always,
                            Ring.

        The specific events of the next two weeks are
    unclear, until Ring writes in the following letter that
    he has taken a position as sports reporter on the
    Boston AMERICAN. What seems probable is that, after
    terminating his three month ordeal under Charles Spink,
    he travelled to Goshen, where he found Mr. Abbott
    unalterably opposed to the Louisville job.   In
    searching elsewhere for employment, Ring probably
    consulted his old friend Hugh Fullerton, who had
    recommended Ring for his first Chicago newspaper job on
    the INTER-OCEAN. Fullerton recommended Ring for the
    vacant post at the Boston AMERICAN, one of the Hearst
    chain, and Ring accepted, at the respectable salary of
    forty-five dollars a week--only five dollars less than
    he had been earning in St. Louis, and ten dollars more
    than he had received from the TRIBUNE. In any case, we
    discover Ring on the 24th writing to Ellis from Boston
    to describe his new work:

Copley Square Hotel
Boston, Mass.
Friday night
[24 February 1911]

My own Girl,-
Writing to you from this room seems like old times and it
would be natural to think I was going to see you in Northampton
in a day or two.
My experience this afternoon was almost as funny as you are.
I called up the paper this afternoon (emphasis by repetition) as
soon as I got in and the managing editor asked me to come right
down. When I got there I discovered I knew the sporting editor
perfectly well, a welcome discovery. Before I had a chance to
show humility befitting an employe, they began to exhibit
gratitude at my condescending to take the job. They said they
would be glad if I would go south with the National league team,
but assured me they wouldn't make me do so against my will. I
didn't want to give in too easily, so we left it open for
discussion on Monday. I really don't care one way or the other
and am happy in the assurance that I won't have to travel after
the season opens.
I just got through supper, after spending most of the
afternoon with my employers, one of whom is going to take me to
the Follies tonight. There is a lot to tell you, but I'll save
it until tomorrow when there'll be more time.
I went to sleep at Kendallville and staid asleep until
Toledo. I thought of you at eight o'clock and all the rest of
the time too. I retired shortly after eight and surely did
sleep. During my waking hours, I tried to read The Egoist, but
your dear face was always between my eyes and the page so I
didn't make a great deal of progress. Sweetheart, I am horribly
lonesome, desperately lonesome, and I don't know how I'm going to
stand it. I love you a thousand times more than I ever did
before.
I'll write you a long letter tomorrow and tell you lots of
things. I'll tell you now that I love you, love you, love you,
and you must love me.
                         Yours always,
                              Ring.
I think it's safer to address this to Culver. Do you love
me?

                         [February 24, 1911]

Sweetheart,-
This is the same night and I'll try to impart to you the rest
of my new knowledge. Mr. Murdoch, new boss, took me to the
show. He is to be married soon and gave me much information. He
thinks it must be better to live in a suburb and says there are
plenty of them, within fifteen minutes of town by train, which

have desirable flats and apartments. However, I'm in no hurry
and will do some looking around of my own; also some consulting
with various people; before I make any move. If you want me to
meet Miss Gibson[1] some time, perhaps she may be able to give me
some dope. If they ship me south next week, I can call on her
when I come back, which will be the second week in April. Here
is something I think you wanted to know: During the baseball
season, the first edition of the paper goes to press at eight in
the morning. Some "gossip" is needed for this, gossip about the
preceding day's game and the game to come. They think it's
better to have that prepared the night before and I guess it is,
for to get it ready in time in the morning, I'd have to be at the
office at six. According to present plans, I won't have to be on
the job until 10:30 or 11 A.M., then will work until between half
six or seven at night, depending on the time the games are over,
and games start earlier here than elsewhere. So, dear, I guess
you'll have to learn to stay up later at night and get up later
in the morning. In the off season, it will be different. That's
about all I've learned since I came to Boston.

Except one thing--I love you better and better every minute
and this evening has been about the longest I ever endured
despite the theater.

Love me, my own dear girl.

Ring

Sunday
[Boston,
26 February 1911]

My Sweetheart,-

The longing for you gets worse every minute and I'll be glad
to go to work tomorrow[2] so there'll be something sharing my mind
with the thought that I want you and you are not here.

I walked down town after supper last night and ran into Bert
Williams, who was on his way to the theater. I told him about an
idea I had for a song and he approved it. He provided an idea
for another one and told me to work on both of them and report to
him later in the week. So I must try to do something this
afternoon, although it's just about impossible to think of
anything but you.

Your picture is standing here in front of me and while it's
nice to have it, looking at it makes me crazy for the original.
Please remember, honey, that I want one of the big ones.

I'm rather hoping they'll send me south, as that will be a

---

[1]Helen Gibson, Ellis's friend from Smith College. She and
Arthur Jacks met at Ring and Ellis's wedding, and married each
other the following year, with Ring and Ellis as attendants.

[2]Ring's first article for the AMERICAN appeared in the 28
February issue.

diversion and a help in killing time. I'm not like you at all.
I wish it were June 15 right this minute and that I still had all
my "plans" to make so that I'd have to hurry every minute. But
my favorite occupation right now is planning and I have four or
five different sets of arrangements already in my mind.

I'll send you my list of invitations and announcements in two
or three weeks. I don't suppose there's such a rush for it, but
such things make the event seem more real and nearer and that's
the way I want it to seem.

I love you, dearest.

                                               Ring

The allusion above to Bert Williams is significant,
for Williams, a popular black singer, dancer, and
comedian, had been one of Ring's friends from Ring's
early days in Chicago. Ring, Jr. speaks of his
father's "contradictory" views of blacks.[1] Though he
seems to have accepted the prevailing prejudice of his
age that blacks were inferior, he greatly admired
Williams and a number of other black performers.[2] In
the Chicago days Ring and Williams frequently drank
together at Stillson's tavern, a newspaper crowd
favorite, and at numerous other saloons. It is known
that Ring wrote a number of lyrics for Williams,
especially while Ring was in Boston and Williams was a
star of Ziegfeld's Follies. There was apparently
correspondence between the two, but only the following
letter from Williams to Ring survives:

                                        New York, March 14, 1911
Hello there Big Boy:
        Thanks so much for the laying out. But it was
deserved. Have revamped the song so I am sure its
a positive hit will write the music this week while
I am in Baltimore. Its not so cold here now but
its not time yet to leave the overcoat home.
Please during this spring practice get the KINKS
out of your arms--because I am going to beat you
bowling and beat you GOOD. I know you're having a
GOOD time "mongst the Pines" and when you see Bro'
Dorey my regards-- This week Baltimore, next
Syracuse. If I hear from you there shall send you
all the route into Frisco.
        Good luck and health are the worst I can wish
you.

                                        Bert Williams
                                        ----/-----

----

[1]Ring Lardner, Jr., p. 27.

[2]See Ring's letter of 7 March 1922 to Heywood Broun on
Williams' abilities.

Wednesday night
[Boston,
1 March 1911]

Sweetheart,-

I'm writing to you before supper again because my whole
evening is set aside for trying to make another verse and chorus
for a song. I met Mr. Williams last night and was encouraged,
but I won't tell you any more about it because it's very
uncertain. When I'm about forty and you are still in your teens,
we may make some money.

I wish you could meet a fellow worker of mine, who is the
pessimistic limit. He told me this morning that no one could be
sure of a job on the American because the men higher up were
constantly firing people for no apparent reason. Then he asked
me if I was going south with the team. I told him I was and he
said he was sorry for me "You know that team was in a railroad
accident last spring," quoth he, "Nobody was badly hurt, but
somebody will be on a trip like that some time." I told him I had
accident insurance.

I'm going out to Brookline next Sunday and look things over.
If I like it I think, perhaps, I'll get a room there when I get
back from the south on April twelfth. Then you see, I'll be
right on the ground, ready to take advantage of anything there is
to be taken advantage of.

I won't be settled till I get back. As soon as I am, I'll
tell you where Miss Gibson can find me.

I'm enclosing some valuable coupons which Dorothy told me to
give you. Please don't tell her I kept them so long.

Honey, your letters are great and make me really believe you
love me. But you haven't told me how that awful cough is getting
along nor whether or not you are obeying orders. I want to know.
One thing I do know and that is that long engagements, when you
are the party of the first part, are awful for the party of the
second part. If ever again I ask you to marry me and you say you
will, the deed will have to be done the same day. I never could
have believed time could pass so slowly if I hadn't suffered the
agony of waiting for you. I'd give anything to be able to go to
sleep and sleep till the twenty-eighth of June. Furthermore I
don't believe that day ever will get here.

The Egoist is very well written, I admit, but I have a faint
suspicion that Sir Willoughby reminded you of me occasionally,
because he reminds me of myself.

It will be fun, dear, to put our house in order, but here are
two queries: What does "making curtains" mean, and what pictures
are we going to hang? If you leave it to me, I'll put pictures
of you all over the walls.

Mother says Mr. Loeffler likes both of us, I don't blame
him. I won't say a word about myself, but you are the dearest
and most lovable person that ever lived, even if you are funny.

Do you love me?

Ring

At Ring's insistence, Ellis finally sent to him a
letter which Captain Willhite had written to her:

Saturday night.
⌈Boston,
4 March 1911⌉

Dearest Girl,-
Please notice that I'm too honorable to keep the captain's
letter, much as I'd like to. But I've marked a passage in it--I
want to know what you promised him Thurs night.
Also, I'm sending you the lists.[1] If they're too long please
tell me and I'll give you a list of names that can be cut off.
There are about twenty more to come. If you lose this list, it's
all off, for I'll never make another one. The Cubs will be at St
Louis and the White Sox at Cleveland on the day, so there's no
danger there, and I'm sure that members of my family will be the
only ones in attendance--from my side.
Tomorrow afternoon I'm going to pack up and tomorrow night
I'm going to supper in Brookline--I have a newspaper friend and
his wife there--not meaning that I have his wife. On Monday
morning I'm going to get a letter from you and Monday night I
start south.
Brookline is on the way to West Newton--about 14 minutes'
ride on the train. I'll do my best on the tan, pink and blue
combinations. Isn't there any choice about dining room
decorations? If there is, you'd better tell me. The gentleman I
talked with said he thought he could fix me for about $35 dollars
per month, which is better than we could have done in St Louis.
I don't know about book shelves yet, but they have janitors, gas
ranges, steam heat and refrigerators.
My Brookline friend made a wonderful suggestion today. If it
can be carried out--and I think it's possible--it will be great.
It is for me, during the baseball season, to go directly home
from the game--both parks are about fifteen minutes' ride from
Brookline on the street cars, write my stuff at home for next
morning's paper and hire a boy by the week to carry it down to
the office every night. He says a boy could be secured for $1.50
a week including carfare. You see I would save almost seven
cents a day railroad fare, so the cost would really be only a
little over a dollar a week, and we could pretend we were making
that much less per week than we really are. It would give me
over an hour and a half more with you every day and I'd be
willing to pay a lot more than $1.08 (Sunday isn't considered) a
week for nine hours extra with you. Do you like it? Whether you
do or not, I'm going to try to put it over, and will begin trying
as soon as I get home from the south--for I'm going to room in
Brockline till June--and after.
I can't tell you about the condition of my heart, Mam'selle,

_____

[1]The lists of people to be invited to the wedding.

but I'm conceited enough to think that if you were here, I'd kiss you and kiss you and kiss you, and look into eyes that are prettier that noon-day skies ever dared to be. I've left my heart with you and I guess it must be a little one, else there wouldn't be room for anything else in that small body. I love you more than he does or could--more than anyone else could, for not a second passes when I'm not longing for you and you are everything in the world.

Kiss me, because this is a long, sensible, practical letter.
                                                    Ring.
In case you've forgotten--Albion Hotel, Augusta, Ga.

        In her letter of 9 March, Ellis laid   to   rest   the
specter of Captain Willhite:

        I did tell you once about what I promised
        Captain Willhite that particular Thursday evening.
        He gave me a book and said that the owner went with
        it. And I said, 'thank you I'd be glad to take
        both. And he said, 'its a promise,' and I laughed.
        There is the whole story. . . .

                                        Tuesday
                                        [Augusta, Ga.,
                                        14 March 1911]

Dearest Girl,-
    I have a new accomplishment. Yesterday I purchased some needles and thread and a piece of chamois skin, which I sewed around the bowl of my pipe. It was such a successful job that I bought some buttons and sewed them on where they were needed--not on my pipe. The result is that I now can wear all the shirts I possess, whereas there were formerly two ineligibles in the outfit. I don't suppose it is wise to tell you this--you may take advantage of it--but I'm so proud I can't keep it to myself.
    It is customary down here to visit a soda fountain every night before retiring. Doc Miller and I have acquired the habit and that is our only dissipation. Usually we have chocolate sodas, but we broadened out last night and ordered nut sundaes, and we ate them, too. I went to bed and had a nutty dream--something like those you have had. I was engaged to you and to one of the girls I went with in high school. I was to marry her first and she was to die in two years. Then I was to marry you. But I was true to you in the dream, for it seemed very hard on me to have to wait two years.
    Three months plus is hard enough, dear; in fact, it's a lot too hard. I couldn't stand two years and I won't. Sometimes you hear of a man and a girl's being engaged five years, but I don't believe they care anything about each other. If I should lose all my wealth and not be able to buy a single chair, you'd have to marry me in June just the same.
    I'm staying home from practice this morning because I am sick

of it. I hurried down to the office to get a letter, but there was none and now I'll have to wait until late this afternoon. There'll have to be one then.

Your picture--the smaller one--is on the table in front of me. I love it, but it makes me want you more and more. Please hurry and come to me, sweetheart.

Ring.

Wednesday
[Augusta, Ga.,
15 March 1911]

Dear, I am worried about you. There was no letter yesterday and none this morning, and there's not another mail until tonight. Please tell me you still love me, and that you aren't sick and that you haven't fallen down stairs. Days on which letters come are lonesome enough; days without letters are unbearable.

I heard from Bert Williams this morning. He said he would have the music finished for one of my songs this week, and that he was going to sing it, but he didn't say when. The show doesn't close till June, and then only for two or three weeks, so I suppose it will be pretty soon. But I'm glad our day doesn't depend on songs. Honey, can't we move up that day a little? Florence and Frank surely could "get off." I want you in May or the early part of June--just as soon as I can have you. Please don't make me wait until the twenty-eighth.

I'm trying hard today to believe you care as much for me as ever and that doubts aren't visiting you again, but there's no letter to help me. And it's three long, long weeks since I saw you. If I'd staid in St Louis, I wouldn't have seen you at all probably, because you aren't going to have any more vacation. I wish you could have one now, because I feel more comfortable when you are in Goshen.

I must go to the game. Write me a long letter to make up for delinquencies.

Ring

Can't I stop addressing you in care of Mrs. G. H. C.? I don't want you in her care.

Thursday
[Augusta, Ga.,
16 March 1911]

Dearest Girl,-

Who gave you permission to skip Sunday, the day on which you ought to write letters twice as long as usual because there's so much more time? I'm afraid you've forgotten a promise you made just three weeks ago today. I know it's hard for you to write every day, dear, but it isn't half as hard as it is for me to get through a day without a letter from you, so I cast myself on your

mercy. Your Saturday letter came Monday and your Monday letter
this morning, so Tuesday and Wednesday were barren and horrible.
I dreamed about you all last night and couldn't think of anything
else this morning. I was going to telegraph, but I asked the
clerk to send up my mail and there was a letter in it, which fact
saved us whatever a telegram would have cost. But if you neglect
me again, I'll refuse to meet your Gibsons and I won't read to
you, nor let you sew. Which reminds me--what are you going to
sew all those evenings?

I'm going to be a teacher, too. There's a girl from New
York, a very pretty one, of course, who, with her father, attends
all our practice games, and she wants to learn to score. So the
owner of the club is to introduce me this afternoon and the first
lesson will follow.

Mr. Rockefeller and Mr. Taft are down here and Mr. Taft is
coming to the game day after tomorrow. I wish you could take his
place.

Have you any objection to Plymouth? (Not Plymouth, Ind.) If
you have, I'll find some other place, but that's supposed to be
quiet, and I don't want anything to disturb us.

Here's a funny thing: We will meet people some time who will
know you only as Mrs. Lardner. They won't know there ever was
such a person as Ellis Abbott. You see you are going to lose
your identity and I'm not. But I'll always remember Ellis
Abbott, and that I loved her and that she was the dearest girl
that ever lived, even if she was funny.

Ring

Ring's frustration must have been increased by
Ellis's reply:

We are invited to a lovely party Monday night.
Captain Stewart's wife has gone home to stay until
summer and he and Dr. Neilson have asked Mr. and
Mrs Crandall, the Gignillats and me down to the
Stewart cottage. The two of them are going to make
cake and ice-cream and a lot of stuff all by
themselves. I am to wash the dishes for them
afterward. Captain Stewart is the kind who is apt
to flirt with almost anyone but I like him and we
get along beautifully together though Mrs.
Crandall does'nt approve of him.

Augusta, Ga.,
Sunday, March 19, '11

Dear Miss Abbott,-

I sincerely hope you will enjoy yourself at Captain Stewart's
party. There are flirtations that are harmless, but I don't
advise you to go very far with a married man.

I was glad to hear from you and to know you were still having
good times at Culver. As for me, I don't recall that I ever

spent so pleasant a winter. The weather down here is ideal, my friends are most congenial and the Southern girls are really charming.
  I hope you will find time to drop me another line soon.
                    Sincerely,
                        Ring. W. Lardner

                              Wednesday
                              [Augusta, Ga.,
                               22 March 1911]

Dearest Girl,-
  I suspect you of having skipped another day and I am positive your letters are getting shorter and shorter. So I have, in desperation, formulated a get even and keep even plan. This is it: On days which bring letters from you, I am going to count the number of words in them and write the same number in reply. On days which don't bring letters, I'm not going to write. There were 193 words, including signature, in this morning's letter. There will be 193 words in this, even if I have to break off in the middle of a sentence.
  The pretty girl isn't quite as nice as you are, but she's so nice that you can't get even by using Billy Lambert, whom I remember. But she isn't dangerous, because she has a husband, although he's in New York and she hasn't seen him since December. Among the athletes she is known as The Queen, and I guess they are wishing for once in their lives that they were newspaper men instead of ball players.
  Our schedule, after leaving here, has been changed. I will send corrections when -------

        On the 25th Ellis wrote from Goshen of her plans
    for the wedding:

        I'll tell you some of the plans for 'your' wedding. You are to be married in the back or north side of the library. You know you and the best man are just <u>there</u> and Ruby and father and I come downstairs and through the middle room. We are going to take the frames out of the windows that go out onto the front and side porch--and drape the porch with something, and hang lights out there. It will enlarge the space on that side of the house a lot. Then the wedding is to be in pink with pink sweetpeas and bride's roses for the flowers. I dont know whether you are interested in all that or not if you are I'll keep you posted as things develope. . . .

Sunday
[Greensboro,
2 April 1911]

Dearest Girl,-
    The rats and I are spending a quiet Sunday in our room.
Everybody attended the Elks' fair last night and I had three
chances on a buggy. What would we have done with it if I'd won?
The Southern Belles were very cordial as long as they were
selling us chances, but froze up when they could get nothing more
out of us. Such is hospitality in the South.
    You know--or you ought to--that Saturday is my hardest day,
because I have a Sunday paper, as well as the regular afternoon
one, to look out for. You would have known that I was familiar
with hell and high and low class swearing in all its branches if
you could have heard me yesterday, for the operator was a
bonehead, the Boston club used nineteen players and the score was
34 to 0. When things like that happen after June, I'm going to
give vent to my anger by beating you when I get home.
    Anne informs me that Ethel Witkowsky Pick and Dora[1] want to
know if you look well in the street. That's cruel and
unaccustomed.
    You made good on your poker prophecy. Here's one of mine
which also will come true if it hasn't already: Captain Willhite
will bring you one or more big red apples. He will say that he
has been regretting all winter that he "declared himself" and
thus deprived himself of the pleasure of evenings with you, but
that his heart ran away from him; that if you will be so kind, he
will resume his calls on a friendly basis and try to keep <u>love</u>
out of his speech and his eyes, for his intercourse with you has
been his only pleasure at Culver and he would give anything if he
had never been so rash and wasteful of the precious hours. Then,
after the friendly basis has been firmly reestablished, his heart
will run wild once more and the former scenes will be repeated
and then some. I'm not setting the hours and days on which these
things will transpire, and I realize right this minute that
jealousy is sharing my room with the rats and me; but, still, I'm
willing to bet on my dope. You may name the amount of the wager
and I'll trust you to decide whether or not I win. But please
love me just the same.
    My brain tells me that the twenty-fifth of June is twelve
weeks from today, but my heart thinks that no time at all has
been cut off my sentence since last Sunday although the week has
been a year. I've quit waiting for the twenty-eighth and am
thinking only of the twenty-fifth, for that date seems much
nearer and much less impossible. You know I've seen you before
and it's reasonable to expect I'll see you again; but I've never
married you before and it's very hard to realize that I ever
will.

_____

[1]Dora McCarley Lardner, Rex's wife.

Two weeks from today will be Easter. I'm going to Church at Brookline in the morning and, in the afternoon, I think I'll get my real estate and renting man to show me around. I'll tell you the result of my search provided you are very good in the meantime and not neglectful of your betrothed husband.

Before I forget it, please tell me the correct names of the Banta and Hawks furniture companies and of John Banta and Edward Hawks.[1] I think I have them right, but I want to be sure. Also, could you find out if I could tell one of them about the other, without violating anything, so they could get together on the shipping proposition; although I don't suppose it will make much difference.

You see, if I find an apartment that fills the requirements, I'll want to grab it in May if necessary, to prevent anyone else's getting it. And, after I get it, I'll want something to put in it. I used to think moving into a place would be a horrible job, but I know I'm going to enjoy this. I will be moving into the home which is going to be to me the happiest home there ever was, and the process may make me realize that I'm really going to have you with me there.

I was doing some figuring awhile ago and I was convinced that we would be almost broke when our home life really started in spite of my economical Southern trip. But I'm not worrying about it because I'm too selfish to think much about your side of the case. If I were really and honestly unselfish, I wouldn't marry you at all. My only excuse, and it's a poor one, is that others have done it and got away with it.

This letter didn't mean to be such a long one. I wish you would forget yourself some time and write me one as long.

If you want me to meet Miss Gibson, I'll tell you my telephone number as soon as I know it.

I would like to hear Anne's instructions about the ring. My hand probably will lose its sense of aim entirely and I'll miss your finger when I shoot at it. It wouldn't be so hard if you had life-sized fingers. And that reminds me that I want the measurement of the finger. You can send me a piece of string or that little ring, the one that's absolutely guaranteed. Don't you dare to forget it.

We'll be in Roanoke only a short time tomorrow and I don't know whether I'll be able to write or not, but I'll try.

Tell me the latest "plans," all about Goshen, and that you love me, my dear, pretty girl.

Ring

Ellis responded:

You must'nt put anything in our house but the furniture we bought and perhaps your books. And

[1]John Banta of the Banta Furniture Company and Edwin W. Hawks of the Hawks Furniture Company

don't you <u>dare</u> to buy anything else until I get there. I am very sure that I will change everything you arrange. Is'nt that encouraging? What difference does it make if we dont have anything in the bank when we start? I am going to keep just a few dollars--about twenty five--and if you have that much we'll start even. It is a very delicate subject--but I wish that sometime when you feel very confidential and practical you'd tell me <u>about</u>--you need'nt be exact if you don't want to--how much '<u>our</u>' monthly income is going to be. You see when I am learning to cook and sew etc. I'd like to know what sort of things we can afford to cook etc. And then of course I'm just naturally curious.

Less than three months before the wedding, Ring still had not revealed to Ellis the precise amount of his income. In his obvious idealization of Ellis, Ring clearly saw her as someone to be protected, and saw himself as the one who should assume all such responsibilities. The fact that Ellis was apprehensive and tactful in raising the question says much about their relationship. Ring replied with the details:

Saturday
[Lynchburg, Va.,
8 April 1911]

Sweetheart,-
I almost missed today, for it rained and we decided all of a sudden to take a five o'clock train for Baltimore. But the train is over an hour late and I have borrowed a hotel across from the station in which to write. If the train goes without me it's your fault.
Dear, I never feel practical and never confidential while I'm on the water wagon. We'll not wait for one of those moods, because you really have a right to know things. So I'll discuss the "delicate subject" briefly. I can't talk by months, for newspapers don't pay that way. The Tribune was giving me $35 a week and I went to St Louis for $50 and came down again to $45 at Boston. It's $45 now and still it isn't, and that's the delicate part. My family used to be "well off," but got over it. My father is kept busy paying for insurance and taxes, and he and my mother and Lena have to have something to live on. Lena makes something and there's no use arguing with her about it. My brother Billy helps when he can. Harry has a crowd for a family of his own, so you see it's up to Rex and me. Each of us ships home $10. Balance for me--$35. If you had been anyone but you, I would have felt obliged to say something before. But I know you. Lena would rather die than ask us (Rex and me) for anything and I guess she thinks I'm going to "stop" when I'm married. But

I'm not. R. W. Lardner and Company, which is you, now possess about $800. About $200 of this will go for the Goshen furniture and probably $150 or $200 for the furniture we are still to get. Another $200 for my typewriter (which I must have) and for my trousseau etc., and we'll be lucky to have $200 left when June comes, because I won't be able to save from now on. And I used to swear I'd never get married before I had $1,000 laid away. I hadn't known you when I swore that.

There'll be a pay-day on "Little Puff of Smoke" in July and perhaps something from other things some time. These can be used in helping to pay for a piano. I guess you know as much as I do now, and it's awful to leave you with all this. But you brought it on yourself. Perhaps I won't mail this letter, but I guess I will, for you'll have to know about things some time.

I don't want to meet Miss Gibson till you come. If you'll trust me with the flat choosing, there'll be no need of my bothering her. I thought you wanted her approval--of the flat and me.

I am interested in your dresses and you must tell me all about them.

In order that this may not be a business letter exclusively, I'll ask you to tell me you love me. You can pretend it isn't your business to.

I'm in a hurry to get back to Boston, but I suppose the days will drag just the same up there.

I love you and love you and love you and you owe me a long, long letter, with nothing in it but that you love me.

Ring

In April the Culver Military Academy school year was terminated early because of epidemics of measles and scarlet fever, so Ellis returned to Goshen earlier than Ring had expected.

[Boulevard, Mass.,
23 April 1911]

Sweetheart,-
This is a combination Saturday and Sunday letter and I imagine it will be a rather long one.

You can't guess how glad I am that you are through with measles, scarlet fever, Marian, Maidie, Mrs. Crandall, Cap Wilhite and all the other diseases. I mailed a letter yesterday to Culver. If the Crandalls are crazy enough to forward it, you must burn it up, or have some one else do so, immediately, and you mustn't read it, for really there is nothing in it except, perhaps, the germs. Also, you must write at once and tell me your headache was just a headache. I'm going to be scared to death if I don't hear from you Monday.

Now that you are home, you can set aside one whole hour every day for writing to me. There's absolutely no excuse for neglecting me any more.

This is Saturday night and the afternoon was glorious. The wind blew horribly from the East, it snowed and they had an extra inning game. I was absolutely coaqulated and I haven't got over it yet. It's lucky for you that you didn't marry me in January.

Do you remember my telling you about a New Year's card from a mysterious Emma Sargent in Malden? The mystery is solved and the romance is busted. There is a "girl" forty years old who lives in Malden and who is insane on the subject of baseball. She is worth $10,000 and promises it to anyone connected with baseball who will marry her. One of the Boston baseball writers delights in introducing her to anyone he can corner. He got me last Summer and I had to go through a back exit to get away from her after the game. I suppose she saw my name in Sporting News and wanted to renew the acquaintance. I'd forgotten all about her when she pounced on me today and I had an awful time. I was obliged to write down her telephone number, although I told her I was married. It seems the Boston man had assured her I wasn't.

Dear, do you know you are a brave girl to have stuck to the finish at Culver? Your small pupils will be happier all their lives for having known you. Also, they will be absolutely spoiled for another teacher, for there aren't any one-tenth as dear and good. And we won't mention Culver any more, for it makes my eyes and ears hurt.

You are to tell me at once about bed-springs, mattresses, bouquets and your visit to Niles, and all about your costumes. I don't know how much mattresses and springs cost and I don't care. For I've given up the idea of having any money in the bank. We'll try to have enough for the first week's provisions and that's all. It's too much trouble to worry about saving any.

I'm going to be presented at the home of a Jewish lawyer named Auerbach tomorrow. It's for your sake. Mr. and Mrs. Dallam think a lot more of you than me and are constantly planning your entertainment. Mrs. Auerbach is a nice person for a strange girl from Indiana to know and so I have to pave the way for the strange girl. Mr. and Mrs. Dallam are, according to them, going to play cards almost every night with Mr. and Mrs. Lardner, but some nights, they're going to take Mr. and Mrs. Lardner to the theater and, afterwards, to a very much Bohemian cafe, where Mr. and Mrs. Dallam can drink something while Mr. and Mrs. Lardner eat something, or look on, for Mr. and Mrs. Lardner don't drink. You see we won't have any time for the Gibsons and not a second for ourselves. I love you.

    Ring

In turn, Ellis argued: "Your idea that I should take an hour off, everyday, to write to you is perfectly ridiculous. I love you dearly and think of you every minute of the day--but I simply have not an hour to spare."

Friday night.
[Boulevard, Mass.,
28 April 1911]

My own Girl,-
If your Wednesday "letter" had been the only one I got today,
I would have skipped tonight, but your Tuesday one arrived this
morning and wasn't so bad. The Wednesday one was unspeakable,
and you can't make me believe it was Ruby's fault either, for
Ruby is a darn nice girl and an intimate friend of mine. Please
thank her for her thoughtfulness regarding the six foot two inch
bed, but I don't think there's any use speaking to Mr. Hawks
about it, for I believe that's regulation size and I've never
slept in any other kind but once, when Pa stretched one for me.
If I find I can't use the Hawks bed, I'll just stay out all
night, every night.
A constable came to the office today and presented me with
$1.80 and a summons to appear as witness in a slander suit.
About two years ago, Ban Johnson said some uncomplimentary things
about a man in an interview which appeared under my name in the
Tribune. The man sued him for $50,000 damages and the case comes
up in New York next week. The man wanted me to go over there and
testify, but I knew they couldn't force me to go, so I told him
it was impossible for me to get away. So they are going to take
my deposition on Monday here in Boston. I'll have to tell the
truth, which may hurt Mr. Johnson, but really I don't remember
much about it. If you don't hear from me next week, you'll know
I'm in Jail for perjury or contempt.
I came past <u>our house</u>[1] on my way home tonight. I wish we
were in it together right this minute.
You haven't told me about Monday night, the twenty-sixth of
June, in Niles. And I love you.
Ring

Thursday night.
[Boston, Mass.,
11 May 1911]

Funny Fiancee,-
I think my search is nearly over. I saw three places this
morning and all of them were pretty good. I'll make my selection
tomorrow I guess, and then, on Sunday, I'll draw you a map of it
with measurements of the windows and the dining-room floor. I
like one of the three particularly because it's only about five
minutes' ride from one ball park.
Perhaps I'll go to Northampton a week from Sunday, but I
don't know. I don't believe Florence will do anything desperate
if I don't. That will be about my only chance to go anywhere,

_____

[1]Ring had chosen an apartment in Brookline, but for reasons
now unknown, he did not proceed to obtain a lease.

for the White Sox will have one Sunday and I'll be busy <u>settling</u>
on the others. You would know that I'll be here only four
Sundays after next, if you took any interest in me at all.

My deposition was thrown out of the libel suit because the
lawyer's questions were "leading and incompetent." Now the
plaintiff wants me to go to New York and testify, but I won't.
There isn't much of a case without my testimony, if I do say it
as shouldn't.

I'm going to keep that ring till I see you, for the thought
of doing it up to send back overwhelms me with terror.

Dear, I don't know whether you love me or not. Lots of times
I think you don't. I think you think you do, but I'm not at all
sure you know. You don't pay any attention when I ask you in
letters, but I'm going to try to find out when I see you. You
are to undergo a rigid cross-examination and my questions may be
leading, but they won't be incompetent. I don't believe I could
give you up, but I do want to know the truth. Won't you try to
help? I love you every minute.
                                            Ring

                              Sunday Evening
                              [Boulevard, Mass.,
                              14 May 1911]

Sweetheart,-
     I enclose another map and some measurements. I like the
place more the more I see it and it's ours if you approve. The
"built-in thing" isn't in the dining-room, but in a sort of
vestibule that leads into the kitchen. The woodwork in the
living-room, alcove and front bedroom is white and in the rest of
the house oak, but a little darker than usual. The alcove is
rather big--about seven feet by twelve and the people who live
there now use it for a bed-room. It has a small, high window.
The living-room windows are two in a row and the ones on the end
of the dining-room are three--the middle one wider than the
others. There are two clothes-closets opposite the bath-room,
in the hall, and one in the front bed-room. The floors are to be
done over and the living-room (including alcove) dining room and
front bed-room repapered.

     I wrote to John Banta and Mr. Hawks today, giving them
directions, and I still have letters to write to my mother, Lena
and Arthur Jacks.

     Do you know what I did this morning? No, you don't. I read
every letter I've had from you since I saw you. There's
something particularly funny in one of them. I'll show it to you
some time.

     I didn't get a letter from you yesterday, so I guess you
don't love me. But I guess you'd better learn to, for it will
pretty hard for you to live with me if you don't. It'll be
pretty hard anyway, I guess.

     Do you know what I'm going to do forty-two days from tonight?
I'm going to kiss you. But it's going to be desperately hard to

wait forty-two days. I love you, honey.
                        Ring
I forgot to tell you--this apartment is on the first floor.

                        Monday night.
                        [Boston, Mass.,
                        15 May 1911]

Dearest Girl,-
    I'm sorry, but I don't think we'll have time to go to the
lake on Monday. I'll have things to do in Goshen in the
morning--a marriage license must be procured for one thing--and
we're going to Niles on the interurban because I'll have an
errand or two in South Bend. But you've got to start when I do
because I won't be separated from you any more than is absolutely
necessary.
    I know you're not interested in baseball, but I am, in one
particular phase of it. They are using a new ball this year.
It's livelier and that means more hitting, and more hitting means
longer games, and that's the devil. It appears to be impossible
to finish a game in less than two hours. It's bad enough now,
but it's going to drive me crazy when it keeps me away from my
own home.
    Today's interminable game and other things have spoiled my
usual sweet good nature and sunny disposition, and tonight my
highest ambition is to kick somebody or something. Also, I'm
lonesome and the time is passing slower than ever. I know that
everything would be all right if you'd just come and kiss me.
Never, as long as I live, will I forgive you for making it the
twenty-eighth of June, when it could have been day after tomorrow
just as well.
    But I love you, and I can't write any more tonight.
                        Ring.

                        Monday night.
                        [Boston, Mass.,
                        22 May 1911]

My own Girl,-
    I'll write to Mr. Van Nuys[1] as soon as I write to you. I'll
be glad to do it because things like that make it seem nearer.
It's a risky thing to do, for if you've lost that invitation list
our engagement is at an end so far as I'm concerned. So for your
own sake you'd better find it.
    Does "Wilmer" have to appear? Whether he does or not, please
don't put any gold on the end of the Ring. It's bad enough
without that. Ring W. or Ring Wilmer is p-lenty.

_____

    [1]The Reverend Van Nuys was the minister of the Goshen
Presbyterian Church.

Our address is No. 16 Park Drive, Brookline.[1] You mustn't send "at homes" to anyone who'd be likely to come, because I want to be the only caller for a year.

Arthermometer is just 92 this minute and it's ? almost nine. And I don't think it's ever going to rain.

You can feel affectionate about eight times as often as you do and I won't mind at all. That's how I look at the matter.

Dear Miss Abbott, my friends, the Cubs, are coming tomorrow and perhaps I won't have time to write tomorrow night. But I will be loving you all the while and please don't skip a day. Next time they come you will be here and I'll have a pleasanter way of spending an evening.

My Boston team has lost twelve straight games and writing about it is a hard task. I wonder how I'm going to spend an hour working every evening when you're in the house. I guess you'll have to keep out of my sight.

If you're interesting in knowing what I'm going to say to Mr. Van Nuys, here it is,

Well, say, old Van Nuys,
Please quote me your price
For doing the splice
For two little mice.
You'd better be nice
And low in your price--
I may want you twice;
"   "   "   " thrice;
"   "   "   " four times, Van.

R

Tuesday night.
[Boulevard, Mass.,
30 May 1911]

Sweetheart,-

I now have absolute, conclusive proof that you don't read my letters, but having gone thus far, I may as well continue to write them.

Listen, dear, if you want a husband who isn't a nervous wreck and a large, ill-tempered grouch, please don't skip any more days. It makes more difference to me because I do read what you write and the days which don't bring letters are awful. This waiting is bad enough without depriving me of the only thing that makes it endurable.

I don't believe Mr. Van Nuys is going to marry us. I wrote to him over a week ago and he hasn't answered. Who is Goshen's most reasonable justice of the peace?

I am hoping that this coming Sunday will be busy. I'm going to spend the morning in our house, "arranging" furniture, and the

---

[1]Ring had finally signed an apartment lease.

afternoon and evening with the White Sox. I see by the Trib that
the bum baseball song is published. Doc hasn't told me anything
about it, but he'll be here day after tomorrow. You and I will
always be living in hope of a windfall from one of our
masterpieces.

I'm going to pay the first month's rent tomorrow and I'll pay
for July before I come West so we won't have that to worry about.
All I'm worrying over just now is you and whether you really want
me or not. Do you know I'm going to be with you in just
twenty-five days? And do you care?

Arthur Jacks is going to meet us in Niles Sunday. Is he
invited to the party? I guess he is, for I told him about it.
Mrs. Tobin and her child will also be in Niles to greet us.

I'm tired to death of being alone, dear, and the queer thing
about it is that I'd rather not be with anyone at all if I can't
be with you. Hurry, and come to me.

Ring

The "bum baseball song" was "Gee, It's a Wonderful
Game," which, as the following letter indicates, the
Remick company publicized by having a quartet sing it
at the White Sox ballpark before a game.

Wednesday night.
[Boulevard, Mass.,
31 May 1911]

My own Girl,-

I was hoping against hope that my mother would carry out my
instructions regarding invitations, but she hasn't. She has sent
some names to me and will send others to you--probably the same
ones to both of us. I know it's too late to send the whole batch
back to me for revision, so I guess you'll just have to take my
list and her list and compare them and see that there are no
duplicates. I hate to bother you about it, dear, but there's no
help for it now.

Furthermore, there's no escape for you now, for Mr. Van Nuys
has consented to do his worst. From what he has heard, Mr.
Lardner will prove a worthy husband for Miss Ellis. That's a hot
one on you and shows that folks have been talking about you to
the minister.

Doc White comes tonight and I'll see him and your friend, Mr.
Tannehill, tomorrow. Doc owed me a letter and was evidently
afraid to meet me before he had answered it. Anyway, a letter
came from him today, along with my contract from the publishers.
I'm acquiring a great little collection of contracts. The Remick
company, a decent concern, is it this time. It started
advertising by having a quartet sing the song at the ball park in
Chicago the other day. If Doc has any professional copies along,
I'll send you one, absolutely free.

There was no letter from you today and I guess you'd pass me
up if you had a chance. But it's too late. I'm going to marry

you three weeks from a week from tonight and then I won't care if
the postman never comes.
        *I l--- y--.
                        Ring
    *A prize for you if you can guess the missing letters.

                        Monday night.
                        [Boulevard, Mass.,
                        5 June 1911]

My darling,-
    Perhaps you don't believe I work at all, but I do and I can't
possibly meet every ten o'clock train from now on until Jeannette
comes. It will help a lot if you'll tell me what __day__ she's
coming. I do want to see her and I will if I can. I presume
she'll get off at Huntington Avenue.
    Dear, the rugs don't make a bit of difference to me--I mean
you are the authority on them--and I wouldn't know any more if I
did go down to look at some. I'll send you the dimensions and
paper samples tomorrow and then, if you will, you can order them
to suit yourself. Address them, or have them addressed to my
Winthrop Road number--"Huntington Avenue delivery." That also
goes for your box, which I think I will open before you come. Do
just as you please about the bed. I do think you are having a
great deal more than your share of bother. It will be nice to
have the rugs in before you arrive because they'll improve the
looks of things.
    If I leave here before the rugs come, I'll fix it with Mr.
Dallam to see that they are delivered.
    He and his wife and I are going to the Friars' Frolic
Wednesday night. We had to pay for our tickets this time, but I
want to see all the celebrities at once. It would be a million
times nicer if you were along.
    Small George[1] is awfully sick I guess. He is a nice kid and
Harry has had trouble enough without that.
    We had a concert down at the White Sox' hotel last night. It
was my first pianisting since March, but, believe me, I'm just as
good as ever.
    It's rather hard to realize, Miss Abbott, that I'm going to
see you two weeks from next Saturday and to __own__ you three weeks
from Wednesday. But it's nice to think about it, even if it
doesn't seem real.
    Do you love me?
                        R ⌒

    You must tell me about the bed--how much it costs--and I'll
send you the money, or else you can tell them to keep it for us
till I come.

----

    [1]Henry (Harry) Lardner's son

Friday night.
[Boston, Mass.
9 June 1911]

Dearest Girl,-
I met Jeannette in spite of you. The Bacon and Eggs family met her too. Mrs. B. and E. and I had a long talk and I made the remarkable discovery that she didn't like me. She asked me to come out to her house during Jeannette's stay, but I'm not going because she doesn't l. m. However, it was nice to see Jeannette and also to carry that funny little pocket edition suitcase.

It's very fitting that you should send me an invitation to my own wedding. Otherwise I would feel as if I were butting in.

Two weeks from tonight I'm going to start. I thought I was tired of traveling, but for some reason or other, I'm crazy to make this trip. But I'm almost sure something's going to happen to prevent. Please don't let it happen at your end. I will be awfully careful of myself. You are probably working harder than you ought to, and you mustn't. When I get there, I'm going to make you take a vacation. You are to do nothing but talk to me. Perhaps that isn't your idea of a vacation, but it's mine.

And three weeks from tonight, you and I will be in our home, and it will be a nice home because it will have you.

I'm finding out every day how little I know about practical things and I have overlooked details so important that I'm really ashamed to tell you about them. It would take me a year to get wise to all the things our apartment lacks and needs, but I'm afraid you'll discover a lot the matter at first glance. I only know I need you, my own sweetheart.
                    R---

Tuesday night.
[Boston, Mass.
13 June 1911]

My own Girl,-
It was kind enough to rain today and I did some shopping. First I made the required deposit with the gas company and then I went after a box springs and a mattress. I got, or ordered, the best they had of each. The springs cost five dollars less than the mattress, which is a hair affair. I was just wondering what I would do for funds when the man asked me if I wanted credit. I told him I certainly did. The dramatic critic on the paper has some sort of an interest in the place and that's why I was trusted. Now we can get the other things we need as soon as we want them, and the "Little Puff of Smoke" money, which comes on the fifteenth of July, ought to be enough to pay for the whole works. The mattress and springs are being made to order and will be delivered next Monday, which is going to be my busy day. It's a big store and seems to have everything.

I'm going to meet Jeannette, without the Bacons, Friday, and convey her from one station to the other. That's the day she leaves for Northampton. She says she has heard nothing from home since she left. You Abbotts are a fine bunch of correspondents and I'm glad I'm almost through with you.

Miss Gibson must surely visit us in August and for more than a few minutes. You will be very weary of just me by that time and, besides, perhaps she can cook.

I'll be with you in eleven days and two weeks from tomorrow night, you'll be all mine.

Write to me, dear.

Ring

Tuesday night.
[Boston, Mass.
20 June 1911]

This is my penultimate letter to you, sweetheart. And these days and nights are, without doubt or exception, the longest in history. Tomorrow is supposed to be the longest day in the year, but it can't possibly be any worse than this one.

I packed my trunk last night, and tonight I went down to our house and unpacked it again. I filled all the drawers in the chiff., but there's a little room left for you in the dresser. The place looks much better at night than in the day-time. I ran across many loving couples in the surrounding parks. Some night we'll pretend we're not married and we'll meet at one of the benches. Then we'll flirt. Oh yes, we will.

We'll have to make some very careful plans for our getaway. We ought to be able to manage somehow with the aid of Frank and Rex. The latter is perfectly trustworthy. He'll do a little lying for us if necessary.

Richard Tobin Sr. is not going to honor us with his presence. That's the one time in the month he has to work nights. I suppose he could make it if he had been on the job longer, but as it is, he's afraid to take a chance.

I think we'll put the Hawks table under the bed or between the dresser and chiff., so it will be among friends.

Please love me for four more days and then some. And remember you have an engagement for Saturday night.

Signed--Ringgold Lardner,
          Horace Nordyke
          Irvin Coppes
          Stewart Gibson
          Loring Hoover
          Dean Taylor
          Ray Lindsay
          Fred Hurtz
          Harold Fonda
          Hugh Newell
          Jerry
              and
          Old Cap Willhite

Ring was listing, besides himself, all of the men whom he knew to have courted Ellis in the past.

Wednesday night.
[Boston, Mass.
21 June 1911]

I'm very tired of writing to Ellis Abbott, and I guess this is the last letter she'll ever get from me. Our correspondence has been a very pleasant diversion--really a necessity--but I don't think I can carry it on any longer, for paper and stamps cost money. I'll drop in and see her at Goshen Saturday night, on my way to South Bend and Niles, and see what she thinks about it.

I'm sure I've done my part toward keeping up our pleasant acquaintance. My letters have been as regular as the devil, and very interesting. Hers, I'm sorry to say, have been irregular as the devil, and sometimes they read as if they had been addressed to a stranger instead of a true and loving friend. But I suppose she was doing her best, and that is the most anybody can do. I always respect a man or woman who does his or her best. Nobody can do more, and one is prone to overlook faults in a person who is really trying.

I shall leave Boston--South Station--at 4:50 P.M. Friday afternoon. Pittsfield, 9:24 P.M., Utica, 1:13 A.M., Saturday morning, Erie, 8:28 A.M. Toledo, 2:05 P.M., Saturday afternoon. Train due at Goshen, 5:37 P.M., Saturday evening, but will be two or three hours late on account of heavy snows west of Toledo.

I went to our house tonight and put the springs and mattress to bed. The bed is now the prettiest thing in the house. It looks like Mount Tom.

I hope your boxes do arrive tomorrow, for I'll feel lots safer about them if they're here before I leave. But I may have time to look them up Friday.

Good-bye till Saturday, my own sweetheart. I want to kiss you and tell you I love you more than anything else in the world.

Ring

Ring and Ellis were married in Goshen on 28 June 1911. The marriage received prominent coverage in both the Niles and Goshen papers, and in the TRIBUNE. The following is from the Niles DAILY STAR:

At eight o'clock last evening at the home of the bride's parents, Mr. and Mrs. Frank P. Abbott of Goshen, Ind., occurred the wedding of Miss Ellis Abbott and Mr. Ringgold Lardner, youngest son of Mr. and Mrs. Henry Lardner of this city. The ceremony was performed by Rev. Mr. Van Nuys, pastor of the Presbyterian church.

The bride was given away by her father and was attended by her sister, Miss Ruby Abbott. Mr.

Arthur H. Jacks of Chicago was best man. The
ribbon bearers were Miss Wilma Johnson of this
city, Miss Helen Gibson of Boston, Miss Julia Dole
of Evanston, Miss Margaret Meyer of South Bend,
Miss Ruth McGee of Toledo, and Miss Florence
Abbott, another sister of the bride.

The wedding march was played by Noble Kryder,
a young musical prodigy of Goshen, which was of his
own composition.

The bride was gowned in Japanese
hand-embroidered silk, trimmed with real lace, with
tulle veil caught with orange blossoms. She
carried a bouquet of bride's roses and lilies of
the valley, and wore a cameo in antique setting,
the gift of the groom.

The bridesmaid wore pink marquisette over pink
satin and carried pink roses.

The ceremony which was witnessed by 175
guests, was performed in front of a beautiful
screen of elderberry blossoms. Roses and
hydrangeas were also used effectively.

The color scheme in the dining room was pink
and green, where a three-course collation was
served by caterers from Toledo.

Beautiful gowns were worn by the guests and
the affair was one of the most elaborate ever given
in Goshen.

The gifts were numberless and very beautiful,
among them being a solid silver vegetable dish from
"Doc" White, the noted Sox pitcher, who is a
particular friend of the groom; from the Cubs, a
200-piece Haviland set of dishes; from Ban Johnson,
Pres. of the American League, a cut glass dish;
Chicago Tribune, of which the groom was formerly
sporting editor, electric lamp; from Jimmie
Callahan, another celebrated base ball man, set of
glass-cut tumblers and pitcher.

Mr. and Mrs. Lardner left last night for
Boston, where they will go to housekeeping at once,
the groom having the home all ready. Mr. Lardner
is now sporting editor of a Boston paper. The
young man's many friends in Niles, where he was
born and reared, extend best wishes, and offer
hearty congratulations to the bride, who has also
many friends here, having visited in Niles a number
of times.

1911-1926:

YEARS OF FRUITION

Since there is no record of any honeymoon, one may
assume that Ring acquiesced to Ellis's earlier request
that they move immediately into the Boston apartment.
In any case, one week after the wedding Ring wrote from
Boston to Ellis's mother, telling her how much he
enjoyed married life:

> [Boston, Mass.]
> The Fourth of July.
>
> Dear Mother II.,-
> My wife and I are having a quarrel. She says I must show her
> this letter and I say I mustn't. I suppose she will win the
> argument.
> People who said she didn't know much about keeping house and
> cooking were trying to deceive me. Last night's supper and this
> morning's breakfast--our first meals at home--were absolutely the
> best I ever tasted.
> I wish I could make some sort of return to you for giving her
> to me, but I know I can't, so I'll just have to be grateful to
> you all the rest of my life.
> You must come to us the first minute you can get away. I
> want you to, for my own sake as well as Ellis'. And you must
> stay a long time when you do come.
> I'm having the best time of my life now. The next best times
> were spent at your house and I'm thankful to you for them, too.
> It's desperately hot here now, but it can't last long. I
> hope it won't anyway, for I don't want Ellis to be utterly
> discouraged right at the start.
> Give my love to yourself and the girls and tell Mr. Abbott
> I'm grateful to him, too, for my everlasting happiness.
> Ring

The following letter was probably written sometime
later in the same summer. Ring, who had been promoted
to sports editor at the AMERICAN at the time of the
wedding, was busy at what appeared to be a promising
position, while Ellis may have been a bit bored with
only the duties of being a housewife. However, since
she became pregnant a month after the wedding, her life
shortly was to become more complicated.

Sunday night.
⌈Summer 1911⌉

Dear Mother II,-
Your small daughter fell asleep while I was reading to her,
so I am stealing a little time to write to you. I'm not allowed
to do anything but read and try to play the piano while she is
awake and I am at home.
I suppose you've heard that Mr. and Mrs. Lardner are to
chaperone a house-party at Helen Gibson's the latter part of this
week. It will be a novel experience but if it's half as nice as
all the other novel experiences I've been having, I won't object
a bit.
A new arrangement at "my" office requires me to work late
every Saturday night. To make up for it, I don't have anything
to do until Tuesday morning, and you may be sure I enjoy the
Sunday-Monday vacation at home.
I think Ellis has been a little homesick once or twice,
although she wouldn't admit it. It's a cinch she'll be glad to
see Ruby and Frank and John--and any other members of the family
who can be enticed away from home--when they come. It would be
wonderfully nice if you, yourself, could come to see us.
We went to Andover a couple of Sundays ago to call on "Cousin
Mary" and she proved to be quite the nicest person of her age I
ever met. I'd like to go back there once a week, but my wife has
a fiendishly jealous disposition, as was evidenced this instant.
She awoke and asked me what I was doing and when I informed her I
was writing to a girl, she went right back to sleep again.
All but two people have quit writing to me. The two are Mrs.
Henry Lardner and Mrs. Abbott, and I hope they won't give up the
practice.
Love to everybody, including yourself.
Ring

Early in September Ellis wrote to her mother with
the news of her pregnancy:

My Dearest Mother,
This is going to be a very private letter so
you'd better take it into the bath room to read.
You have'nt written to me for a long time and I am
afraid father is'nt so well or you are sick
yourself. Do write and tell me everyone is well.
Mother, dear, I have the most wonderful news
for you. What would you think about being a
grandmother? Well I think there is a very great
probability that it wont be very, very, long before
that happens. We are so happy about it mother,
dear. Ring is just perfect. I wish you could know
how nice he is. Just think of having a little baby
all my own. I wont ever be lonesome any more--and
it is lonesome all by myself in the day time. We

had a doctor about a week ago and he said it was
sure. I was sick last the tenth of July which
makes it just eight weeks yesterday.
    I am not a bit afraid, mother though I dont
care much for this horrid feeling I have every
morning. Its hard to sit down and plan dinner and
order food when the very thought of it makes you
ill.
    Ruby must stay with me until Christmas and
then you will come after Christmas wont you--if
father does'nt need you. Anyway you will come for
the last month won't you?
    Please dont tell any one but Ruby and Florence
and father and <u>dont</u> let anyone else find out for
two or three months. I wish you would write me all
the things I should and should'nt do because your
little girl is all alone and does'nt know any
thing. And ask Ruby if she knows the name of that
book Diana & Nell have by Dr. someone--Holt I
think. I want to get it.
                        love to you all
                        your happy happy daughter

    Though Ellis's pregnancy meant new financial
responsibilities for Ring, he abruptly resigned his
post with the AMERICAN that October, out of a sense of
family loyalty and personal honor. As sports editor,
Ring had, earlier that summer, added both his Chicago
colleague Frank Smith and his brother Rex to the sports
staff, but when he went to New York to cover the 1911
World's Series between the Philadelphia Athletics and
the New York Giants, the Hearst newspaper in his
absence fired both men as an economy move following the
close of the baseball season. A letter from Ellis in
Brookline to Ring in New York at this time reveals her
anxiety about the situation:

    I am wondering what you are going to do about
this business at the office. I'd like to go out
and murder Mr. Shore--or whatever his name is. I
never <u>knew</u> anything so horrid as to wait until you
got out of town and then make all this trouble. I
dont think Rex cares very much as long as he has
this job in Cleveland and I only hope Mr. Smith
can get out of it as well. But it is the very
devil for you and I'd like to kill people for
making all this trouble for you--when you are
working so hard any way.

On principle Ring immediately resigned, though he had
little money on hand. Three weeks later, he wrote
reassuringly to Ellis's mother:

Thursday, November ninth.
[9 November 1911]

Dear Mother II,-
    You are hereby ordered not to worry about us, although I'm
free to admit that it is natural you should. We are through with
the Boston American, but are finding out that we get along nicely
without its help. I am doing some work for magazines that are
not particular what they print, and waiting for a call to
Chicago, New York, or some other city of size and importance. We
have three meals daily, and some of your grand pickles and
preserves are on every bill-of-fare.
    Ruby and Ellis have gone to their bridge club. It's a very
interesting organization now that Helen is out of town, for none
of the surviving members knows the others personally. Inasmuch
as they can't get back before seven o'clock, I am going to get
supper, and it will be good.
    Ruby is the only one in our family who gets any mail. But
she is good enough to read most of it to us. If you don't mind,
we'll keep her here always.
    My mother and father celebrated their golden wedding
anniversary last Monday, the celebration consisting of staying at
home and entertaining their grandson, Richard L. Tobin, and his
mother.
    I must go to market.
                        With love,
                            Ring

        Shortly afterward, the Lardners returned to
    Chicago, where Ring worked briefly at the only job he
    could find--as a copy reader with the Chicago AMERICAN.
    It must have been a difficult time both professionally
    and economically, until, in February 1912, Ring went to
    work again with the EXAMINER as a sports reporter,
    covering the White Sox.

                        Tuesday
                        [May 1912]

Dear Mother II,-
    I have returned to a state of activity and am going to the
ball game this afternoon after a ten days' lay-off. I haven't
yet learned what my ailment was, although the doctor gave me a
big variety of things from which to choose, including typhoid
fever, spinal maginnis, cerebro-spinal fever and grip. The last
named seemed more simple than the others, so I picked it and got
well much sooner than I would have from one of the others.
    Did you know Ruby was going to live with us hereafter? She
has become indispensable to the welfare of our small family and
will not be allowed to go to Goshen except for short visits
    Ellis is awaiting the event with external patience. She
seems well and I'm sure she'll be all right. She's the bravest

young lady I ever met.
    Tell Mr. Abbott we all may surprise him by paying him a call
some time before Summer.
    Love to you and the rest of the family.
                                Ring

    The Lardner's first child, John Abbott Lardner
(much later to establish outstanding credentials as a
sportswriter; he was also a noted World War II
correspondent, and a columnist and essayist for
NEWSWEEK, THE NEW YORKER, and other magazines before
tuberculosis and heart trouble resulted in his death in
1960) was born on 4 May 1912 in their Chicago apartment
near the Tobins. The following letter to Ellis was
written not long afterward, sometime during the 1912
baseball season, while Ring was on the road with one of
the Chicago teams. It describes humorously the dinner
dialogue during an evening spent at a friend's home.
The letter must be read carefully to distinguish when
he is speaking as himself and when he is reproducing
conversation in much the same manner as in some of his
later stories.

                        Friday.
                        [1912]

Sweetheart,-
    As predicted, I attended supper at the Leaming's last night.
Roast beef, mashed potatoes, gravy, BEETS, peas in little round
cups cooked with cracker crumb frosting, nut salad with something
like maple syrup on it, biscuits, because Mr. Dehman, Mary's
father, can't eat plain bread, coffee and strawberry shortcake,
which needed sugar, but when it first came on Mary said she
hoped, she certainly hoped, she had made it sweet enough this
time because Harry was such a sweet tooth, and so, although I
wanted sugar, I couldn't use any, and after dinner mints and
cigars for me, you know Harry doesn't smoke at all and Mr. D.
doesn't either, although he's a fiend for chewing tobacco, and
has taken the cure twice and been cured of the habit, but has
gone back to it again; he started chewing when he was sixteen and
he is pretty old now, and the tobacco must have had the effect of
making him nervous, for he talks in his sleep and sometimes even
walks; you know he went with the band to Niagara Falls last year
and it was the first time he had been on a sleeping car for eight
years, and he and the cornet player shared a lower berth, and the
rumbling of the car wheels made him dream that the machinery on
the floor above the coffee room of the wholesale grocery in which
he works was going to fall through the ceiling, and he dreamed
that he was trying to escape by jumping out the window, and so he
hauled off and smashed his fist through the car window, cutting
his hand badly, and was going to throw himself out, when the
cornet player awoke and grabbed him. It's hard to sleep on

Pullmans when you're not used to it, but of course you're used to
it. Don't you get tired of travelling? Mary often sits up in
bed and talks and one night last week she dreamed Harry had hit
Jack Johnson, the nigger, and that Jack had sworn vengeance, and
so Mary thought Jack would kill Harry and she cried in her sleep.
Does Ellis ever bother you at night? Gee, I love those Abbott
girls. Gee, I love Florence. Gee, I love Ruby. You tell Ellis
that I'll break her head for not coming here with you. Is Ruby
engaged? When is she going to be married? What kind of fellow
is Paull? Will he be good to Florence? Why, says Mary, I
thought you knew him. Well, I just met him. Don't you think
Wood Spitler is good looking? He's going to marry a little
country girl, but she's a peach. He rides his bicycle out to see
her. He says he'll trade his bike for my pony if the pony can
get over the ground better. Mary sent him a pipe for Christmas
and he said he thought at first that it wouldn't be any good
because it was too fancy, but after smoking it, he decided that
Mary must have pretty good taste in pipes. Mildred certainly
likes her beer and she likes to tell how much she can drink. Did
you ever meet Aunt -----? Well, then you missed the best of the
lot. She isn't what you could call pretty, but she's all heart.
She gave us this silver and the dining room set. Elizabeth's
going to marry a pretty rich fellow, so I suppose Aunt ----- will
spend a lot of money on something small but nice, instead of
giving them any furniture. They want a sort of family reunion at
Elizabeth's wedding, but it costs too much money to go. Marion
and Margaret can travel as much as they please, for Marion gets
passes. How can the paper afford to send you all around with the
team? says Mary. Why, Lord, don't you know that nine out of
every ten people read the sporting page first? Lillian is crazy
about baseball, says Mr. D., and I wanted to ask you if it would
be all right for a girl to go to the games alone in New York.
When do you go to New York? Well, that's very good of you. I
got a letter from her yesterday. I'll give it to you, for it has
her telephone number and address. Don't you want the letter?
says I. Well, yes, I'll tear off the part with the address on
it.

I'll bet when you went home last spring you told Ellis all
about the tough chicken we gave you. My, but Mary was ashamed of
that. We have spoken of it a hundred times since.

Are there any crabs among the ball players? Does Ellis like
to take care of the baby, or is it drudgery for her? I've got a
picture of Ellis that looks just like a nigger. Why, Harry, it
does not. Well, she looks dark.

Lillian finishes her study with Damrosch in June and then
she's coming home. Mrs. D. says she thinks she'll make her do
all her playing hereafter in the servants' quarters because she's
so tired of listening to it.

Perhaps I'll get a letter from you in St. Joe.

R-

On 13 July, when Ring was again on the road with
the Sox, Ellis wrote to tell him that her sister
Florence was to marry Paull Torrence in seven weeks,
and she reminisced about their own courtship:

It does'nt seem over a year since we were
counting the days does it? Do you remember you
wrote me once from Boston that in so many weeks we
would be together never to be separated again? I
think that was a pretty poor guess. Do you think
that time will ever come? I love you so much,
dear, and I need you every minute. Life is too
short to waste so many days apart. I wonder so
many times if you are really as happy as you
expected to be. Life means so much more to me than
I ever thought it could - with my own husband and
my baby - I am a very very happy girl--but I would
be infinately happier if you could put your arms
around me now ---- Ellis.

In March 1913 Ellis left John with her parents in
Goshen and accompanied Ring to the White Sox training
camp in Oakland, California, so as to enjoy a lengthy
vacation in a warmer climate. Also with the Sox that
spring was William Veeck, Sr. and his wife. At the time
Veeck, who was to become president of the Chicago Cubs
in 1917, was writing the Bill Bailey sports byline for
the Chicago AMERICAN. This California vacation marked
the beginning of the Lardner-Veeck family friendship, a
friendship which continued throughout the Lardner
residence in Chicago.[1]

When Ellis's father died early in September 1912,
she had inherited some money with which she and Ring
now bought property in west suburban Riverside and
began to build a house.

> Friday
> [Chicago, Ill.
> 18 April 1913]

[To Miss Ruby Abbott]
Dearest Lillian,-
You see Ellis already has written to your Ma and told her
everything except a few inside facts. My Missus and boy spent
Wednesday night at the home of my sister on South Park Avenue. I
stopped there for them yesterday morning and we had breakfast
consisting of boiled eggs, toast and coffee.

---

[1]See Bill Veeck Jr.'s autobiography, VEECK--AS IN WRECK
(New York: Bantam, 1963), pp. 14-16.

John was very glad to see me. He nearly says Daddy and Dickie. I think he likes Dickie better than anyone, except, of course, his parents and his dear aunts.

One of my annual practices is to see the Follies so that I can study the songs and acting of Bert Williams, my colored friend. So I deserted home and kindred last night and went. In the seats next to me were a man, middle aged or more, and his daughter. They talked of Helen Irwin several times and I sort of recognized them, but realized that they wouldn't know me from a dog (What an expression!). Finally a little Japanese girl came on the stage and the lady on my left said, "That must be the girl Helen saw on the train--the one who could say in English only 'Shut up' and 'I should worry,'" or something like that--and right then and there I recalled Miss Irwin's account of her California trip, and as sure as my name is Gus I knew those two must be from Goshen. What a small World this is after all.

One week from Sunday night I'm going to Detroit and perhaps, who knows?

If you want to carry on a regular correspondence with me, well and good. But I don't think it's fair to either of us to hold communication in this desultory way. I wrote you a long letter in February. You wrote me a short note late in April, and you wrote on account of no interest in me, but merely because you wanted to know where your sister had slept. For your further information let me say that she is sleeping right now--on a couch--in her own home--where she belongs.

You want us to build in Goshen. Why? Because you don't expect to be there long. Is that friendship? Is that sisterly?

    X

In June 1913 Lardner replaced Hugh Fullerton (at Fullerton's suggestion) as author of the daily "In the Wake of the News" column in the sports section of the TRIBUNE. The popular Hugh Keogh, who had written the column for years, had died some months earlier. The TRIBUNE managing editor, James Keeley, hired Ring on a three-months trial basis, and Ring wrote his first column on 3 June 1913. Though Ring, being on trial, had some uneasy moments, he was almost from the beginning a huge success, and his salary was raised shortly to $100 a week. He wrote the column for the next six years.

                              Tuesday
                              [Winter 1913]

Dear Mother II,-
As you have undoubtedly discovered, Ellis forgot to enclose the Moffett Studio card. She wants me to tell you to write your letter to Mr. Anderson, c/o Moffett's Studio, 57 East Congress Street.

Ruby is in Evanston, but we expect her back some time today.

Her purchases are so pretty that even I know it.

When John saw the white snow on the ground this morning, he said, "Muck," which is his word for milk. We told him that it was snow and he pointed to his nose.

Everybody sends love to everybody.

Ring

Thursday
[January 1914]

Dear Mother II,-

A stiff neck has prevented my writing before to thank you for your kindness to me at Christmas time. I didn't deserve so much, and I appreciate it more than I can tell you.

I don't suppose I'll sleep, eat or otherwise enjoy myself in the old house again, but I assure you that I had some of my best times there and wouldn't have missed knowing it and its inhabitants for the world. The farm is bound to be a mighty pleasant place to visit, as would any house in which you and the rest of your nice family elected to live.

We have received all the property we left behind us in Goshen and ask your forgiveness for having caused you so much extra work. John is still wild about his hobby-horse and spends much time gazing at it and saying "Hoss" and "Duke."

The child has a new habit of sleeping soundly at night and continuing in slumber until eight in the morning, which makes life more enjoyable for Ellis.

Frank called on us Monday morning, but had to rush away on fraternity business.

Ellis made a mince pie the other day that was very good. She is repeating the performance today.

Love from all of us to you and Bill and "Hawn" and "Abe."

Ring

Early in 1914, apparently in an effort to bring in some extra money, Ring began to write his epistolary "busher" stories consisting of fictional Sox pitcher Jack Keefe's self-centered, insensitive letters to his friend Al. Clearly drawing on his association with an illiterate Sox pitcher for whom Ring had compassionately read dinner menus aloud during the 1908 season, on his camaraderie with Frank Schulte, and on his general experience in the baseball world, Ring depicted Keefe with a tolerant pen which renders him vividly real and oddly sympathetic. Later that year Ring achieved a breakthrough when George Horace Lorimer, editor of the SATURDAY EVENING POST, accepted Ring's stories for publication in that magazine, probably on the recommendation of Charles Van Loan, a POST writer whom Ring knew through Hugh Fullerton. A

number of stories have circulated concerning the
circumstances of the acceptance of Ring's stories, but
Ring's own version, in his letter below of 7 October
1926 to Burton Rascoe, must be considered
authoritative. Ring received $250 for the first piece,
and subsequent increases of $250 per story between 1914
and 1921, until he was receiving $1250 a story, the
POST's ceiling at that time.

The following letter to Franklin P. Adams
(popularly referred to as F.P.A.), a colleague who had
already transferred to the New York newspaper world,
foreshadows the move Ring himself would make five years
later.

Chicago, March 12 [1914]

Dear Mr. Adams:
I'm glad you liked the Post stuff and also glad that you took
the trouble to write to me. It may not sound reasonable, but
sometimes I almost prefer appreciation (from real guys) to dough.
However, it's dough and the prospect of it that would tempt me to
tackle the New York game. I think a gent in this business would
be foolish not to go to New York if he had a good chance. From
all I can learn, that's where the real money is. I'm not
grabbing such a salary from the Trib. that I have any trouble
carrying it home. But I do make a little on the side owing to my
acquaintance with people hereabouts who want special stunts
done--such as vaudeville acts, ads and alleged lyrics for stage
songs. (Of course one might expect to get some of that work in
New York after a reasonable length of time.) Moreover, I've just
finished building a little house in Riverside, the suburb Briggs[1]
lived in until he heard I was coming. I suppose I could sell it
or rent it, and I mention it merely as a thing I have to
consider. I could be torn away from here--and Riverside--for
$8,000, and that's probably more than I'm worth. But you see how
things are. It's not that I'm swelled on myself as much as some
of our well-known diamond heroes, but that I'd have to get
something like that to make the change pay. However, I suppose
the sooner a person lands in New York, the sooner he feels as if
he had a permanent residence. This letter, I'm afraid, is
unintelligible in spots. I hope you may be able to make some
sense of it. It might have been clearer if Ted Sullivan[2] hadn't
come in to see me twice during its composition.
                    Sincerely,
                    Ring W. Lardner
Happiest respects, as Jimmy Sheckard[3] says, to Briggs and Rice.[4]

---

[1]Clare Briggs, Ring's friend and a cartoonist for the
TRIBUNE sports pages, before he moved on to New York.

[2]Ted Sullivan was one of Ring's colleagues on the TRIBUNE.

The following letter refers to the birth of the
Lardners' second child, James Phillips Lardner, on 18
May 1914 (In September 1938 James was killed in the
Spanish Civil War while fighting with the Abraham
Lincoln Brigade--a group of American volunteers--on the
side of the elected Republican government against
General Franco's Fascist forces). The letter is
written in dialect as if by Ellis to her family.

                         Tuesday.

Dear Family:-
     This here baby I've got now is probably the best looking baby
that every happened.   He weighed 7 3/4.   While he is good
looking, he also is mad looking.   His expression is one of
permanent anger. I don't know why. He cries very little, but
thinks a whole lot. All the nurses say he is the prettiest baby
they ever saw.
     The alarm sounded about five o'clock Monday morning.   I
immediately told Ring to call up Dr. Courtright. Ring did so
(He always does his duty) and also got me a taxi at some expense.
The doctor was mad, as usual. He hurried with his shaving and
cut himself twice. Then he had a quarrel with the hospital about
the condition of the room, etc. Ring was mad because the taxi
didn't come soon enough and the nurses were mad because the
doctor bawled them all out. James Phillips was therefore born in
an atmosphere of rage and he shows it.
     I expect to be in the hospital (Washington Park) two more
weeks.   Then I will move to Riverside, where James Phillips and I
will be glad to see each and every one of you.
                         Ellis.

                    The Chicago Tribune
                    Chicago, Ill.
                    Friday.
                    [May 1914]

Dears Florence and Ruby:-
     This letter is written on an Underwood Typewriter No. 4.
     We will be glad to see you, Florence, especially if you don't
forget to bring John.
     (We would also be glad to see you, Ruby)
     Ellis is very grateful, Ruby, for the candy. You, Florence,
didn't send her any. But we'll be glad to see you just the same.
     The baby looks like John. He is supposed to be called Phil

_____

     ³The Chicago Cub centerfielder from 1906 through 1912.

     ⁴Grantland Rice, at this time a sportswriter on the New York
HERALD. After 1924 he was Ring's closest friend.

and not Barbara, as Ruby thought. He cries very seldom, sleeps
very much and doesn't ask to be fed between ten o'clock at night
and six in the morning.
Ellis wasn't very well for the first two days afterwards.
But Dora came to see her the third day and, on her departure,
promised to give Ellis absent treatment. Sure as you live, it
worked. Ellis now feels perfectly well and says she is much
stronger than this long (or short) after John's arrival.
The house will be done tomorrow, so I'm told. Not for a
minute do I believe it.
Write again soon.
                                    R. W. L.
        P. S. I presume Paull meant that I should send him more
details in telegraphic form, but, girls, I can't afford it.
        P. S. No. 2-- Weight, 7 3/4.

                                    The Chicago Tribune
                                    Chicago, Ill.
                                    Wednesday.
                                    [End of May 1914]

Dear Mother II:-
        Will you please forgive the typewriter? I left my perfectly
good fountain pen at the Grant Hotel, where I am now stopping.
        Ellis wants me to ask you if you will be kind enough to start
shipment of the furniture and other stuff as soon as possible.
It should be addressed to Riverside, but the bills of lading may
be sent to me at the Tribune.
        The house is nearly done, but everybody is doing his part as
slowly as possible. I suppose we'll have to wait a long time for
electricity and gas.
        The new baby, James Phillips, has ears that stick close to
his head. He hardly ever cries and doesn't eat between ten at
night and six in the morning.
        Ellis is much better than she was yesterday, when she had bad
after-pains and cramps.
        Love to everybody.

        Ring and Ellis's house was not finished until the
    summer of 1914. Ring drew on the economic frustrations
    of having a home built for a story, "Own Your Own
    Home," originally published in REDBOOK in 1915, about
    the antics and anxieties of fictional Chicago detective
    Fred Gross during Gross's housebuilding venture. But
    Ring appears to have been especially happy for a period
    of time immediately following completion of the house,
    with a secure position not requiring much travelling,
    and the companionship of a wife and children.

        The following letter was written to Ellis's sister
    Ruby, now married to Robin Hendry and the mother of a
    son named James Abbott Hendry.

[ca 1914]

Copy Cat! Copy Cat! I thought you certainly would be
original and have a girl. And when I heard it was a boy, I
thought, "Well, she'll at least display her natural ingenuity in
naming him." But my Heavens! you've swiped his front name from
my youngest son and his middle name from my eldest. My
Heavens! And as he didn't come in the spring, poor thing, we
can't even call him Robin.

What can we call him? Nothing. We'll never be able to speak
to him if he isn't looking at us, unless we yell, "Say, there!
Listen!" My Heavens!

While in Boston, I called on Helen, removing my shoes and
stockings before entering her apartment. And I backed in and out
to make her feel more at ease.

"Hello, kid," I said.

"Hello there, Ringlets," said she. "How's Ruby?"

I told her you were married and living in Detroit. She is
going there to do her Christmas shopping--hosiery and the
like--and will call on you.

You owe me a debt of gratitude. I reached Detroit on the
homeward journey at eight o'clock Sunday night. I then did an
hour's work. I then had two hours and a half to wait for my
train. But it was past Abbott bedtime when I got through work
and I refrained from paying you a call.

We hope to see you and yours at the lake next summer. JAMES
phillips and john ABBOTT lardner send their happiest respects.
Your friend Reese McCarley.

The third of Ring's four sons, Ringgold Wilmer
Lardner Jr., nicknamed "Bill," was born on 19 August
1915 (The only surviving son, Ring Jr. won his first
Academy Award as a Hollywood screenwriter at the age of
26. In 1947 he was subpoenaed as one of the "Hollywood
Ten" before the House Un-American Activities Committee,
where he chose on principle not to reveal whether he
had ever been a Communist. Imprisoned for nine months
and blacklisted by Hollywood for fifteen years, he has
now reestablished himself as one of Hollywood's
outstanding writers, recently winning a second Oscar
for the script of the movie M* A* S* H*.).

As early as 1916, Ring was writing for the movies,
in an attempt to increase his income. The following
letter to R. L. Giffen, an authors' agent associated
primarily with theater and movies, refers to twelve
short comic baseball scripts which Ring had agreed to
write:

Riverside, Illinois
April 10. [1916]

Dear Mr. Giffen:-
    In reply to your letter of the first, which I should have
answered before, I will write the scenarios you desire (twelve in
all, delivered one per month) at $250 apiece and an advance of
$250.

Sincerely,
Ring W. Lardner

    The first five busher stories, all of which had
appeared in the SATURDAY EVENING POST in 1914, were
collected and published by the George H. Doran Company
in 1916, under the title of YOU KNOW ME AL. The
stories published together became an epistolary novel
which gradually achieved a sustained popularity,
primarily because of the comic effect of its semi-
literate protagonist with his monumental ego, but also,
as H. L. Mencken was the first to proclaim, for the
uniquely accurate way in which Ring had captured the
written language of the lowbrow American.
    After the appearance of YOU KNOW ME AL, a larger,
midwestern publishing house, Bobbs-Merrill, arranged
with Ring to publish his stories in book form. In all
Bobbs-Merrill published eight volumes of Ring's work,
before Scribners purchased the rights in 1924.
    The following telegram, obviously a response to a
request for copies of Ring's stories, exhibits again
the often-stressed fact that Ring did not bother to
keep copies of his own work, once it was accepted for
publication.

To Bobbs-Merrill Publishing Company
Collect

RIVERSIDE ILL 6P NOV 29 [1916]

BOBBS MERRILL PUBLISHING CO
INDIANAPOLIS IND
    I HAVE NO COPIES OF STORIES ASK POST FOR THEM
RING W LARDNER

    Most of Ring's correspondence with Bobbs-Merrill
was through its general editor, Hewitt H. Howland, who
came to be a friend and, even in these early days of
their relationship, a drinking companion. "Three
Without, Doubled" was the last of five SATURDAY EVENING
POST stories collected to form GULLIBLE'S TRAVELS, ETC.

December 4, [1916]

Dear Mr. Howland:-
    I have no copy of "Three Without, Doubled," but I sent the

proof back to the Post about ten days ago, so if you don't want
to wait for it to come out, I think you will have no trouble
getting it from them.
      Have seen Artie[1] but once since you were.   He was in good
voice, but I, being on the wagon, was not.
                          Sincerely,
                          Ring W. Lardner

      The narrator of GULLIBLE'S TRAVELS is, as Carl Van
Doren observed, "a case-hardened low-brow . . .
seeing the world with his slightly snobbish wife."   The
title story deals with the wife's unsuccessful attempt
to elevate their social standing by spending a vacation
at Palm Springs: "We'd be stayin' under the same roof
with the Vanderbilts and Goulds, and eatin' at the same
table, and probably, before we was there a week,
callin' 'em Steve and Gus." They succeed only in
getting acquainted with the hired help, and the
devastating blow comes when Mrs. Gullible is mistaken
for a maid. Another story relates the ludicrous
efforts of the Gullibles and the Hatches to attain
social status by attending an opera.   "Three Without,
Doubled" illustrates that the Gullibles do not fit into
a higher social stratum even after they are tentatively
accepted.   They are invited to join the "San Susie"
bridge club for one meeting, but Gullible plays
miserable bridge and insults most of those present, so
they are discreetly dropped from membership. Two other
stories deal with Mrs. Gullible's attempts to help her
sister catch a husband--a theme to be repeated with
greater skill in THE BIG TOWN.

                          Chicago Tribune
                          March 2, 1917.

Dear Mr. Howland:-
      I apologize for not having answered your letter before.
Inasmuch as I had resolved that February was going to be my last
liquid month for some time, I was busy preparing for the dry
spell.
      The book is, I think, very attractive and ought to be a go on
its appearance alone. Our book department last Sunday said it
had been one of the six best sellers in Chicago last week, but
perhaps our book critic was using her imagination and merely
wanted to help me out.
      I haven't sent a copy to F.P.A., but will do so; also will
hand one to B.L.T., our own column conductor, who is widely read
in these and other parts. Or No. I'm afraid I haven't another
one to spare and will ask you to send him one. Just B.L.T., care

────────────────────────────────

[1] Artie Hofman

of the Chicago Tribune, will reach him.
    I enclose a brief letter to dealers, as you requested.
    Others to whom you might, to our mutual profit, send copies,
are Grantland Rice of the New York Tribune, and the sporting
editors of some of the larger metropolitan papers.
                    Sincerely,[1]

                                    Chicago, Ill.
                                    June 4, [1917]

Dear Mr. Howland:-
    I just found in my desk your letter enclosing the cut which
you wished to use in connection with advertising "Gullible's
Travels." For some reason I overlooked the letter and never saw
its contents till just now. I presume it is too late for me to
write the stuff you wanted, but if not, please let me know and
I'll try not to delay so again.
                    Sincerely,
                    Ring W. Lardner

    In the summer of 1917 Ring went to France as a war
correspondent. Ring and Ellis sold their Riverside
house, and she and the boys stayed that summer at a
lake resort in St. Joseph, Michigan. Ring was gone
for eleven weeks.

                                    Chicago, Ill.
                                    January 9, [1918]

Dear Mr. Howland:-
    I have just found your note unopened in a remote corner of my
desk where a too-careful copy boy stored it.
    The manuscript business is very punk. I am just beginning a
drive on the Post, but don't know whether they'll give way or
not.
    Do you think my experiences in France, which are about to be
wound up in Collier's, are worth printing in book form? Or have
you read them? Lots of people haven't, I find.
                    Sincerely,
                    Ring W. Lardner[2]

    The "Lardner matter" was the "experiences in
France" which Ring had described in a series of
articles written as part of an overseas assignment by
COLLIERS and published under the title "A Reporter's

---

[1]Unsigned.

[2]A note penciled on this letter reads: "Mr. Howland-
Please get the Lardner matter in shape as we need it if it is
good - and I may go east anytime - WBC"

Diary" in eight installments from 29 September 1917 to
19 January 1918. They are not especially noteworthy
articles, except insofar as they reveal Ring's views
that war is generally pointless and that the backwash
of war, which was actually what he wrote about, is
boring. Nevertheless, Ring's popularity in the midwest
was such that Howland did, as the following letter
shows, set about immediately to obtain copies of the
installments for publication as a book:

Chicago, Ill.
January 21, [1918]

Dear Mr. Howland:-
     You are shy two installments of the stuff--one of them about
my visit to the American camp and the other, my stay in the
vicinity of the British front. They were Nos. 4 and 5 in the
series. I tried to save copies at home, but they have been torn
up or hidden by offspring. They would come between the one about
the first attempt to get to the American camp and the one about
trying to get the major's car out of Paris.
     Because I didn't hear from you for quite a spell, I replied
to a letter from one Paul Reynolds in New York, who said he could
make a deal with the Century Company for the book. I told him I
would listen to reason and this morning, with your two letters, I
received one from him, saying Century would give me a fifteen per
cent royalty with an advance of $500.00, would get the book out
within two months, and use Wallace Morgan's[1] illustrations, which
I think are very good. I will not answer him until I hear from
you. I, too, am dissatisfied with the title. My own title was
"A Neophyte's Diary", but Collier's changed it. Also, Collier's
cut out some verses that were in the sixth and eighth
installments, and if I do say it as shouldn't, the verses did not
deserve to be cut out. Perhaps I can remember or rewrite them.
     My Evanston address[2] is 740 Hinman Avenue, but as a rule, I
get things sooner at the Tribune.

Sincerely,
Ring W. Lardner

----

     [1]An illustrator for such well-known novelists as Richard
Harding Davis and Julian Street. Morgan was noted for his
realistic drawings. When he died in 1948, he was described in
the New York TIMES as "the dean of American illustrators."

     [2]When Ring returned from France in the fall of 1917, the
family had rented a house at this address in Evanston.

The Chicago Tribune
Chicago, Ill.
March 12, [1918]

Dear Mr. Howland:-
I mailed the galley proofs--with one insert and some rather important corrections--this morning.
I have been unable to think of a suitably brief title that conveys the Innocents Abroad idea. How would "OVER THERE AND BACK" or "OVER THERE AND RIGHT BACK" do?
Sincerely,
Ring W. Lardner[1]

The titling of the book was quite a problem, the subject of several letters.

Chicago, Ill.
March 19, [1918]

Dear Mr. Howland:-
I don't believe the "world's series" title fits very well. There is no baseball in the book, nor any war as far as that is concerned, and people thinking I was going to treat the war in a baseball way might be disappointed. Can I have a day or two more to think it over?
Sincerely,
Ring W. Lardner

Chicago Tribune
March 25, [1918]

Dear Mr. Howland:-
I was out of town for a couple of days and didn't get your letter till this morning.
I have been trying hard to think of a title, but can't seem to get one that would hit anybody "right in the eye." Would "My Four Weeks in France"--a sort of parody on Mr. Gerard's[2] "My Four Years in Germany"--be any good? The "Allies vs. Huns" one doesn't seem to get me. If I have an inspiration I will wire you. However, you are the best judge and if you think any of the ones we have discussed will do, I have no objection to your going ahead with it.
Sincerely,
Ring W. Lardner

----

[1] A pencilled note is below Ring's signature: "Mr Chambers What do you think of these suggestions? HHH 3/13"

[2] James Watson Gerard, a former ambassador to the German imperial court. His book was published in 1917 by Hodder and Stoughton.

Ring's suggestion was accepted, and the book became
MY FOUR WEEKS IN FRANCE.

In the summer of 1918 Howland collected another
series of Jack Keefe letters Ring had written after
publication of YOU KNOW ME AL for the SATURDAY EVENING
POST, dealing with Jack's army training camp
experiences. Jack remains as stupid as he was on the
baseball field. In the following passage, as he is
about to be shipped overseas, he exhibits a strident
patriotism, after having exhausted all attempts to
avoid military service:

> Well Al this may be the last time you will
> ever hear from me or at least for a long time and
> maybe never. I'm going over there old pal and
> something tells me I won't never come back . . .
> . Well Al it's a big honor to be 1 of the men
> picked and it means they have got a lot of
> confidence in me and you can bet they are not
> sending no riff and raff over there but just picked
> men and I will show them they didn't make no
> mistake in choosing me.

                    The Chicago Tribune
                    Chicago March 28th.
Dear Mr. Howland:-
    I am mailing you an alleged picture of me, taken by "a staff
photographer" yesterday. If you can wait a little while, I can
send you one, taken by a flattering artist, which looks more
human. But if you are in a hurry, this is the best I can do. I
haven't an old one of any kind to my name.
                    Sincerely,
                    Ring W. Lardner

                    AUG 20 AM 12 21
                    CHICAGO ILLS

H H HOWLAND
    BOBBS MERRILL PUB CO INDIANAPOLIS IND I AM GLAD STORIES DONT
HAVE TO BE CUT NO OBJECTION TO USE OF "TREAT EM ROUGH" IN
CONNECTION WITH TITLE IF IT IS MADE PLAIN THAT I AM NOT CLAIMING
CREDIT FOR AUTHORISHIP[1] OF THE PHRASE
                    RING W LARDNER.

                    Chicago, Ill.
                    August 30, [1918]

Dear Mr. Howland:-
    I enclosed a copy of the book contract, which I have duly

----

[1] Telegrapher's error.

signed in the presence of a beautiful young lady.

I don't understand exactly what you want in the nature of a verse. Is it to be an ad for the book or something?

Sincerely,
Ring W. Lardner

The references below are to more accounts of the overseas antics of Jack Keefe, which were published in book form in 1919 as THE REAL DOPE.

Chicago Tribune
November 5, [1918]

Dear Mr. Howland:-

I haven't saved the Posts of dates previous to the first of October. As I remember, there have been four in the "overseas" series, the titles being "And Many a Stormy Wind Shall Blow---," "Private Valentine," "Stragety and Tragedy," and "Decorated." The Post now has one more, called "Sammy Boy," and about two others will wind it up.[1] But if you are contemplating publication of another book, I would like to pass on the title and the illustrations. I don't think it was brought out clearly enough in the last one that I didn't claim authorship of the slogan "Treat 'Em Rough," and I did think it was understood that Mrs. Preston's[2] illustrations were to be used.

I had a letter from Bobbs-Merrill about two months ago, saying there was $280 or some such amount coming to me in October from "My Four Weeks in France" and "Gullible's Travels" and so far no check has arrived. Will you please ask somebody about it?

Sincerely,
Ring W. Lardner

The next letter, written at the close of World War I to Ring's old friend and fellow baseball reporter John Neville Wheeler, while Wheeler was still with the Army in France, indicates that Ring was even at this time contemplating a move to New York. After leaving the TRIBUNE some years earlier Wheeler had established the Bell Syndicate to sell the work of well-known

---

[1] Six stories were published as THE REAL DOPE: "And Many a Stormy Wind Shall Blow," "Private Valentine," 'Stragety and Tragedy," "Decorated," "Sammy Boy," and "Simple Simon" (previously published in the SATURDAY EVENING POST issues of 6 July 1918, 3 August, 31 August, 26 October, 21 December, and 25 January 1919, respectively). "The Busher Reenlists," to which Ring is probably also referring, was not included in the book.

[2] May Wilson Preston, who had illustrated GULLIBLE'S TRAVELS, ETC. She did the illustrations for THE REAL DOPE, in conjunction with M. L. Blumenthal, and later for THE BIG TOWN.

journalists, and clearly he had invited Ring to write
for him.

                              The Chicago Tribune
                              Chicago Nov. 8th.
Dear Jack:-
    I haven't forgotten the "good old Bell Syndicate," but what
can I do for it? However, I'm through here the first of next
July and I presume you'll be through with the army by that time,
and maybe we can put something over then. I don't want any
regular job (if I can live without one), but what I would like to
do is occasional stunts like national conventions, etc.   I'll
probably move east next summer and hang around N. Y. city till
I can find a better place.
    Mr. Howard, president of the United Press, cabled his
company from Paris yesterday morning that the armistice had been
signed and almost everybody got drunk. Mr. Crusinberry[1] and I,
who have a bet up, decided to wait for Associated Press
confirmation, and when the story was officially denied we were
still bone dry. However, we've stood it six months and can wait
a few, très few, days longer.
    Of course you must come to Chicago as soon as you get back
and Mr. Griffin will be invited to give us a party.
                              R. W. L.

                              Chicago, Ill.
                              December 9, [1918]

Dear Mr. Howland:-
    I am trying to find a title for the new one and will fire it
along as soon as the inspiration comes; not that I think "Let's
Go" is at all bad, but there may be one that will fit better.
The Post now has the closing two installments and I presume will
print the first one in two weeks or so.   I know Mr. Lorimer
wants to get through with his war stuff as soon as possible.
    Is there any law in the Bobbs-Merrill company against sending
a poor bird a check before it is due. If not--Well, it promises
to be an unmerry Christmas on Buena Avenue.[2]
    I had the pleasure of seeing Chicago with your townsman,
Meridith Nicholson, Saturday night. We were fellow attendants at
the farewell dinner to Ray Long, who, as you doubtless have
heard, goes to Cosmopolitan as editor.
_____

    [1]James Crusinberry, a Chicago sportswriter. He and Ring
were old friends, and in the summer of 1909 had been members of a
singing quartet which also included Artie Hofman and Jimmy
Sheckard.

    [2]After another summer in St. Joseph, the Lardners had
rented an apartment on Buena Avenue in Chicago.

Remember me to Mrs. Howland and tell her Laurette sends love.

Sincerely,
Ring W. Lardner

Chicago, Ill.
December 23, [1918]

Dear H. H. H.-
"The Real Dope" seems to me a better title than "Let's Go." I am returning the galley proofs with some rather important corrections and the postscript you requested. I do wish that instead of just the three stories, the whole six could be combined, winding up the series right and all at once. The Post has only one more installment, the final one, which no doubt they would send you ahead of their publication. The six installments together make a complete story of Jack's adventures from the time he sailed until he was invalided home, and I think purchasers of the book would be less likely to consider themselves "stung" if they got it all at once, no matter what the price. Besides, if the last three installments were published separately, it would be pretty late for war stuff, and I do want to be sure that the whole series is published if part of it is.
The check was very welcome; also Mrs. Howland's message of cheer.

Sincerely,
R. W. L.

On 24 December 1918 Howland wrote offering Ring "a flat royalty of ten cents a copy" on THE REAL DOPE, on the grounds, that Bobbs-Merrill could thereby offer the book at one dollar, rather than at a dollar and a half a copy. Greater sales, Howland explained, would make up the difference in the amount of royalty Ring would receive.

Chicago, Ill.
December 27, [1918]

Dear Mr. Howland:-
The "thin dime" royalty is all right with me. The main idea, I think, is to have the clients satisfied, which I'm afraid they wouldn't be if only the three stories were published. I'm glad you will try to get some of Mrs. Preston's pictures.
Will you ask the editors or whatever they are to cut out the postscript which I wrote to tack onto the end of the three installments I received in galley proof. With the latest three stories added, there's no use of it.
We had a dry Christmas, too, as I climbed back onto the cart

the 18th., with a ticket good until the first of May.
                    Sincerely,
                      R. W. L.
                 R. W. Lardner[1]

     David Ellis, the Lardners' fourth child (and fourth
son, who while serving as a NEW YORKER correspondent in
1944 died in a land mine explosion in Germany as he was
returning from the American First Army front), was born
on 11 March 1919. Feeling the need for more income,
and cognizant that his old contract with the TRIBUNE
was to expire in June, Ring went to New York early in
the year to negotiate an agreement with John Wheeler,
to write a weekly column for Wheeler's Bell Syndicate.
This arrangement meant moving to New York. Ring
anticipated that his salary, which would be dependent
on the number of newspapers that ran the column, would
be substantially larger than the slightly more than ten
thousand dollars a year he was receiving from the
TRIBUNE in 1919. Because the agreement between Ring
and Wheeler was a verbal one, Wheeler apparently became
worried some weeks later and offered to provide Ring
with a written contract. Ring wired him:

If you knew anything about contracts you would realize we made
one in the Waldorf bar before five witnesses, three of whom were
sober.[2]

     Feeling the need for money to finance the impending
move, Ring wrote to Howland:

                           Chicago, Ill.
                           May 5, [1919]

Dear Mr. Howland:-
     I was in St. Louis two weeks ago and spent last week
recovering; else I would have answered your letter before. I
wrote a series of short stories about building a home three or
four years ago. The series was printed in the Red Book and I
don't know whether or not it could be obtained now; nor whether
it would be worth printing.
     I saw by the paper that you and Mrs. Howland were here last
week, but my telephone told me nothing to that effect. Next time

_____

[1]Signature is both signed and typed.

[2]Quoted by John Wheeler, "The Unforgettable Ring Lardner,"
READERS DIGEST, 89 (October 1966), p. 115.

[you] come, you are supposed to call up.
                    Sincerely,
                        R. W. L.
                    R. W. Lardner[1]

        After some delay Howland telegraphed Ring on June
30 requesting his permission to obtain the four stories
from REDBOOK to be published as a book titled OWN YOUR
OWN HOME.

                    TOLEDO O   3 05 P JUL 3 1919
H H HOWLAND
        BODDS[2] MERRILL CO INDIANAPOLIS IND ITS ALL RIGHT WITH ME
                    RING LARDNER.

                    CHICAGO ILL   1919 JUL 10 PM 3 16
H H HOWLAND
        CARE BOBBS MERRILL PUBLISHING CO INDIANAPOLIS IND
WILL YOU PLEASE ASK TREASURER TO SEND ME ROYALTIES DUE IN JUNE I
NEED THE MONEY
                    RING W LARDNER.

        By the fall of 1919 the Lardners were settled in a
rented house in Greenwich, Connecticut (Ring's first
"Weekly Letter" for the Bell Syndicate, titled "Moving
to the East," appeared on 2 November 1919):

                    33 Otter Rock Drive
                    Greenwich, Connecticut
                    [26 October 1919]

Dear Mr. Howland:-
        I enclose a copy of the "Own Your Own Home" contract, signed
but not witnessed. The books came and are now on their way east
by freight.
        Will you please tell your treasurer that I have a couple of
royalty checks coming and the cost of living down this way is
terrific?[3]
                    Sincerely,
                    Ring W. Lardner

----

        [1]Initials signed, signature typed.

        [2]Telegrapher's error.

        [3]Royalties due Ring in October, for sales of GULLIBLE'S
TRAVELS, MY FOUR WEEKS IN FRANCE, TREAT 'EM ROUGH, and THE REAL
DOPE during the first six months of 1919, amounted to $1017.36.

The Lardner Family Home in Niles, Michigan.

Niles, Michigan, 1906

(L to R) Ellis, Helen Irwin,
Ruby. Goshen, Indiana,
2 October 1910. (See letter
from Ellis, p. 75).

Chicago, 1913

(L to R) Warren Harding, Grantland Rice, Ring, Henry Fletcher. At the White House before a round of golf, 1921.

Ellis and Ring, Ca. 1920

(L to R) Jim, Ellis, David, Ring Jr.,
Ring, John. Great Neck, 1923

Ring, Ca. 1925

Off to Europe,
10 September 1924

Leaving London for Home,
November 1924

John Golden and Ring in a Publicity
"Fight." Miami Beach, 1921

(L to R) Tex Rickard, Rube Goldberg, Gene
Tunney, Grantland Rice and Ring on the
Palm Beach Golf Course. February 1928

Ring Visiting the Lion Farm
Near Pasadena. March 1926

A Publicity Composite of Ellis
and Ring. 1926

The Lardner Home at East Hampton, 1928

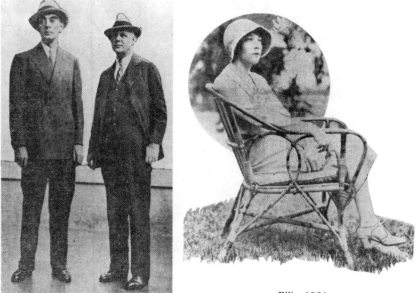

Ring and Grantland Rice,
Miami Beach, 1921.

Ellis, 1931

Ring, 1931

Round-robin letters among the Abbotts were a
practical family convention. The eight Abbott
siblings--Ruby, Ellis, Florence, Frank, John,
Jeannette, Dorothy, and William--and their mother kept
in touch by writing round-robins to which each
recipient would add news and forward the whole to the
next. Ruby, the oldest child, married Robin Hendry.
Florence married Paull Torrence (their courtship was
renowned among the family for the fact that Florence
fainted in a boat on Lake Wawasee upon receiving
Paull's proposal). Jeannette married Francis R.
Kitchell, and Dorothy, the youngest sister, married
Howell W. Kitchell, Francis's brother. Late in 1919,
just after the U. S. Navy had commissioned a new
destroyer the JAMES L. LARDNER, in honor of a Rear
Admiral who was a great-uncle of Ring's, Ring wrote the
following:

Mrs. Abbott, Girls and Kitchell:-
   I note in the current "Round Robin" a suggestion from Mrs.
Torrence that the husbands do the writing for once. Well, at
least they wouldn't be illegible, though the only husband that
has tried it to date is unintelligible which is worse. But I
want to say that I would do the writing for this house only for
two reasons:
   1. Why do they call it a Round Robin? When you think of the
adverb round, what do you think of next? You think of Ring, not
only that, but who was the first that married into the Abbotts?
Torrence may have been the first to propose marriage and Hendry
the first to consider, but who was the first that had the nerve
to go through with it? Who set the pace by showing that his
intentions were honorable? Furthermore who else does the adverb
round fit? The only thing round about Paull outside of his
physique is round Riverside, and who showed him round? The only
thing round about Kitchell is his specs which he wears to keep
people from taking a punch at him. (When Kitchell is mentioned
in this letter, it means F. R. Kitchell. The other Kitchell is
disregarded on account of his wife not taking part in the Round
Robin. (What a name for it!) on account of being ashamed because
she married the only man in the Navy that didn't get a medal
except William Abbott. And speaking of the Navy, they recently
christened a new destroyer "Lardner." The records don't show that
there's even a cat boat named Torrence or Hendry or Kitchell.)
   2. If the husbands are supposed to write, what about John
Abbott, who certainly can't claim shame-facedness on Dorothy's
grounds, as he at least has a Victoria Cross, or at least she was
down to the lake last summer when her so-called husband bid four
and got set four and bawled her out for it, though she was dummy.
Also what about the would-be husbands, Frank and William
Chauncey? Why don't they write? Perhaps they will answer,
"Because we have nothing to say." But did that ever prevent their
talking?

In conclusion let me say that there is a show running in New York called "No More Blondes" and I consider it the truest word ever spoken as far as I am concerned, and when I say that I don't mean you, Victoria, nor you, Mrs. Abbott's favorite daughter, but the one I mean married the only man in the Navy that didn't get a medal except William Abbott, and won't write.
Guess who this is talking.

By the following February, Howland was also seeking Ring's permission to publish as a book "The Young Immigrunts," which had appeared as a lengthy story in the 31 January 1920 SATURDAY EVENING POST.

                    GREENWICH CONN   1920 FEB 9 PM 8 49
H H HOWLAND
    CARE BOBBS MERRILL CO INDIANAPOLIS IND
IF YOU THINK "YOUNG IMMIGRANTS"[1] IS LONG ENOUGH TO MAKE A BOOK I HAVE NO OBJECTION BUT I THINK CRAZY OLD FASHIONED PHOTOGRAPHS WOULD BE BETTER AS ILLUSTRATIONS
                    RING W LARDNER.

"The Young Immigrunts," based on the family move from Goshen to Greenwich, is one of Ring's funniest stories. Presented as if "written" by four-year-old Ring, Jr., the account focuses on the obstacles encountered during the auto trip, and upon the numerous exchanges between husband and wife:

A little latter who should come out on the porch and set themselfs ner us but the bride and glum.
Oh I said to myself I hope they will talk so as I can hear them as I have always wandered what newlyweds talk about on their way to Niagara Falls and soon my wishs was realized.
Some night said the young glum are you warm enough.
I am perfectly comfertible replid the fare bride tho her looks belid her words what time do we arive in Buffalo.
9 oclock said the lordly glum are you warm enough.
I am perfectly comfertible replid the fare bride what time do we arive in Buffalo.
9 oclock said the lordly glum I am afrade it is too cold for you out here.
Well maybe it is replid the fare bride and without farther adieu they went in the spacius parlers.

---

[1] Probably a telegrapher's error.

I wander will he be arsking her 8 years from now is she warm enough said my mother with a faint grimace.
The weather may change before then replid my father.
Are you warm enough said my father after a slite pause.
No was my mothers catchy reply.

The book also contains this classic bit of family dialoque:

The lease said about my and my fathers trip from the Bureau of Manhattan to our new home the soonest mended. In some way ether I or he got balled up on the grand concorpse and next thing you know we was thretning to swoop down on Pittsfield.
Are you lost daddy I arsked tenderly.
Shut up he explained.

The story is also a parody of THE YOUNG VISITERS, a book supposedly written by nine-year-old Daisy Ashford, for whom Sir James Barrie had written an introduction in which he hailed her as a child prodigy. Ring, and others, suspected (probably incorrectly) that the whole affair was a joke perpetrated by Barrie (see letter of 22 February 1925, to William Orton Tewson).

NEWYORK NY   1920 MAR 10 AM 2 15

H H HOWLAND
BOBBS MERRILL CO INDIANAPOLIS IND
DO NOT THINK THERE IS ANY REASON FOR CHANGE OF TITLE BUT IF YOU
MUST CHANGE MAKE IT THE YOUNG MOORERS[1] INSTEAD OF YOUNG TRAVELERS
RING LARDNER.

The letter below responds to an inquiry by Howland as to whether a rumor he has heard from a friend in California is correct, that Ring had run a series of fairy tales in the POST several years earlier.

Greenwich, Connecticut
April 2, [1920]

Dear H3:-
I enclose the signed contract for "The Young Immigrunts."
As for any fairy tales I ever wrote, the guy who said so is just a plain California cuckoo.
Remember me to the family.

----

[1]Telegrapher's error for "MOOVERS."

And Oh, yes. Another cuckoo here wants two copies of "Gullible's Travels." Are there any left?
>   Sincerely,
>   R. W. L.
>   R. W. Lardner[1]

In the spring of 1920 the Lardners purchased a large house on East Shore Road in Great Neck, Long Island. His neighbors there included many of his friends, such as his brother Rex, Arthur Jacks, Frank Adams, Herbert Swope, and, from October 1922 to early May 1924, Scott and Zelda Fitzgerald.

>   Great Neck, New York
>   July 29, [1920]

Dear H. H.,-
I hear that "The Young Immigrunts" has been out for some time, but so far I haven't seen nothing of it, as they say. I presume my copies were shipped to the various eastern coast points at which I have lived for the last 3/4 of a year, but they haven't caught up with me yet. I hope the above is our permanent address and if you have a few copies left, could you send them along?
Please tell Mrs. Howland that I had a very pleasant two conventions with a guy named Irving R. Cobb[2] from Parduchar in spite of the fact that his r's are all misplaced.
>   Sincerely,
>   Ring W. Lardner
Did you read about the reception that Laurette Taylor[3] got in London? I felt so sorry that I nearly broke down or up.

>   Great Neck, New York
>   September 16, [1920]

Dear Mr. Howland:-
I have yet to see a copy of "The Young Immigrunts" and I would like a few to distribute among my kin. I suppose I could go to New York and buy some, but I haven't been there for five

---

[1]Signature both written and typed.

[2]Irvin S. Cobb, journalist and humorous columnist. He wrote numerous books of humor, probably the best known of which is OLD JUDGE PRIEST (1915).

[3]Famous actress and commedienne. She starred in such stage successes as PEG O' MY HEART (1912), OUT THERE (1917), HAPPINESS (1918), and ONE NIGHT IN ROME (1919). In her last stage role she created the character of the mother in THE GLASS MENAGERIE (1945).

weeks and hate to spoil the record. I don't accuse you of not
having had my allotment sent, but Mr. Burleson[1] seems set on my
not receiving same. Remember me to Mrs. Howland.

Sincerely,

Ring W. Lardner

The following letter was written to William C.
Abbott, Ellis's youngest sibling, then in his last year
at the University of Michigan:

Great Neck, N. Y., Nov. 29 [1920]

Dear sir:-

Your sister, my wife by marriage, is too proud to write and
asks me to tell you that yourself and friend (who we trust is of
the male sex) will be welcome whenever you are ready to come.
Let us know two or three days ahead so we can have the dishes
washed.

I'm sorry I was obliged to decline the kind invitation to
make a speech at Ann Arbor, but if you'd ever heard me make one,
you wouldn't have asked me.

Trying to remain your brother-in-law,

R. W. L.

Great Neck, New York
March 5, [1921]

[To Ellis's mother]
Dear Madam:-

I enclose a check for the interest due you on March 6 and I
trust my prompt attention to same will be appreciated in the
proper spirit.

My own Madam and I got back this morning from Washington
where she made herself very conspicuous by trying to start
conversations with all the prominent men. And on one occasion it
was all I could do to restrain her from forcing a way into the
White House. Hereafter she shall remain in woman's place--the
home.

Love to yourself and the Torrences and please overlook my
expert use of the typewriter.

R. W. L.

P.S. Ellis says that whatever you do with the cottage[2] is
all right with her.

_____

[1] Postmaster General Albert S. Burleson, who was unpopular
with the newspaper world because he favored higher bulk mail
rates which would have affected newspaper prices.

[2] The Abbott summer home at Lake Wawasee.

Great Neck, New York
March 5, [1921]

Dear Mr. Howland:-

Will you please remind the bookkeeper of a $515 "Young Immigrunts" check that I was told was due in February?

I have just finished for the Post the last of a series of five stories dealing with three newly rich Indiana people who moved to New York. Four of them--"Quick Returns," "Beautiful Katie," "The Battle of Long Island" and "Only One"--have been published. The fifth gets Katie married off and is called "The Comic." How would this bunch do for a book under the title of "The Big Town."

Sincerely,

We declined an invitation to Herb Swope's[1] house the other night and found out afterward that Laurette and Hartley[2] were there. My God.

THE BIG TOWN, published later in 1921 by Bobbs-Merrill, is superior to any of the fiction Lardner previously had written, except YOU KNOW ME AL. The themes are again social-climbing and husband-finding, but the characters of Finch, his wife, and sister-in-law are somewhat more broadly depicted than previously. Finch is another version of Babbitt, always sure of himself, never indulging in self-analysis, thick-skinned, prudish, and never lacking in nerve. As a member of the nouveau riche, he knows nothing of books, and speaks only the jargon of business, card parties, and the sports world. All five chapters of the book deal with the love affairs of Katie, the sister-in-law. The first is with a Wall Street broker, who, however, exhibits more interest in Finch's wife, until Finch beats him up. The second

---

[1]Herbert Bayard Swope, as a reporter on the New York WORLD, won the first Pulitzer Prize for reporting (1917). While he was executive editor of the WORLD, in 1922, the paper was awarded a Pulitzer Prize for public service for its series on the Klu Klux Klan. In 1929 Swope left the WORLD, and later became a "policy consultant" to such major figures as Bernard Baruch and Dwight Eisenhower.

[2]J. Hartley Manners was the second husband of Laurette Taylor. Manners wrote many of her plays, including PEG O' MY HEART, THE CROSSWAYS, THE PATRIOT, THE HOUSE NEXT DOOR, and THE GIRL IN WAITING. They were married in 1912. After his death in 1928, she retired temporarly from the stage and isolated herself with a substantial supply of liquor. Reemerging some months later, she is reputed to have described the period as "the longest wake in history."

suitor is an elderly millionaire who has "seen baseball when the second bounce was out," but Katie foolishly falls for the chauffeur instead, and swoons when she discovers the chauffeur has two children and a wife. The third suitor is an aviator who seems destined to marry Katie, until he is killed when his airplane develops engine trouble over Long Island. Callously, Finch's wife observes: "Sis is taking it pretty calm. She's sensible. She says if that could of happened why the invention couldn't of been no good after all. And the Williamses probably wouldn't of give him a plugged dime for it."

The fourth suitor, an owner of racing horses, turns out to be as mercenary as Katie, and their "love" sours when Katie thinks he has given her a bad tip at the race track. Katie marries the fifth suitor and gets exactly what she deserves--a fortune hunter who works as a comic in the Follies. There is nothing really new in THE BIG TOWN, but the social satire is perhaps more sharply depicted--the social-climbing nouveau riche, the snobbish upper class, the idiotically avid bridge players, prohibition--and the lowbrow's language is perfected.

One should also note in the letter below another of the many examples of Ring's nonchalance about keeping copies of his work.

                              Great Neck, New York
                              March 14, [1921]

Dear Mr. Howland:-

I suppose I ought to keep copies of my stuff, but I never have, so I guess the Post will have to be called on to provide you with the five that would go into "The Big Town." The titles are "Quick Returns," "Beautiful Katie," "The Battle of Long Island," "Only One" and "The Comic," the last named not yet published. May Preston did the pictures for all of them and don't you think it would be a good idea to have her illustrations in the book?
                              Sincerely,
                              Ring W. Lardner

                              Great Neck
                              April 11, [1921]

Dear Mr. Howland:-

I haven't heard when the Post is going to publish "The Comic," the last story in The Big Town series, but presume it will be in two or three weeks.

I enclose the contracts, which I haven't signed on account of Clause No. 2, providing that I offer the next two books to Bobbs-Merrill. If this clause is in every contract I sign, it

means that I sign with Bobbs-Merrill not only for life, but also for the two books afterwards, and while I have no fault to find with Bobbs-Merrill's treatment of me and see no immediate prospect of switching to another company, where would I be at if Doran or Appleton or some one else should go crazy and offer me a million for book rights to some future set of stories?
    Can you have this clause removed?
                Sincerely,
                Ring W. Lardner

    In a letter dated 14 April 1921, Howland agreed to remove the clause to which Ring objected.

      As the following exchange of letters, with George Horace Lorimer, editor of the SATURDAY EVENING POST, demonstrates, Ring's magazine articles were much sought-after, though he had from the time of the acceptance of the busher stories favored the POST:

                Great Neck, New York, April 11. [1921]

Dear Mr. Lorimer:-
    Some time ago, at Hughie Fullerton's solicitation, I wrote one of those things for The American Magazine on "How it Feels to be Thirty-five." Mr. Siddall has asked me several times since to write him two or three more of the same kind. I've told him that my time was limited and I didn't have much to spare for any but my Post and syndicate stuff. When he called up the other day, however, I said I'd see if I could arrange to do two or three short stunts for him. I don't want to do them unless it's all right with the Post, so I'm writing to see how you feel about it. It really doesn't make any difference to me one way or the other.
                Sincerely,
                Ring W. Lardner

    Lorimer answered: "If you have time to write two or three pieces for the American, why not do them for the Saturday Evening Post?" Whereupon Ring wrote:

                Great Neck, New York, April 15.

Dear Mr. Lorimer:-
    That's very complimentary, and to return the compliment--I thought perhaps the pieces I intended writing for the American might not be good enough for the Post. However, if I do write them (I have no ideas for them yet), I will send them to you.
                Sincerely,
                Ring W. Lardner

    Lorimer replied: "My dear Lardner: The answer is to make them better. We must not degrade our art."

Great Neck, New York
May 11th.

Dear Sister--and Brothers--and Night School-in-Law:-
I don't suppose anybody will be surprised to hear that we
have another baby. I had it myself this time and it's a girl and
we have named her Frederika Beauvais. I started for the hospital
Saturday night and found it Sunday morning and was back home in
time for Sunday night supper. The doctor said he had never
enjoyed a more obstetrical week-end. The baby weighed 9 1/2
pounds stripped. The boys are wild about her and she has already
taken a fancy to David, whom she calls "Curly."
Mr. and Mrs. Fred Nymeyer and mother-in-law, Mrs. Crewell,
were here the night after the baby came and I played bridge with
them till nurse made me stop. Ellis is in town today, having
lunch with Grace and Helen Hawks.
Speaking about bridge, Ralph Crews, our Riverside neighbor,
and considered a very good player out there, told me a while ago
that he was totally lost in a New York bridge game and warned me
to keep out of same, but I got roped into one at a party next
door the other night, and before we started, the lady who was to
be my partner, asked me what conventions I played. So I kind of
stalled and said I always liked to play my partner's conventions,
so she rattled off seven of them. Then it was announced that we
were playing for 2 1/2 cents. I won $24 and I don't have to tell
you that I held good hands, and whatever her bid was, I raised
it. After the first lead, the declarer generally slapped the
cards down on the table and said it was a grand slam or a small
slam and that ended it. Ellis and I have since bought two books
on bridge by New York experts and in three or four years I will
expect her to know that when I lead the four of spades, it means
I haven't the trey of diamonds.
Dear Vic:- If you are as empty as you say and John is
bankrupt, I'm very much afraid we'll have to call you the vacuum
cleaner, and next time I telephone you I'll say, "Hollow."
Dear Howell:- There are two l's in your Indianapolis
brother-in-law's first name. Let's try to keep our spelling pure
and be as different as possible from the children's round robin.
Dear Paull:- If you do want to help that Link Belt friend of
Kitch's, I'd strongly advise against your mentioning the fact
that he went to Wisconsin with a couple of hoodlums.
Dear Robin:- My golf seems to have gained in accuracy and
lost none of its brilliance. The other day I was playing over in
New Jersey and George Ade[1] insisted on my trying his spoon. I
did, and the ball hit George in the colon bacillus. Vic can tell
you where that is. Also, Bill Fields of the Follies said he met

----

[1]George Ade was a well-known newspaperman (on the old
Chicago MORNING NEWS in the 1890's), writer of humorous stories
in dialect (e.g. FABLES IN SLANG, MORE FABLES, FORTY MODERN
FABLES), and, later, a musical comedy writer (e.g. THE SULTAN OF

a brother-in-law of mine on a party in Detroit. Don't let Ruby
open this one.
 Dear Kitch:- I pray God you'll have nerve enough to dictate
to a stenographer next time. It will save everybody time and may
make you less obscene.
 I didn't feel like writing this today, but the other letters
had been in the house since Monday and were just beginning to
spell.
R. W. L., five times a Father.

 The following letter, to Churchill Williams, an
associate editor at the SATURDAY EVENING POST, is
evidently a response to an expressed fear by the POST
editors that publication of Ring's story "The Battle of
the Century" might result in the POST's being sued for
libel. Sarcastically so titled, the story was a thinly
disguised narrative based on the Dempsey versus
Carpentier heavyweight title mismatch of 2 July 1921.

Great Neck, New York
August 4.

Dear Mr. Williams:-
 Before I forget it, will you please tell whom it may concern
that my address is <u>Great Neck, New York</u>, <u>not</u> Greenwich, Conn.
The last three or four communications from the Post have been
sent to Greenwich and forwarded to me from there.
 I have gone over the proof of the fight story carefully and
this is my dope on it:

SULU). Clearly Ring's interests paralleled Ade's, and they seem
to have been good friends, though Ade was nineteen years older.
The high esteem in which Ring held Ade is evident from Ring's
apparently serious comment during a 1917 New York TIMES magazine
section interview:

 "Well, I wouldn't consider Mark Twain our greatest
humorist. I guess that George Ade is. Certainly he appeals
to us more than Mark Twain does because he belongs to our own
time. He writes of the life we are living, and Mark Twain's
books deal with the life which we know only by hearsay. I
suppose my forebears would say that Mark Twain was a much
greater humorist than George Ade.
 "But I never saw one of Mark Twain's characters, while I
feel that I know every one about whom George Ade writes. You
see, I didn't travel along the Mississippi in Mark Twain's
youth, so I don't know his people. Harry Leon Wilson is a
great humorist, and Finley Peter Dunne is another. But I'll
bet Finley Peter Dunne is sick of writing in Irish dialect."

There is nothing Tex Rickard[1] possibly could object to, as
all the references to him, as "Charley Riggs," are boosts for
him. He is the man Kearns[2] (Larry Moon) wants as promoter
because he is the only man big enough for the job. And later
there is a boost for the way he handled the fight.

As I see it, the fall guys in the story are Crawley and
Guthrie, who are supposed to have been fooled by the Cuban
waiters.[3] "Crawley" and "Guthrie" are supposed to be Cochrane,[4]
the English theatrical man, and William A. Brady.[5] I don't
believe there is anything even remotely libellous about them, but
it is possible they might not relish being represented as
gullible. If you think best, I will fix the story so that their
identities will be more obscure.

As for Jack Kearns (Larry Moon), I don't like to brag, but he
is a friend of mine and wouldn't be offended at anything I wrote,
even if he happened to read it. Moreover, I think he is proud of
his part--a mighty big one--in "building up" the fight. Besides
all that, he is too busy defending suits to start any. But to
play it perfectly safe, I'll show him the proof of the story, not
saying anything, of course, about the possibility of libel, but
merely telling him I don't want to have it printed if there's
anything in it that he objects to, and will let you know what he
says. He is at the Belmont in New York and I think I can see him
in a day or two. I'll do it as soon as possible and then return
the proof to you.

Please let me know if you think it necessary to "cover up"
the Crawley and Guthrie characters.

---

[1]Boxing promoter, largely responsible for developing boxing
into a million-dollar sport. The Dempsey-Carpentier fight which
he promoted had the first million-dollar gate in boxing history.

[2]Jack Dempsey's manager from 1917 to 1925.

[3]According to Nat Fleischer's 1972 biography JACK DEMPSEY,
the deception practiced through the Cuban waiters was connected
with the Dempsey-Willard fight of 4 July 1919. Rickard was
unwilling to match Jess Willard with the unproven Dempsey.
Kearns introduced the Cubans, who could not speak English, to
Rickard as representatives of a syndicate which would promote the
fight if Rickard would not. The ploy worked, and Rickard began
serious negotiations for the championship bout, which Dempsey won
by a TKO after three rounds. Ring simply appropriated this
incident for his attack on the promotion of the later fight.

[4]Charles B. Cochran, a British theatrical producer and
sports promoter.

[5]New York theatrical impresario who had managed both James
J. Jeffries and James J. Corbett.

I enclose Runyon's Wednesday stuff[1] which corroborates the opinion of everybody that knows the fight game--i.e. that the Dempsey-Carpentier match wasn't a match at all.

Sincerely,
Ring W. Lardner

If you think it advisable, I can also show the story to Rickard, who is friendly, too.

Great Neck, New York
August 10th.

Dear Mr. Williams:-

I enclose the proof of the fight story. You will notice that I have indicated a couple of changes on Page 3 which would cover up the identity of Cochrane and Brady. I don't believe the changes are necessary, for safety's sake, but if you want to make them, all right.

I saw Jack Kearns, Dempsey's manager, yesterday. As I thought, he saw nothing in the story to object to; in fact, seemed to take it as a boost for him. He wanted to know how I had found out about the Cuban waiters, which he said was true. By chance two friends of mine were with me and heard all he had to say, the important part of which was, as truly as I can report it: "You don't have to show me nothing that you write. Anything you write about the champ and I is O.K. with us. I don't know how you found out all them things or remembered them. But they's nothing in there that ain't right."

He also told me (this not for publication) that he is going to Europe soon to try to arrange another bout between Dempsey and Carpentier in Paris. I asked him how he expected to get away with a thing like that and he said he thought the French would be as eager to see it as if the Jersey City fight had never taken place. "They don't believe nothing that happens over here," he said.

Sincerely,
Ring W. Lardner

When Williams still expressed the fear that Tex Rickard "has good grounds for a suit if he chooses to bring one on the ground that he had promoted a phoney fight," Ring sent the proofs to Rickard's secretary:

Great Neck, New York
Friday.

Dear Ike:-

Here is the dope and if you will ask Tex to take time to read it (it isn't long) and say whether it's all right with him, I'll

---

[1]Damon Runyon, the famous columnist, who obviously shared Ring's view of the fight.

be much obliged.
     Will you please send it back to me as soon as possible in the
enclosed envelope?

                         R. W. L.[1]

     Ring then enclosed that letter with another to
George Horace Lorimer:

                         Great Neck, New York
                         September sixth.

Dear Mr. Lorimer:-
     Here is the fight story again, with the note I wrote to Ike
Dorgan (Rickard's secretary and press agent) and his and
Rickard's expressions of approval. The cipher message in blue
pencil means "O. K., G. L. R. (George L. Rickard)."
     If the libel experts have others in mind who they think might
be sensitive, I wish they'd send the whole list at once, as the
story is in danger of losing something of its timeliness.
                         Sincerely,
                         Ring W. Lardner

     "The Battle of the Century"[2] appeared in the 29
October 1921 POST.

     When Hewitt Howland passed on to Ring an invitation
from the Advertising Club of St. Louis to come
expenses paid and speak for twenty minutes on anything
he might be interested in, Ring made clear his typical
reluctance to make such public appearances:

                         GREATNECK NY   1921 SEP 23 AM 11 44
H H HOLLAND[3]
BOBBS MERRILL CO INDIANAPOLIS IND
NOT A CHANCE TELL THEM AM BUSY WITH BASEBALL STUFF
          RING W LARDNER.

     At this time Howland also wrote to inquire whether
Ring would write an article of five or six hundred
words on "anything you have to say about books, the
reading public, styles in literature, revival of
interest in books, what in a book creates conversation
among those who have read it; does the American public
give English authors preference, etc., etc." The

----

     [1]Inscribed on the page in large letters are "OK / GLR" and
"Ring- / Listens good / Ike."

     [2]Reprinted in SOME CHAMPIONS.

     [3]Telegrapher's error for "Howland."

article was to be one of a series syndicated by the
"All-the-Year Round Bookselling Committee," for the
purpose of "stimulating the buying of books."

                              Great Neck, New York
                              September 28, [1921]

Dear Mr. Howland:-
    Please let me beg off on that assignment. Whenever I attempt
anything in the line of serious discussion it sounds like a
seventh grade essay on The Ethics of Veterinarianism.
                         Sincerely,
                              R. W. L.

    When D. Laurence Chambers, president of Bobbs
Merrill, wrote, during Howland's visit to New York at
World Series time, to propose syndication of OWN YOUR
OWN HOME to newspapers if the rights were available,
Ring responded just after the Series:

                              Great Neck, New York
                              October 14, [1921]

Dear Mr. Chambers:-
    I would have replied more promptly to your letter, but the
world's series has had me jumping.
    My newspaper syndication rights are all in the hands of the
Bell Syndicate, with which I am tied up. Moreover, I'm afraid
the "Own Your Own Home" stuff is out of date. In it are many
references to prices of material etc. which were considered out
of all reason when I wrote the stories, but which would be mighty
cheap nowadays.
    I saw Mr. Howland at one world's series game and expect to
have a chance to visit with him before he goes.
                         Sincerely,
                              Ring W. Lardner

    Below is the first of several extant letters to H.
L. Mencken, one of the first literary critics to
regard Ring as a major American fictionist and to
praise especially Ring's ear for capturing dialogue
accurately. In the first edition of THE AMERICAN
LANGUAGE, in 1919, Mencken had written:

        In his grotesque tales of base-ball players,
    so immediately and so deservedly successful and now
    so widely imitated, Lardner reports the common
    speech not only with humor, but also with the
    utmost accuracy . . . . The result is a mine of
    authentic American.
        In a single story by Lardner, in truth, it is

usually possible to discover examples of almost
every logical and grammatical peculiarity of the
emerging language, and he always resists very
stoutly the temptation to overdo the thing.[1]

In 1920, while they were both covering the
Republican Convention, Ring and Mencken became good
friends. They shared a number of views, notably
distrust of the American politician and skepticism of
an electoral process dependent on the good judgment of
the American "boob." For the second edition of THE
AMERICAN LANGUAGE (1921), Ring wrote two "amusing
specimens of the common speech" (see fourth edition, p.
425n).

> Great Neck, New York
> October 24th. [1921]

Dear H. - L. -
"The Girls"[2] is in the house, but I haven't had my turn at it
yet. I just got through with "If Winter Comes"[3] and thought it
was over-touted, possibly because I was fed up with English
stories.
I'm glad you liked the Post story.[4] I didn't hate it myself,
but I have a hunch that the editor wasn't so keen for it.
Are you going to the disarmament conference? I am, for some
reason another.
> R. W. L.
The above is where I live.

The next letter was probably written in 1921 just
after Ring had returned from covering the Disarmament
Conference in Washington.

> Great Neck, New York
> November 23.

Dear sir:
Thanks for the Declaration, which I read and enjoyed. I
_____

[1]H. L. Mencken, THE AMERICAN LANGUAGE, first ed. (New
York: Alfred Knopf, 1919), pp. 190-91.

[2]A novel by Edna Ferber about three spinsters, each
symbolizing an era. Published by Doubleday, 1921.

[3]A novel of sentiment by Arthur Stewart-Menteth Hutchinson,
published by Little, Brown and Company, 1921.

[4]"Some Like Them Cold," which had just appeared in the 21
October SATURDAY EVENING POST.

intended to tell you this face to face at Washington, but didn't
run across you, probably because I stuck to the dry spots.
    I think it only fair to warn you that a certain back biter
whom we will call Harry Hyde[1] and whom I have nicknamed Dr.
Jekyll and Harry Hyde is spreading a report about you the
substance of which is that no matter what you seem, you have a
kind heart.
                                    R. W. L.

    Ring's addressing Howland below as "Hewitt" is
probably a result of the social meeting predicted in
the letter to D. L. Chambers of 14 October above.
Subsequent letters to Howland exhibit a more relaxed
tone.

                                    Great Neck, New York
                                    November 24, [1921]

Dear Hewitt:-
    I'd like two or three copies of "The Young Immigrunts" if it
isn't too much trouble.
                                    R. W. L.

    The following is a letter to Heywood Broun[2] (as
quoted by Broun in his New York MORNING WORLD column of
9 March 1922) in response to Broun's column of 7 March
on Bert Williams,[3] who had died on 4 March:

    When I read your line, "It did not seem to us that Williams
was a great comedian and certainly not a great clown," I thought
to myself--
    But then I thought, "This guy ain't stupid so the answer must
be that he never saw a Williams and Walker show, and is judging
Bert by Bert in the Follies, well, sir, you might just as well

_____

    [1]Henry M. Hyde, a reporter on the Chicago TRIBUNE from 1915
to 1920, and went from that newspaper to the Baltimore SUN
(Mencken's home base for years), for which he was Washington
reporter.

    [2]Broun began his career as a rewrite man on the New York
TRIBUNE. He became a sportswriter, drama critic, and columnist,
moving to the New York WORLD in 1921, where he began writing "It
Seems to Me." In 1930 he was a losing candidate for the House of
Representatives on the Socialist ticket. He was one of the
founders of the American Newspaper Guild and its first president.

    [3]See Williams' letter to Ring of 17 March 1911, with
preceding commentary.

judge Babe Ruth's pitching on his 1920-1921 showing with the Yankees."

And besides being the greatest comedian and one of the greatest clowns I ever saw, Bert was a great natural musician and a masterly singer of "coon songs," and when I say singer, I mean singer.

The people who wrote the Williams and Walker shows knew how to write for Bert. The Follies people didn't, and he lacked the energy to write for himself. Besides, he was under the impression, the delusion, that Follies audiences were drawn by scenery and legs and didn't want to laugh. He used to say, "I'm just out there to give the gals time to change."

In my early Chicago days, Williams and Walker played long runs, mostly at the Alhambra and Great Northern theaters. My allowance for spending money was about $5 a month. I used to spend $3 of it on their show, going once a week at 75 cents a trip. It was Williams who drew me and he meant to me a sacrifice of sixty beers a month. He had a song--"My Castle on the Nile"--in the chorus of which there wasn't a funny line; yet they (we) made him come out and sing, or dance, that refrain twenty-one times in one show.

Speaking about his dancing, if you'd seen him just dance in the old days, you'd have pronounced him comedian and clown as well as the champion eccentric "hoofer" of all time.

In my record book he leads the league as comedian and can be given no worse than a tie for first place as clown, pantomimist, story-teller, eccentric dancer and a singer of a certain type of songs. Otherwise, he was a flop.

Great Neck, New York
January 9, [1922]

Dear Mr. Chambers:-
I have today forwarded the book[1] as requested to Professor Weaver, Madison, Wisconsin.
Sincerely,
Ring W. Lardner

At income-tax time Ring wrote to the POST:

Great Neck, New York
February twentieth.

Dear Mr. Lorimer:-
Will you please ask the cashier to send me, for income tax purposes, a statement of what the Post paid me in 1921?

---

[1]The book forwarded was SYMPTOMS OF BEING 35, which Ring had autographed at the request of Bobbs-Merrill and sent to Professor Andrew Thomas Weaver, then Assistant Professor of Speech at the University of Wisconsin in Madison.

Also, I was in Cuba the early part of this month and thought of writing a piece about it. But two or three people have told me they thought the subject was covered not very long ago by Mrs. Putnam[1] or somebody. Will you let me know whether it was or not?

Sincerely,

Ring W. Lardner

The statement Ring received shows a total payment of $6,000 ($1500 for each of four pieces--"The Comic," "A Frame-Up," "The Battle of the Century," and "Some Like Them Cold"). Lorimer also expressed encouragement to write about Cuba "if the subject is handled in your well known josh style."

Ring also wrote to Hewitt Howland:

Great Neck, New York
March 1, [1922]

Dear Hewitt:-

Will you be good enough to ask the bookkeepers to let me know how much Bobbs-Merrill paid me in 1921?

Also, thanks for that letter you wrote to the guy on the Brooklyn Eagle.

Sincerely,

R. W. L.[2]

At the suggestion of W. L. Baker of the New York Bobbs-Merrill office, Howland wrote to ask what Ring thought of making a booklet out of "A Caddy's Diary," which had appeared in the 11 March 1922 SATURDAY EVENING POST.

Great Neck, New York
April 1, [1922]

Dear Hewitt:-

I think we'd better lay off'n the caddy's diary. In the first place, it's too short and in the second, I may follow it up, though probably not.

Sincerely,

R. W. L.

----

[1]Nina Wilcox Putnam, a well-known contributor of stories and articles at that time to periodicals such as AINSLEE'S MAGAZINE and THE SATURDAY EVENING POST. Like Ring, she wrote for the motion pictures, and also later wrote a syndicated news column.

[2]Notations, probably by someone at Bobbs-Merrill, on the letter above indicate that Ring received a total of $522.09 from Bobbs-Merrill in 1921.

Great Neck, New York
June 12, [1922]

Dear Hewitt:-
    I received notice in February that a royalty on the "35"
story, amounting to $293.66, would reach me in May. It hasn't
arrived, so will you please nudge the bookkeeper?
    Nina Wilcox Putnam and I have written one of those double
stunts,[1] like the one Irvin Cobb and Mrs. Rinehart wrote on men
and women;[2] ours will appear in the November American and Doran
wants to make a book of it. Mrs. Putnam, as you doubtless know,
is signed up with Doran, so I told them it was all right with me,
though I was going to tell you about it first. Between you and
me, I don't think the book will set the world afire, but it may
help toward the mortgage.
                    Sincerely,
                    Ring W. Lardner

        In March Lorimer had, astonishingly, rejected
    Ring's "The Golden Honeymoon" on the grounds that "the
    humor in it is so quiet that . . . the average reader
    would miss it." In April Lorimer rejected another piece
    (probably "My Week in Cuba"), indicating that "this
    story and the one before it are rather a slip-back for
    you considering what you have done for the Post." When
    Ring consequently began sending his work to
    COSMOPOLITAN, T. B. Costain, one of the POST's
    associate editors, wrote suggesting that they "talk
    matters over."

                    Great Neck, New York
                    July seventh.

Dear Mr. Costain:-
    I am going to have young visitors from the middle west all
week, so I'm afraid I can't make a lunch or dinner date. But
I'll try to get to town some time Wednesday or Thursday and look
you up.
                    Sincerely,
                    Ring W. Lardner
----

    [1]The "double stunt" was a combination of Ring's SAY IT WITH
OIL; A FEW REMARKS ABOUT WIVES with Putnam's SAY IT WITH BRICKS;
A FEW REMARKS ABOUT HUSBANDS. The two books were bound together
back to back, inverted, with separate title pages and pagination.

    [2]OH, WELL, YOU KNOW HOW WOMEN ARE! by Irvin S. Cobb, with
ISN'T THAT JUST LIKE A MAN, by Mary Roberts Rinehart, inverted,
with separate title pages. Published by George H. Doran
Company, 1920.

Ring did meet with Costain, at which time they apparently discussed the idea of a series of football stories. Although Lorimer and the POST continued to solicit Ring's work, he did not publish again with the POST until 1931.

                                    Great Neck, New York
                                    August 7, [1922]

Dear Hewitt:-
    Will you please ask the boys to send along the $574.44 which was supposed to be due on "The Big Town" last month?
                            Sincerely,
                                R. W. L.

    Zelda Fitzgerald's scrapbook contains the following Christmas poem which Ring sent to her in 1922:

A CHRISTMAS WISH--AND WHAT CAME OF IT.

Of all the girls for whom I care,
And there are quite a number,
None can compare with Zelda Sayre,
Now wedded to a plumber.

I knew her when she was a waif
In southern Alabama.
Her old granddaddy cracked a safe
And found therein her grandma.

A Glee Club man walked up New York
For forty city blocks,
Nor did he meet a girl as sweet
As Mrs. Farmer Fox.

I read the World, I read the Sun,
The Tribune and the Herald,
But of all the papers, there is none
Like Mrs. Scott Fitzgerald.

God rest thee, merry gentlemen!
God shrew thee, greasy maiden!
God love that pure American
Who married Mr. Braden.

If it is dark when home I go
And safety is imperilled,
There's no policeman that I know
Like Zelda Sayre Fitzgerald.

I met her at the football game;
'Twas in the Harvard stadium.
A megaphone announced her name:
"It's Mrs. James S. Braden!"

So here's my Christmas wish for you:
I worship Leon Errol,[1]
But the funniest girl I ever knew
Is Mrs. Scott Fitzgerald.

The following letter was to Kenneth Gilbert, a
newspaperman who was in 1922 the editor of the Seattle
Press Club's annual publication, EL TORO. Gilbert had
invited Ring (along with Irvin S. Cobb, George Ade,
and Hugh Wiley) to write anecdotal pieces to be
published that year in EL TORO, but neither Ring nor
the others were interested in writing for free.

Great Neck, New York
December 30, [1922]

Dear Mr. Gilbert:-
My desk is a mess and your letter, written in December, got
lost in it. I'm sorry. And I hope you haven't thought I was in
the habit of just not paying any attention to correspondence.
Sincerely,
Ring W. Lardner

Miami Beach, Florida
Sunday, February eleventh
[1923]

[To George Ade]
Dear Geo,-
This will introduce a old pal of mine Mr. J. C. Andrew.[2]
He is a member of the Pardon Board of the Indiana State
Penitentiary. So if you ever get in the state which he is in,
beg his pardon. I was sentenced for a year, but he commuted me
48 pints. He is a Indiana boy and played a half back on Purdue
the year they scored. They call them the Boilermakers on acct.

---

[1]Comic in the first Ziegfeld Follies (1911), and starred in
the Follies regularly through World War I. His most notable
success was in SALLY, with Marilyn Miller. He went to Hollywood
to make the film version, and became a star in short film
comedies.

[2]A member of the Indiana Prison Board, Jess C. Andrew went
on to serve eight terms in the Indiana House of Representatives
and to become president of the International Livestock
Exposition.

of him getting everybody boiled.   Please treat him as a equal.
                            Respy,
                            A Michigan Boy.

                            Great Neck, New York
                            February 21st. [1923]

Dear Mencken:-
    Your letter was waiting for me on my return from your old
friend the South.   "Champion" (a story of which I am a great
admirer) was published first in Metropolitan and later
syndicated.   The gent who had the syndicate rights is trying to
unearth a copy for me and if he does, I'll send it on.   The
German Authors' League is welcome to the receipts.
                            R. W. L.

                            Great Neck, New York
                            February 26. [1923]

Dear Mencken:-
    Here's "Champion," copied by a $2.50 stenographer who paid no
attention to jumps in the story which were indicated by spaces.
I have put in x's to show where they were.   If it isn't too much
trouble, will you return the copy when you are through with it?
    I guess the Who's Who is all right.   My four grandparents
were all born in America, of Irish descent on the father's side
and English on the mother's.
    I'll pay you back the $7 in liquid form at the next
Democratic convention.
    If you go to Miami, get far enough ahead in your work so that
you can spend the week following your visit in bed.
                            R. W. L.

                            Ring Lardner
                            Great Neck, New York
                            June fifteenth [1923].

[To Francis R. Kitchell, Jeannette Abbott's husband]
Dear Kitch:-
    I'd send this to your office if they didn't insist on all
communications being addressed to the A. C. Lawrence Leather
Co.   NOT to an individual.
    If Mr. Ely is in his dotage he might like "Gullible's
Travels," but I'm afraid there is no way of trying it on him.
The author has no copy.   The bookstores evidently never heard of
it.   I wrote to the publishers two or three months ago,
requesting that they send me six copies, but have had no reply.
If I ever get hold of one, I'll send it.
    I'm sorry we didn't see more of you and Hingham, but I had to
get back to work, and when one is touring with the Abbott girls,
one has to allow for retreats every two or three hundred miles to

recover what they left at the last stop.

Tell Jane she might as well make up her mind to the western trip en famille; there is an overwhelming majority in favor of same.

I am one of the grafters sailing from Boston Tuesday on the Leviathan, but won't get there till Tuesday morning and the last tender is supposed to leave at ten o'clock.

Ruby, Ellis and I were at Fitzgerald's Sunday night, but left early on account of dullness. Half an hour after we had gone, Scott nearly killed Gene Buck's[1] sister-in-law's husband. The last named had confided to me earlier in the evening that there weren't no real decent fellas nowheres but in the south. He himself is from Texas where men are oil men. Scott is nursing a broken hand as a result of hitting him in the head. This was the semi-final bout. The wind-up was won by Mrs. Buck, who hit Mr. Buck three times in the nose for not taking his brother-in-law's part. My sympathies are with Mr. Buck. What is this world coming to if you have to take your brother-in-law's part?

Thanks for the Collier clippings. The Herald will lose some day.

                                    R. W. L.

The following was written to C. O. Kalman. The Kalmans were old friends of the Fitzgeralds from their St. Paul days. Beginning on the same paper is also a note from Fitzgerald. Both notes were apparently written during a drinking session:

                        Great Neck
                        Long Island
                        5.30 A. M.
                        (Not so much up
                        already as up
                        still)[2]
                        [ca. November 1923]

Dear Kaly:-

I hear that you have given two seats to this nonsensical game

---

[1] Gene Buck was Ring's Great Neck neighbor, and a songwriter and producer for Florenz Ziegfeld's Follies and Midnight Frolics. His songs included "Hello, Frisco," "Tulip Time," "Maybe," "No Foolin'," and "Garden of My Dreams." As a male talent scout for Ziegfeld, he "discovered" Ed Wynn and Eddie Cantor. Buck's range of acquaintances is indicated by diversity of the one hundred honorary pallbearers at his funeral in 1957. They included Bugs Baer, J. Edgar Hoover, William Randolph Hearst, Jr., Fritz Kreisler, Deems Taylor, David Sarnoff, Oscar Hammerstein, and Eddie Rickenbacker.

[2] This return address and comment in Fitzgerald's hand.

between the Yale blues vs. the Princeton Elis, to F. Scott Fitzgerald. For what reason, is what I want to know.
                              Ring W. Lardner

        The note by Fitzgerald follows:

Dear Kaly:
        This is a letter from your two favorite authors. Ring & I got stewed together the other night & sat up till the next night without what he would laughingly refer to as a wink of sleep. About 5.30 I told him he should write you a letter. The above is his maudlin extacy.
        The tickets arrived and I am enclosing check for same. I'm sorry as the devil you didn't come. We could have had a wonderful time even tho the game was punk.
        We took Mr. & Mrs. Gene Buck (the man who writes the Follies & Frolics.) This is a very drunken town full of intoxicated people and retired debauches & actresses so I know that you and she to who you laughingly refer to as the Missus would enjoy it.
        I hope St Paul is cold & raw

I discover this telltale evidence on the paper[1]

        so that you'll be driven east before Xmas. Everything is in its usual muddle. Zelda says ect, asks, ect, sends ect.
                              Your Happy but Lazy friend
                              F Scott Fitzgerald.

        Fitzgerald was from the beginning of the friendship a great admirer of Ring, though he deplored Ring's apparent lack of regard for his talent and lack of desire to achieve a serious reputation as a writer of fiction. The following letter, Ring's first in a lengthy correspondence with Scribner's famous editor Maxwell Perkins, was the result of Fitzgerald's enthusiastic recommendation of Ring's work to Perkins. Perkins had initiated the correspondence by saying, in a letter dated 2 July 1923: "I read your story 'The Golden Wedding' ["The Golden Honeymoon"] with huge enjoyment. Scott Fitzgerald recommended it to me and he also suggested that you might have other material of the same sort, which, with this, could form a volume." Ring was obviously agreeable, but since he had,

----

[1]Fitzgerald here draws an arrow to a circular stain obviously made by the placement of a wet glass on the paper.

astonishingly, not bothered to keep copies of his stories, Perkins had a difficult time obtaining copies from the magazines in which they had appeared, and eventually had to photostat back copies of magazines in the New York Public Library in order to assemble HOW TO WRITE SHORT STORIES.

> Great Neck, New York
> December fifth.

Dear Mr. Perkins:-
I enclose a (and, I guess, the only) copy of "Champion", which Scott tells me you have been looking for. I'm sorry to have kept you waiting.
> Sincerely
> Ring W. Lardner

> Great Neck, New York
> February second.

Dear Mr. Perkins:-
The arrangement and terms are satisfactory to me. I'm sorry you have had so much trouble gathering the stuff.
Why not visit Great Neck again? It's safer now, as Durand's pond is frozen over.
> Sincerely,
> Ring W. Lardner

The reference above to Durand's pond has to do with Fitzgerald's auto driving. A favorite eating and drinking place on Long Island was Rene Durand's restaurant at Manhasset, where on one occasion Perkins, Ring, and Fitzgerald apparently discussed the composition of Ring's projected volume of short stories, and where Fitzgerald imbibed too freely and, while attempting to leave, drove Perkins into a nearby pond. A year later, Perkins recalled the incident in a letter to Fitzgerald:

I had yesterday a disillusioning afternoon at Great Neck, not in respect to Ring Lardner, who gains on you whenever you see him, but in respect to Durant's where he took me for lunch. I thought that night a year ago that we ran down a steep place into a lake. There was no steep place and no lake. We sat on a balcony in front. It was dripping hot and Durant took his police dog down to the margin of that puddle of a lily pond,- the dog waded almost across it;- and I'd been calling it a lake all these months. But they've put up a fence to keep others from doing as we did.

On 18 February 1924 Perkins described publication plans for HOW TO WRITE SHORT STORIES to Ring:

I considered first more or less grouping the stories but gave up the idea and went in the other direction ;- that is, I aimed at variety. I thought that the several baseball stories ought to be scattered through the volume, for instance. The question of the first story was a hard one, but it could not be "The Golden Honeymoon" because that had appeared in the "Short Stories of 1922" volume. I did not think it ought to be a baseball story anyhow, because we want to place the emphasis differently in this whole scheme. I finally hit upon "The Facts" because it will please everybody, male and female, of every sort. Then I followed with "Some Like 'em Cold" because it seemed to me to be a masterpiece in that sort of writing. At this point it seemed well to get in one of the baseball stories and "Alibi Ike" is a corker. I am sorry "Champion" comes so late in a way, but publishers probably exaggerate the importance of an early position. People don't begin at the beginning and read a book of stories straight through. The stories that follow I have arranged on the principle of variety.

At Perkins' suggestion, the collection was to parody then-popular manuals on the relatively new art of short-story writing through the title HOW TO WRITE SHORT STORIES and a burlesque preface on the "technic" of writing the short story. This preface contained such advice as:

How to begin--or, as we professionals would say, "how to commence"--is the next question. It must be admitted that the method of approach ("L'approchement") differs even among first class fictionists. For example, Blasco Ibanez usually starts his stories with a Spanish word, Jack Dempsey with an "I" and Charley Peterson with a couple of simple declarative sentences about his leading character, such as "Hazel Gooftree had just gone mah jong. She felt faint."

One might second-guess Perkins by suggesting that the quality of the stories over-all was such that a promotional gimmick was unnecessary, but then Perkins had to consider that Ring's audience at that time consisted largely of newspaper readers rather than literary scholars, and that such satiric introductions were likely to cause a stir, even if they were deplored by such critics as Edmund Wilson, who later accused Ring of "a guilty conscience at attempting to disguise an excellent piece of literature as a Stephen Leacock buffoonery." In any event, Ring went along with Perkins' suggestion.

March 27.

Dear Mr. Perkins:-
I will try to show up in your office on Monday with all the galleys and everything. I think that would be the simplest way of getting things finished up. I will call you Monday forenoon. And that's the last sentence I intend to start with an I till my next letter.

Sincerely,
Ring W. Lardner

In mid-April the Fitzgeralds abandoned the social life of Great Neck for France. Though Scott was earning in excess of $30,000 a year, he had been spending more than that on booze and lavish parties. On their departure Ring sent Zelda another poem:

To Z. S. F.

Zelda, fair queel cf Alabam',
Across the waves I kiss you!
You think I am a stone, a clam;
You think that I don't care a damn,
But God! how I will miss you!

For months and months you've meant to me
What Mario meant to Tosca.
You've gone, and I am all at sea
Just like the Minnewaska.

I once respected him you call
Your spouse, and that is why, dear,
I held my tongue--And then, last Fall,
He bared a flippancy and gall
Of which I'd had no idear.

When I with pulmonary pain
Was seized, he had the gumption
To send me lives of Wilde and Crane,
Twc brother craftsmen who in vain
Had battled with consumption.

We wreak our vengeance as we can,
And I have no objection
To getting even with this "man"
By stealing your affection.

So, dearie, when your tender heart
Of all his coarseness tires,
Just cable me and I will start
Immediately for Hyeres.

To hell with Scott Fitzgerald then!
To hell with Scott, his daughter!
It's you and I back home again,
To Great Neck, where the men are men
And booze is 3/4 water.

My heart goes with you as you sail.
God grant you won't be seasick!
The thought of you abaft the rail,
Diffusing meat and ginger ale,
Makes both my wife and me sick.
                    Ring W. Lardner

      When Perkins asked Ring for a publishable
photograph, Ring invited him and Mrs. Perkins to
dinner:

                        Great Neck, New York
                        May 9, 1924.

Dear Mr. Perkins:-
    Sorry you have a cold. We never have them in Great Neck.
    I will be home all day every day next week excepting Monday.
My wife says (and we speak as one), can you and Mrs. Perkins
come to dinner Tuesday night (or Wednesday, Thursday, Friday or
Saturday night)? The telephone is Great Neck 103. If you drive
out and can't find the place, call up from the drug store and
we'll come and pilot you. Dinner is at seven o'clock and I have
outgrown my dinner clothes. If you accept this invitation I will
give you my photograph.
                    Sincerely,
                      R. W. L.

      This informal evening was apparently a great
success: thereafter both men continue the
correspondence on a first-name basis.

                        Great Neck, New York
                        May 19, 1924.

Dear Mr. Perkins (or Max):-
    I suppose you saw Burton Rascoe's little piece.
    Here are some more names:
    Percy Hammond, 17 West 10th. Street, New York.
    Alexander Woollcott, the City Club, New York.
    Quinn Martin, Greak Neck, N.Y.

Harvey T. Woodruff, c/o Chicago Tribune,
Chicago, Illinois.
W.O. McGeehan, New York Herald and Tribune.
                              Sincerely,
                                R. W. L.

    P.S. Next time you come out here, which I hope will be soon,
I will be different.
    P.S.S. Also- - adding to names - Herbert B. Swope, New York
World.

        When Perkins did not reply immediately to the
    letter above, Ring cautiously resumed a formal
    salutation. After Perkins' letter of the 24th,
    addressed to "Dear Ring," reached him, he always
    addressed Perkins as "Max."

                              Great Neck, New York
                              May 27th.

Dear Mr. Perkins:-
    I enclose what I have nicknamed the perfect blurb.[1] Thanks
for sending me the Post's.
    I also enjoyed Scott's "Absolution" though some of it was
over my partly bald head.

    Mencken writes that he is reviewing my book at length in the
July Mercury.
    Did I put James J.Montague on that list? I meant to.   His
address is c/o The Bell Syndicate,154 Nassau Street,New York
City. And another one is Hugh S.Fullerton, c/o Liberty,25 Park
Place, New York City. I hope I haven't overdrawn my account, but
anyway I promise this is the finish.

                              Sincerely,
                                R. W. L.

        In both the preceding letter and the following one
    to Mencken (then editor of AMERICAN MERCURY), Ring's
    pretense at not understanding "Absolution" is probably
    a reaction to overtones in Scott's story, which deals
    with the sexual frustrations of a priest. For Ring the
    expression "over my head" was often the ultimate
    dismissal. It is debatable whether this reaction is
    due always to prudery or simply to the
    anti-intellectuality of a thoughtful, brooding,

    ────────────────────

    [1]Ring included a piece from the Boston TRANSCRIPT
advertising HOW TO WRITE SHORT STORIES straightforwardly thus:
"Ten short stories by an American humorist, with a brief
prefatory explanation of methods of writing them."

inner-directed man for whom both the world of the flesh
and the world of the mind had fairly prescriptive
limits.

                                    Great Neck, New York
                                    May 27th. [1924]
Dear Sir:-
    Thanks for the tip on the Boilermakers' Journal and the
Journeyman Barber. I'll try to find some copies of them. My
wife says the American labor leader has already got into fiction,
but she can't remember where. That's the woman of it.
    I liked Scott's "Absolution" in the current Mercury (my
favorite magazine) though parts of it were over my head.
    I'm going to Cleveland and if we do meet (I expect to stop at
the Hotel Cleveland), I'll take steps to repay in part the debt I
have owed you since the return trip from San Francisco.
    Your attention is called to "Why I Didn't Die" by Harold Bell
Wright[1] in the June American Magazine.
                                    R. W. L.

    The Mencken review of HOW TO WRITE SHORT STORIES
appeared in the June 1924 AMERICAN MERCURY. After
deploring academia's failure to recognize Ring's
talent, Mencken focused on that talent:

        His studies, to be sure, are never very
    profound; he makes no attempt to get at the primary
    springs of passion and motive; all his people share
    the same amiable stupidity, the same transparent
    vanity, the same shallow inconsequentiality; they
    are all human Fords, and absolutely alike at
    bottom. But if he thus confines himself to the
    surface, it yet remains a fact that his
    investigations on that surface are extraordinarily
    alert, ingenious and brilliant--that the character
    he finally sets before us, however roughly
    articulated as to bones, is so astoundingly
    realistic as to hide that the effect is
    indistinguishable from that of life itself. The
    old man in "The Golden Honeymoon" is not merely
    well done; he is perfect. And so is the girl in
    "Some Like Them Cold." And so, even, is the idiotic
    Frank X. Farrell in "Alibi Ike"--an extravagant
    grotesque and yet quite real from glabella to
    calcaneus.

----

    [1]Harold Bell Wright was a clergyman and novelist, best known
for THE SHEPHERD OF THE HILLS (1907). The article, "Why I Did
Not Die," describes a collision between Wright, while on
horseback, and a car, and a subsequent lengthy but successful
struggle in the Arizona desert with tuberculosis.

When the Fitzgeralds departed, they had left Ring
to rent their hastily abandoned house and to take care
of assorted expenses. Ring did conscientiously restore
order to Scott's chaotic financial arrangements and
even covered his Great Neck bank account later that
year when Scott overdrew.

Thursday, June 5. [1924]

Dears Scott and Zelda:-
Why and the hell don't you state your address, or haven't you
any? I'm going to send this registered to plain Hyéres, with a
prayer.
First the financial news, which I am afraid is bad, but I am
enclosing plenty of documentary evidence to support it.
The day after you left, Miss Robinson called up to say that
she had rented the house to Mr. and Mrs. Gordon Sarre, née Ruth
Shepley, for $1600. "But listen, Miss Robinson," I remonstrated;
"Mr. Fitzgerald told me that if you rented it right away, the
rent was to be $2000." "But listen, Mr. Lardner," said Miss
Robinson: "Mr. Fitzgerald called me up just before he left and
said I was to rent it as soon as possible for $1600 as he had
given up ideas of making a profit and just wanted it off his
mind." Well, she seemed honest so I said all right and I hope it
was. Now then, it seems that William and Sally had kind of let
things get dirty in out of the way places and Miss Robinson said
that both the house and yard needed a thorough renovating, which
ought to be at the expense of the last tenants. Not knowing the
ethics, I asked Ellis and she said this was according to custom.
So I said go ahead and renovate, and all you were soaked for that
was $50. Then there was the matter of the oven door, mentioned
in one of the enclosures. I said I thought it was up to the
owner to repair oven doors, but she said no. I don't think it
will amount to more than a very few dollars and will be
subtracted from the next rent check.
The Sarres paid $500 down. There was subtracted from that
$50 for the cleaning and $80 for Craw's commission, leaving a
balance of $370, which I deposited to your account in the
Guaranty Trust Company.
Then along came a water bill for $22.08 which I paid because
if I hadn't, the company would have shut off the water and Ruth
and Gordon would have had to join the Kensington Association in
order to use the pool. Sarre is a French name and they ought to
get along without baths, but they are kind of Ritzy.
The balance of $1100 in rent is to be paid partly in July and
partly in August. Anyway I'll see that it's paid and deposited
to your account.
In regards to "How to Write Short Stories": The notices have
been what I might call sublime; in fact, readers might think I
was having an affair with some of the critics. I'll send the

most important ones when I get them all--Mencken, Bunny Wilson[1]
and Tom Boyd[2] are yet to be heard from. But listen, if I do send
them, will you please send them back? Burton said I was better
than Katherine Mansfield, which I really believe is kind of raw,
but anyway it got him and Hazel an invitation to come out and
spend Sunday with us. Hazel was on the wagon, but her husband
was NOT. I enclose his Day Book for June 1 which mentions
several of the best writers.

Max Perkins and wife came out to dinner one night. Max
brought along twenty-five books for me to autograph (not to sell)
and it just happened on this occasion that I could hardly write
my name once, let alone twenty-five times. I have promised to be
sober next time I see him and her.

John Golden[3] wants me to write a play based on "The Golden
Honeymoon," but I don't see how it could be done without
introducing a pair of young lovers or something.

Personally I am now reading "The Beautiful and Damned."

We have a parrot which talks, laughs and whistles.

We are going to Cleveland Sunday night for the Republican
convention.

Victor Herbert dropped dead a week or so ago. The papers
said he spent the forenoon with his daughter, then had lunch with
Silvio Hein and died soon after lunch, but Gene says he was with
him virtually all day up to the time he died.[4] How he missed
being with him when he died or put him in the death business is a
mystery to me. Anyway he was the leading pall bearer. I didn't
find out whether or not your stunt was going into the Follies
because all we could talk about was Victor's death which came
like a bolt from the blue.

There's a great murder case in Chicago. Two Jew boys named
Loeb and Leopold, aged nineteen apiece, both of whom had
graduated from both Michigan and Chicago at the age of eighteen
with the best records ever made, were trapped and confessed

---

[1] Edmund Wilson, in 1924 managing editor of VANITY FAIR. He
was then in the process of becoming one of the ablest American
critics and editors of the 20th century.

[2] Thomas A. Boyd, one of Scribners' authors at that time.

[3] John Golden produced more than a hundred plays on Broadway.
His first hit was TURN TO THE RIGHT (1916); his last, THE MALE
ANIMAL (1953).

[4] The death of operetta composer Victor Herbert was a shock
to the New York theatrical world. According to the New York
TIMES of 27 May 1924, he became ill after luncheon at the Lambs
Club, went home after cancelling an appointment with Ziegfeld's
producer, decided to visit his doctor, and collapsed while
climbing the stairs to the doctor's office. Gene Buck was an
honorary pallbearer.

murdering another Jew boy aged thirteen. It has since been
brought out that they had previously murdered two or three other
guys and helped themselves to important glands.

Ellis says she will write as soon as she is through with the
dentist. Personally I have written a thousand words. Love to
one of you.

Mary Esselstyn.

The same day Ring also wrote to the SATURDAY
EVENING POST on behalf of a young writer:

Great Neck, New York
June fifth.

Dear Mr. Costain:-

Nick Flatley,[1] a rising young Boston Irishman, has written a
golf story in which he thinks the Post might be interested. He
asked my advice as to whom to send it to, being one of the boys
who think that a manuscript addressed merely to The Editors is
thrown into the nearest open fireplace unread. Anyway, I've
taken the liberty of telling him to address it you and you'll
probably get it in a few days.

Sincerely,
Ring W. Lardner

The following letter is probably to Kate Rice, wife of
Grantland Rice. By this time the Rices and the
Lardners had become close friends.

Ring Lardner
Great Neck, New York
June 12.

Dear Madam:-

I trust this will put a stop to the innuendoes regarding my
alleged indebtedness to you. Three dollars of it is for what you
say I owe you at golf, God knows how; five cents is for a
telephone call which I was going to make to you, but decided not
to, and twelve dollars is for flowers for the funeral of Mr.
Morse Sr.,[2] though I swear I had nothing to do with his death and
would have preferred the demise of another member of the family.

Cordially,
Sister Stanislaus.

---

[1]No story by Nick Flatley appeared in the POST.

[2]Theodore Morse was a composer. He had just returned from
accompanying Victor Herbert to Washington to testify in the
hearing on the copyright law when he died, on 26 May 1924.

Though Ring was in his mildly cynical political
views rather conservative, his irritation in the
following letter with the Democrats is the result of
his frustration with the machinations of the 1924
Democratic National Convention, which Ring covered as a
reporter. At the Convention he suffered through 103
ballots while William McAdoo, considered the spokesman
for small town protestant America, and Al Smith, the
leader of the eastern liberal establishment, struggled
for political control. Eventually the party labor
groups sought to promote Robert M. LaFollette, and the
moderates supported John W. Davis. Davis was finally
selected (though the "Progressives" later ran
LaFollette as a third-party candidate) but he lost the
election to Calvin Coolidge by seven million votes.

Perhaps more interesting is Ring's reluctance here
and elsewhere to use profanity. As almost everyone
knows, he angered many people in the popular music
field in 1932 when he conducted from his hospital bed a
crusade in his NEW YORKER "Over the Waves" column
against songs he considered suggestive or immoral.
Though his objections were primarily to sexual
overtones, Ring also clearly disapproved of written
profanity, and did not include such language in his
fiction, to Ernest Hemingway's dismay. In a 1934
ESQUIRE piece Hemingway described himself as an "early
imitator and always admirer" of Ring and argued that
this reluctance to use profanity was Ring's only flaw
as a master of realistic dialogue.

Great Neck, New York
July twenty-first.

Dear Max:-
I do hope you will overlook or forgive or something my
rudeness in not replying sooner to your letters or telephone
calls--my alibi is the Democrats, God   them.
Now then (1)I am trying to get up nerve enough to ask for
release from the "comic" strip,[1] which is me bete noir as the

----

[1]From September 1922 to January 1925 Ring wrote a comic
strip for the Bell Syndicate called "You Know Me Al" which
featured Jack Keefe as protagonist (the strip continued to appear
under Ring's name until September 1925). The cartoons were drawn
first by Will Johnston and, after February 1923, by Dick Dorgan,
brother of the well-known cartoonist Tad Dorgan, who was a good
friend of Ring's. The strip appeared in over a hundred
newspapers and brought in about $20,000 a year, but Ring found it
boring and in January 1925 turned it over completely to Dick
Dorgan, who apparently wrote those strips which appeared between
September 1925 and May 1926, when the strip ceased.

Scotch have it; if I do that I will have a lot more time to spend on short stories. (2). I'll come to one of those literary luncheons if you think it advisable, but it is my secret ambition not to. (3). I enclose a letter from Mr. Darrow which I ought to have answered. Will you please tell him that I had a letter from Mr. Beach,[1] in which he not only repeated the request that I write something for his Book Notes, but also he wrote it himself as he thought I ought to write it and I wished you could see it; he put every gag into it except Alabama casts 24 votes for Underwood.[2] If Mr. Darrow thinks I'd better write something for them, I'll do it, but between you and me I have nicknamed the editor the Beach Nut. (4). I very much appreciate the way you are pushing the book. (5). I have virtually gone down on my knees to the Bobbs-Merrill people for a copy of Gullible's Travels, vainly. I haven't a copy myself. Gene Buck has, and if you just want to read it, I'll try to get it away from him for a few days. It isn't that he is so fond of it, but they have got great big bookcases.

I wish you would call up and get into a confidential conversation with me, the gist of which would be that we'd make an engagement for you and Mrs. Perkins to come to Great Neck and I'd promise to be cold sober and nice, but not amusing.

Sincerely,
Ring W. Lardner

HOW TO WRITE SHORT STORIES had sold moderately well in 1924—about 3,500 copies by the end of June, enough for Perkins not only to encourage Ring to write enough stories for another book next year but also to contemplate obtaining the rights to Ring's earlier books so that Ring could become fully another of "Scribner's authors." Since Perkins had not been able to obtain a copy of GULLIBLE'S TRAVELS, ETC., he had appealed to Ring, who in the above letter referred him humorously to Gene Buck. While Ring clearly liked Buck, he was occasionally amused by Buck's professional brainstorms and by his rather pretentious lifestyle.

---

[1] Probably Harrison L. Beach, a newspaperman.

[2] During the struggle through 103 ballots at the 1924 Democratic National Convention, Alabama continually cast its 24 votes for its own Senator Oscar W. Underwood, in hopes either of promoting him as a compromise candidate or of waiting until that block of votes could function significantly in a swing to another candidate.

Great Neck, New York
July 27. [1924]

Dear Francis:-
    I enclose proof that the second payment of $500.00 (being
Ruth Shepley's rent) has been deposited to your account. I also
enclose the letter about the frozen water pipes in the garage and
the plumber's bill for fixing same. I asked Charley Goddard who
was responsible for frozen water pipes in a garage (he being an
experienced landlord) and he said the tenant was responsible;
that the tenant ought to have seen that the water was turned off.
    Meanwhile, I have told Mrs. Sarre (Ruth Shepley) that I had
sent Hines's bill to you and that if Hines bothered her, to refer
him to me. If you want to pay it, all right; if you don't, let
me know, and I'll send the bill to Mrs. Miller.
    Furthermore, Huntington Smith, of Craw's office, wrote me
that you hadn't paid the rent for July, and he wanted me to pay
it for July and August, as Mrs. Miller was squawking. I called
him up and told him I knew it was an oversight on your part and
if Mrs. Miller would be patient a few weeks, she would get her
money. He seemed satisfied and said he would pacify her.
    Now for the bad news:-
    She whom I married and I are going to leave for France on the
Paris, September tenth; will stay in Paris a week or so, and then
go to the south of France, where I have a first cousin, aged
about 60, in Montpelier, and we may possibly drop in at San
Raphael, but if we do, we're going to stop at a hotel, because we
have agreed we don't like the service in private homes. We'll
try to find the Villa Marie, and if we do, don't let me forget to
tell you the many peculiar things that have happened in Great
Neck. Most of them have happened to nobody but me, but I always
like to talk in the first person.
    Give my fondest regrets to her whom you so generously
married.
                                R. W. L.
    If we do come, I'll wire you from Paris or Montpelier the
approximate time of our arrival. Could you go to Biarritz or
Spain with us? I want to see a bullfight.

Great Neck, New York
August 24th. [1924]

[To Scott and Zelda Fitzgerald]
Gents:-
    I'll bring some of the clippings with me and then I'll be
sure of getting them back.
    Met Gordon and Ruth at a wild party the other night and they
gave me a check for the final $600.00 and I will deposit it and
either bring you the duplicate or send it to you, though the
Guaranty Trust Company says it attends to that itself. I am
still arguing about the $29.00 Plumbers bill, but will do my best

to get it passed on to Mrs. Miller. Of course it isn't the
Sarres' business and I don't see why it's yours, but plumbers
will be plumbers.
We leave here September 10 and will stay a week in Paris
before going south. I hope you and Thelma or whatever her name
is can be ready to go with us to Biarritz for a day or two.
The book has now gone into the fifth edition of 3,000, which
is better than I expected.
We'll wire you or write you from g-y P-ar-is
Don't forget to let me tell you the latest Great Neck news
when we arrive.
Our address in Paris from Sept. 17 to 24 will be the
Crillon, in case you can come up.
Sam.

Ring and Ellis visited the Fitzgeralds in France in
the fall of 1924. They left New York on 10 September,
disembarked at Le Havre, and, after spending some days
in Paris and Montpellier, joined Scott and Zelda at St.
Raphael. Scott then drove the four of them to Monte
Carlo, where they won moderately at the roulette wheel.
Ring and Ellis returned to Paris, went on to London,
and finally came home on the MAURETANIA. As before,
Ring seems not to have been greatly impressed by
Europe; his series for LIBERTY based on the trip is a
pale burlesque of THE INNOCENTS ABROAD, lacking the
spontaneity of Twain's work. Curiously, too, Ring says
little about the visit with the Fitzgeralds. Certainly
it was during a trying period for Scott and Zelda.
Zelda's attraction at St. Raphael to the French pilot
Edouard Jozan had caused a crisis not fully resolved at
the time of the Lardners' visit, and Scott in addition
was revising THE GREAT GATSBY for publication the
following year.

As early as March 1924, Perkins had been
considering the possibility of obtaining from
Bobbs-Merrill and Doran the rights to Ring's previous
books, so that Scribners could publish a uniform
edition of Ring's works. Ring had written a letter in
April to Hewitt Howland, indicating his approval of
Perkins' plan, which had evoked the following agonized
reply:

The Bobbs Merrill Company
Publishers -- Indianapolis
April 19, 1924

Dear Ring:
Your letter sent me to the hospital for
repairs; hence the delay in replying. I am still
running a temperature, clear up over the transom,

as Riley used to say, and am dictating this letter
while the doctor and the nurse have their backs
turned--not on each other.
    As Brown says when Smith dies! Why, I can't
believe it. I saw him only three days ago and he
never looked better. If you were going to
some--but are you really going? And why do you
have to "stick with 'em" as you say, just because
they happened to have an idea? This getting an
author with the uniform edition bait is such an old
wheeze. Listen--if I lose you I'll probably lose
my job, and it's a long time since I worked. I'd
starve and you'd have me on your conscience and be
most uncomfortable.
    You ask if we'd set a price on the plates of
your books. As for me, I'd as soon sell my fee
simple in my brother-in-law. But Lawrence Chambers
will be in New York next week. Get hold of him,
and there may be another story, as the girl said to
the soldier.
    The doctor and the nurse have come to and are
saying that if there is any dictating to be done
they'll do it. And if you could see the nurse!

    By October 1924 an agreement was reached, whereby
Scribner's paid the George H. Doran Company $500 for
the plates, existing stock, and rights of YOU KNOW ME
AL, and $2000 to Bobbs-Merrill for the stock, plates,
and rights of TREAT 'EM ROUGH, OWN YOUR OWN HOME, THE
YOUNG IMMIGRUNTS, GULLIBLE'S TRAVELS, MY FOUR WEEKS IN
FRANCE, THE BIG TOWN, THE REAL DOPE, and SYMPTOMS OF
BEING 35. YOU KNOW ME AL, GULLIBLE'S TRAVELS, and THE
BIG TOWN were reissued by Scribner's in 1925 as part of
a five-volume set, including HOW TO WRITE SHORT STORIES
and WHAT OF IT?

                              Great Neck, New York
                              November 11th.

Dear Max:-
    I enclose a letter to Bobbs Merrill as you requested.
    I'm so desperately far behind in work that I don't believe
I'll be able to get to town for a couple of weeks.
    We had a pleasant session with the Fitzgeralds. Scott likes
his new book,[1] which he was revising when we left.
                              Sincerely,
                              R. W. L.

----

[1]THE GREAT GATSBY, published the following year.

The above letter included a copy of the following letter to Bobbs-Merrill.

Great Neck, New York
November 11, 1924.

Bobbs Merrill,
Indianapolis, Indiana.
Gentlemen:-
Charles Scribner's Sons have informed me of an agreement with you, depending on my approval, by which they are to take over those books by me which you have published with the idea of forming a uniform group of them and of others for publication. This is to tell you that the arrangement has my approval and that I am grateful for your cooperation in connection with it.
Sincerely,

On 29 November Perkins wrote to Ring:

I'm delighted with Scott's book. It's got his old vitality,- vitality enough to sweep away the faults you could, critically, find with it;- which relate, in my view, chiefly to Gatsby himself. Large parts of it are almost incredibly good and there is in it a sort of strange mystical element which he has not exhibited since "Paradise",- an element that comes partly, perhaps, from once having been a Catholic. Well -- I am one of these 'jaded' readers, or ought to be and I read it straight through and thought it much shorter than it was.

Great Neck, New York
December second.

Dear Max:-
I am tickled to death with your report on Scott's book. It's his pet and I believe he would take poison if it flopped.

Ellis and I have both read "Three Flights Up"[1] and both liked the two middle stories best. My favorite is "Transatlantic." The last story is way over my head.
I think I am going to be able to sever connections with the daily cartoon early next month. This ought to leave me with plenty of time and it is my intention to write at least ten short stories a year. Whether I can do it or not, I don't know. I started one the other day and got through with about 700 words, which were so bad that I gave up. I seem to be out of the habit

_____

[1]THREE FLIGHTS UP was a collection of short stories by Sidney Coe Howard, published by Scribners in 1924.

and it may take time to get back.

Don Stewart's "Mr. and Mrs. Haddock Abroad" was a blow to me.[1] That is the kind of "novel" I had intended to write, but if I did it now, the boys would yell stop thief.

Five "articles" on the European trip are coming out in Liberty, beginning in January.[2] I don't know whether or not they will be worth putting in a book.

I'm coming to town early next week to call on a dentist. As soon as I know when, I'll telephone you and try to make a date. Not that we don't want you in Great Neck, but I realize that it's no pleasure trip.

Sincerely,

R. W. L.

Great Neck, New York

Dec. 10.

Dear Max:-

I enclose the pieces I think more worthy. I am sending the others in a separate envelope.

I have put new titles on the ones here enclosed, titles of which I am not proud, but which I believe are at least better than the Syndicate's. As soon as I think of a general title, I'll call you up.

It seems to me that the year and month when they were written ought to be put at the bottom or top of each piece.

Sincerely,

R. W. L.

No record survives of Ring's preferences, but presumably the "pieces" to which he refers in the letter above were selections from a list Perkins had compiled of Ring's syndicated articles which Perkins felt were worthy of republication. Titled WHAT OF IT?, this volume of miscellany appeared in 1925 and sold a respectable 8000 copies in its first year. It is notable chiefly for the reappearance of THE YOUNG IMMIGRUNTS and SYMPTOMS OF BEING 35, and for three remarkably contemporary "nonsense" plays--"Clemo Uti--'The Water Lilies,'" "I. Gaspiri," and "Taxidea Americana." These plays exhibit a kind of non-sequitur world in which people talk, but no one listens to anyone else:

---

[1]Donald Ogden Stewart, a friend of the Lardner family, was a well-known humorist, playwright, and screenwriter, and was briefly, at his friend Philip Barry's request, an actor.

[2]Published in the 14, 21, and 28 February, 7 and 14 March issues of LIBERTY, all under the title "The Other Side"

            First Stranger
Where was you born?
            Second Stranger
Out of wedlock.
            First Stranger
That's a mighty pretty country around there.
            Second Stranger
Are you married?
            First Stranger
I don't know. There's a woman living with me, but
I can't place her.

Or:

            Pat
I certainly feel sorry for people on the ocean
to-night.
            Mike
What makes you think so?
            Pat
You can call me whatever you like as long as you
don't call me down.

        It has been suggested that this mad world reflects
a deepening cynicism Ring developed in his later years,
and that it explains why Ring felt unmotivated to
attempt the novel Perkins continually urged him to
write. Some lines in these plays seem also to satirize
specific values; the following stage direction, for
instance, appears to deplore the emphasis on stage
naturalism: "The curtain is lowered for seven days to
denote the lapse of a week."

        In December 1924 Ring sent the following printed
Christmas postcard verse to a number of people,
including Frank Crowninshield (the humorist and critic,
perhaps best known for his work as editor and writer
for VANITY FAIR), whose card survives:

How utterly ridiculous
You'd feel, how damn unpleasant,
If you sent just a card to us
While we sent you a present!

In order that no such a thing
Can happen to you ccmma
This card is all you'll get from Ring,
His kiddies or their mamma.

        The following letter to the Fitzgeralds captures
the tone of Great Neck life in early 1925.

[Great Neck, Long Island]
Friday, January 9, 1925.

Dear Wops:-

You would get a lot more mail from me if you had a decent and permanent address. I hate to write letters and think all the time that they'll never get anywhere.

I have talked with Max Perkins several times since he received Scott's novel. He is very enthusiastic about it, saying it's much the best thing Scott has done since "Paradise," that parts of it are inspired, and etc. He wasn't crazy to have anybody use it serially on account of the delay it meant in getting out the book, but he told me today that "College Humor" had made a good offer which he thought you might accept. "College-Humor" seems to be l---y with money and careless of how it spends it--not knocking Mr. Fitzgerald. My brother was strong for the book and wanted "Liberty" to run it, but some of the readers thought it was better as a book than it would be as a serial, meaning that it couldn't be arranged so that the reader would be left in suspense at the end of each installment.

I've been on the wagon since Armistice Day and Ellis and I have seen a lot of shows. Laurence Stallings' play[1] is a bear, even with a few of the words left out. I see no reason why it shouldn't beat a record or come near it. Dorothy Parker's[2] "Close Harmony" got great notices and was, we thought, a dandy play, but it flopped in three weeks. Dorothy, Beatrice Kaufman[3] and Peggy Leech[4] gave a party at the Algonquin six or seven weeks

---

[1]WHAT PRICE GLORY, by Maxwell Anderson and Laurence Stallings, then playing at the Plymouth Theater in New York City.

[2]Dorothy Parker was a poet, short story writer, and playwright. She was drama critic of VANITY FAIR (1917-1920), but reputedly was discharged because her reviews were considered too harsh. Thereafter she wrote drama and book reviews for the NEW YORKER. Her one play was written in collaboration with Elmer Rice. She was a member of the Algonquin Round Table, where she exercised her caustic wit.

[3]Wife of George S. Kaufman. She was active as an editor with HARPER'S BAZAAR and several book-publishing firms. She herself wrote two plays, the first in collaboration with Peggy Leech (DIVIDED BY THREE) and the second in collaboration with Charles Martin (THE WHITE-HAIRED BOY). Both were near-misses.

[4]Margaret Leech was the author of two novels and a number of non-fiction works. She won a Pulitzer Prize in history for REVEILLE IN WASHINGTON (1941), and another for IN THE DAYS OF MCKINLEY (1960). She married Ralph Pulitzer in 1928.

ago. I was enjoying an intellectual conversation with Mary Hay[1] when Peggy tore me away to talk to a lady who seemed kind of lonely. The lady was Mrs. Ernest Boyd[2] and I'd have been with her yet if June Walker[3] hadn't come in with a bun and rescued me. We got back from the other side (Europe) in time to see the Yale-Princeton game. Art Samuels[4] was host to a huge party of us--Swopes, Brouns, etc.--at lunch at the Cottage club. The Princeton team, which had made a sucker of Harvard the Saturday before, acted on this occasion as if football was a complete surprise and novelty. We stood up all the way home and I swore it would be my last trip to old Nassau.

Instead of working on the ship coming home, as I intended, I did nothing but lap them up. But as soon as I was home and on the wagon, I wrote the five European articles in nine days.

I have quit the strip and Dick Dorgan is doing it, with help from Tad.[5]

The Society of Composers and Authors, of which Gene is president, gave him a clock for Christmas that must have cost $1000 at least.[6]

---

[1]Mary Hay was a Ziegfeld girl and an actress. She married Dick Barthelmess, the actor, in 1920; they were divorced in 1926.

[2]Madeleine Boyd, wife of the critic, eventually wrote a novel based on her life with her husband, titled LIFE MAKES ADVANCES (1939).

[3]June Walker made her debut on Broadway in the chorus of HITCHY KOO (1916). She is especially remembered as the original Lorelei Lee in GENTLEMEN PREFER BLONDES (1926) and for her starring role in GREEN GROW THE LILACS (1931).

[4]Art Samuels worked in an advertising agency from 1920 to 1928; he then became managing editor of the NEW YORKER. In 1930 he became editor of HOME AND FIELD; from 1931 to 1934 he edited HARPER's BAZAAR, and in 1934 he became editor of HOUSE BEAUTIFUL. He wrote one musical, POPPY, starring W. C. Fields, in 1923.

[5]Dick Dorgan was the illustrator of Ring's comic strip "You Know Me Al." Ring had written the continuity for the strip from September 1922 to January 1925, although the strip continued to carry his by-line until the following September. Dick Dorgan took over the continuity when Ring gave it up (though profitable, Ring had found it boring) and carried on until May 1926. Tad Dorgan was a well-known newspaper cartoonist and close friend of Ring.

[6]Gene Buck was one of the founders of the American Society of Composers, Authors and Publishers, and its president from 1924 to 1941.

Gene and Helen were over the other night and in the midst of one of Gene's stories, Helen said, "Stop picking your nose, sweetheart." That's all the dirt I know.

Speaking of noses, Rube[1] and Irma gave a New Year's Eve party to which 150 people were invited and 300 came. Rube said he never saw so many strangers in his life. Billy Seeman[2] had a lot of the Follies people there to help entertain, but the affair was such a riot that little attention was paid to the entertainment. Ellis and I missed this party. Speaking of noses again, I was in the hospital having my antrum cut open. I'm nearly all right again now, I think, though if I get up suddenly or stoop over, a regular Niagara of blood pours forth from my shapely nostrils.

I took "Vanity Fair" (Thackeray's, not Crowninshield's) to the hospital with me and one day the nurse asked me what I was reading and I told her and she said, "I haven't read it yet. I've been busy making Christmas presents."[3]

Ellis is at present in Danville, Illinois, where her last brother is being married tomorrow to a gal named Bredehoft. I was kept at home by my nose. We are leaving next Tuesday, with the Grant Rices, for Miami and then Nassau, to be gone till nearly the first of March. Our address at Nassau will be New Colonial Hotel. I think I'll take up golf again, but won't stick to it if I don't like it.

And I think you've staid away long enough.

Mrs. Nell

The following letter was written during a vacation in Miami and Nassau with the Grantland Rices, from 13 January 1925 through mid-February. Though the Lardners and the Fitzgeralds were devoted friends, their ties were of a relatively short duration (after the visit to France in the fall of 1924, Ring and Scott saw each other only twice more). The Rices were the Lardners' closest friends over a long period of time. Sports and the newspaper world were common ground for Ring and Grantland, and Ellis was especially fond of Kate Rice (Ellis had admired Zelda but never quite approved of the Fitzgeralds' unrestrained lifestyle). In the 1920's the Lardners and the Rices vacationed together for a period of time nearly every winter.

---

[1]Rube Goldberg, the famous cartoonist, and one of Ring's neighbors in Great Neck.

[2]William Seeman was a young man-about-town, the son of a wealthy food processor. He would marry Rube Goldberg's sister-in-law, Phyllis Haver, in 1929.

[3]This experience with a nurse's ignorance of VANITY FAIR is utilized in "Zone of Quiet," a story published originally in the June 1925 COSMOPOLITAN.

The New Colonial
Nassau - Bahamas
January 31, 1925.

Dear Max:-

How about WHAT OF IT? as a title. This is Grantland Rice's suggestion and it sounds pretty good to me.
I'll send you the prefaces in not too short a while.
R. W. L.

The following letter is to William Orton Tewson, then editor of the New York EVENING POST Literary Review section, who had asked Ring to review THE PRINCE OF WASHINGTON SQUARE, a novel reportedly by nineteen-year-old Harry F. Liscomb, dealing with the exploits of a newsboy, and written in a mixture of semi-idiomatic formal and colloquial English. The book obviously reminded Ring of THE YOUNG VISITERS, the narrative supposedly written by nine-year-old Daisy Ashford, which Ring had parodied with THE YOUNG IMMIGRUNTS.

Great Neck, New York
February 22, 1925.

Dear Mr. Tewson:-
I was away for six weeks and I guess some of my mail went astray; anyway, the enclosed note is the only one I received about "walnuts."
As for "The Prince of Washington Square," I think it had better be reviewed by some one less skeptical than I. I didn't, and don't believe Daisy Ashford in spite of Swinnerton's testimony and that of other "witnesses," and this new book is, to me, palpably conscious humor written by somebody much older than they say the author is.
Sincerely,
Ring W. Lardner
P.S. I don't mean to say the Stokes people are trying to put something over, but that they have been deceived. (Though some of the lines and paragraphs in the book are so "raw" that it is hard to know how they could fool anybody)

Great Neck, New York
March 11, 1925

Dear Max:-
The principal cause of delay has been lack of an idea. But I've also been fighting a cold; the kind that relieves you of all pep.
R. W. L.
Did you have the wrap changed on You Know Me Al?

When Perkins read Ring's short story "Haircut" in the 28 March issue of LIBERTY, he wrote to Ring:

March 16, 1925

Dear Ring:
    I read "Hair Cut" on Friday and I can't shake it out of my mind;- in fact the impression it made has deepened with time. There's not a man alive who could have done better, that's certain.
    Everyone will tell you this, or something like it I guess, so there's little use in my doing it.- But it is a most biting and revealing story and I'd like to say so.

Ring's reply was succinct and typically modest:

Great Neck, New York
March Seventeenth.

Dear Max:-
    Thanks.

R. W. L.

    Perkins' judgment has been sustained, since "Haircut" remains today Ring's most anthologized short story. The ironic depiction of the variance between the narrator-barber's insensitive interpretation of an "accidental" death and what actually occurred exhibits powerfully Ring's valuation of sensitivity and human sympathy--a theme which runs through much of his work. Curiously, Ring had written no short stories between "The Golden Honeymoon" (COSMOPOLITAN, July 1922) and "Haircut" (LIBERTY, March 28, 1925), though he had written a number of short fictional sketches (e. g. "What of It?" and "In Conference") for HEARST'S INTERNATIONAL and COSMOPOLITAN. In the next year and a half, however, he wrote twelve stories, nine of which were published in THE LOVE NEST, after appearing in COSMOPOLITAN or LIBERTY. A significant factor in Ring's resumption of writing stories was probably the offer that Ray Long, editor of COSMOPOLITAN, had made to Ring in London in the fall of 1924: "For your next six short stories, $3000 each, or, for your next twelve short stories, to be delivered at intervals of not more than 45 days, $3500 each."[1] During the remainder of 1925 Ring alternated his stories between COSMOPOLITAN and LIBERTY, where his brother Rex was an editor. When Rex was dismissed near the end of the year in one of

[1] Quoted by Donald Elder, RING LARDNER, New York, 1956, p. 219.

LIBERTY's frequent reorganizations, Ring sent all his short stories to COSMOPOLITAN, where Rex shortly was hired as an associate editor.

At this time Perkins, considerably frustrated by the last minute revisions Scott had continued to send, mailed Ring a copy of THE GREAT GATSBY proofs, an action which suggests both the closeness of Ring's friendship with Scott, and Perkins's trust in Ring. Ring proof-read the copy and, as he explained to Scott in the letter below, suggested a few minor changes in the interest of a more accurate representation of New York City.

March 24th. [1925]

Dears Mr. and Mrs. F.-
Max Perkins reports that Mrs. F. is or has been sick, which we hope isn't true, but would like to know for sure.
I read Mr. F's book (in page proofs) at one sitting and liked it enormously, particularly the description of Gatsby's home and his party, and the party in the apartment in New York. It sounds as if Mr. F. must have attended a party or two during his metropolitan career. The plot held my interest, too, and I found no tedious moments. Altogether I think it's the best thing you've done since Paradise.
On the other hand, I acted as volunteer proof reader and gave Max a brief list of what I thought were errata. On Pages 31 and 46 you spoke of the news-stand on the lower-level, and the cold waiting room on the lower level of the Pennsylvania Station. There ain't any lower level at that station and I suggested substitute terms for same. On Page 82, you had the guy driving his car under the elevated at Astoria, which isn't Astoria, but Long Island City. On Page 118 you had a tide in Lake Superior and on Page 209 you had the Chicago, Milwaukee & St. Paul running out of the La Salle Street Station. These things are trivial, but some of the critics pick on trivial errors for lack of anything else to pick on.
Michael Arlen, who is here to watch the staging of The Green Hat,[1] said he thought How To Write Short Stories was a great title for my book and when I told him it was your title, he said he had heard a great deal about you and was sorry to miss you. He also said he had heard that Mrs. Fitzgerald was very attractive, but I told him he must be thinking of somebody else. Mike is being entertained high and low. He was guest of honor at

---

[1]Michael Arlen dramatized his own novel, THE GREEN HAT in 1925. The play starred Katherine Cornell and was the basis for two later films. He wrote thirteen other novels, none of which had the success of THE GREEN HAT. His works were carefully calculated to appeal to the popular taste.

a luncheon given by Ray Long. Irv Cobb and George Doran sat on either side of him and told one dirty story after another. Last Sunday night he was at a party at Condé Nast's,[1] but who wasn't? I was looking forward to a miserable evening, but had the luck to draw Ina Claire[2] for a dinner and evening companion and was perfectly happy, though I regretted being on the wagon. The last previous time I saw her was at the Press Club in Chicago about eight years ago and she says I was much more companionable on that occasion. George Nathan[3] said he heard you were coming home soon. George, they say, is quitting the associate editorship of the Mercury, but will continue to write theaters for it.

So far as I know, Zelda, Mary Hay and Richard are still together; they were when I met them.

Beatrice Kaufman and Peggy Leach have gone abroad.

We had a dinner party at our little nest about two weeks ago; the guests were the Ray Longs, the Grantland Rices, June Walker and Frank Crowninshield. As place cards for Ray, Crownie and Grant, we had, respectively, covers of Cosmopolitan, Vanity Fair and The American Golfer, but this didn't seem to make any impression on June and right after the soup she began knocking Condé Nast in general and his alleged snobbishness in particular. Finally Crownie butted in to defend him and June said, "What do you know about him?" "I live with him," said Crownie. "What for?" said June. "Well," said Crownie, "I happen to be editor of one of his magazines, Vanity Fair." "Oh!" said June. "That's my favorite magazine! And I hate most magazines! For instance, I wouldn't be seen with a Cosmopolitan." After the loud laughter had subsided, I explained to her that Ray was editor of Cosmopolitan. "I'm always making breaks," she said, "and I guess this is one of my unlucky evenings. I suppose that if I said what I think of William R. Hearst, I'd find that even he has a friend here or something."

The annual Dutch Treat show comes off this week. I have a sketch in it which is a born flop.

I met Gene on the train the other day and he said, "Come over and play bridge with us tonight," and I said I couldn't because

---

[1]Publisher of VOGUE, VANITY FAIR, and HOUSE AND GARDEN. Nast was known as a bon vivant, entertaining frequently in his thirty-room Park Avenue apartment.

[2]Ina Claire made her first appearance on Broadway in the Ziegfeld Follies of 1915. She became a star in THE GOLD DIGGERS (1919), and played in vaudeville, musical comedy, and "drawing room" comedy, eventually starring in movies.

[3]George Jean Nathan began his career as a drama critic in 1906. He was associated with H. L. Mencken on both THE SMART SET and AMERICAN MERCURY. His articles appeared in VANITY FAIR, AMERICAN SPECTATOR, SATURDAY REVIEW, ESQUIRE, SCRIBNER'S, NEWSWEEK, THEATRE ARTS, and LIBERTY.

Arthur Jacks was coming to our house. When I got home, I called up Arthur to inform him of this and he said it was tough luck, but it just happened that he had been invited, several days before, to dine at Gene's that very night.
Write.
                              Bob Esselstyn.

                                   Great Neck, New York
                                   March 25.

Dear Scott:-
    Thanks for the idea, which I think I can use. I wrote to you yesterday, but don't mind doing it again as I left out one piece of news which may be of interest, namely that George Jean and Lillian Gish are often seen together these days. And a handsome pair they make.
    Looked up Capri in the encyclopedia and learned that the water supply for drinking was unsatisfactory. Hope to God this is not ruining your stay.
    Mr. Lambert, when questioned, said he was taking the best of care of your stuff. He said he had sent the wrong graphophone south or something, but had got it back again.
    Visited Mr. Perkins yesterday, had myself sketched by a lady named Anderson,[1] and saw the wrap of your book, which looks good. Then dined at the Princeton club with Art Samuels and attended a Dutch Treat rehearsal, after which I went backstage at the Follies and turned down three offers of drinks, one from a lady, or at least a female.
    Must close and nibble on a carrot. Love to the little woman.
                              Buckie.

        The following letter is to Walter Yust, associate editor of The Literary Review and The Literary Lobby in the New York EVENING POST.

                                   Great Neck, New York
                                   April 4, 1925.

Dear Mr. Yust:-
    If you don't mind, I'd like to consider my brief book reviewing career at an end.[2] There is more work ahead of me than I can possibly do, and besides, I can't be even half way entertaining unless I knock, and I don't like to knock.
                              Sincerely,
                              Ring Lardner

    ————————————————————————————

    [1]The original of this sketch, by Ellen Graham Anderson, is now in the University of Virginia Library.

    [2]Ring had written a review four years earlier of J. V. A. Weaver's IN AMERICAN: "What Is the 'American Language'?"

On 24 April Perkins wrote to encourage Ring towards
the completion of another volume of short stories:

> I just ran into John Wheeler at lunch and he
> told me of two stories written and one in early
> expectation. These with "Hair Cut" make four. In
> "How to Write Short Stories" we had ten, but we
> would not need quite that many for another book and
> what Wheeler said was encouraging.

> Great Neck, New York
> April 25th.

Dear Max:-
I do think there ought to be at least nine stories in a book
and I am fairly well on the way to that number. Besides Haircut,
Mr. and Mrs. Fix-it, and Women (a baseball story) for Liberty,
Ray Long has two stories--Zone of Quiet (which, I think, will be
in June Cosmopolitan) and The Love Nest (which I sent him this
week). I intend to have one and possibly two more done for
Liberty by the end of May. The quality of the five already
written averages better than the stories in How To Write Short
Stories and if we give 'em fair quantity too, they ought to be
satisfied.
I'm glad to hear that Scott's book is going.
R. W. L.

BOCKMAN, LIII (March 1921), pp. 81-82. In the following excerpt
from that review, his precise scrutiny of the common American's
careless speech is particularly evident:

> We can't hope to land the old K.O. on the writer's jaw,
> but we can fret him a little with a few pokes to the ear.
> For the most part this organ has served Mr. Weaver
> well. But I think that on occasion it consciously or
> unconsciously plays him false. It has told him, for example,
> that we say everythin' and anythin'. We don't. We say
> somethin' and nothin', but we say anything and everything.
> There appears to be somethin' about the y near the middle of
> both these words that impels us to acknowledge the g on the
> end of them. Mr. Weaver's ear has also give or gave (not
> gi'n) him a bum hunch on thing itself. It has told him to
> make it thin'. But it's a real effort to drop the g off this
> little word and, as a rule, our language is not looking for
> trouble. His ear has gone wrong on the American for fellow,
> kind of, and sort of. Only on the stage or in "comic strips"
> do we use feller, kinder, and sorter. Kinda and sorta are
> what us common fellas say.

Great Neck, New York
May 4, 1925.

[To H. L. Mencken]
Gents:-
Your stuff about Scott in the Sunday World was, it seemed to me, close to perfection in criticism.
And you have the right dope on the pains he took with Gatsby. He rewrote the whole book four or five times and had Scribner's crazy at the finish with revisions by cable.
R. W. L.

THE GREAT GATSBY had been published on 10 April. Though it generally would receive the best critical reviews Fitzgerald ever received, the sales were disappointing by Fitzgerald's standards--just over 20,000 copies during the first year, perhaps, as Perkins thought, because the public reacted negatively to a book that was quite short compared with Fitzgerald's previous books.

Great Neck, New York
June 25, 1925

Mr. H. L. Mencken
1524 Hollins Street
Baltimore, Md.

Dear Sir:
If you will be a little patient I will autograph all my books and all Dickens's and most of Cobb's.
I have been kind of sick but I did like what you said about me.
Sincerely,
R. W. L.

On 27 July Perkins advised Ring that they should delay publication of the next volume of short stories. He cited as an example THE GREAT GATSBY, which he felt was not selling as well as Fitzgerald's earlier books because it was relatively short:

The temptation is to get the book out . . . and it is certainly very hard for me to resist it, because I think the stories almost incredibly good. "The Love Nest" is a marvel. But I do honestly think from a farsighted view, that we should act more wisely if we waited -- and after all, it would mean only four months -- until you had several more stories, so that the book would not look slim and perhaps padded, in half titles, etc. and a widely spaced page and all, along side of "How to Write Short Stories". It is bound to be compared with that and the fact that it was not its equal in

quantity,- at least it would not in the eyes of the
trade:- they began by washing their hands of the
whole matter when they saw how few pages there were
in "The Great Gatsby" compared with his other
books.

The following is again to Fitzgerald:

Great Neck, August 8, 1925.

Dear Sir:-
    I enclose a fragment from one of your former letters.   Zelda
isn't here, but when I see her I certainly will give her your
best love.
    I might consider visiting Paris if you will guarantee me   an
introduction to Miss La Gallienne[1] who is my favorite actress and
with whom I have been secretly in love ever since Liliom.
    Thanks to the Great Neck Playhouse we hardly ever have to go
to New York any more. Nearly all the shows play a night or two
here before going to Broadway. Twenty-two try-outs are booked
for this season and you can buy season tickets if you want to.
    Gene didn't make any comment on "The Love Nest," but
evidently had no suspicion.[2] Anyway, we are still pals. He told
Dorothy Parker in my presence one night that the new house had
been bought as a memorial to the kiddies.
    Dorothy visited the Lardners for a week at my invitation.
She had been having an unfortunate affair and for some reason or
other, I thought a visit to us would cheer her up.   I got into
this sympathetic mood on the seventh of May and it lasted till
the tenth of July; during the two months I was constantly
cock-eyed, drinking all night and sleeping all day and never
working. Fortunately I was eight weeks ahead in syndicates
before the spree started.
    One night during Dorothy's visit, Herman Mankiewicz[3] called
up from Petrova's and said he would come and see us if we'd come

_____

    [1]Eva LeGallienne established herself on the New York stage
with NOT SO LONG AGO (1920). She also starred in LILIOM (1921)
and THE SWAN (1924). She founded the Civic Repertory Theatre in
1926.

    [2]Though Ring admitted that "The Love Nest" (a portrait of an
apparently happy marriage in reality blighted by the husband's
possessiveness, his wife's sense of unfulfillment, and her
subsequent dipsomania) was actually based on the Buck household,
Buck never gave any sign of having read the story or of having
been offended in any way. His wife was the former Helen
Faulkner, a Fred Stone showgirl before her marriage.

    [3]Herman Mankiewicz was a foreign correspondent for the WORLD
who subsequently became drama editor and critic for the New York

after him. We did and I took them, Mank and Dorothy, to
Durand's, Ellis (very sensibly) refusing to go. The place was
full of Durand's big, husky Irish clients. After a few drinks,
Mank remembered that he had been in the Marines and ought to
prove it by licking all the inmates of the joint. I (as usual)
acted as pacifist and felt next day as if I'd been in a football
game against Notre Dame. We finally got Mank home (our house)
and put him to bed and he arose next day at ten and said he had
to go right to town and do some work for the Sunday Times. Ellis
gave him a few highballs to brace him up and he finally left at
five in the afternoon.

George Nathan and Lillian are still very thick so far as I
knew.

Harry Frazee,[1] who is making millions out of "No, No,
Nanette" (with four companies in America, three in England and
two in Australia), promises to stage a small revue, written by
Jerry Kern and me, late this fall. But you know how those things
go.

Dick Barthelmess[2] is living in Great Neck and we see him
occasionally. The papers announced that Mary was through with
him, though she didn't intend to get a divorce.

Mrs. Lardner and I will be highly honored by the dedication
of your book to us.[3] I hope "The Great Gatsby" is going better.
It certainly deserves a big sale. I think it probable that the
reason it got no notice from Frank Adams was that he was on a
vacation and getting married about the time it came out. Max
Perkins said he thought the size of the book was against it (in
the eyes of the buyers). That is a great commentary on American
life and letters. What is your new novel going to be about?

Gene called up the other day and said he had sold the play
"we" wrote to Ziegfeld, but that it would have to be rewritten
into musical comedy form. Ziegfeld had given him contracts for
us to sign. There were clauses in them which I wouldn't sign
even with a manager I could trust. I told Gene so and he cabled
Ziegfeld, who is now in France, and said we objected to certain
clauses. Ziegfeld cabled back that he wouldn't make any changes.
Gene then wanted me to sign the contracts as they stood and I

TIMES. He went on to become a screenwriter for Paramount. He
shared an academy award for the screen play of CITIZEN KANE
(1941).

[1]Harry Frazee was producer of NO, NO, NANETTE (which was
written by Vincent Youmans). He was the owner of the Boston Red
Sox from 1916 to 1923.

[2]Dick Barthelmess was a leading man in many movies from 1916
to 1941.

[3]Scott had dedicated ALL THE SAD YOUNG MEN to Ring and
Ellis.

wouldn't. So that's that. I've got a story coming out in
"Liberty" for October 3, of which Flo is the hero. When, and if,
he reads it, he won't offer me any more contracts, even lousy
ones.[1]
    On the Fourth of July, Ed Wynn[2] gave a fireworks party at his
new estate in the Grenwolde division. After the children had
been sent home, everybody got pie-eyed and I never enjoyed a
night so much. All the Great Neck professionals did their stuff,
the former chorus girls danced, Blanche Ring[3] kissed me and sang,
etc. The party lasted through the next day and wound up next
evening at Tom Meighan's,[4] where the principal entertainment was
provided by Lila Lee and another dame, who did some very funny
imitations (really funny) in the moonlight on the tennis court.
We would ask them to imitate Houdini, or Leon Errol, or Will
Rogers, or Elsie Janis; the imitations were all the same,
consisting of an aesthetic dance which ended with an unaesthetic
fall onto the tennis court.
    Charley Chaplin's new picture, "The Gold Rush," opens here
next week and we are going to a party in his honor at Nast's.
    I seem to have written a good many words, most of them about
myself, and not many of them of much interest.
    We do miss you and Zelda a great deal. Write again and tell
her to write, too. And I might add that I have a little money to
lend at the proverbial six percent, if worst comes to worst.
                                                       Bucky.
    Signing this letter "Bucky" reminded me that Bucky bought
himself a Chevrolet or something and nobody would ride with him
but Isabelle, so he took her riding and drove her into a tree and
raised hell with the bridge work.[5]

    On 29 October Perkins wrote suggesting the title
THE LOVE NEST AND OTHER STORIES for the collection in
hand of Ring's short stories.

---

    [1]The story, which depicts an insensitive, mercenary
producer, was "A Day with Conrad Green."

    [2]Ed Wynn played in the Ziegfeld Follies from 1914 on. In
1921 the title role in THE PERFECT FOOL established his style as
a comic.

    [3]Blanche Ring was a star in numerous musicals of the 1920's.
She introduced such hits as "In the Good Old Summertime" and
"Come, Josephine, in My Flying Machine."

    [4]Tom Meighan lived in the Grenewolde section of Great Neck.
He was a leading man in silent movies and was married to Blanche
Ring's sister.

    [5]For lack of room elsewhere, this postscript is typed at the
top of page one of this letter.

Great Neck, New York
November 1, 1925.

Dear Max:-
I think your title is all right. It would be better, I
believe, to have a straight title like that instead of a trick
title, this time.
Have you Scott's up-to-date address? The last I have is 14
rue de Tilsitt, but he said something in his last letter about
moving. I hate to write a 1,500-word news letter to him and have
it go astray.

R. W. L.

On 3 November the WORLD carried the following
Chicago news:

Speeding Capias Out for Lardner;
He Says Not Guilty in Own Court

Chicago, Nov. 3.--Ring Lardner's humor made no
appeal to Clyde Dyckman, Inspector of Records in
the City Hall. He was reading to-day an ad written
by Ring for a big hotel opposite the City Hall.
Ring said whenever he returned here he took a room
in this hotel "so I can look across the street,
view the County Building and see how the other half
lives without working."
"I'll fix him the next time he comes," said
Dyckman. Then he flashed a record from the office
of the Clerk of the Municipal Court wherein was set
forth that one Ring W. Lardner had been fined $50
and costs for speeding, June 17, 1919, and had
never paid the fine. The court clerk went before
Judge George and obtained a capias for the arrest
of the writer.

Ring Says Not Guilty in His Own Night Court

Ring Lardner, holding Night Court in his Great
Neck home, pleaded not guilty to the Chicago charge
and ordered himself discharged last evening.
"I didn't do it," he said. "It must have been
a couple of other fellows. However, I'm ready to
take my medicine and begin all over again. If they
prove it on me I'll pay the $50. I've never been
fined for speeding--Oh, yes, I've been arested for
speeding but never fined. That's different.
"They charge me with speeding in June 1919. I
didn't move away from Chicago until the following
October. My creditors never wait four months to
give me time to leave town."

Ring then wrote the following letter to Chicago
Mayor Dever:

Great Neck, New York
November 4, 1925

Dear Mr. Mayor:-
I enclose a clipping from the New York World of this morning.
The story was in the other New York papers, too. I don't like to
have a thing like this against my record in Chicago which was
clean, financially, at least. I never, to my knowledge, was
fined for speeding in Chicago or elsewhere. I was living in
Chicago the entire summer of 1919 and up until October of that
year. If the fine was assessed in June, surely I ought to, and
could, have been told about it. I certainly was not making any
effort to hide.
I hate to bother you about a trivial thing like this, but I
don't know whom else to bother. And I wonder if you could have
your secretary or somebody look it up and find out who fined me
and why I was kept in ignorance of it. I'll be very grateful.
Sincerely,
Ring Lardner

The Mayor responded to this "surprising information" by
writing to Ring on 9 November:

I do not know Mr. Dyckman, whose statement is
included in the clipping. I suppose he is an
employee of the Municipal Court, over which we have
no jurisdiction whatever.
As you suggest I am having my Secretary look
the matter up and have directed him to advise you
if he obtains any information serviceable to you.

But Ring had no success in his struggle with City Hall.
The Mayor's secretary replied on 12 November:

I am writing to inform you that the records of
the Clerk of the Municipal Court show that you were
arrested by a Lincoln Park Police Officer on June
17, 1919 for speeding; that you appeared before
Municipal Judge Stelk on the same date, waived a
jury trial and pleaded guilty; that you were fined
Fifty Dollars and Six Dollars costs; that you made
a motion to vacate judgment, the hearing of which
was set for September 30, 1919. As you did not
appear in Court on that date the motion to vacate
was overruled and a warrant was issued for your
arrest.

Sunday, Nov. 8. [1925]

Dear Scott and Darling Zelda:-
     I swear to my God I would write to you oftener if you'd stay
in one place. Even when you give me an address, you always say
you don't expect to be there long.
     Max Perkins reports that Gatsby has established you (Scott;
not you, dearie) or re-established you or something; that your
book of short stories is very good, and that you are at work on
another novel. My next book is to come out in March with the
title, perhaps, "The Love Nest, and Other Stories."
     Ellis, Kate Rice, the Percy Hammonds,[1] my crazy sister and I
drove to Princeton yesterday and saw the "Tiger" (Princeton) beat
the "Crimson" (H-rv--d) 36 to 0. I won a six dollar pool by
predicting a Princeton victory of 30 to 0. But don't get it into
your heads that Princeton will have any frolic with Yale.
Harvard had the most childish team I every saw representing a big
school. A week before they played William and Mary, winning 14
to 7. Bill McGeehan[2] says it was Mary who scored the touchdown.
A week ago, Ellis and I and our sons John and Jim went to
Philadelphia and saw Red Grange make a monkey of the "Red and
Blue." He is the greatest ball carrier I've seen since Heston.
     The other night Heywood and Ruth[3] gave a party at which one
of the guests of honor was Rosamond Johnson, the coon, who, as
you doubtless know, wrote "Under the Bamboo Tree," "The Maiden
with the Dreamy Eyes," and other songs. They asked him to sing
the Bamboo Tree song and when he got to the line, "I lika change
your name," Ruth, loyal to the Lucy Stoners,[4] hissed. Poor
Johnson was what you might call nonplussed.
     We are going to the opening of the new Charlot Revue Tuesday
night. Jack Buchanan, Mundin, Beatrice and Gertrude are all back
here with it.[5]

_____

     [1]Percy Hammond was a drama critic from 1908 to 1921 for the
Chicago TRIBUNE. Then, like Ring, he moved to New York, where he
wrote for the New York TRIBUNE. Later, he was one of Ring's East
Hampton neighbors.

     [2]Bill McGeehan was sports editor of the New York HERALD. He
was chiefly noted for his column "Down the Line."

     [3]Ruth Hale was an outspoken supporter of feminist principles
and author of several articles on women's rights. She married
Heywood Campbell Broun in 1917 but retained her "maiden" name.

     [4]Lucy Stoner was an early advocate of sexual equality.

     [5]The Charlot Revue of 1926 (it opened on 10 November 1925)
starred Beatrice Lillie, Jack Buchanan, Gertrude Lawrence, and
Herbert Mundin. It received generally favorable reviews.

New York is all agog over Michael Arlen and Noel Coward.[1] Heywood, George Nathan and one or two others have taken some awful socks at Mike, but the large majority are mushy over him. Noel I haven't met, but those who have tell me he is--well, you know. I can hardly wait. His "The Vortex" is going big, but "Hay Fever" has flopped. "Hay Fever," I am told by real people, is much the best thing he has done, but was handicapped by having Laura Hope Crews as lead. As for "The Green Hat," it's a good thing for Mike that Katharine Cornell and Margalo Gilmore are in it. Les Howard is also in it, but it really isn't the right kind of part for him.

I had forgotten what terrible things world's series were so I consented to cover this year's. I got drunk three days before it started in the hope and belief that I would be remorseful and sober by the time I had to go to it. But when I got to Pittsburgh it seemed that I was the only newspaper man in America who had reserved a room; all the others moved in with me and there wasn't a chance to eat, sleep, work, or do anything but drink. The result was two fairly good stories and seven terrible ones out of a possible nine, including rainy days.

Please don't hold it against me, but I have just written a picture scenario for Tom Meighan.[2] The plot, which has to do with baseball and Florida real estate, was originated by one of the Famous Players' regular men, but they wanted me to elaborate it or something. I didn't want to, so when they said $5,000, I said it wouldn't be worth my while, but I might do it for $7,500. They said that was fine. So I did it, taking four days to the job. They begin making the picture next week. After it's done, I am to write the titles. I suppose some would consider this easy money, but it was a damn bore and unless the picture is very good, I'll be sorry I did it. The reason I said $7,500 is that Tom gets that amount per week, work or no work, and I thought perhaps I could do it in a week and be as well paid as he is.

Speaking, as we were, of Ruth Hale, some of her best friends (closest friends) have nicknamed her country place Halo-itosis.

Did May Preston look you up?

If you give a damn, we are going to Florida in January, coming back here in February and going to California in March.

But I know you are in a fever to hear the latest Buckshot, which is the title I have just thought of for my column of news about the Bucks. Well, Gene, after threatening, for several

---

[1]THE VORTEX established Noel Coward as a playwright and actor. In 1925 he had five plays running in London. In all he wrote forty-two plays.

[2]This film was THE NEW KLONDIKE, for which Ring wrote the script as a favor to his actor neighbor, Tom Meighan. As the letters to Scott of 23 February and 10 May 1926 indicate, the titles which finally appeared with the film bore little resemblance to what Ring had written.

years, to go into the producing end of the "game," finally bought
a play by J. C. Nugent, called "Gunpowder." The thesis was that
when an elderly man marries a young girl, she may some day become
a mother at the hands of somebody her own age. The play opened
in Washington and ran a week, a record-breaking week. The house
for opening night was $300 and for the Saturday night, $8.00.
Gene decided something was the matter with the show and took it
off to have it rewritten by (you'll never guess) Brandon Tynan,[1]
who was also engaged to play the elderly husband's part,
replacing Nugent. Well, they opened here in New York on Thursday
night and we all got dressed up and went and I wish you could
have been there. The audience, trying its best to be decent,
laughed hysterically and uproariously at the saddest parts and
when the girl finally announced that she was in a two-family way,
there was almost a panic. Two tickets were sold for Saturday
night and then Gene took it off.

"I wasn't kiddin' myself," said the young entrepeneur. "I
thought I saw somethin' in the play that wasn't there. I thought
I read somethin' between the lines, but it wasn't there. But I
wasn't kiddin' myself. I said to myself, 'What's the use takin'
this troupe to Reading or Stamford and foolin' with it another
week? I'll bring it right into New York and see if it's there or
not.' That's what I figured. No use wastin' any more money on
the troupe if it wasn't there. I wasn't kiddin' myself for a
minute. Well, it wasn't there. But it was good experience. And
I'll know where I'm at next time. If you got any notion, any
comedy notion, just real stuff, you come to me and I'll go
through with it. I don't want no great big troupe, but just a
homey, real comedy notion. I ain't kiddin' myself."

Well, on top of this debacle, his mother and aunt and five
cousins we'd never seen before swooped down on him in rapid
succession for long visits, and he hasn't been able to sell the
old house and the new one must be a millstone. In the face of
which, he and Frank Craven[2] "invested" in some shore front at
about $18,000 or $20,000 an acre (five acres of it), making a ten
percent payment which, I presume, Frank put up, and are now
trying to make "a quick turnover" at $27,500 an acre. I have no
doubt it will be worth that in ten years, but meanwhile the
interest will just be added to his other burdens. "But it's the
relatives that are the poison," he says. "They're what breaks a
man's back. I'm glad to own all this real estate; it'll make the
kiddies independent some day. But I wish some of my aunts and
cousins would lay off, to say nothin' of that sapadola Marguerite

---

[1]Brandon Tynan was a well-known actor and playwright. He
was the "serious relief" in the Follies from 1923 on. He wrote
seven plays and a number of screen treatments.

[2]Frank Craven was an actor, playwright, and director, mostly
for John Golden. He wrote dialogue for the Laurel and Hardy
movies, and was the original stage manager in OUR TOWN (1938).

married." Also, to say nothing of "Red" and Bucky.

Now, then, we come to my latest theatrical successes. Harry Frazee agreed to put on a revue by me and Jerry Kern if we could land Bill Fields. Bill said it was all right with him and I started to work, only to discover that Bill had already signed contracts (synchronous contracts) with Goodman, with Ziegfeld and with the Famous Players. He's going to spend the winter in court. Goodman is suing him for $100,000, Ziegfeld has him and he is supposed to be working for Famous Players and getting $6,000 a week.

Well, in August Gene called up and said Ziegfeld was "hot" for the Palm Beach show "we" wrote two or three years ago; he wanted it rewritten into musical comedy form; he "had to have it" to put in the Cosmopolitan theatre to succeed "Louis the Fourteenth," which was slipping. I said it was ridiculous to pretend the show could be fixed up by the first of September (which was the date set by Ziegfeld); besides, I didn't trust him and wouldn't even think about working on it till I saw a check. So then Ziegfeld extended the time limit to October first and gave us $500 apiece, with a written promise to give us $500 apiece more when the completed play was turned over to him, provided it was within the time limit. I got busy and rewrote the play into a musical comedy book; also wrote some lyrics which I thought were not bad. On the first day of October, Ziegfeld had not yet signed a composer, and as you know, it is impossible to turn in a complete book and lyrics these days unless you have a composer with whom to work on the numbers. On the second of October, Ziegfeld engaged Vincent Youmans[1] to write the music. I showed him my lyrics and he didn't seem to care much for them. Neither did Gene. In fact, Gene wanted to write all the lyrics himself, though he didn't say so. Finally I said, "Well, I'm going to write the lyrics of three or four comedy songs and I want them to get a trial anyway." Then I went to the world's series and when I came back, not one tap of work had been done and Gene hadn't even turned over the book to Ziegfeld. Moreover, I think, though I'm not sure, that Youmans told Ziegfeld he had seen the book and didn't like it. Anyway, both Gene and I got telegrams saying we had broken the contract and I was sick and tired of the whole proceeding that I was glad of it, but Gene said he was going to give Ziegfeld a terrible bawling out. He saw him and Ziegfeld soft-soaped him and said that what he wanted to do was get rid of Youmans and when he did, he would produce the show, probably about the first of the year. So Gene thinks that is what is going to happen, but between you and me, dear Scott and darling Zelda, Ziegfeld is not going to produce the

---

[1] Vincent Youmans was a composer and producer of musicals. Among his many hit songs were "Tea for Two," and "I Want To Be Happy." NO, NO, NANETTE was his best known musical. He also produced the movie FLYING DOWN TO RIO (1933), starring Ginger Rogers and Fred Astaire.

show at any time, whether he wants to or whether he doesn't. And
I have written him a letter, to the effect that my stuff was
probably known to more people than was that of any of the popular
song writers of the day with the possible exception of Irving
Berlin and that said stuff never would have got before the public
if magazine and newspaper editors had jazz composers engaged to
pass on manuscripts. I guess that will make him think, eh,
girls?

At present I am Americanizing Offenbach's "Orpheus in the
Underworld," which, if I do it well, is supposed to be produced
by the Actors' Theater with Otto Kahn's backing and under the
direction of Max Reinhardt. I have no confidence that this will
come to pass, but I am looking forward to some pleasure in the
work because there is no other lyric writer concerned and the
composer is dead.

Ellis and I have bought a farm four miles southeast of here.
It is 44 acres.[1] We don't intend to farm, but if possible, to
hold onto it for five or ten years and sell it at a big profit,
the theory being that New York City will grow out to it by that
time. We are doing it as a memorial to the kiddies. After I get
it all paid for, in two or three years I hope, I'm going to quit
saving money and drink in a serious way.

Ed Gallagher of Gallagher and Shean is in an asylum. Not
soon enough.

"Sunny," with Marilyn Miller,[2] Jack Donahue,[3] Mary Hay, etc.,
is a big hit, but it so expensive that they have to take in over
$35,000 a week to break even. Mary isn't so good in it,
according to me and other critics. Donahue is wonderful and, in
my estimation, the most valuable comedian in America.

A play called "Young Blood," with Norman Trevor[4] and Helen
Hayes, opened here in Great Neck Friday night. A young man
sleeps with a maid and later on in the show are these lines:
"Are you sure?" asks the young man. "Yes," she says. "It's been
over six weeks."

Have you heard the story about the Frenchwoman who wanted to
go to America just to see the Statue of Liberty and also meet the

----

[1]Ring sold this farm at a substantial profit some time
before the 1929 stock market crash.

[2]Marilyn Miller came out of the Follies to star in such
musicals as ROSALIE, and SMILES (the 1930 musical for which Ring
wrote some lyrics).

[3]Jack Donahue began as a dancer in the Follies. His first
starring role, as a comedian, was in SONS O' GUNS (1929). He
died suddenly, in 1930, while on tour with the play.

[4]Norman Trevor was an Olympic athlete in 1900 who entered
the theater in England in 1907. He made his Broadway debut in
1913, and began making movies in 1924.

Bitches, who had all those boys in the American army?
Speaking of Liberty, John Wheeler has been removed as editor.
J. M. Patterson of the Chicago Tribune has come to New York to
run it and the Daily News. Harvey Deuel, a Chicago newspaper
man, will succeed Jack as editor of Liberty. I guess my brother
Rex is all right for a while, but if they do anything to him, I'm
going to jump to Cosmopolitan.
Do you know that this is about 2,500 words and I'm not
getting a nickel for it? You must repay me with love.
Bob Esselstyn.

The following verse to H. L. Mencken suggests
that Ring was now mailing the autographed copies of his
books which Mencken had requested over six months
earlier.[1]

Great Neck, New York
[December 1925]

I will send you in December what you asked in May;
I will send it by the U. S. mails today (the mails today)
Oh, when I have passed away,
Please seek out my pals and say
That I sent you in December what you asked in May.

On 2 December Perkins sent Ring a proof of the
dust jacket for THE LOVE NEST AND OTHER STORIES, a
royalty check for $1608.68, and a gift copy of Will
James's THE DRIFTING COWBOY. Perkins thought that Ring
might enjoy lunch sometime with James, whose western
narratives, all published by Scribner's, remained very
popular through the 1940's.

Great Neck, New York
December 4, 1925.
Dear Max:-
Thanks for the check and the wrap, both of which looked good.
I'd like to meet Mr. James, but it will have to be a little
later; I've promised to do a stunt for the Actors' Theater and
have sworn an oath not to leave this house for immoral purposes
till it is completed.
R.W.L.
Ray Long now has my last story--"Rhythm"--which will be in
April Cosmopolitan, out March 10.

On the 23rd Perkins wrote to ask Ring if he might
have another story to lengthen the projected book, and
to encourage Ring to write as long a preface as could
without "forcing it."

---

[1]See Ring's letter to Mencken dated 25 June 1925.

Great Neck, New York
December 26, 1925.

Dear Max:-
    I don't think there is a chance of my writing another short
story in time for publication before the book comes out. You
see, I am now tied up pretty definitely with Cosmopolitan and it
is already scheduling the July issue. I'll write as long a
preface as I can. When do you have to have it? I can't think of
any comments that would go between stories.
    We had a merry, though dry, Christmas and hope you did too
(not necessarily dry).
                            Sincerely,
                            R. W. L.

    The following letter refers to another of Ring's
agreements with film companies:

                            Great Neck, New York
                            January 12, 1926.

Dear Max:-
    I am sorry to trouble you, but the Century Film Corporation
which has brought the rights to my "busher" stories, says it is
necessary, for the records at Washington, to have the enclosed
assignment signed by Scribner's. Will you be good enough to have
it signed and returned to Mr. Siegfried F. Hartman, 120
Broadway, New York?
                            Sincerely,
                            Ring W. Lardner

    Ring wrote a similar letter to Lorimer at the
SATURDAY EVENING POST on the same day. But though
Scribners and the Curtis Publishing Company (publisher
of the POST) did agree to the contract, the saga of
Jack Keefe was never filmed. Some of Ring's works did
become films, though--JUNE MOON in 1931 and (retitled
BLOND TROUBLE) in 1937; ELMER THE GREAT in 1929 (as
FAST COMPANY), in 1931, and (as THE COWBOY QUARTERBACK)
in 1939.[1] "Alibi Ike" was done in 1935, with Joe E.
Brown, and after World War II THE BIG TOWN (retitled SO
THIS IS NEW YORK, starring Henry Morgan) and
"Champion," with Kirk Douglas, appeared. A fine film,
CHAMPION was the most faithfully reproduced of Ring's
works, and the most successful. Unfortunately, Ring
had no part in the movie adaptations of any of his
fiction.

----

    [1]See Ring Lardner, Jr., pp. 152-53, for an anecdote
explaining how Elmer was transformed from a pitcher to a
quarterback.

The Bellview
Belleair Heights, Florida
January 25, 1926.

Dear Max:-
Several proofs have been forwarded to me down here. If it is
all right with you, I will bring them, together with the preface,
when I come up to New York, which will be about February 8. I'm
going to be home two or three days and then set out again for New
Orleans and California.
R.W.L.

Grove Park Inn
Asheville, N. C.
Wednesday.
[February 1926]

Dearest:
Here are a few more things for you to remember:
1. Bring along your check book so that you can pay your
income tax when the time comes.
2. Telephone Mr. Kelly (Vanderbilt 6737) and give him our
address so he can tell us the amount of the tax.
3. Mrs. Landis.
4. Give your trunk check to the man who gets on the train a
few stations before Asheville.
5. Bring along the March American Mercury if it arrives in
time.
In regards to your queries--The weather down here is winter
weather, though never getting extremely cold. I haven't seen any
of the women (there are about fifteen of them in the hotel)
wearing light colored dresses in the daytime, but it has either
rained or snowed nearly every day and they may brighten up when
the weather does. Most of them dress for dinner, even when the
men don't, but their dinner dresses are medium, not startling.
I started to exercise daily, but ever since Sunday the
weather has been impossible. I hope it will be all through
misbehaving before you come. Just now it would be ideal for the
boys, four inches of snow and plenty of steep hills. I don't
know whether you are going to like Asheville at all, but if you
don't we can go somewhere else.
Thanks for sending me the insurance blanks. I have signed
them and returned them to Fred Van Ness, who will mail the
policies back to Great Neck. Better tell Miss Feldmann[1] to put
them away in some drawer when they come.
My daily schedule is very quiet. I get up about nine-thirty,
have breakfast in my room, work, shave and bathe. Go down to

----

[1]Gusti Feldmann, a trained nurse, had been employed by Ring
and Ellis after David's birth in 1919, and remained with the
family for most of the next twelve years.

lunch about one-thirty, return to my room and work and read. Go
down to dinner at seven-thirty, return to my room, go to bed and
read. At odd moments I am busy being inverviewed or refusing
invitations to speak.
Tell Bill and Jim that the strip has been sold to the Evening
Sun and Globe. They were very curious about it. Also tell them
and David that I will write soon and wish they would write to me.
Also John.
Love to you and remember me to Miss Feldmann.
Husband.

Grove Park Inn
Asheville, N. C.
Friday.
[ca 1926]

Dearest:
Thanks to you I have been wholeheartedly welcomed into the
Asheville aristocracy. A lady called up last night and asked if
I was the husband of Ellis Abbott of Goshen and I said yes, so
she and her husband and twelve-year-old child came and got me and
drove me out to a roadhouse. My hostess was formerly Grace
Nisonger and her mother used to be the Abbotts' washerwoman. She
knows Frank and Florence better than you, but you will have a
chance to get acquainted when you arrive.
I forgot to bring Volume 4 of the war history and I wish
you'd bring it if you have room. I'm nearly out of reading
matter.
The snow is practically gone and warmer weather is predicted.
I've been out only once since Sunday and that was on Grace's
party.
This will be my last letter to you, as the mail service
between here and Great Neck doesn't seem very swift. I will
certainly be glad to see you Thursday as I am very lonesome.
Husband.

HOTEL DEL CORONADO
Coronado Beach, California
Feb. 23, 1926.

Heap Big Zelda and Scott:-
I am in the Indian and Mexican country and am learning the
language rapidly.
The elegant picture, "The Fitzgeralds' Christmas," was
forwarded to us here and we really did and do like it. We agree
that Scotty is the second best looking one in the outfit, or
shebang, to use the colloquial.
We and the Rices, including their daughter, went to Belleair,
Florida, the first week in January and staid there three weeks.
Then I had to go home for a few days and view a Tommie Meighan
picture, to which I was engaged to write the titles. The
picture, I believe, will be the worst ever seen on land or sea,

and the titles are excrutiatingly terrible. They will look as if Jack Hazzard[1] had written them.

On the tenth of February, if you are still interested, we set out for New Orleans, stopping fifteen minutes in Montgomery, where we shed a tear. (But I almost forgot to say that while in New York, Ellis and I saw "The Great Gatsby." It was a matinee on a day of the worst weather ever seen in the city or anywhere else; yet the house was over three-quarters full. The blizzard was so bad that all the schools were closed and the commuters had a terrible time getting to New York at all. The man who plays Buchanan lives on Long Island and arrived during Act 2. But we thought the show was great and that Rennie[2] was just about perfect. I regretted that they left out the drunken apartment scene, but I presume Davis[3] figured that one party scene was enough. Every now and then one of Scott's lines would pop out and hit you in the face and make you wish he had done the dramatization himself.

Well, anyway, we got to New Orleans for the Mardi Gras and were rushed by a bunch of morons and I couldn't stand it and fell off the wagon and we all got the flu and had a very sick trip from New Orleans to this place, where we are resting. From here we go to Los Angeles (including Hollywood), Monterey and San Francisco; then home, arriving there the first week in April. The Rices have been with us right along and we are still all speaking.

Write soon, both of you. You, Zelda, come home and show up the Charleston dancers. You, Scott, also come home and write a play.

And Oh, yes, we had two long and entertaining sessions with Sherwood Anderson and wife in New Orleans. We took them along with us to one of the dinners given, for no reason, in our honor and Sherwood was very frank in stating his opinion of the host and local guests.

Tallulah.

The following is the first of a number of surviving letters written over the next several years to Burton

---

[1] An actor neighbor in Great Neck, John E. Hazzard played the lead in THE GOOD FELLOW (1926), George S. Kaufman and Herman Mankiewicz's unsuccessful play.

[2] James Rennie played Gatsby. He was a star of the London stage and on Broadway. He made a number of movies, several with Dorothy Gish, whom he married in 1920. They were divorced in 1935.

[3] Owen Davis's dramatization of THE GREAT GATSBY had opened in New York on 2 February 1926. In his lifetime Davis was the author of over two hundred plays, including ICEBOUND (1923), for which he won a Pulitzer Prize.

Rascoe, Ring's old colleague on the TRIBUNE who was now
also a New York newspaperman, the author of a
syndicated column, "The Daybook of a New Yorker."

Great Neck, New York
Monday, May 10.

Dear Burton:-
Ellis and I traveled constantly from the first of January to
the first of April and have no intention of leaving Great Neck
again for months and months. So it is up to you and Hazel to
come out here. Can you endure waiting till our alterations are
completed? Ellis is taking my room and I am taking hers, but of
course she couldn't live in a room that looked like a man's room
and vice versa; hence the alterations, which, they promise will
be done in three weeks. When they are, I will write to you and
you must bring your overnight bag. Allow me, as an expert on
ferries, to advise against the Greenwich line, which runs
infrequently and lands you way out at Oyster Bay, and to
recommend the Clason Point-College Point line, which is a
municipal institution, runs every forty minutes, brings you from
the Bronx to Flushing and costs you about forty cents, car and
all.

Love to Hazel.

R. W. L.

The reference to Ring and Ellis's arrangement of
separate bedrooms is an interesting revelation on which
Ring Jr. comments.[1] Ellis preferred single beds and,
in 1917, while Ring was serving as a war-correspondent
in France, seized the opportunity to arrange separate
bedrooms in their just-rented Evanston house. It may
or may not have been a shock to Ring when he returned
to find his things moved to another room, but one
should not misinterpret such information. Especially
among the upper social classes, separate bedrooms for
married couples were by the 1920's entirely
conventional.

Monday, May 10, 1926.

Dear Scott and Darling Zelda:-
I just got through reading the current Bookman and it
certainly gave me the impression that you, Scott (or Fitz), are
having a violent affair with Johnnie Farrar.[2] I was touched

_____

[1] Ring Lardner, Jr., pp. 75-76.

[2] In 1926 John Farrar, later to be a successful book
publisher, was editor of THE BOOKMAN. The reference here is to

particularly by his assertion that he was glad you were coming
back this fall, though you and he quarreled a great deal.

Ellis and I are exceedingly grateful to you, Scott, not you,
Zelda, for dedicating "All The Sad Young Men" to us. I had read
all of it except the first story, which, I think, is the best
story. I think also that you were a sap not to have made a novel
of it.

"Gatsby," I see by the papers, closed Saturday night owing to
Rennie's impending trip to England. It's too bad it couldn't
have run on, but it would have been a mistake to continue it with
somebody else in the lead. If there was ever a man that fitted a
part and vice versa, etc.

In case you haven't heard of the Pulitzer awards--George
Kelly got first prize for his play "Craig's Wife." Aleck
Woollcott said he would have given it to Marc Connolly's "The
Wisdom Tooth," which is a damn good play, and Percy said he would
have placed both "Gatsby" and "The Wisdom Tooth" ahead of the
winner. The fact that Owen Davis was on the committee may have
ruined "Gatsby's" chance. It's too bad you couldn't have seen
"Gatsby." I think you'd have been pleased. Red Lewis got the
book prize with "Arrowsmith" and turned it down. I can see his
point. I am against all that kind of stuff, meaning the Pulitzer
awards and the All America football team and "The Best Short
Stories of so-and-so," even when Mr. O'Brien honors me with a
place or three or four stars in the last named.[1]

Reviews of "The Love Nest" have been perfectly elegant. I
don't know whether you've seen the book, but I had an
introduction to it written as if I were dead. The Sunday Times
ran a long review and played up the introduction strong, saying
it was too bad I had died so young, etc. and the result was that
Ellis was kept busy on the telephone all that Sunday evening
assuring friends and reporters that I was alive and well. It
just happened that I was at home and cold sober; if I'd been out,
she might have worried a little. Or maybe not.

Max Perkins tells me you have sold "Gatsby" to the movies.
It ought to make a great picture and it would be a knock-out if
they got Rennie to play in it.

Speaking of pictures, I rewrote a lousy baseball-Florida real
estate story for Tom Meighan, some one else having written it
first, and I also wrote the titles after seeing the uncut film.
When the picture came out, it was a complete surprise to me and
one of the worst pictures I ever saw. But it seems to be going

---

Farrar's review of ALL THE SAD YOUNG MEN, which he termed the
"very best" of Fitzgerald's short stories.

[1]From 1919 through 1941 Edward J. O'Brien annually edited a
volume of of the year's best short stories, with an index in
which one, two, or three asterisks were prefixed to the titles to
indicate distinction. Three asterisks meant that the story was
listed in the "Roll of Honor."

all right and I am told that it compares very favorably with most
of Tom's recent releases.

I can't remember when I wrote to you last, so I may be
telling you old stuff. (Stop me if you have heard this one).
Ellis and I toured California with the Grantland Rices and their
daughter. I'd have had a much better time in Hollywood if I'd
been drinking. Anyway, Charlie Chaplin had us out to dinner and
was more or less amusing and we met all the nuts.

Gene and Helen spent six weeks in Palm Beach while Gene was
working on Ziegfeld's "Palm Beach Nights," a girl show which Flo
put on down there with somebody else's money and which proved a
dismal flop. However, Gene and Jimmy Hanley had a good song in
it-- "No Foolin'"-- and I think he (Gene) will make some money
out of the song. He has bought a Lincoln "town car," but the old
homestead is still on the market. I suggest that you two take it
off his hands when you come back. Anyway, I insist on your
living somewhere in Great Neck. You have no idea how I miss you,
Zelda, not you, Scott.

Tom and Peggy Boyd are expected in New York soon and will be
invited out here to dinner.

Burton and Hazel are also threatening to visit us. I think
Burton is doing pretty well, writing a daily syndicate letter for
Johnson Features and also acting as editor for the concern's
other features.

Harry Hansen has quit the Chicago News and taken Laurence
Stallings' place on the World.

Max Perkins gave me your address over the telephone and I
hope I got it approximately right.

Write and tell me your plans. If you want me to be looking
up a house in Great Neck, let me know and I'll be glad to serve.

I went on the wagon April 18, theoretically for a year, but I
might get a week off when you come back.

                              Gil Boag

     The following letter is to Bob Davis, the
well-known writer and photographer of the 1920's, who
had just published RUBY ROBERT, a book on Bob
Fitzsimmons, former heavyweight boxing champion:

                         Great Neck, New York
                         June 15, 1926.

Dear Bob:-
     Though the defeat of Corbett in 1897 broke my young heart, I
was always interested in his conqueror, curious about his
offstage personality, character, habits, etc. Fitz, it seemed to
me, must have been one of the most diverting of the champs, but
until you came across with "Ruby Robert" there was no first hand
dope on him available. It's an entertaining, readable book, Mr.
Davis and fills a l. f. w.
                         Sincerely,
                         Ring W. Lardner

Between you and me, Bob, I was intrigued by some of the disagreements as to fact between your book and Corbett's "The Roar of the Crowd." I copied off a few for G. Rice, who said he might use them in his column. If he does, it won't hurt the sale of either book.

1926-1933:

YEARS OF ADVERSITY

In the summer of 1926, Ring first discovered during a routine checkup that he had tuberculosis, the disease which, coupled with his alcoholism, was gradually to destroy his health in the following years. Characteristically, Ring did not mention his illness in his letters, and kept it as much as possible to himself.

The following letter to Ellis's older sister indicates clearly Ring's disgust with the outcome of the 1926 Dempsey-Tunney fight, which Tunney had won by a judges' decision. No evidence has ever been revealed to support Ring's view that the fight was fixed. Ring had bet heavily on Dempsey.

> Great Neck, New York
> October fourth. [1926]

Dear Rube:-

I have never talked on a radio and it is my ambition to keep that record spotless.

I don't know how much of my story got into your paper. About a third of it missed the New York World and most of the other papers because of wire trouble. However, the readers are probably just as well off.

None of us could write what we (Eighty percent of us, at least) really thought--that the fight was "one of those things;" a paper printing such a story would lay itself open to a libel suit, and about the only way a boxing match can be proved a fake is to have one of the parties confess. I don't blame Jack much--He needed money; he figured everybody was trying to fleece him; if he won, there was no other fight in sight, and whatever he got for "laying down" was money that the income tax collectors won't know anything about.

Otherwise, everybody here is well. The absent John is evidently homesick and I think Ellis will have to pay him a visit. Love to Robin and the kids.

> R. W. L.

In the following letter Ring corrects Burton Rascoe's account of how Ring's busher stories were first accepted by the POST:

Great Neck, New York
October 7, 1926.

Dear Burton:-
It isn't often I care what the boys and girls say about me in print,
    (Author's note: That's a dirty lie!)
        but honestly, Burton, that stuff you wrote under date of October 2, well, you must have got the information from Willie Stevens.[1] The first "busher" story was never sent back by the Post; it was accepted promptly by Mr. Lorimer himself. I didn't show it to Hugh Fullerton or Charlie Van Loan first; I sent it to Mr. Lorimer at the Post's office, not to his residence; I didn't write "Personal" on the envelope in even one place; I didn't write any preliminary, special delivery, warning letter to Mr. Lorimer; no sub-editor ever asked me to correct the spelling and grammar, and I never sent any sub-editor or anyone else a bundle of letters I had received from ball players. Otherwise--
Ellis' mother died in July and we have had a quiet summer. But we do want you and Hazel to come out some time. Love to her.
                    R. W. L.

The following letter is perhaps most remarkable for its bored, cynical tone. In sports outside baseball, Ring was reputed to have two passions--Notre Dame and Jack Dempsey, both of whom he regarded as representatives of the midwest. The bitterness of the assertion that Dempsey had thrown his first championship fight with Tunney is intensified by the stoical comment at the beginning of the letter that "nothing happens." The tone may also be partially the result of Ring's knowledge that he was ill. For that reason and because he obviously was tired of writing his weekly Bell Syndicate column, he gave up the column in March of the following year to concentrate on magazine pieces, short stories, and plays.

October 13, 1926.

Fitzgeralds one and all:-
I have said to myself a hundred times, "Ring, you just must write to those sweet Fitzgeralds," and then I have added (to myself, mind you), "Better wait, perhaps, until there is something to write about." But the days come and the days go and nothing happens---nothing may ever happen. Best not delay any longer.
Very, very glad to hear you are returning soon to God's Country and the Woman. Don't you dare live anywhere but Great

---

[1] An eccentric figure in the Hall-Mills murder case.

Neck, but if I were you, I'd rent awhile before I thought of
buying. If you want me to, I will be on the look-out for a
suitable furnished house.

Ellis had two babies this summer. They are both girls,
giving us two girls and four boys, an ideal combination, we
think.

On a party with the Rices, at the Sidney Fishes'[1] in East
Hampton, we ran into Esther Murphy and her father and mother. I
had an interesting talk with Miss Murphy (Interesting to me, mind
you).

The Ziegfeld show (Gene's) didn't do well in New York, but is
going better (they say) on the road.

I was in deadly earnest when I said I liked "The Peasants." I
knew damn well it would be over your head (Not yours, Zelda).

May Preston reports that she saw you (not you, Zelda) on your
way to the hospital, in Paris, and that you were carrying a
bouquet of corsets to give your wife.

I enclose a copy (nearly complete) of the story I wrote about
the "fight" in Philadelphia. Heywood Broun refused, at the last
moment, to cover it and as a favor to Herbert, and to my
syndicate, I said I would do it. We had terrible wire trouble on
account of the rain and only about half my story got into the
World. It broke off (the story) in such a manner that people
must have said to themselves that I was very drunk. It made me
so mad that I am going to quit newspapers as soon as the last of
my present contracts expires, which will be in six months. After
that I am going to try to work half as hard and make the same
amount of money, a feat which I believe can be done. I bet $500
on Dempsey, giving 2 to 1. The odds ought to have been 7 to 1.
Tunney couldn't lick David if David was trying. The thing was a
very well done fake, which lots of us would like to say in print,
but you know what newspapers are where possible libel suits are
concerned. As usual, I did my heavy thinking too late; otherwise
I would have bet the other way. The championship wasn't worth a
dime to Jack; there was nobody else for him to fight and he had
made all there was to be made (by him) out of vaudeville and
pictures. The average odds were 3 to 1 and the money he made by
losing was money that the income tax collectors will know nothing
about.

You ought to meet this guy Tunney. We had lunch with him a
few weeks before the fight and among a great many other things,
he said he thought the New York State boxing commission was
"imbecilic" and that he hoped Dempsey would not think his
(Tunney's) experience in pictures had "cosmeticized" him.

I think now (if you care what I think) that the
Gibbons-Tunney fight was fixed and that the Dempsey-Gibbons
fight was fixed, to let Gibbons stay, and that it was all leading
up to this climax--to give the public a popular war hero for

---

[1]Sidney Fish was a prominent attorney from an old New York
family.

champion. Well, he's about as popular as my plays.

We have just had a world's series that neither club had any right to be in, let alone win, and that is all I will say about sports, excepting that Heywood, who has become quite a Negrophile, wrote column after column on the fistic prowess of Harry Wills and the dread that he was held in by Dempsey et al. and how unfair it was not to give Harry a chance, and -- Well, last night Wills deliberately fouled Jack Sharkey in the 13th. round after Sharkey (who isn't even as good as Tunney) had beaten the life out of him from the very beginning.

I have been on the wagon since early in July, when Ellis' mother died. Before that I had a spree that broke a few records for longevity and dullness.

A couple of months ago, the Metro-Goldwyn people asked me to write a baseball picture for Karl Dane, the man who made such a hit as "Slim," one of the doughboys in "The Big Parade." We talked matters over several times and finally the man asked me how much I would want. I told him I didn't know what authors were getting. He said, "Well, we are giving Johnnie Weaver $7,500 and Marc Connelly the same," so he asked me again what I wanted and I said $40,000 and he threw up his hands and exclaimed, "Excuse me, Mr. Lardner, for wasting your valuable time!" Maybe I told you that before; I have no idea how long ago it was I wrote to you.

It might not be very lively for you, but why not come and stay with us awhile before or after you go to Montgomery.

Keep me posted on your plans and accept the undying love of the madam and

                    I.

    When Rascoe informed Ring that he had published a correction of his earlier story, Ring wrote to him again:

                    Great Neck, New York
                    October 29, 1926

Dear Burton:-

    The clipping bureau[1] hasn't come across with the second story, but probably will in its own good time. However, so long as you made the correction, it doesn't matter. I don't like to have the impression spread, more than it has, that it is hard for new writers to break in, when the fact is, as you know, that editors are tickled to death to get anything printable, even if it is written by a day-old child. The false impression impels countless young writers to send their stuff to veteran writers

---

[1]Paradoxically, though Ring did not keep copies of his work, he did from the early twenties subscribe to a clipping service. The clippings which he regularly received have now been donated to The Newberry Library by Ring Jr.

with the request that they (the vets) use their "influence" with
editors to have it read, approved and published.
What I probably told you was that I talked over the idea of
the busher letters with Charlie Van Loan, and that he liked it
and said he would write to Lorimer to be on the look-out for the
first batch. That was when he was merely a Post author; long
before he was an associate editor or scout.
Are you reading Stagg's[1] memoirs? I wish he had written them
himself.

R. W. L.

The following fragment of a letter to the
Fitzgeralds, containing the news of the Chaplin-Davies-
Hearst scandal, was probably written just before Scott
and Zelda returned to the United States, on 10 December
1926, after two and a half years abroad:

Great Neck, New York

Anyway, the "low down" as Gene calls it is that Hearst found out
that Chaplin was giving Marion the "run around" as Gene calls it
and Hearst closed the Davies studio and leased the Cosmopolitan
theater, where Marion's releases were wont to be released, to
Ziegfeld because he, Hearst, had been given the "air" as Gene
calls it by Marion, and he also ordered his papers to cease
mentioning her name. And poor old W. R. as Gene calls him is
alone on his ranch in California and doesn't dare come to New
York because Fallon is laying for him to serve papers in a libel
suit and Fallon is the boy who has the birth certificates of the
W. R.-Marion offspring. Chaplin and Marion are, of course,
obliged to live out of wedlock as I call it on account of the new
Mrs. Chaplin who certainly made a monkey out of Charley. "With
all his money, there's two things W. R. can't buy--One is
Marion's love and the other is Bill Fallon. There's one square
fella (Fallon) and he can't be bought!" (Well, Zelda, you know
yourself what a nice, straight, clean-cut, decent fella Fallon
must be. But a Catholic). "W. P. wanted the worst way to
marry Marion, but Mrs. Hearst wouldn't divorce him. She was too
smart, see? She was too smart. Mrs. Hearst was too smart. She
wouldn't divorce him. She was too smart. And now Marion gets
stuck on Chaplin and Chaplin gives her a $25,000 stone (diamond
not gall) and W. R. hears about it. Can you imagine! Where is
the damn fool Chaplin goin' to fit if the Hearst papers gets
after him? Can you imagine! That's the low down."
I think you've stayed away long enough for all the scandal to
blow over and if you'll come home I'll fall off the wagon for a
week or as long as you think necessary.

---

[1] Amos Alonzo Stagg was the famous coach of the University of
Chicago football team. He had a high opinion of Ring as a
football reporter, and Ring respected him as a coach.

There's a new paper in Great Neck--a tabloid affair called
the News. Jack Hazzard runs a funny column on it. Funny ain't
the word for it.
Here is some more "low down:" Some of the Algonquin bunch was
sort of riding Michael Arlen, I don't know why. Anyway, when
Edna Ferber was introduced to him, she said: "Why, Mr. Arlen,
you look almost like a woman!" "So do you, Miss Ferber," was
Michael's reply.

Mrs. Nell.

That Christmas, Ring sent some postcard verse to
the Rices:

We haven't heard from you in three long years;
Christmas just comes, and Christmas disappears,
But little's came from you in Yuletides recent.
For God's sakes, sweet, start sending something decent!

Perkins, who realized that Ring's mock
autobiography, THE STORY OF A WONDER MAN, which he was
about to publish, was merely a potboiler, was urging
Ring strongly at this time to do a longer fictional
work:

I wish though, that for the next book of
stories, we could have one long one, and the longer
the better. I know that while you are writing for
the Cosmopolitan, this is impossible for periodical
use but couldn't you do one long one just for a
book? If it were twenty or twenty-five thousand
words, we would have something entirely new, and we
could make ever so much of it, and we might be able
to even get a financial return that would warrant
the sacrifice of magazine publication.

When Ring did not respond to the urging, Perkins tried
again:

Jan. 18, 1927

Dear Ring:
Why don't you write about the boy who believed
the 'ads'; read up on all the highbrow stuff and
tried it on the gals!!- And the boy who didn't.

Yours,

Great Neck, New York
January 19.

Dear Max:-
That sounds like a good idea and I'll see some time what I
can do with it. Thanks.

Sincerely,
R. W. L.

In the following letter to Burton Rascoe, Ring refers to an article he had written at the request of John Siddall, editor of AMERICAN MAGAZINE. He refused to write the standard success story for which the magazine was famous. Instead, he wrote an account of his career as a songwriter. The article was rejected.

> Great Neck, New York
> March 30, 1927.

Dear Burton:-
   The article was on "How I Won Success as a Song Writer" and I wrote it more to kid John Siddall than anything else. I destroyed it long ago.
   I am glad to hear you are going to have "The Bookman." I think it is just the spot for you and you ought to make it a wow, as the boys say.
   Love to Hazel.

> Sincerely,
> R. W. L.

The following letter is addressed to Mrs. Grantland Rice, East Hampton. Ring had given up writing "Ring Lardner's Weekly Letter" for the Bell Syndicate at the end of March, and the Lardners vacationed in the summer of 1927 at Lake Placid, where it was hoped the air would be beneficial to Ring's health.

> [Lake Placid, New York]
> Sunday afternoon.
> [25 July 1927]

Dear Mrs. Rice:-
   I enclose a note from your hero.
   Who should be in our car Friday night but Karl and Sylvia and two boys, one of them named Parsons, who looked like Fred Godwin and said he knew Floncey.[1] Sylvia's chin and eyes reminded me so much of Sharkey that I nearly fouled her.
   We spent Saturday with the Conways, meeting all the children and accessories. I played the piano to accompany Sylvia's violin and wish to state that her violin playing is at least as good as my piano playing. In plain words, it is excellent.
   Well, what I started to say was that on Friday afternoon, I had to go way downtown to buy an algebra book for John, and I came uptown on a bus. I sat on the roof and a lady sat down beside me. Her costume looked as if it had been cut out of a wash cloth. She said: "What time is it?" I said. "It is half past three." She said: "Oh, I thought you were a Mexican."
   Conversations like that can never be explained.

----

[1]Grantland and Kate Rice's daughter Florence.

Tomorrow I am going under the knife. The doctor's name is Trembley, and so am I.

Salami I Salute You.

The description in the above letter of the chance conversation is a beautiful example of Ring's ability to capture the human habit of inattention to what others have to say. This sort of non-sequitur dialogue may have inspired "Dinner Bridge," another of Ring's nonsense plays, which he wrote for a Dutch Treat show in 1927, and which Edmund Wilson published in THE NEW REPUBLIC, to the chagrin of H. L. Mencken, who would have published it in AMERICAN MERCURY. When Mencken wrote about it to Ring, Ring replied:

August 2.

Dear Mencken:
The thing in "The New Republic" was written for the Dutch Treat show. Bunny Wilson wanted to print it so I gave it to him. Next time I have anything of the sort, I will think of you.
Meanwhile --
I'll pardon your calling the Comstockers "wowsers,"
But not your attiring yourself in red trousers.
Dr. Lardner.

The following is the only surviving page of a letter Ring wrote to Scott and Zelda at Ellerslie, the old mansion outside Wilmington, Delaware, to which the Fitzgeralds had moved after an unhappy stay in Hollywood:

Sunday, Sept. 25.

Dear Sir and Madam:-
Our son Jimmie has joined our son John at Andover, and Jimmie is pretty homesick, so Ellis is going up there to spend next week-end with him. If she broke that engagement, he would die. So, you see, we can't visit you and we are both sorry. I hope you are, too.
If you care to know anything about my affairs, I had quite a wet summer, but have now been on the wagon since the 22nd. of August. During the dry intermissions, I wrote a baseball play[1]

---

[1] ELMER THE GREAT, a three-act play, in collaboration with George M. Cohan, based on Ring's story "Hurry Kane." The story of a baseball pitcher who, captivated by a chorus girl, momentarily agrees to throw a game (he later changes his mind), it was not to be a success. After opening in Boston and Chicago, with Walter Huston in the leading role, it ran for only forty performances at the Lyceum in the fall of 1928. Cohan and Ring

which George Cohan accepted. He says he is going to put it on
this fall, but you know these d------------------------------d
producers. If he does, and if he should happen to try it out at
Atlantic City, I'd expect the Fitzgeralds to be in attendance as
a belated reward for the Lardners' sacrifice of time and money in
1924 or whatever year "The Vegetable" was staged.
   I have written three short stories this month in an effort to
ease the financial situation brought about by weeks of idleness
and weeks of work on the play. To make that situation a little
more desperate, the Pittsburgh ball club seems ready to lose the
National League pennant and finish behind the Giants. Last
spring I bet $800 to $2400 that Pittsburgh would win the pennant
and $800 to $800 that it would beat out New York. A week ago, it
looked as if I could begin spending my $3200 winnings, but now,
with New York having all the best of the remaining schedule, I
appear to be sunk.[1] To offset that, I am thinking of covering the
world's series for Jack Wheeler. Two years ago I swore I would
never work on another one, but when poverty . . . .

        On 11 October, after visiting the Fitzgeralds,
   Perkins had written expressing his fears to Ring about
   Fitzgerald's health. Ring replied:

                              Great Neck, New York
                              Thursday, Oct. 13, 1927

Dear Max:-
   I am sorry to hear that Scott isn't well. I wouldn't
recommend Muldoon's as a cure for nerves, especially Scott's kind
of nerves. From what I have always heard, it is so strenuous
that when a person is released, he is inclined to go on a bat to
make up for it. I don't believe I have any influence over Scott,
but I'll try to see him some time soon, either down there or
here.
   The play isn't finished. I have done it through the first
time, but it is still to be torn to shreds by Cohan and done over
again by him and me.
   Cosmopolitan has enough stories, already printed or to be
printed, to fill a book, but only about two of them are worth

---

were ill-matched as co-authors, since Cohan was not sensitive to
Ring's subtle humor and deleted most of it, so that the play
became a melodrama, and Elmer became the "honest-Abe" savior of
the game. "Hurry Kane" is not one of Ring's better stories,
though it is indicative of Ring's deepening pessimism towards
baseball.

[1]Pittsburgh did win the pennant, by 1 1/2 games over
St. Louis and 2 games over New York. The Pirates then proceeded
to lose the Series in four straight games to the Yankees.

putting in a book. I'd rather wait until there are enough decent
ones or until I've done something "different." If ever.
R. W. L.

GREATNECK NY   1927 OCT 14 AM 11 52
H L MENCKEN.
1524 HOLLINS ST BALTIMORE MD.
A PLAY CALLED WILD HONEY OPENS IN BALTIMORE NEXT MONDAY NIGHT FOR
A WEEKS RUN THE AUTHOR SOPHIE TREADWELL[1] WOULD LIKE TO HAVE YOU
SEE IT IF YOU WISH TO PLEASE WIRE ME WHAT NIGHT YOU CAN ATTEND
AND SHE WILL MAIL YOU SOME TICKETS.
RING LARDNER.

Perkins next wrote to ask Ring's permission to
publish the play which Robert Sherwood had adapted from
"The Love Nest." This play would not be a stage
success; it would run only three weeks, beginning on 22
December 1927, though June Walker was to receive good
reviews as the dipsomaniac wife. The play was faithful
to the short story, with the exception of the
resolution, when in the play Mrs. Gregg leaves her
husband and elopes with the butler.

Great Neck, New York
December 17, 1927.

Dear Max:-
I honestly haven't the slightest objection to your pub-
lishing "The Love Nest".
Some time this winter I may write one decent short story and
if I do, we can talk about a book for next fall.
I thought Hemingway's book was great and am glad it went, and
is going, well. Also that Scott is in better shape.
R. W. L.

At Christmastime Ring sent another of his annual
postcards of printed verse to several of his friends,
among them H. L. Mencken and the Fitzgeralds:

[20 December 1927]

We combed Fifth Avenue this last month
A hundred times if we combed it onth,
In search of something we thought would do
To give to a person as nice as you.

----

[1]Sophie Treadwell was married to William McGeehan in San
Francisco in 1910. She had a long and active career as a
dramatist.

We had no trouble selecting gifts
For the Ogden Armours and Louie Swifts,
The Otto Kahns and the George E. Bakers,
The Munns and the Rodman Wanamakers.[1]

It's a simple matter to pick things out
For people one isn't so wild about.
But you, you wonderful pal and friend, you!
We couldn't find anything fit to send you.
                              The Ring Lardners

          Scott replied in kind the following Christmas:

              To the Ring Lardners
         You combed Third Avenue last year
              For some small gift that was not too dear
         --Like a candy cane or a worn out truss--
              To give to a loving friend like us
         You'd found gold eggs for such wealthy hicks
              As the Edsell Fords and the Pittsburgh Fricks
         The Andy Mellons, the Teddy Shonts
              The Coleman T. and Pierre duPonts[2]
         But not one gift to brighten our hoem
         --So I'm sending you back your God damn poem.

                              Great Neck, New York
                              December 21. [1927]

Dear Scott and Zelda:-
     Thanks for your telegram, which arrived this morning. This
ain't my play, though of course I will share in the receipts
(There won't be many). I saw a dress rehearsal last night. Bob
has done some very clever writing and the second act is quite
strong, with June Walker great as a drunk. But I'm afraid most
of it will be over peoples' heads. This, of course, is under
your hat (to use a slang expression)
     Gene has another of those things, I fear.
     Scott, Lynne Overman[3] said he had written to you in regard to
a dramatization of "The Jelly Bean" and you had named your terms.
He wanted my advice as to whom to get to collaborate with him and
I suggested that he get you yourself. His knowledge of stage

---

     [1]All these people were prominent socialites in Chicago and
New York.

     [2]Fitzgerald is supplying his own list of prominent people,
in response to Ring's references.

     [3]A character actor in more than fifty films. He played in
burlesque, in vaudeville, and as a minstrel man between dramatic
engagements.

tricks and your lines would make a good combination. He's a
pretty good actor. He is about to appear in a Shubert musical,
which he thinks is bad but will be successful, so there is no
immediate hurry. However, he would like to hear from you. In
care of the Lambs will get him.
    My thing with Cohan is supposed to go into rehearsal in
February, but you never can tell. Walter Huston is to be our
star. You will be notified in plenty of time for that opening
and you've got to attend it.
    John and Jim are home from Andover. John "made" the
Phillipian (the semi-weekly paper) board, being rated No. 1
among the contestants.
    I have been on the wagon since August 22 and haven't smoked
since October 31. All I know about you is that a novel is near
completion. What is its title and what is it about?
    And you, Zelda, my queel, are you as beautiful as customary?
Write me a decent letter and tell me your news.
Ellis sends love.
                        F. Farmer Fox.

    The reference to abstinence from smoking recalls
that Lardner apparently had almost as much difficulty
avoiding smoking as he did drinking. On one occasion,
Lardner prefaced his return from a trip with a telegram
to Mrs. Lardner: "I DON'T SMOKE," but when he arrived
he had a cigarette in hand.[1]

    The following letter was written to Burton Rascoe
probably in the spring of 1928:

                        Great Neck, New York
                        Thursday.

Dear Burton:-
    Miss Feldmann had your notebook all wrapped up and ready to
address when I got downstairs Monday, so I didn't have a chance
to read it.
    I think the French would be mystified by a translation of my
book, but I have nc objection to your sending a copy to whoever
M. Galantiere is. If he is interested, he can take the matter
up with Charley Scribner's boys.
    We are leaving for Cleveland and points west Sunday evening,
to be gone until the twenty-second. If I live through the trip,
we'll be glad to see you in the city.
    I still maintain that Great Neck is the proper place for you

_____

[1]See Donald Elder, p. 199.

and Hazel to live. Also that you are criminally insane not to
save the Day Book.[1]

                              R. W. L.

     In the spring of 1928 Ring and Grantland Rice
bought adjoining tracts of land in East Hampton, about
ninety miles east of Great Neck, where they built
neighboring houses fronting on the ocean. The move
reflected Ring's desire to remove himself from the
excessive social demands of Great Neck to a more
peaceful location. Ring called this new home "Still
Pond"--"no more moving."[2] Associated with the move was
a reduction of time spent in New York, a confining, at
first, of his socializing to the circle of his close
friends such as the Rices, the Percy Hammonds, the
James Prestons,[3] and the John Wheelers, and a
concentration on writing plays, songs, and stories,
instead of newspaper articles.

     Perkins was now putting together a collection of 35
of Ring's short stories, later to be titled ROUND UP,
containing all of those printed in HOW TO WRITE SHORT
STORIES or THE LOVE NEST, and sixteen new ones. Most
of the new stories had been written in the interval
between his temporary retirement from newspaper work
and his return to write for the New York MORNING
TELEGRAPH in December 1928. The volume, which was
selected by the Literary Guild as one of its monthly
offerings, had the aura of a contemporary classic, and
solidified Lardner's position as one of the outstanding
fictionists of his day.
     The new stories are mostly variations of earlier
stories and themes, though they are perhaps somewhat
more satiric in their commentary on American life and
character types. In "Contract," for instance,
Shelton's disgusted remarks about the "educational
complex" of bridge players sound suspiciously like
Lardner speaking:

     It's a conviction of most bridge players, and
     some golf players, that God sent them into the

_____

[1]Rascoe had written a syndicated column, "The Daybook of a
New Yorker," from 1924 through early 1928.

[2]Elder, p. 306.

[3]James Moore Preston was an artist and illustrator who made
his first impact in the Armory Show of 1913. He had one-man
shows in New York and London, as well as in East Hampton.

world to teach. At that, what they tell you isn't intended for your edification and future good. It's just a way of announcing "I'm smart and you're a lunkhead." And to my mind it's a revelation of bad manners and bad sportsmanship.

In "Nora" Hazlett, writer of a musical comedy, endures the destruction of his play by a philistinic producer and his staff who change the Irish heroine's nationality because they have a Spanish actress idle under contract, and who rewrite the script to insert various tunes they have composed. These caricatures are so damning that one immediately recalls Lardner's frustrations in theater ventures with Florenz Ziegfeld and George M. Cohan. One suspects that Lardner's reaction may have been similar to Hazlett's:

> Hazlett said good-by to his producer and collaborators, went home by taxi and called up his bootlegger.
> "Harry," he said, "what kind of whiskey have you got?"
> "Well, Mr. Hazlett, I can sell you some good Scotch, but I ain't so sure of the rye. In fact, I'm kind of scared of it."
> "How soon can you bring me a case?"
> "Right off quick. It's the Scotch you want, ain't it?"
> "No," said Hazlett. "I want the rye."

Among the better new stories is "I Can't Breathe," the often-anthologized diary of a rather predatory young female flirt, in which Lardner captures masterfully the hyperbole of the average adolescent, during, in this case, the recounting of her romances with four young men. Another is "Liberty Hall," about a writer of musicals who, with his sympathetic wife, must during a weekend in the country endure hosts who insist on imposing their tastes upon their visitors. Ben Drake is forced to drink coffee with cream; he must smoke a cigarette brand he dislikes; and he cannot play the piano because he is there for a rest. Drake finally resorts to faking a telegram calling him back to work. In contrast "Ex Parte" deals with a marriage in which there is no real bond or understanding. The narrator is a bridegroom with conventional tastes, whose wife prefers Early American antiques. When they visit some friends living in a renovated barn, she admires their furnishings extravagantly, with the clear implication that she regards her groom's furnished house as vulgar and common. Her husband resentfully gets drunk on "Early American rye" and tries to "antique" their new house by applying a blowtorch and an axe to the dining room table.

The "traffic policeman story" is "There Are Smiles," a rather sentimental treatment of a semi-literate, good-natured traffic cop who becomes infatuated with an attractive female speeder who is amused by his trite jokes. Since the policeman's life and marriage is depicted as one without much direction or communication, the girl seems to represent an escape from a life which the cop vaguely senses to be without purpose. Thus, when he reads of the girl's death in a traffic accident, the reader pities him in his wonderment: "I can't feel as bad as I think I do. I only seen her four or five times. I can't really feel this bad."

The best of the new stories is "The Maysville Minstrel," which deals with the same theme of the trapped common man who discovers an illusory escape. Stephen Gale is a small-town bookkeeper for the Maysville gas company who reads poetry (Amy Lowell and Edgar A. Guest, whose work Lardner disliked with equal fervor) and writes his own verse, on the order of the following "classic":

The Lackawanna Railroad where does it go?
It goes from Jersey City to Buffalo.
Some of the trains stop at Maysville but they are few
Most of them go right through
Except the 8:22
Going west but the 10:12 bound for Jersey City
That is the train we like the best
As it takes you to Jersey City
Where you can take a ferry or tube for New York City.

In this condition of ignorance and vaguely dissatisfied preoccupation with insignificant time tables, Stephen is duped by a water-heater salesman into believing that he can sell his poems for a dollar a line. His eventual realization that he has been tricked draws our sympathy, because he has been led to believe, like Thomas Hardy's Jude, that he can escape from the mundane existence to which not just his poverty but his own natural limitations condemn him. Unlike "Haircut," this story entails no possibility for revenge. Stephen makes an effort, but, in the last line of the story, realizes the hopelessness: "But even as he spoke, Stephen realized there was nothing he could do about it." It is at once the most sympathetic and the bleakest of Lardner's stories.

It is to the projected preface for this collection that Ring refers below:

East Hampton, Long Island
June 3.

Dear Max:-
    Sure I'll do a preface if you don't want it too soon.   I am
still trying to think of a title.   I believe the traffic
policeman story, which people seem to think is best, ought to
have a good position.
                    R. W. L.

East Hampton, Long Island
July 9, 1928.

Dear Burton:-
    I didn't do any work whatever between February and the first
of June and as a result, I won't be able to catch up with myself
for months. So will you please excuse me from the Almanack.
    I hope that what I heard in Chicago (from Maude Evers Ellis
or somebody) is true--that the Rascoe family struck oil and is
growing filthy rich.
    Love to Hazel.

      The following letter is to Ted Coy, former Yale
University fullback (1907-1909) and twice All-American
(1908-1909). Coy, a New York stock broker in August
1928, had just married his third wife, Lottie Bruhn, in
El Paso, where they were probably still staying when
Ring wrote to him. During their 1912 spring training,
when Ring was with the club, the White Sox had spent
some time in El Paso.

12 East 86th Street
America's Pre-Eminent Apartment Hotel[1]
New York City
October 23, 1928.

Dear Ted:-
    Your letter finally caught up with me here.
    It is all right for Grant to send you his picture; he has
looks.   But I am not going to send you mine as the physical
distress it would cause your wife might spoil the honeymoon.   I
will ship you a book as soon as I can get downtown and buy one.
My madam does not allow them in the house.
    You are living in my favorite town, but I hope you can tear
away from it and come east soon so I can hear the piano played
all night--and I'm on the wagon at that.
              Sincerely,
              Ring Lardner

----

[1] The New York Croydon

In December 1928 Ring for financial reasons
returned briefly to newspaper work as a columnist on
the New York MORNING TELEGRAPH, which had offered him
$50,000 a year to write four articles a week on any
subject he wished. However, the column, "Ring's Side,"
lasted only two months, before the paper's financial
problems forced a termination of the agreement.

The following letter was written to Mrs. Mildred
Luthy, the sister of Kate Hollis Rice (Mrs. Grantland
Rice). Through the Grantland Rices, Ring and Ellis had
come to know both Mrs. Luthy and Mrs. Lizabeth
("Myrt") Vereen, another of Kate Rice's sisters.

12 East 86th Street
New York City
January twelfth.
[1929 or 1930]

Dear Millie:-
Granny has gone to Alabam' to shoot mules and Ellis and I
have advised Kate to take the telephone receiver off the hook
during his absence, but she is a Hollis and stubborn.
If you and Myrt are going to quarrel over my letters, there
is only one thing I can do - use a carbon and send a copy of one
letter to each of you. But please try to get hold of yourselves.
I am quite nice, but not as nice as you think.
You can't expect me not to sympathize with Jane over her
attitude toward your absences from home. If you left me for an
evening, I'd cry, too. In fact, I've cried every evening since
September. And most mornings.
Honestly I don't think you ought to treat Myrt the way you do
in the matter of food. She is growing and building up tissue,
and besides, she is by nature a great big eater. I recall one
evening I took her and the Rices to the theater, and before the
theater we went to dinner somewhere and I kind of hoped that
inasmuch as I was paying for the theater tickets, Granny would
settle for the meal, but as usual on such occasions, he was
writing poetry when the check came, so it was brought to me, and
it amounted to $24.00 of which the Rices and Ellis and I had
eaten four and a half dollars' worth. You can't cut a woman like
that down to a plate of beans in one day.
I ought to have spent this whole day working and I guess it's
just as well I am not on corresponding terms with Mrs. Hand,
Mrs. Lanier and Mrs. Crisp.
Ringgold.

A title for the collection of short stories was
again a problem. The one chosen, ROUND UP, was
Perkins' idea, and was chosen from such other
suggestions as "Our Kind," "Some of Ours," "Such as
We," and "Sorts and Conditions." Perkins anticipated
the criticism that the title was "especially western"

and argued that "it is now used about almost every sort of gathering together,- even that of crooks." In fact the title is inappropriate, though its cowboy connotations may have enhanced sales. When Ring offered a better title, it was too late:

NASSAU   1929 FEB. 9 PM 11 27

MAXWELL PERKINS=
    CHARLES SCRIBNERS SONS FIFTH AVE NEW-YORK (NY)=
I PREFER ENSEMBLE TO ROUND UP DONT YOU.
                          RING LARDNER.

        In addition to printing 20,000 copies of ROUND UP, Scribner's also did an additional 70,000 (with an alternate cover) for the Literary Guild, whose selection committee of Carl Van Doren, Hendrik Willem Van Loon, Elinor Wylie, Joseph Wood Krutch, and Burton Rascoe had chosen Ring's book for one of the Guild monthly selections. The choice was a sign of Ring's stature by this time as a writer of fiction, and Perkins wrote to say: "We have never thought that you have had the sale your books are entitled to, and we are going to try to get it now, and to build for the future."
        In fact ROUND UP had a combined sale of nearly 90,000 copies in its first year, and Ring's royalties for 1929 alone amounted to $11,873.21. His status was further assured by unanimously positive reviews. The TIMES review, by John Chamberlain, was typical in stating: "'Round Up' gives the full measure of his talent--a talent that is mature and sure-footed." Lewis Mumford, in the New York HERALD TRIBUNE, asserted that "the short stories brought together in 'Round Up' must be counted among the few that will be readable twenty years hence."

        The following letter, to a director of the Bread Loaf Conference, a writers' summer conference in upper New York state, reiterates Ring's distaste for public speaking:

                              New York, New York
                              May 2, 1929.

Dear Mr. Davison:-
    I am sorry to say I cannot possibly come to the Bread Loaf Conference this summer. It is not a question of money, but I am utterly incapable of talking, even to a small audience. It is something I tried years ago and "swore off."
                          Sincerely,
                          Ring Lardner

East Hampton, Long Island
June 19, 1929.

Dear Max:-
I had a letter from Mr. Bennet,[1] whom (it seems) I met in
Waco, Texas, years ago. He said he hadn't been able to peddle
any of the "Round Up" stories to the talkie people. I am not
tied up for movie rights and would be glad if Scribner's could
sell some of the stories.
"Show business" has kept me so busy that I haven't even
considered the novelette. But show business is slow on financial
returns and maybe I'll be asking you for some advance soon.
I haven't heard a word of Scott. Hasn't he ever finished the
novel?[2]

Sincerely,
R. W. L.

During much of 1929 Ring was collaborating with
George Kaufman on their play, JUNE MOON. It seems
significant that, even after the substantial success of
ROUND UP, it was to drama and popular music that he
wished primarily to devote his energies.
JUNE MOON was presented in the fall of 1929 with
considerable success, running for 273 performances in
New York. The reviews were favorable, and Burns Mantle
included the play in his volume BEST PLAYS OF 1929-30.
Two songs from the play, "June Moon" and "Montana
Moon," also achieved some separate popularity.
Consequently, Perkins wrote:

> I am delighted with the reviews of your play.
> Don't you think we ought to publish it?-- if it's
> to be the success it looks like, we should for
> there should be sufficient sale, at least.
> I have much better news about Scott. He is
> getting on well.

During much of September 1929 Scott was momentarily his
old self and worked hard on the new novel (though he
would not finish it until 1934).

---

[1]An agent to whom Perkins had given a copy of ROUND UP, in
hopes of negotiating film adaptations with movie producers. The
advent of talkies in this year seemed to offer considerable
opportunity for the presentation of Ring's fictional world.

[2]Fitzgerald had dropped the matricide novel on which he had
working for so long, in favor of "The Drunkard's Holiday," a new
novel which by 1934 would evolve into TENDER IS THE NIGHT.

                              The Croydon
                              12 East 86th Street
                              New York City
                              December 31, 1929.

Dear Max:-
     George Kaufman is trying to get a script into shape for
publication, but it is such a mess now that it may take a little
time.
     Have you seen Scott since he came back, or is he back?   I
haven't heard a word from him.
                              Sincerely,
                              R. W. L.

          The next letter was to Ring's eldest son John, who
     was then a freshman at Harvard:

                              The Croydon
                              12 East 86th Street
                              New York City
                              January 17, 1930.

Dear John:-
     You haven't written to me, but I am without pride and will
write to you just the same. You are cordially invited to spend
your off-week at the Croydon and your mother, the financier,
encloses a check to pay for your trip and extraneous expenses.
Please wire or write us what train you will come on, and if it is
a train that stops at 125th. Street, get off there, informing us
in your telegram or letter just where you are going to get off
and when.
                              R. W. L.

     The letter contains a handwritten P. S. by Ellis:

          As you didn't tell me Mr. Gornator other name
     or I dont remember, I am sending you $95.00 -
     $75.00 for him and $20.00 for you and the railroad.

                              New York, New York.
                              January 22, 1930.

Dear Scott:-
     Mrs. Mabel Johns, a friend of mine (as who isn't?) will be
in Paris in a month or so and she doesn't know a soul there. She
will mail you this letter from wherever she happens to be at
whatever time she wants to mail it, and your job is to reply to
her in care of the American Express Company, tell her where she
can find you, and then advise her where to go and what to see.
     I hear from Max Perkins that your book is nearly finished.
What are you calling it, the Encyclopedia Brittanica? (That
seems to be spelled wrong.

I won't write any more because you owe me a letter. Love to Zelda.

R. W. L.

The following note appears at the bottom of the above letter:

I certainly hope to meet you in Paris because Ring said you are <u>wonderful</u>.

Mabel Johns.

Will be in Paris about Mar. 20-   Feb. 28-

The Croydon
12 East 86<u>th</u> Street
New York City.
February 27, 1930.

Dear Scott:-

I've forgotten who owes whom a letter. Anyway there is a girl (three or four years younger than I) who expects to be in Paris, at the Continental, on or about March 19--it is her first trip abroad and she asked me to pick on a friend or two in each port to look her up so she would not be entirely unacquainted. Her name is Mrs. Mabel A. Johns; she is divorced; I met her twenty years ago; she used to be from St. Louis, but now lives in Long Beach, California. If you and Zelda could call her up or write to her and give her part of a day, or night, you would put me in a fever of gratitude.

I hear (from Max Perkins) that your book is nearly done and (from Walter Winchell) that you have sold the serial rights to Liberty for an unheard of sum. I hope this is true and that you will see fit to pay us a visit soon.

"June Moon," the play I wrote with George Kaufman, will run about six more weeks here, I think; then will play Philadelphia, Boston and perhaps Pittsburgh before folding up. It is still doing all right, but nearly everyone will have seen it in a little while. We have no kick coming; it opened in New York on Oct. 9 and, until the first of the year, broke all records for a non-musical show. We put out a second company, which played a week in Cleveland and is now in Cincinnati, after ten weeks in Chicago, where it did well. It will play a week each in Milwaukee, St. Louis and Kansas City and then go to the Coast. The notices, here and in the other towns, were grand. George and I worked on the play nearly all last spring and summer and when the New York opening was over, I went on a bat that lasted nearly three months and haven't been able to work since, so it's a good thing that the play paid dividends. I wish you had had George to collaborate with you on, or to direct, "The Vegetable," and not Sam Forrest, who, to me, is one of the mysteries of show business.

I'd like to hear first hand what your plans are and news of a personal nature; and I'm anxious to know all there is to tell

about the premiere danseuse and her daughter, to both of whom I
send love.
R. W. L.

Unlike the Cohan collaboration, the work with
George Kaufman was a compatible and profitable one.
Ring wrote most of the play, and Kaufman provided the
sort of revision which resulted in a strong dramatic
structure. Basically, the difference was that Kaufman
understood Ring's humor and satire. Ring's finances
were improved considerably by the success of JUNE
MOON--a fortunate development, since he became
increasingly ill in 1930 and spent considerable time in
hospitals for treatment of tuberculosis and heart
trouble.

The following letter must have been written on
older stationery, since the move to East Hampton had
occurred over two years previously. Rascoe was
interested in publishing one of Ring's "nonsense"
plays. Ring's reply indicates that he seems not even
to have kept copies of his books!

Great Neck, New York
July 25, 1930.

Dear Burton:-
You are welcome to I Gaspiri (if Scribner's says so). I
think it was in a book called "What Of It?" and I have no copy.
R. W. L.

Ring also had some correspondence (apparently much
more than now survives) with Jean Dixon, the Broadway
actress who had been a member of the original cast of
JUNE MOON, and who was at this time starring in ONCE IN
A LIFETIME. Ring sent the following telegram the fall
after JUNE MCON:

24 Sept. 1930

Miss Jean Dixon
Music Box Theatre
New York, N.Y.

Shuberts just turned down my musical show Stop Will you play lead
Ring Lardner[1]

Letters to Ring's sons occur more frequently now.
In the fall of 1930, when the Depression was adversely
affecting so many other people, the Lardners were still
enjoying the benefits of a highly successful book and a

---

[1]From a copy transcribed by Ring Lardner Jr.

play in the previous year. After his freshman year at
Harvard, John had persuaded his parents to allow him to
go to France that fall, to study French at the
Sorbonne, because he felt a knowledge of the language
would further his newspaper career.[1]

Jim and Ring Jr. ("Bill") were now both at the
Phillips Academy, a preparatory school located in
Andover, Massachusetts. David had been enrolled (as a
boarder) in the seventh grade at the Riverdale Country
School in upper New York City.

Sunday, September 28.

Dear Jim:-
I am afraid you will have to wait years for your share of the
royalties. The producers say that times are too hard to risk an
expensive musical play. It is just possible that the real reason
for their shyness is that they don't appreciate what we have
written.
John is going to Philadelphia for the first two games (at
least) of the world's series, and he sails for France on the 17th
of October, aboard The France itself.
It seems to me you have a very tough schedule and I don't see
how you are going to have time for the Phillipian, football and
sleep.
I subscribed for the Phillipian, but told King Howard not to
start sending it until we know where we will live this fall and
winter.
You might as well reserve two rooms (if you can) for
commencement. Your mother will write to you in detail about it.
Let me know if you and Bill fail to receive The New Yorker,
and write again soon.
Buddy Beale.

Later that fall Ring wrote an unlocated letter to
John in Paris, from which, fortunately, Donald Elder
quotes extensively:[2]

The thing that took me to Boston and gave me a chance to
visit Andover, and the Kitchells at South Byfield, was a summons
from Ziegfeld to "help out" with the lyrics of the Marilyn
Miller-Astaires show, "Smiles." While the company was still in
rehearsal here in New York, the Astaires threatened to walk out
because they didn't have a single song together and demanded two.
I wrote them two, to Vincent Youmans' music, for a flat price,
and thereby got myself into a world of trouble because one of the

---

[1]Ring Lardner Jr., p. 199.

[2]Elder, pp. 265-67. The words in brackets are Elder's.

two was so very comical that, on opening night in Boston, it
stopped the show. This was too much for Marilyn's temperament
and she told Ziegfeld she would walk out unless I wrote her a
comical one (she being as well equipped to sing a "funny" as Miss
Feldmann). Ziegfeld called me up from Boston and asked me to
come there and write a song for Marilyn and rewrite three other
lyrics that were not so good. I, knowing him well, asked for an
unheard of advance royalty. He accepted my terms and I went to
Boston and wrote eight songs instead of four, and have written
two more since I came home (Youmans singing me his tunes over the
long distance telephone). Your knowledge of mathematics will
tell you that I have written twelve songs altogether (three of
them purely production numbers), but there isn't a chance that
more than seven of them will be used because there won't be room
for even that many. My work in Boston was rendered quite
feverish owing to the fact that it was next to impossible to get
Youmans (who was quarreling with Ziegfeld) out of bed and to the
piano.

The book of the show, by William Anthony McGuire, was
unbelievably terrible as I saw it in Boston, but it may be better
when it opens here next Tuesday night. I will send you my songs
when, and if, they are published.

[The book of the show concerned four American Army buddies
who adopt a French orphan girl and bring her back to the United
States where she is brought up as a Salvation Army lassie.]

. . . Paul [Lannin] resigned his job as musical director
at Youmans' suggestion (everybody knew there was something the
matter with the show and picked on Paul, who was not at fault),
but I gather from latest reports that he is reinstated and that
some of the quarrels have been patched up. The real trouble is
the book and the fact that the three stars are cutting one
another's throats and each trying to help him- or herself instead
of the production. For example, the best of my contributions, a
duet and ensemble for the opening of the first act, will be left
out through the protests of Fred Astaire--the number calls for
the presence of some Park Avenue women in evening dress and he
doesn't want anybody to appear dressed up before his own
entrance.

All and all my trip to Boston was kind of wearing, but I
wouldn't have missed it because it was so ludicrous. I got two
hours of sleep out of each twenty-four and spent the rest of the
time coaxing Youmans to the piano. One morning when I was
retiring at four o'clock, Harland Dixon, who was directing some
of the dances, came into my room and said, "I'm drunk and I'm
going to tell you some tragic incidents in my life, though I know
I'll regret it tomorrow." I said, "I know I will, too," but that
didn't stop him and he went on relating tragic incidents until
suddenly I had a bright idea--I drank some paraldehyde and went
to sleep with him still standing there with his incidents.

                                   Hotel Elysée
                                   New York City
                                   Sunday, November ninth.

[To Jeannette Abbott Kitchell]
Dear Jane:-
     This is a belated bread and butter (or rather, chicken and
jello) note. Thanks for the only meal I had in New England. And
please tell Kitch that the three-lettered Cornell man I tried to
think of was Kaw.
     It would take me years to relate the incredible things that
happened after I got back to Boston, and since I have got home.
Here is the barest synopsis: I finished the "happy" lyric on the
train from Newburyport. It was acceptable (though terrible).
Then Flo, on Sunday evening, told me what I and everyone else had
been telling him for weeks--that Marilyn's first dance with Fred
(to the tune of "Young Man of Manhattan") took her entirely out
of her character and, besides, was too hot for her. I must get
together with Vince and write a "light" duet that would give the
pair a chance to do a dance that she could do. Also, I must get
Vince to write a tune to which I could set a lyric, a "smart"
lyric, with which to open the first act, in place of that
remarkable "East River Flows" number where the girls appeared
with tail feathers or something. Vince was still in his room,
where he had been since Friday, in pajamas. From seven till ten
Sunday evening, I struggled to get him at the piano, and the
instant I got him there, an explosion in a cleaning and dyeing
establishment across LaGrange Street, right outside his window,
knocked both of us off our chairs. Before we could get to the
window to see what had happened, the dyeing establishment was a
mass of flames. We had a beautiful place from which to watch a
big fire, and of course there was no hope of getting back to work
till it was all over. Vince got statistical and counted over
thirty pieces of fire apparatus. It was cold leaning out the
window and I had to be his nurse and force a bathrobe and
overcoat on him.
     After midnight, I succeeded in interesting him in music and
was about to accomplish something when several girls and the
nutty dance director came in and made it a party. I gave up at
two o'clock and went to my room and to bed.
     On Monday I made him get up before noon and dress. Then he
went to the theater and rearranged the first act finale. Flo
told me to forget the duet for Marilyn and Fred and concentrate
on the opening. I wrote a lyric that would go to the old
"Bambalina" rhythm and tried to make the lyric good enough so
that the tune wouldn't matter. Between five and nine I got a
tune out of Vince; then I went to the show. Paul Lannin had
forgotten the rearrangement of the first act finale. The curtain
came down on confusion and I went back stage and found the three
stars in hysterics. Flo naturally called Vince up about Paul's
mistake and Vince made Paul write a letter of resignation for his
own (Paul's) sake, so Vince said. I don't know yet whether Vince

was double-crossing Paul. Anyway I felt kind of low about Paul and decided to take some paraldehyde to make me sleep (it works instantly). I asked a boy to get me some orange juice to mix with the paraldehyde, which is terrible tasting stuff. There was a knock at my door and I said, "Come in," thinking it was the boy with the orange juice. Instead, it was the dance director with a confidential, weeping jag. He said: "I'm going to tell you some tragic incidents in my life, and tomorrow I know I'll be sorry I told them to you." I said: "I know I will, too," but that didn't stop him and he went on for an hour. The boy came with the orange juice and I got into bed and drank the paraldehyde and fell asleep with the dance director still telling me tragic incidents.

I wrote another lyric Tuesday and finally got out of town Tuesday midnight. I had been home less than three hours when Flo called up from Boston and said he wanted the Fred-Marilyn duet after all. Fortunately Vince had an old tune in his New York office and I got it. Flo called up again at half past one Thursday morning. I was asleep and Ellis refused to arouse me. He asked her if she would allow me to come back to Boston. She said I wasn't feeling so good, but maybe I would come if it was necessary. He called me up Thursday forenoon and said Marilyn was going to quit the show unless she got a song to sing in place of "Carry On, Keep Smiling." Would I write a lyric? I said, yes, but I must have a tune. Flo said Vince was mailing me a tune. The tune didn't come and Flo asked me to come up to Boston and make Vince write it. I got reservations on the five o'clock Saturday afternoon train, but at noon Saturday, Vince called up (from Boston, of course) and sang me the tune, with some dummy words. I stayed here and did the best I could with it and mailed it to Flo last night. He has mercifully let me alone today, but I have a hunch I'll be back in Boston for a few hours later in the week.

And did I tell you that Fred Astaire pouted over my opening ensemble idea because it required the presence of some Park Avenue women on one side of the stage and he didn't want anybody to appear dressed up before his entrance? And I wrote a lyric for Eddie Foy to sing in place of that dismal thing the girl sings in front of the curtain just ahead of the marvelous bedroom scene. I have written eleven numbers instead of the six I was asked write, and they can't possibly get more than seven of them in, and I have written you the longest letter (about tragic incidents in my life) I ever wrote to any Abbott girl excepting Ellis.

Love to the boys, who seem quite nice.
A Refugee.

The letter above is ominous for its reference to Ring's taking of Paraldehyde to overcome the insomnia which increasingly troubled him during his later years. Also portentous is an observation by Ellis in a letter she wrote to John on 14 December 1930 when John was in

Paris: "Dad is not very well. I get so discouraged about him. He is eating and trying to take care of himself but the results are not what they should be."

New York
February 11, 1931

[To H. L. Mencken]
Gent:
   It is too late to congratulate you on your wedding, so let's just forget all about it.
   When I was in my nonage I "went with" a Jewish girl. Now she is writing verse and will probably send you some. Will you please read it? I read it myself and know just as much about poetry as I did before.
                              Sincerely,
                              Ring Lardner.
   Her name is Ethel Miriam Pick.[1]

   However, the tuberculosis, heart trouble, and alcoholism of Ring's later years were by early 1931 depleting Ring's strength both physically and creatively:

The Vanderbilt Hotel
Thirty-Fourth Street East at Park Avenue
New York
February 13, 1931.

Dear Max:-
   My health hasn't been so good. I guess I am paying for my past--and I'm not averaging more than four short stories a year. None of the recent ones has been anything to boast of and I'm afraid there won't be enough decent ones to print by fall. Maybe I'll get more energetic or inspired or something in the next few months.
   This is just a temporary address. you can always reach me in care of the Bell Syndicate, 63 Park Row.
                              Sincerely,
                              Ring Lardner

   That February, after returning from their usual vacation to Florida with the Rices, Ring agreed in spite of his declining health to do a short daily Bell Syndicate piece, in association with the Chicago TRIBUNE and the New York DAILY NEWS (circulated by wire service), titled "A Night Letter from Ring Lardner," for $750 a week. It was an unsuccessful effort and was

----

[1]The source of this letter is a copy in the New York Public Library.

terminated in April. In addition to his illness, Ring
was laboring under the difficulties of not being up to
date on current events, and of trying to be funny in
the darker days of the depression. He began writing
the "Night Letter" from his and Ellis's suite at the
Vanderbilt Hotel, to which they had been forced by a
severe Atlantic storm which had washed away nearly two
hundred feet of beach and seriously damaged the
foundation of their East Hampton house. A few weeks
later, Ellis wrote describing the damage to John in
Paris:

> There is some maligne power that keeps me from
> writing to you. This time it took shape as the
> Atlantic ocean which rose up in two terrific storms
> and washed away practically all of our dune leaving
> over half the house hanging out over the ocean and
> taking most of the basement foundation out to feed
> the fishes. We had props put under her but she
> will either have to be moved at great expense or
> left to float out to sea.

In New York   The Vanderbilt Hotel
3 a.m. Sunday, Feb. 15, 1931   Park Avenue at Thirty-fourth
8 a.m. the same day in Paris   Street
                               New York

Dear John-
Keep a hold of this letter
For fear you won't get anything better.
It is written in the "wee small" hours of the morning
Without an instant's warning;
I just suddenly took a notion,
Having sworn off the nightly self-administration of
    a sleeping potion,
To get out of bed and use my Underwood portable
Rather than go out and walk the streets and perhaps
    court a belle.
We are back from the South and stopping at the
    Hotel V-nde-b--t,
A place that some goose or gander built.
The food here would annoy you and pain you
More than that procurable at the Pennsylvania,
And my opinion, which is seldom wrong,
Is that we won't be stopping here long.
If you should care to write us, through a sense of
    duty or pity,
Address us in care of the Bell Syndicate, 63 Park
    Row, N. Y. City,
Which, in association with the Chicago Tribune and
    New York Daily News,
Both of whom have plenty of money to lose,
Has engaged me to write a daily wire a la Will Rogers,

Designed to entertain young folks and old codgers.
I am supposed to write a hundred words or less per day
On timely topics, at very fair pay,
Though you are safe in betting
That I am not getting as much as Mr. Rogers is getting;
However, it keeps the wolf from the door
And while I may not be getting so much now, some day
      I might be getting more.
The reason I accepted this position
Was that my food was not giving me proper nutrition
And I seemed to lack the strength
To write short stories or plays or other works of
      any length.
When I am feeling fit again and everything is nice
      and tidy,
I intend to write the book of a musical show with a
      brand new idea.
A while ago I received a letter from a young man who,
      I am sure,
Had recently seen my own elegant signature,
And some time last autumn, ere the leaves were off
      the limb,
You had written my autograph and sent it to him;
He sent this autograph back and said he didn't
      want it;
By the vicious words of his accompanying letter I am
      still grieved and haunted.
David and your mother are in the next room,
Sleeping soundly, I trust, through the inexorable gloom.
The little one came in from school yesterday to meet us
And greet us with an advanced case of tonsilitis.
His throat is so sore that it irks him to swallow,
And if the ailment were to continue eight or ten years,
      his insides would become hollow.
Yesterday afternoon, your mother and I went to a matinee:
"America's Sweetheart," the new Fields, Rodgers and
      Hart musical play.
Gus Shy, John Sheehan, Jeanne Aubert and Inez Courtney
      are in it
And some of the songs are pretty enough to take home
      and play on your spinnet;
In fact, it is the best Rodgers score I have heard
      for a long time
And I'll send you the three best numbers when I
      think it is song time.
I thought you very deftly and wittily
Described your visit to s---y Italy.
This spring, if you have another holiday,
I wish you would spend it in Montpellier
Where my mother's niece Amy Serre
Lives unless she has moved from there.
She is a widow about seventy and has a daughter

Who grew old before a suitor caught her.
But they are nice and the daughter is a musician
Who prefers playing the pianoforte to going fishing.
I shall find out whether they're still there, yes or no;
Meanwhile, you inform me whether you'd like to go.
At Miami Beach, I saw very
Much of Paul Waner and Max Carey.
Paul is holding out for a larger salary
And poor Max is about through playing for a baseball gallery.
He is a free agent and would make a swell coach;
Barney Dreyfuss would keep him if he (Barney) were not
     a roach.
"June Moon" closed in Boston a week ago
After making quite a lot of money for such a small show.
I still think they were rather silly
To let it play four weeks in Philly,
But we beat Holiday records in Detroit,
Greatly to the stockholders' delight.
My experience with "Smiles" is too funny and too long
     to put in a letter;
When I see you I can tell you better.
And now when you think it isn't too much bother,
You might write a letter to sincerely your father.

          In spite of his distaste for Florenz Ziegfeld, Ring
     had written several lyrics for Marilyn Miller and Fred
     and Adele Astaire, six of which finally remained in the
     show, SMILES. But this activity too was cut short by
     his doctor's recommendation that Ring spend some time
     at the Desert Sanitarium in Tucson, Arizona. Ellis had
     to stay in New York, to oversee the moving and repair
     of the East Hampton house.

                         The Vanderbilt Hotel
                         New York
                         Feb. 23. [1931]

[To James Lardner]
Son whom I esteem nearly the best:
I am about to venture into the far-flung West;
They are about to turn your father loose on
The desert in Arizona near Tucson,
In the hope that he will regain that manly vigor
So noticeable in the liver-lipped nigger
Beloved by Shakespeare's heroine, Desdemona.
My address will be the Desert Sanitarium, Tucson, Arizona;
Not that that makes any difference to you.
I might as well be in Timbuctoo
So far as is concerned the reading of your letters,
Which are probably written to those you consider my betters.
As you may have heard from the mouths of birds,
I am now writing a daily sixty or seventy words

(A sort of Will Rogers message it is,
Though doubtless not as good as his);
It appears in papers from Portland to Austin,
And I think the Globe carries it in Boston;
At least, the Globe has always bought my stuff,
Throwing the Post and Herald into a rip-roaring huff.
Speaking of rip, has Dartmouth accepted you
Or have you changed your "mind" and decided on the Blue?
David came home last week with an attack of tonsilitis.
Even milk was hard to swallow, and you know how tough meat is.
His sore throat is now nearly gone;
The only time it hurts is when he has to yawn.
The only time he yawns is when anyone speaks French around
    the house,
Which, as you can readily fathom, makes me quiet as a louse.
It is now time to superintend the packing of my trunk;
It will be a big job owing to my last-minute decision to
    take along a skunk.
Write soon and often to the Desert Sanitarium, Tucson, Arizona,
And if I ever wake up in the night particularly lonesome,
    I will phone you.
                    Father in Heaven.

                        The Desert Sanitorium
                        Tucson, Arizona
                        March 6, 1931.

[To Ring Lardner Jr.]
Bravado:-
    A telegram from you and Jim, congratulating me on my
twentieth birthday, just arrived. I congratulate you for
remembering the date; also for being chosen in the upper bracket
of the Means contest.
    I hope your essay
    Is not too messay.
    There was a night letter from your mother, too, telling me
abour our houseboat in East Hampton and hinting that she was
going to Andover to hear your oration. I wish I might hear it,
but as I can't, you would please me by writing about it or
sending me a Phillipian containing a report of same.
    This joint is 2,500 feet up in the air and surrounded by
mountains that are close to a mile high. It is in the middle of
the desert and has queer flora and fauna. Among the latter are
coyotes and the funniest looking rabbits I ever saw. The full
grown ones are as big as ponies and have ears that are at least
half a foot long. They say that one of the female patients saw
one and thought it was a deer.
    I received a letter from an inmate of the Arizona state
prison, saying he had met me several times when he was one of the
hangers-on of Jack Dempsey and Jack Kearns years ago. All he
wants now is money with which to buy himself an artificial leg.

I could better afford to give him one of my own.

On the train coming down, a Dartmouth alumnus introduced himself and when I told him one of my sons was probably going there next year, he said, "There's no place like it," which I don't doubt a bit.

Write soon and often and keep out of the infirmary.
                                        Uncle Henry.

                                        The Desert Sanatorium
                                        Tucson, Arizona

Dear Jim or his brother:-
The spouse of your mother
Thanks you for the books,
Which, to judge from their looks,
Will furnish good reading,
A thing I've been needing.

        The following letter was written to Mrs. Mildred Luthy:

                                        [The Desert Sanatorium
                                        Tucson, Arizona]
                                        Wednesday, March 11 [1931]
Dear Millie:-
        You are a nice girl to take time from your gardening and your games with Jane to write to me. Most of the letters I get are from lawyers or income tax agents who seem to think I am a born embezzler. Yours (your letters, I mean) take the curse off the others.

        You had better not offer your services as nurse unless you are in earnest. I would give a fabulous sum (if I had it) for one like you, even though I know you would try to force those funny drinks on me. The nurses here are a hard-boiled lot and evidently selected for their ugliness. There is only one pretty one and she, strange to say, is from Georgia. Stranger to say, she is incompetent.

        Something tells me I am not going to linger here long. The doctors know their business and the weather is perfect, but the Lord didn't intend me for sanatorium life two thousand miles from home. What I'd like and hope to find is a suitable place within easy telephoning and visiting distance of New York. I suppose it would be sensible to obey orders and stay here six months, but I'm just not sensible.

        Ellis and I would have come to Americus and stayed there until we were driven out if Sister Kate hadn't objected to the idea so strenuously. I guess she wanted all the attention herself. We will come at a time when there is no danger of stealing the spotlight from anybody.

        Love to you and your mother and all the other Hollises.
                                        R.

[The Desert Sanatorium
Tucson, Arizona]
Sunday, March 15 [1931]

Dear John:-
        Believe it or not, your letters are much better reading than
the Arizona Star or the Tucson Daily Citizen. I have learned
from the latter, however, that Old Homme Seine is running amuck
and, perhaps by this time your dormitory has become a house boat
like the Lardners' hovel in East Hampton . . . .
        My wardens, not knowing I am a born rover, think I intend to
stay here all spring and most of the summer, but right after the
middle of April les Etats Unis will   be   placarded   with
announcements that I have escaped. As Lincoln said, you can
stand Arizona part of the time, you can even stand Arizona some
of the time, but you can't etc.
        My daily "night letter" is not in as many papers as it is out
of. It would be more readable if I weren't always four or five
days behind the news, but I do think it's as good as Bill Rogers'
or Coolidge's stuff.
        All my neighbors have radios (a recent invention) and just as
I get ready for my sleeping potion at nine P. M. (Mountain
Time) they turn on Amos and Andy, who, as you may not know, are
now broadcasting twice per night. I can't hear them distinctly
and wouldn't mind if I could, but what wrecks me is the kind of
laughter with which one of said neighbors greets their gags. It
is like the bleat of the coyotes in the surrounding mountains and
keeps me awake long after it is hushed for the night . . . .
        Write whether you feel like it or not and keep going to them
concerts.
                              A Vagabond[1]

                              The Desert Sanatorium
                              Tucson, Arizona
                              April Fool. [1931]

[To John Golden]
Dear John:-
        After a careful examination of the list of productions at the
bottom of your stationery I am constrained to ask, "W'at about
'The W'eel'"?
        Mrs. "Sid" is in the arthritis section of this jail and I
have had a couple of pleasant visits with her. She is a lot
worse off than I am because she suffers physically. My suffering
is entirely mental and mostly, I guess, ridiculous; besides, I
can have it stopped promptly by hollering for my "personal
physician" who is sufficiently understanding and sensible to know
that a shot in the arm is less harmful than the heebie jeebies.

----

        [1]This letter quoted by Elder, pp. 325-26. Original
unlocated.

If it weren't for the pain, I think Jean Siddall would enjoy it here - She likes company and there are lots of congenial women in her part of the asylum. As for me, I have been anti-social for a long, long time and wondered why. It is, they tell me, a characteristic of the ailment in a good many cases.

Do I seem to be answering your letter? A thousand times No. Well, then, I think it was mighty nice of you to relay Mr. French's[1] message and to volunteer your services as agent. The trouble is that Mr. French must be thinking of four or five other fellows. I never wrote a one-act play. I have an idea for one act _of_ a play and only need ideas for the other two acts. I have written short sketches for gambols and Dutch Treat shows and the like, but I have no copies of them and they are way out of date and weren't so hot in the first place. Also I have had short things, in play form, published in newspapers and magazines, but they were absolutely unplayable and never intended for the stage. Will you be good enough to convey this information to Mr. French?

Give my love to May. And thanks for writing. You are excused from writing again because willy-nilly, I am coming home in a very short time. I can't do daily syndicate work in this joint, where news arrives by pack mule about two weeks after it is news.

Sincerely,
R. W. L.

The following letter to Ring, Jr., or "Bill," comments on the injuries (a fractured pelvis and shoulder) he had sustained from a fall from the ledge of a fourth-floor dormitory window at Andover while attempting to crawl to the window of the next room. Ring Jr. was then recuperating at the Phillips House hospital in Boston, while Ring, having returned in mid-April from Tucson, was at Doctors Hospital in New York.

> [Doctors Hospital
> New York]
> Monday night, April 27 [1931]

Dear Bill:-

I don't intend to allow a son of mine to show me up. If you can live in a hospital, so can I. I _would_ like to trade ailments with you, for I have no excuse not to write letters; you have, which means that I shall hear from you almost as often as before.

I am on the ninth floor of this structure so that if I ever take a notion to step out of the window and stroll along the walls, the X-rays are likely to show a couple of fractured

---

[1] Samuel French, probably the most active publisher of plays for production by amateur or community theaters.

fingernails as well as the conventional arm and leg breaks.

Out in Arizona, the gent in charge of me said I mustn't do any work for six months at least, and preferably for a year. I had hoped for an order like that, from a competent physician, for a lcng, lcng while, but I didn't like it so well when it was actually issued. So I said I wouldn't do anything excepting for a daily syndicate "feature" of about one hundred words; it was no strain, paid very well and couldn't really be classed as work. He said anything I had to think of every day was sure to be a strain and a handicap. I said maybe that was true, but I intended to keep it up. Well, you can imagine my blushes when I got back to this city (New York) and discovered that the various newspapers throughout the country were in thorough agreement with my Arizona doctor; not only did they feel that I mustn't do any work, but also they doubted that I had been doing any. The only reason I can think of is that readers of the few papers to which my stuff had been sold were dying with laughter in such numbers that the editors were afraid the entire circulation would soon be in the col', col' ground. Anyway, massa is temporarily amongst the unemployed and awaiting offers from magazine editors. I presume I shall have to ask for a squad of mounted police to keep them in line at the door.

A very unfortunate thing just happened to you. Your mother called up and reported that she had received a letter from you, written on a one-armed typewriter. If you can write to one parent, etc. But don't do it if it tires you.

Sr.

Doctors Hospital
Tuesday evening
[May 1931]

[To Mrs. Mildred Luthy]
Dear Mildred:

A Mr. and Mrs. Lanier called on me yesterday morning. Mrs. Lanier claimed to be one of the Hollis family of Americus, but I couldn't quite believe it because I never saw anyone from Americus, least of all a Hollis, move so fast. Before I had a chance to say hello, they were saying good-bye and were gone. They seemed to be very nice people and I would have enjoyed a longer visit with them, but they evidently were under the impression that they were disturbing me. The only thing about a Hollis that can disturb me is its obstinacy. I have never met one I wanted to say good-bye to. If they are really relatives of yours, I wish you would ask them to come back and give me a chance to get acquainted with them before I am ordered out of here to make room for some one who is sick.

The other night I had a visitation from five members of the Lambs Club. They were all in extremely high spirits and the house doctor refused them permission to see me. They pushed him aside and came in anyway. Among them was Gitz Rice whom you will remember as composer of "Dear Old Pal of Mine." Chairs were

plentiful, but Gitz preferred sitting on the floor, from which he
arose at too frequent intervals to come to my alleged bed of
pain, kiss me on top of the head and say, "You old sweetheart!"
They had all given their names down at the office, and when they
had gone, my nurse, who had witnessed the proceedings, said, "I
had no idea Grantland Rice would act like that." Of course I
immediately corrected her error, but it was too late to deny the
rumor which she had spread all over the place and I am afraid
Grannie will go down in Doctors Hospital history as a man who
sits on the floor and springs up every little while to kiss the
patient on top of the head.
    Aside from the Laniers' split-second call, I have been
pleasantly surprised here just once. Vince Youmans came in and a
house doctor took it on himself to conduct us to the
housekeeper's rooms, where there was a piano. I made Vince play
everything he had ever written, and it was grand. If I could
afford to hire a composer-pianist like him to stay with me all
the time, I could laugh at doctors and nurses.
    John gets home next Sunday. Ellis is going to meet him and
bring him right up here. I hope he still speaks English.
    Love to the family. (And to you).
                    R.

        The following telegram is again to Mildred Luthy:

NEWYORK NY   1931 MAY 11 AM 8 52
MRS KENNETH LUTHY=
    133 TAYLOR HILLS AMERICUS GA=
AM NOT NEARLY AS DISCOURAGED NOW AS SINCE WE TALKED A FEW HOURS
AGO STOP I MUST LIVE IN HIGH DRY CLIMATE THIS SUMMER FOR GOOD OF
THE PUBLIC STOP IT OCCURED TO ME HOW LEAVENLY IF LIZ NEEDED THE
SAME SORT OF CLIMATE STOP MISS FELDMAN WOULD WORK AS NURSE AND
HOUSEKEEPER AND COOK FOR NOTHING STOP I TELEPHONED YOU WHETHER
LIZ WOULD CONSIDER ANY SUCH ARRANGEMENT AROUND NEWYORK OR VERMONT
OR CANADA AND I SWEAR I THOUGHT I HEARD NOT ONLY YOU BUT LIZ SAY
YES AND I GOT QUITE A THRILL STOP WHEN I HUNG UP OPERATOR SAID
ELLIS WANTED ME AND ELLIS ASKED WHOM I HAD BEEN AFTER SO LONG
STOP THEN [WHEN?] I TOLD ELLIS I THOUGHT SHE SAID KATE HAD
INVENTED THE SCHEME STOP EVERYBODY WAS IN HIGH SPIRITS OVER
SCHEME STOP BUT IT SEEMS MISS FELDMAN CLAIMED AUTHORSHIP SO YOU
CAN SEE THAT [WHAT?] I AM UP AGAINST STOP LIZ CAN GET WELL QUICK
OR STILL STICK TO BARGAIN BUT POSTPONE

        The following letter is addressed to Ring's nephew
(his sister Anna's son) Richard Lardner Tobin (now
senior vice-president of SATURDAY REVIEW) in care of
the University of Michigan DAILY, of which he was
editor, in his senior year. Tobin had placed Ring on
the complimentary circulation list of the paper.

Doctors Hospital
East End Ave. at 87th St.
New York
October 2, 1931.

Dear Cousin:-
     A very swell elegant paper, Cousin. Keep up the good work.
But don't let your sports editor think for one moment that he can
fool this old codger by putting Bottomley's name under Hoyt's
picture and vice versa. Also, hasn't it occurred to you that you
could relieve the unemployment situation by hiring a few night
editors?
     On and after next Wednesday, Mr. and Mrs. R. W. Lardner
and son John will be living at 25 East End Avenue. It's a
furnished apartment seven blocks down the street from here.
                    Cousin Ring

          As the above letter indicates, Ring and Ellis were
     about to move into a furnished apartment in New York,
     while their house was still being repaired. John had
     gone to work for the HERALD-TRIBUNE.

                                   Saturday, October 31 [1931]

[To son James at Harvard]
Dear Sir,-
     I can recall a Wigglesworth[1] who played on your team;
otherwise I should have to keep asking Ronghild.
     You may get up in the middle of Harvard Square and tell the
Reds that I never wrote a picture for Chevalier and expect never
to be asked to. If I were, I know I should swoon. At the
present moment, I am awaiting a telephonic yes or no from Harold
Lloyd as to whether I am to write the dialogue (not the scenario)
for his new picture at an outrageous (not for Hollywood) price.
If he says yes, I shall have to go out there in a couple of days
and stay three or four weeks. If he says no, well and good.
Again, if he says yes, I shall try to find some sappy Southern
Californian who wants to bet against Notre Dame, so I can get
even with my baseball sharpshooters. Otherwise, it will be
necessary for me to back you vs. Yale.
     Since starting this letter, I have had a telegram from
Harold, who thinks my price is too high. I telegraphed back that
I disagreed with him. He replied that he would give me a
definite answer on Monday.[2] I know he is right, so if we get into
a conversation on the telephone, I shall bargain with him until

----

[1]James Lardner resided in Wigglesworth Hall at Harvard.

[2]The arrangement with Harold Lloyd was never successfully
negotiated.

we come to terms. I need the money to pay the galumps who moved our house back to Sag Harbor. I shall try to ease in a stipulation to the effect that he pay an extra fare out there and back, so I can have a compartment and work all the way going and coming. Your mother or older brother will let you know the result.

John is making good at the Herald Tribune and will probably be managing editor by the end of the year if the paper fails, as seems inevitable. He and Dicky Tobin went to the Princeton-Michigan game today. The game was for the championship of the slums and Michigan won, 21 to 0. If, as I presume, you depend on the Boston papers, you may not know this.

If King Howard wins the managership of the team and you are any kind of business man, you will strip him of enough tickets to pay your board, lodging and tuition.

The meals, nursing and beds here are much better than at the hospital. The day I left there, Dr. Erdmann, who works about five days a year, performed three operations, while fifteen doctors stood around and watched. His total fees were $25,000. One op was the removal, manicuring and replacement of the stomach of a seventy-year-old rake, who is now able to go out and get cock-eyed again.

Other East Hampton news is the death, by pneumonia, of Mr. Coppell. Why couldn't it have been she, is the question being asked in all the quail coveys.

Write to me here. If I'm gone, the letter will be forwarded by mail.

In a week or two, maybe this week, a series of mine[1] will begin in the Saturday Evening Post. Save the covers.

Mrs. Coppell.

The following letter is to Mrs. Florence Hollis (who was about seventy-five at the time), the mother of Kate Rice, Mildred Luthy, and Lizabeth Vereen:

25 East End Avenue,
New York City.
November twentieth, nineteen thirty-one.

Dear Mrs. Hollis:-

No matter what any or all of your daughters may have told you, I am not a chronic grumbler. But occasionally I do feel constrained to lodge what I consider a just complaint.

---

[1]The "series" consisted of six autobiographical articles: "Meet Mr. Howley" (in the November 14 POST), "Me, Boy Scout" (November 21), "Caught in the Draft" (January 9, 1932), "Heap Big Chief" (January 23), "Chicago's Beau Monde" (February 20), and "Alias James Clarkson" (April 16). Elder calls these pieces Lardner's "only real autobiography" (p. 337). They also are available now in SOME CHAMPIONS.

Sensing the need of a Hollis in our home, I recently extended an invitation to Mrs. Luthy or Mrs Vereen or both to come and visit us. They replied with a terse "No." The reply came by telegraph and was addressed not to me, but to my wife. Has the Master of the House no standing? If I were to ask you (as I do here and now) to pay us a visit, would you answer Ellis or me. I hope you would, and will, answer me and say "Yes."

Once in a while (I believe the last time was three years ago), we make up our minds to invite the Rices to a theater. When this happens, I telephone to Grant and he says "Yes" without consulting his wife or Floncey or Helga or Charles. He has rights which the Hollis girls seem to think I lack. This is a very serious matter with me and I would appreciate your decision.

Otherwise I hope you are in better health than most people I know. Sincerely,

Ring Lardner

[late November 1931]
Saturday, 3 A. M.

Dear James:-

As I have told your brother at Andover in a belle lettre I wrote him yesterday morning about this time, I have a new habit; I grow very, very sleepy every evening at dinner, stay up after dinner, nodding and blinking, until your mother scolds me into going to bed, fall asleep at eleven, awake at 1:30, all through with sleep, and spend the balance of the night working or writing mash notes such as this. The habit has persisted ever since I left the hospital, where a kindly night nurse gave me shots in the arm to insure me a night's sleep (thereby also insuring herself of one), but I have a hunch that during the coming week, I shall return to something near normalcy and then my correspondents (God help them!) will wonder why they aren't even receiving postcards from me any more.

Now don't imagine for one moment that I am suffering from a delusion that I owe you a letter--well do I remember replying to your last one and advising you to take advantage of King Howard's appointment to the post of football manager and make yourself and family independently wealthy by scalping. (I judge from recent events, however, that no tickets will be sold for Harvard games after this fall; the public will be barred, as Husing was,[1] for the use of naughty words or for other misbehavior--In passing,

---

[1]Ted Husing, the radio sports broadcaster with CBS, used the word "putrid" to describe the play of Harvard quarterback Barry Wood in a game against Dartmouth in 1931. William Bingham, Harvard athletic director, banned Husing from Harvard Stadium because of his language. Despite the disagreement, Husing placed Wood on his all-star team at the end of the year. Husing was permitted to return after two years banishment.

my child, I might say that if you weren't a Harvard man, I'd
write a little piece for The New Yorker regarding your school's
haughty attitude toward the outside world. I know Bill Bingham
and like him, but his refusal to have anything to do with the
benefit games for the unemployed, his high hat stand in the
Husing case, etc.--these and other items of the same sort have
kind of cooled my love for your institution. Nevertheless, I
have tried all week to bet on you and only last night succeeded
in finding anyone with more than ten cents in Yale money. I had
to give 8 to 5 (nonsensical odds) and the amount of the wager is
$80.00 to $50.00. I lost my shirt and underwear on the world's
series and not through bad judgment either, but incredibly bad
luck. The defeat of Earnshaw in the last game was nothing short
of murder--There was only one real hit (Watkins' home run) made
off him.[1]

Anyway, I says to myself, "I'll get even on football." There
was no chance to bet until November 7; then a bookmaker whom I
know made this generous offer: Of all the games scheduled for
that day, he would select fifteen; he would submit to me the list
of fifteen and I could select six of them. If my six teams all
won, he would pay me 6 to 1, but the betting limit was $10.00.
(However, for friendship's sake, he would permit me to bet
$20.00.) Well, just on the chance of having the laugh on him, I
told him to send his list. John and I studied it carefully and
picked the probable winners--nine instead of six so we would have
three to argue about. I showed our selections to Mr. Rice, and
he and two of his friends went in with us. I bet $20.00 and the
others bet $10.00 each. Our six final choices all won. They
were Colgate, Alabama, Lafayette, Temple, Nebraska, and
Northwestern. (And our three alternatives--Michigan, Williams
and Pittsburgh--were winners also). I thought I was very bright,
and so did my bookmaker.

On that same day, Georgia, which had already beaten Yale,
licked New York University 7 to 6, a very lucky victory. But the
Georgians and their followers were extremely cocky and thought
they had a national championship team.

During the following week, Dan McGugin, who used to be a
great guard at Michigan, is Yost's[2] brother-in-law, and coach at
Vanderbilt, confided that Tulane was two touchdowns better than
Georgia; his team had played them both. Mr. Rice was going
south to cover the Georgia-Tulane game, so I gave him a check for
all I had in the world and told him to bet it on Tulane,
believing he would have a better chance to place it down there
than I would up here. He wired back from Atlanta that he could

----

[1]In the 1931 World Series the St. Louis Cardinals defeated
the Philadelphia Athletics four games to three, with Burleigh
Grimes defeating George Earnshaw 4-2 in the deciding game.

[2]Fielding Yost was head football coach at the University of
Michigan from 1901 through 1925.

find no takers, so all day Friday, the 13th., I hung on the
telephone trying to unearth a bookmaker who had heard of Georgia
money. I discovered it was impossible to lay a bet on Tulane at
any price.
    Beginning Monday morning of this week, I set out to bet on
Harvard, succeeding, last night, as I have told you, in wagering
$80.00 to $50.00. Once or twice I mentioned the Notre Dame-
U. S. C. game; the bookies said Notre Dame was odds-on at 1 to 2
1/2. I wouldn't fall for any monkey business like that.

Sunday, 4 A. M.

    I presume I ought to kneel down and thank the Almighty for
getting by as fortunately as I did yesterday. I am thoroughly
convinced that your hero, Barry Wood, got his Phi Beta Kappa key
from a locksmith and that Notre Dame's coach, Hunk Anderson, will
be driving mules in an Indiana coal mine next fall.
    Forgetting (if we can) that first scrimmage, in which Harvard
had a first down on Yale's seven-yard line, and the selection of
plays that couldn't have scored a touchdown against Niles High
School, let us leap into the fourth quarter where all the
allegedly bright boys (Wood Casey at Harvard and Anderson,
Jackswhich and Schwartz at Notre Dame) suddenly became the
victims of brainstorms.
    In war or in football, the first lesson is that the attack is
more wearisome than the defense. In football it is a cardinal
principle that the team just scored against shall kick off and
not receive the kick-off. If the man who kicks off is any good,
the receiving team will have eighty yards to go for a touchdown.
When it is finally forced to punt, your team will have the ball
close to midfield. The blunder occurred only once at Harvard.
At Notre Dame, it happened three times. And listen to this:
When Notre Dame was leading 14 to 6, the broadcaster said, "Notre
Dame wisely elected to receive the kick-off so it would be in
possession of the ball," and on the first play after Notre Dame
had received the kick-off, Schwartz threw a sixty yard pass from
his own twenty-yard line, and the pass was knocked down. He
proceeded to get himself into a hole and finally made a bad punt
that gave U. S. C. its chance for a second touchdown. Even at
that, Notre Dame could have kept its one-point advantage if it
had slowed up its play. What is a five-yard delay penalty
compared with defeat? Or three or four penalties?
    Oh, well, let's not get mad. But I did get mad yesterday
afternoon. Your mother, John and I were listening to both games
over the radio (a new invention) and I am afraid your mother
heard some "putrid" language.
    In closing, I hated to see Harvard lose on your account and
John's, and I hated to see those swell-headed Californians beat a
superior team because it's Schwartz's last year.

There is one safe bet--that poor old Rock turned over in his
grave at least three times yesterday P. M.
Remember me to the Howards and write.
                    A Second Guesser.

    The letter below was written at two o'clock in the
morning to Richard Lardner Tobin, who describes it as

        the work of a desperately ill man who has
        nonetheless an abiding interest in the sports world
        from which he came. The quote 'Mrs.
        Hoag' mentioned at the beginning was a small-town
        character in Niles, Michigan, whom I would have
        recognized as the silliest of all possible
        salutations to me. Also, I rather like the use of
        the postal telegraph press copy on which he is
        writing. As you will see, he is at this moment
        doing some pieces for the New Yorker, date line:
        'No Visitors, New York,' which, of course, is
        Doctors Hospital. Since I was in Ann Arbor and
        Fielding Yost was still coaching out there, Uncle
        Ring is asking me to say hello to him personally,
        since they were once great pals.

                        Postal Telegraph - Cable Company
                        Press Telegram
                        Dec. 10, 1931, 2 A. M.

    Mrs. Hoag (Mabel's mamma):- This isn't even a Western Union
press telegram let alone a Postal press telegram, why should you
let alone a Postal press telegram? Mackay may be a Catholic, but
after all his daughter married a Heeb who plays everything in the
key of F sharp. And can't play even in that key.
    I guess I told you that I don't sleep o' nights any more, and
my ankles are so swollen and itchy that all I can do is sit in a
scratching position and turn out words, either for publication or
for some one's private ear. This press telegram may be placed in
the latter category and, as usual, what I write you is
confidential. Mr. Rice's All-American team (to be in the
December 26 issue of Collier's, which, appropriately enough, goes
on sale the 18th.) is composed of the following rugby stars:
Ends-Dalrymple, Tulane, and Catnip Smith, Georgia;
tackles-Schweger (?), Washington, and an unspellable
Pittsburgher, something like Quoutchi or Pouchi; guards-Hickman,
Tennessee, and Munn, Minnesota; center-M-rr-s-n, Michigan; backs-
Wood, Schwartz, Rentner and Shaver. No team represented by more
than one man and may God have mercy on my soul and yours if you
breathe a word even to your mother-in-law. There is nothing,
however, to prevent you from digging up pictures for use at the
proper time.

A few hours ago I did my annual radio broadcast. I called Morton Downey a soprano, which he is, but when he sees me and starts to sock me in the jaw, I'll tell him I have just been sick.

John has had five stories in the paper in the last three days and one of them each day carried a by-line. We are all swollen up like my ankles.

He (John) and I lost nothing on Notre Dame for the reason that no one would bet on the opposition.

The Princeton-Columbia-Penn-Cornell round robin yesterday was a terrific flop and the unemployed had to drive the visiting players home in their Hispano-Suizas. John Philip Suiza's band is on the Goodyear hour nearly every Tuesday and Saturday night. So are the Revellers, under a pseudonym. I read in the Michigan Daily that the Revs were in your town last week. Lah-de-dah.

In one of the next two or three New Yorkers will appear a comical parody on "Mourning Becomes Elektra."[1] It was a tough thing to write as two-thirds of it is menu cards which I copied from the program.

Love to Dean Yost.

A Cadaver.

I gather (you gather, he, she or it gathers) that B. Friedman is in kind of wrong at Yale owing to his lack of respect for Albie, and it is doubtful that he will be asked to return as assistant coach. Moreover, he has been more or less dissatisfied at New Haven, where the morons in charge have paid little heed, man, to the suggestions of B. Friedman. I realize that, until death do us part, a person named Fielding Yost will have a lot to say about the coaching at Michigan; nevertheless, I should like to see Benny get in (out) there. He could at least act as a formidable scrub team all by himself, just as Germany Schulz[2] used to do.

Ring*

*for icewater

Richard Tobin heeded the information his uncle had given him. The MICHIGAN DAILY of December 18, 1931, carried a story, with pictures, on Grantland Rice's All-American football selections. The COLLIER'S story appeared the same day.

[1]Quadroon," THE NEW YORKER, 19 December 1931. Collected in FIRST AND LAST.

[2]Adolph George "Germany" Schultz played football at Michigan. He was noted for his passing ability and for his defensive play as a "roving center." After fourteen years of coaching at such universities as Wisconsin, Michigan, and Tulane, he retired in 1922 from football.

As a result of an October interview Ring had given
a WORLD-TELEGRAM reporter, the 9 November 1931 TIME had
quoted Ring, perhaps incorrectly, on Theodore Dreiser
as saying: "The prince of all bad writers is Dreiser.
He takes a big subject, but so far as handling it and
writing it--why one of my children could do better."
When Burton Rascoe defended Dreiser against Ring's
"attack" in his New York SUN column, Ring wrote to him:

                          25 East End Avenue,
                          New York City.
                          December 16, 1931.

Dear Burton:-
    I believe that a great many football fatalities might be
averted by the adoption of the following rule:
    "Before commenting on a statement attributed to an
interviewee, the commentator must seek out the interviewee and
ascertain what the latter really did say. Penalty--Loss of two
paragraphs."
    Love and a merry Christmas to the Rascoe parents and progeny.
                          R. W. L.

    Rascoe wrote back on Christmas Day from California
explaining that he had quoted verbatim from the TIME
article and urging Ring to "rebuke" the TIME reporter
and write a denial to the magazine.

    In the meantime, Ring sent a telegram of
encouragement to Jim at Harvard just before a varsity
wrestling match (in his senior year, just after Ring's
death, Jim would become New England intercollegiate
wrestling champion in his 145-pound class):

                          1931 DEC 17 PM 9 53
JAMES LARDNER=
    WIGGLESWORTH HALL HARVARD UNIVERSITY CAMBRIDGE MASS=
DON'T LET ANYBODY THROW YOU STOP AM BACKING YOU HEAVILY STOP
PLEASE SEND NIGHTLETTER RESULT OF MATCH ALSO WHEN YOU WILL BE
HOME AND BRING YOUR DINNER CLOTHES=
                          DAD.

NEWYORK NY   [1931 DEC 24 PM 1 44]
MRS FLORENCE HOLLIS=
    133 TAYLOR HILL AMERICUS GA=
JUST TO WISH YOU A MERRY CHRISTMAS AND TO ASK YOU TO TAKE CARE OF
YOURSELF SO THAT I MAY COME AND SEE YOU NEXT TIME AMERICUS HAS A
CENTENNIAL=
    RING LARDNER.

    On 2 January 1932 Ring wrote to Dreiser:

25 East End Avenue,
New York City.
January 2, 1932.

Dear Mr. Dreiser:-
      This is an effort to get the record straight.
      Six or seven weeks ago a World-Telegram man, who wanted an
"interview" and whom I had stalled until he convinced me that he
was stall-proof, crashed my gate and discovered what I could have
told him in advance - that I am a complete flop as copy.   We
drifted to the subject of what I was reading; it was a book about
Jake Lingle, who was a friend of mine when I worked on the
Chicago Tribune. (I left Chicago a year before Capone took
charge).   The idea I tried to convey to the W.-T. man was that I
got more of a kick out of an actual transcript of testimony in a
real murder case than from anything of that nature I had ever
read in fiction, adding that one of the most fascinating
documents I had seen was the stenographic report of Judd Gray's
confession.[1] We discussed you and "An American Tragedy," and, to
the best of my recollection, I said that no one, not even one of
my children, could fail to make a human story like that
uninteresting, and the more simply it was written, the better.
In the "interview," as it appeared, I was quoted as calling you
"the prince of bad writers" and saying other things about you
which I certainly did not say.   When I read it, I got all excited
and was calmed down by my wife and my doctor who assured me that
people who knew me would know I had been misquoted.
      Well, it seems that "Time" lifted and reprinted one paragraph
(the worst) and Burton Rascoe read it and jumped on me in his
daily column.   I wrote to him and suggested an amendment to the
constitution, making it a punishable offense to quote from a
quote from a quote, when it was such a simple matter to find out
first hand what the victim of the interview really had said.
      I assure you I am not in the habit of knocking writers (God
help us all), and particularly novelists, whose patience and
energy are far beyond any good traits I can claim.   You don't
know me and therefore will have to take my word, or the word of
some of my friends, that I am incapable of the offense charged.
On the other hand, Burton has known me twenty-five years and when
he gets home, I'll "rebuke" him, as he suggests that I rebuke the
interviewer.
      As for "Time," in another recent issue it said I was slowly
recovering from "pernicious anaemia." Aside from glanders, that
is the only ailment I haven't had.   But at least a dozen

_____

      [1]Judd Gray was the lover in "the Dumbbell Murder," a
sensational case in March 1927. He and his mistress, Ruth Brown
Snyder, were convicted and electrocuted for the murder of her
husband.

sufferers from it wrote to me asking what treatment I took, and I
had to reply to all of them.

                        Sincerely,
                        Ring Lardner
    I seem to have made quite a fuss over what you doubtless
consider nothing, but I do want you to know that I'm not a
knocker.

        Dreiser responded:

                            Hotel Ansonia
                            New York City
                            Jan. 5, 1932

        Courtesy and good will shine through your
    explanation of the World-Telegram and Time
    comments, and I thank you, though you need not have
    troubled. It is a long while since I have taken
    umbrage at any comment made either on myself or my
    work, since, good bad or indifferent, both are as
    they are, and, as for my work, the best I can do.
        Surely only critics are intolerant of those who
    do the best they can in so trying a world.
        None the less, the phrase "the prince of bad
    writers" cheers me. It is glistering irony that
    ought to be said if for no more than the saying. I
    am grateful to you for having called my attention
    to it.
                Cordially and with assurances of my esteem,
                        Theodore Dreiser

    Dreiser's letter was so ambiguous that Ring felt
the need to write again:

                        Wednesday, January sixth.
                            [1932]

Dear Mr. Dreiser:-
    When I was in my teens, schoolmates and other acquaintances
used to say of some one they particularly liked (some one who
spent his money lavishly for drinks, ready-made cigarettes,
etc.), "He's a prince," and for some reason the phrase nauseated
me so that I have always avoided the word "prince" except when
referring to the Prince of Wales, a thing I have seldom found
occasion to do. So whether or not "The prince of bad writers" is
glistering irony, it isn't my irony and I cannot accept the
credit for somebody else's glistering.
    It is only fair to warn you that when spring comes, your
hotel will be a hotbed of Giant and Yankee ball players - unless
they have decided to jump to the new Waldorf.
                        Sincerely,
                        Ring Lardner

Dreiser answered as explicitly:

> Hotel Ansonia
> New York
> Jan. 7, 1932

Dear Lardner:
Plainly I did not make myself clear. But you
m<u>ust</u> believe that I accept--and did--fully your
assurance of innocence. More, <u>that</u> I appr<u>eciated</u>
<u>fully</u> and <u>gratefully</u> your troubling to write me and
explain. Can I make this more definite? At the
same time I rejoice in the phrase "The Prince of
Bad Writers." The newspaper man who concocted it
should have a medal of some kind--a real one.
Let's call it "the phrase of the year" or "the
year's best bit of irony."
Anyhow you are a neighbor of mine. If you
would trouble to walk so far we might drown this
slight misunderstanding in hard likker. The mystic
hour of five usually finds me turning from
composition to speculation & drink.
> Theodore Dreiser
As for the base-ball wonders,--at worst they can
only drown out the tuneful Latins herein resident
at this hour.

Lardner concluded the correspondence (and the
"friendship," since the two writers in fact never did
meet) with this note:

> 25 East End Avenue,
> New York City.
> January 11, 1931.
> [misdated; actually 1932]

Dear Mr. Dreiser:-
On the contrary, you did make yourself plain and I am
grateful to you for taking my word.
I want to ask for a rain check on that hard likker
invitation. It is my misfortune that when I get started, I seem
to find it necessary to fight it out on those lines if it takes
all winter, and having spent a whole year among the unemployed, I
must now work until I am somewhere near even.
We would be neighbors if I lived on <u>West</u> End Avenue, but as
it is, the whole width of Manhattan divides us. I am within
wading distance of Welfare Island and hope to finish there.
> Sincerely
> Ring Lardner
> The Prince of Doltish Drinkers.

The following letter is again to Richard Lardner
Tobin at the University of Michigan. The play Ring
mentions was a one-act play by Tobin which had been
included in a book of plays published by the
University. Of the reference to shirking his work, Mr.
Tobin writes:

The mention of "Dowagiac" is a reference to a
small town near Niles, Michigan. Stanley Walker,
the famous City Editor of the New York Herald
Tribune, had just hired me to start on the paper in
June after graduation and, when this fact was made
public, the Dowagiac paper ran a big editorial
about the importance of working on college papers,
using me as a prime example. It was, after all,
the bottom of the depression and not many people
were getting jobs that spring and summer.
Apparently it impressed Mr. Lardner, too. The
Bill Dickey whose name appears at the bottom was,
of course, the famous New York Yankees' catcher, a
drinking friend of Mr. Lardner, and well-known to
me, naturally.

Thursday.
[ca. March 1932]

Dear Dickie:-
The book of plays arrived from Ann Arbor yesterday. I read
"Masquerade" last night and liked it, though it didn't "leave me
laughing," as George Cohan says a play should do.
If you are ever tempted to shirk your work, remember that
Dowagiac has its eye on you.
And if you know of another record I would like you might,
when you have time, ask the Schirmer boys to send it along.
It was tough luck for you to have that postponement Monday,
but not so tough for me and my unspeakable Giants.
Bill Dickey.

March 16, 1932.

[To Adelaide W. Neall, an editor with George Horace Lorimer's
SATURDAY EVENING POST]
Dear Miss Neall:-
You are almost forgiven and will be entirely so if you will
see that the one-line insert (appropriately marked Insert A) in
the sixth galley of the proof is attended to, and if you will
rush me the proofs of the second installment.[1] The insert will

----

[1]Ring's reference is to "When the Moon Comes Over the
Mountain," the second in a series of six new "busher" stories
published by the POST in 1932 and as a book titled LOSE WITH A

show the readers if any that we are more or less up to date, and the second installment will require some revision because Babe Herman[1] was included in the Cincinnati trade, something I had not been warned against. "Insert A" is near the bottom of this sheet.

My mark of elision in proofreading is ‿ as you have probably guessed. I shall try to master the Post's.

Whether or not you are interested, I went visiting the Philadelphia sick after leaving your office Wednesday, and wound up sicker than any of them, without breaking a resolution or a law and on the train coming home an utter stranger told me a joke about the Lindbergh baby, which I laughed at so heartily that he left the washroom offended.

Sincerely,
Ring Lardner

Insert A--6th galley of proof:
   because they trade it Herman to Cincinnati.

New York, New York
May 13, 1932.

Dear Mr. Meconnahey:-
Please pardon my tardiness in replying to your letter. I have not been able to write or even dictate.

Sid Skolsky's stuff was more nearly accurate than those things usually are.

I believe that I like "Golden Honeymoon" best of my immortal works, but I don't know why.

Sincerely,
Ring Lardner

The letter below was written to John McGraw, baseball manager of the New York Giants and an old friend of Ring's, who had just been forced by ill health to retire.

SMILE by Scribners in 1933. The stories are imitative of the Jack Keefe series, consisting of letters between rookie Brooklyn outfielder Danny Warner and his girl Jesse. Though the stories are a pale version of YOU KNOW ME AL, and not at all the novel which Perkins had hoped Ring might produce, they do exhibit all Ring's earlier mastery of the "busher" dialect and the epistolary form, and they are a remarkable effort by an extremely sick man who was unable now to write for any sustained length of time.

[1]Floyd "Babe" Herman was a star outfielder for the Brooklyn Dodgers, who was traded to Cincinnati before the 1932 season. He had a batting average of .393 in 1930, and a cumulative average for thirteen years in the major leagues of .324.

Doctors Hospital
New York City
June 4, 1932

Dear John:
    This is just to say that I'm terribly sorry to hear of your resignation as manager and of the serious nature of the illness that caused it. Baseball hasn't meant much to me since the introduction of the TNT ball that robbed the game of the features I used to like best--features that gave you and Bill Carrigan and Fielder Jones and other really intelligent managers a deserved advantage, and smart ball players like Cobb and Jim Sheckard a chance to do things.
    You and Bill Gleason and Eddie Collins were among the few men left who personified what I enjoyed in "the national pastime." Moreover your retirement has ruined my hope of a resumption of amusing (to me) relations with Frank Belcher when, and if, I am ever physically and financially able to go into the Lambs club-house again. Two or three years ago, when the Giants lost a game or a series, I used to torture him by saying that it was due to bad management. When I had him on the verge of tears, I would "break down and confess" that I was kidding and that I really considered you the greatest of managers, and it was honestly pathetic to see him brighten up at my sudden change of front. If you ever had a loyal supporter, he was and is it.
    Often I have wondered whether you ever enjoyed the feeling of security and comfort that must be a manager's when the reporters assigned to his club are "safe" and not pestiferous--a gang such as Chance and Jones and Jim Callahan were surrounded with for a few years in Chicago, and I don't say that just because I happen to be one of the gang. We had a rule, and lived up to it, that none of us would ever act as assistant managers, would be worthy of whatever confidence was reposed and would never ask, "Who's going to pitch tomorrow?" The result was mutually beneficial. We were kept posted on whatever changes, deals and trades were "in the air" and therefore knew what we were talking about when the trade or deal was put through or called off. The managers referred to didn't wince when they saw one of us approaching. They were our friends and we were theirs. So far as I was concerned, Frank Chance knew that I was very close to Schulte and lots of times when Schulte was not "behaving," Chance would drop a hint to me, knowing that I would warn Schulte, and I am positive I was thus enabled to save Schulte money and Chance the unpleasant task of fining and suspending him . . . .
    I do hope you get better soon and that eventually you get "back." I am lucky in that I have no physical pain. My chief trouble is an increasing hatred of work, and it happens that work

is necessary. Please remember me to Mrs. McGraw, or, as the internes would call her, Mrs. "McGror."
                              Sincerely,
                              Ring Lardner[1]

     The letter below is to Ellis's sister, Ruby Abbott Hendry:

                                             July seventh. [1932]
Dear Rube:-
     Thank God for John, if only because he made you write. I thought I was the Hendrys' Forgotten Man; Ellis evidently thought so, too, for when she saw your writing, she opened the letter--and read it.
     Arthur Jacks used to have an exasperating (till you knew him) trick of always "topping" people. If I complained of a headache, he had a worse one. If Rex mentioned a sore throat, Arthur had all the symptoms of diphtheria. So I will proceed to annoy you by pointing out that Robin's present unemployment is not nearly as "bad" as my plight throughout 1931 and several weeks of this blessed year. There was work to be done, but the mere sight of a typewriter gave me the heebie-jeebies. When I was able to subdue them and attempt to work, I was immediately overcome by sleeping sickness, though nothing short of chloroform would put me to sleep in bed. I would lie awake and think of debts and expenses; jump up determined to work; begin to work and either get the shakes or doze off, and then go back to bed and start the whole performance over again. I maintain that when a person is idle through no fault of his own, it is less irritating than when he realizes that "loose living" is "the cause of it all."
     Dickie Tobin, having got through Michigan, is rooming in town with John. They are both, as you probably know, reporters on the Herald Tribune. They have the same off-day and will probably come out here about once every two weeks during the summer. David will be our contribution to Andover this fall; Jim will go back to Harvard and Bill will enter Princeton, IF the magazines don't "ask" the old man to take another cut. Magazines and newspapers are, of course, face to face with the Grim Reaper, their only consolation being that radio, which beat them out of a lot of advertising, is now as badly off as they.
     The New Yorker, being a "class" publication, doesn't pay much, but it's kind of fun to be a radio critic. If I don't get fired, I will crusade against the vulgarity and stupidity of some of the comedians and the immorality and illiteracy of most of the songs. It won't do any good, excepting to my disposition, which is soured by listening to the atrocities perpetrated by jokers, lyric writers and alleged singers.
     I sympathize whole-heartedly with Boots on the subject of

---

     [1]This letter quoted from Elder, pp.361-62. Unlocated elsewhere.

July Fourth, and I was mean enough to be glad that it rained all day hereabouts. The most fun I have all year is tossing into the waste basket the annual request for a contribution to the Village Fireworks Fund.

You ought to make a proposition to your friend, Mr. Marr. During dull times--and it must be dull times for good architects--have him draw new plans and remodel the cottage with the understanding that he will receive ten percent of any amount over $100,000 that it sells for when good times return. I have always thought it was extremely attractive--both the cottage itself and the site.

The bus cure for insomnia would work on me with a vengeance. Once I rode in one from Miami to Palm Beach, a trip taking only a couple of hours. An hour more and I would have shot all the other passengers and gone to sleep permanently in the electric chair. Buses and berths were not designed for people over five feet eleven. When I go to bed in sleeping cars now (which I don't), I wonder how in the world I stood it an average of two or three times a week all those years. Probably I was encouraged by the knowledge that there were always four or five pitchers who couldn't get through a car door without crawling on their hands and knees.

Please give my love to Mrs. Hendry and the kids and Robin, and keep a lot for yourself. And please don't ask Florence--I wrote her a five hundred-word letter once and she hasn't sent me a postcard in reply.

I am addressing this to Detroit on advice of Ellis, though my own very good judgment tells me you are still at the lake. Well, you will live just as long if it never reaches you.

Come and see us and I will cook you a meal such as only I can cook--lamb chops, potato salad, pie--just as I cooked for you in Brookline twenty-one (Good heavens!) years ago.

                                        RWL

                              East Hampton
                              Bastille Day
                              [1932]

[To Mildred Luthy]
Dear Millie:-
    Two or three years ago I scolded you for using a comma where a semi-colon belonged (or something) and you were _furious_, so I'm afraid to tell you how your last letter impressed me, or rather, depressed me. Honestly it sounded as if you considered me a perfect or imperfect stranger and when I had finished it, I was amazed that the salutation hadn't been "Dear Mr. Lardner" or "Dear Sir." I won't answer such questions as how do I like my house in its new position or is my interest in radio something new. Listen, Miss, I ain't Dr. Erdmann,[1] with whom you are

_____

[1]A surgeon at Doctors Hospital (see letter of 31 October 1931 to James Lardner).

trying to make dinner conversation. I remember you quite well and can talk to you on much more familiar topics--Ovaltine, for example. Aren't you the lady who once recommended it as a cure for my Intractable Insomnia? Well, the other night (July fourth) I was listening in on Little Orphan Annie and the man said, "If you are going to stay up and see the fireworks tonight, take a glass of Ovaltine before supper and another glass an hour later, and it will keep you wide awake and fresh for the evening's entertainment. Now Millie, this man is employed by the Ovaltine company and he ought to know what the lovely stuff is good for. Yet I can scarcely believe you would try to coax me into consuming a beverage that not only must drive a person to beverages more pleasant, expensive, habit-forming and devastating, but also keep him wide awake and, above, all things, FRESH. I simply am too fond of myself to entertain the thought that you don't remember me a little, and if you do, you surely are aware that I seldom have an ambition to keep wide awake, unless there is a game of setback in prospect, and never fresh. I do think an explanation is in order.

Moreover, I have this against you: One of the reasons I left the hospital before my time was to be in a position to serve as a member of the reception and entertainment committee when you and Jane came to East Hampton. I don't believe the Rices are ever coming but Helga is here and so hard up for work that she insists on inviting our two Danes to have a meal with her once or twice a week. Ellis seldom goes out in the evening and I am afraid she gets quite lonely without Kate. Even when she goes out, I would insist on your staying home and entertaining Jim, Bill and me; I am not suggesting that you wouldn't be invited other places, but merely hoping that your attitude toward parties is the same as it used to be. Dave misses Jane, as also do Liz Wheeler and the other Lardner boys. If you ever did want to go out, I would love to serve as Jane's nurse because it would give me a comfortable sensation of having to do something that isn't work. Please think it over, Millie, and consider carefully that the summer will be over before we know it . . . .

I know a person doesn't always, or often, feel like writing. But please try it again, Millie, and don't treat me as if I were a silent policeman.

R.[1]

In the midst of the Depression, the 1932 political campaigns were especially intense. When Heywood Broun ran for mayor of Hartford on the Socialist ticket, Ring, though nominally a Republican, supported him out of friendship, after which a misunderstanding developed, and Ring was listed in the 9 July 1932 NEW LEADER among a number of contributors who had agreed to

----

[1]No original discovered of this letter. Quoted by Elder, pp. 364-65.

write an article supportive of the Norman Thomas-James
Maurer campaign for a four page weekly tabloid to be
edited by Edward Levinson, then an assistant editor of
the NEW LEADER and to be published during the sixteen
weeks of the campaign. Ring objected in the following
note:

East Hampton, Long Island
July 29, 1932.

Dear Mr. Levinson:-
    I agreed to contribute to the Thomas and Maurer campaign
publication, but did not say I would write on my reasons for
supporting Norman Thomas. If there is any misunderstanding,
please let me know.
                    Sincerely,

    At Broun's request Ring did finally write a rather
facetious letter, which the NEW LEADER published on 5
November 1932 as a statement of political support for
the Socialist party:

RING LARDNER EXPLAINING WHY HE WILL VOTE SOCIALIST

    On November the 8th my vote, as such, is liable to be cast
for the Socialist candidates for president. I have the
impressive figure of Heywood Broun in mind when I say this. The
big fellow, I am told, is very thick with your candidate for
national honors, Norman Thomas, and it seems probable that if the
latter is elected he will take Broun, the rail-splitter, to
Washington with him to occupy some comfortable berth in the
cabinet. As a citizen of New York I feel that Broun's place is
in Washington, and I would be willing to cast three or four votes
and any number of aspersions to get him there.
    My friends reel back in amazement when I tell them, after a
certain amount of preliminary fencing, that I am going to vote
the Socialist ticket. Their comments are not printable, but the
gist is as follows:
    "Your [sic] are just wasting your vote, kid. Who do you
like in the fifth at Empire City?"
    Throwing out the last sentence for reasons of policy, I am
moved to ask in turn:
    "What am I doing when I vote for Hoover or Roosevelt?"
    This, you understand, is strictly between myself and the
Socialist National Campaign committee U.nder [sic] no
circumstances would I care to have such old golfing buddies as
John McCooey and Everett Sanders know that I am planning to knife
them at the polls.
    The other day my doctor, while strapping me to a bed,
pointed out that if Mr. Thomas is elected Mr. Hoover and Mr.
Roosevelt will be out of a job.

"Don't worry, doctor," I replied, recognizing him without
difficulty. "There is a big demand for comedians, and both those
boys will be able to land swell jobs on the radio."

He parried this thrust with a gag from one of the Old Music
Box Revues, and left me composing this campaign plea, which
should stir up no little discussion around White's drug store in
East Hampton. Until you are ready to hand me my piece of
America, I remain,

> Without rancor,
> Ring Lardner.

After a lapse of nearly a year in his
correspondence with Perkins, Ring wrote the following
letter which hints strongly of self-doubt and
depression:

Tuesday, August 16

Dear Max:-

Early in the summer, one of the Post's associate editors
wrote me such a tactless letter, suggesting that the new series
of baseball letters be brought to a conclusion in two more
installments that I, then in a low mental condition, thought the
whole series must be pretty bad though I had felt quite proud of
part of it when I had sent it in. His words were chosen with a
view, I guess, to lessening the shock of the premature
conclusion, whereas if he had written frankly, saying that the
Post could no longer afford to pay the very liberal price it had
set on the series, I would have understood perfectly and thought
little of it. For a time I banished the idea of offering the
series to you for a book, but later on I reread some of the
acceptance letters from Lorimer and other Post editors, as well
as a bunch of nice "fan mail," and got steamed up about it again.
I honestly don't know how the present interest in baseball
compares with the past, but I presume that Brooklyn's recent
spurt (the "hero" is a Brooklyn player) ought to be a help.
Please read the whole thing when you feel strong and healthy and
tell me what you think. I enclose the final installment, which
should be published in a week or so. If Brooklyn wins the
pennant, a book appearing simultaneously with the world's series
might go.

R. L.

Perkins received Ring's letter the next day and
immediately wrote to say that Ring's royalties were due
in December, but that he would send them sooner if Ring
wished. He also commented:

I had always supposed that we would publish
your Saturday Evening Post baseball articles in
early 1933, but because of all the things I have
had to do lately, I only read one, the early one.

I am getting all there are, and probably now the last one has been published. I thought your radio pieces in the New Yorker were extremely good, and read all of them in the idea that they might make a book, but I hardly think so because they deal with such transitory matters.

The "radio pieces" were the often-attacked series of articles Ring wrote in 1932 and 1933 for the NEW YORKER on standards of radio entertainment. They constitute a curious crusade by a dying man against faulty grammar, tastelessness, and sexual allusions in the popular songs over the radio to which Ring listened from his hospital bed. Among the more effective passages in these articles are the memorable parodies of Cole Porter's "Night and Day": "Night and day under the fleece of me/There's an Oh, such a flaming furneth burneth the grease of me . . . . Night and day under my dermis, dear,/There's a spot just as hot as coffee kept in a thermos, dear . . . ."

Thursday, August 18.

Dear Max:-
A check for that $222.73 early next week would be a life-saver; or rather, a life insurance saver. However, if it isn't convenient I can manage to get over the hurdle in some other way.
I mailed you the proof of the final Post installment yesterday or the day before. I hasn't been published yet, but certainly ought to be within three weeks. You are right about the New Yorker stuff--It is much too topical and local for publication in a book.
I am very much steamed up over the news of Zelda's novel[1] and hope you will keep me posted on the date of publication, etc.
Sincerely,
R. L.

Included with the royalty check which Perkins sent five days later was a report from Scribners which indicated a total sale at this point of 20,366 copies of HOW TO WRITE SHORT STORIES, 8,633 copies of WHAT OF IT?, 12,904 copies of THE LOVE NEST, 6,764 copies of THE STORY OF A WONDER MAN, and 15,261 copies of ROUND UP (in addition to the 70,000 copies sold through the Literary Guild).

---

[1]SAVE ME THE WALTZ, which was about to be published by Scribners. It is a strikingly autobiographical account written in about six weeks during Zelda's confinement in a Baltimore hospital after her second breakdown.

Doctors Hospital
East End Avenue at 87th Street, New York
November 5, 1932.

H. L. Mencken,
704 Cathedral Street,
Baltimore, Md.

Dear Henry:
   Your suggestion that we meet far too seldom has been in my
head for ten years. If I ever escape from here I will see what
can be done about it. Meanwhile, kindly publish another book.
                     Sincerely,
                         Ring Lardner
RL:HR
   I think we ought to make it a trio and include that ole devil
H. R. M. Landis of Philly.[1]

        In the following letter to his son James at
   Harvard, Ring demonstrates the high standards that he
   applied to the art of writing popular music:

                         Doctors Hospital
                         New York
                         Sunday.
                         [6 November 1932]

Dear Jim:-
   I enclose an amended version of your song. As I said in my
telegram, I _think_ your refrain begins on the wrong word and on
the wrong beat--Anyway, it's unsingable as you have it, as you
will find out if you try. Your music demands a two-syllable
rhyme scheme (except in the middle eight bars, where you have
written "ritardo"--incidently, you don't want any retard; it
ruins the number as a dance tune). If I were you, I'd rewrite
the music to those middle eight bars, simplifying it: you can
almost do it with a couple of monotones, allowing the harmony to
embellish it, or you can go into an entirely different key--A
flat for instance.
   As the song stands, no one but a man can sing it. To rectify
this fault, write a verse (holding it to eight bars if possible,
but making it sixteen if necessary) in the third person, along
these lines: "Joe Serviss was a handsome brute," then words to
the effect that he had a girl, but he didn't like to work, etc.,
winding up with something like, "And so when he proposed to her,
why this is what he said:" (I guess you'll need sixteen bars to
tell the story). The last word of the verse must come on the
first beat of the eighth or sixteenth bar, and the "Oh,"

----

   [1]Comment in ink at end of letter. Possibly a reference to
the baseball comissioner--"His Royal Majesty" Kenesaw Mountain
Landis.

preceding the refrain, is the last beat in that same bar. The
last note in the verse can be either a quarter, a half or a
dotted half. If not a dotted half, you must put a half rest or a
quarter rest between it and the word "Oh."

In the third bar of the refrain, you will notice that I have
changed the tune to get away from the resemblance to "River
Shannon" and innumerable other songs. If you don't like my
alteration, you can make it four straight Cs, with the harmony to
help it, or C,B,C,B or C,A,C,A or C,F,A,C. (While on the
subject, never mind about the harmony unless you have some
special idea regarding one or two spots. If and when the song
gets to an arranger, he'll do just what he pleases.)

As I told you, your afterthought seventh and eighth bars was
an improvement, and it should also be kept that way in the final
bars of the song.

I think your broken time is a mistake and I have rewritten it
in straight time. As a matter of fact, I wouldn't be surprised
if the tempo oughtn't to be changed to two-four--I am considering
it from the dancing angle. This can be determined, and easily
fixed, later on.

In my version, the title appears in the first and last lines
of the refrain, which always helps a song commercially. However,
you mustn't think this song is commercial in a "big way"--Very
few are these days. But it's too good not to work on, and I may
find one or two people who will introduce it on the radio.

I have taken a few liberties with your words, necessitated by
the swing of the melody and the two-syllable rhymes; I have also
taken a slight liberty with the pronunciation of "robust," but I
think it makes a good finish the way I have it.

One explanatory verse will be enough, but you might be
pondering a second refrain.

On whistling over the refrain, I am "struck" with the thought
that if you use the C,A,F and A third bar, you ought to duplicate
those four notes in the fifth bar (and of course, all the
corresponding bars). But suit yourself.

I think you have a good start and I'm glad to see you working
at something like this. Make the verse simple musically and
COMICAL lyrically. Don't rush.

It's good news that you have even a chance to get on that old
davil dean's list, but if you miss this time, don't let it worry
you.

Who were those ringers that posed as Harvard's team
yesterday? There is one consolation--I won't have to give 3 to 1
on Notre Dame against the Army.

Write when you have time. Your mother is moving into town
day after tomorrow. If you intend to write to her, you'd better
address her here, in care of me. Don't forget to wire me how you
come out with the dean, and when you have fixed this song, send
it back and I'll see what can be done with it.

                    Pa.
Keep me posted on your football. Are you inclined to try

baseball? Fred Mitchell[1] is an old (and queer) friend of mine
and I might get him to pay you a little attention.[2]
    Later: It occurs to me that your idea is to make it a mock
ballad. If so, of course we'll keep it in 4/4 time and mark it
slow.[3]

        On 9 November Mencken wrote saying he would visit
    shortly and promising "some dreadful scandal to tell
    you, some of it relating to persons hitherto regarded
    as impeccable Christians." Ring wrote back:

                        Doctors Hospital
                        East End Ave. at 87th St.
                        New York
                        November 13

Dear Henry:-
    I think the chiropractors will let up on me in about two
weeks. If you will tell me what days you are in New York, I will
telephone and insist that you keep your promise. Meanwhile,
please don't forget the scandal.
                    Sincerely,
                        RL.

        Ring was overly optimistic. His conditioned
    worsened, and at the end of January, he was still
    hospitalized and his doctors were advising that he seek
    a better climate in California.

                    New York, New York
                    December 22, 1932.

Dear Mr. Glaenzer[4]:-
    If you don't mind, I would rather not give permission for the
use of any of my work in Laugh Club publications. I have always
been opposed to any story or volume of stories that guaranteed
the reader laughs, a practice which puts him on the defensive and
is likely to end in alienating whatever affection he may have had
for one's writing. If I had known that "Comic Relief" was to be

----

    [1]Fred Mitchell was a former major league pitcher-catcher who
was then coaching at Harvard.

    [2]This paragraph is a postscript in ink at the close of the
letter.

    [3]This paragraph is a postscript in ink at the top of the
first page.

    [4]Seymour Glaenzer edited the Laugh Club publication, a
series of paperbound anthologies of humor.

peddled on such a basis, I never would have consented to the
inclusion in it of any work of mine.
                    Sincerely,
                    Ring Lardner

NEWYORK NY JAN 30   1933 JAN 31 AM 9 20
H L MENCKEN=
        =704 CATHEDRAL STREET 3RD FLOOR (RD)=
=HAVE SEVENTY FIVE HUNDRED WORD FICTION STORY SO GOOD THAT POST
CCSMOPOLITAN AND COLLIERS DONT WANT IT STOP WOULD YOU LIKE A
CHANCE AT FOURTH REFUSAL STOP IF SO WHERE SHALL I SEND IT STOP
PLEASE WIRE ME CARE DOCTORS HOSPITAL STOP AM LEAVING FOR DESERT
RETREAT NEXT SATURDAY
        =RING LARDNER.

        The next day Ring mailed the story, "Poodle," to
Mencken, with the enclosed letter:

                    Doctors Hospital
                    East End Avenue at 87th Street, New York
                    January 31, 1933.

Dear H:-
        Here's the one-part serial. The Post just didn't seem to
care for it, Bill Lengel[1] said it was swell, but he ain't the
boss, and Collier's objected to its length and tenuousness. What
can you think of? I really advise you not to return it because I
am leaving (by boat) Saturday for the Mojave Desert and it
doesn't look to me as if it would stand a trip that long, or even
one as far as the waste-basket. My address will be La Quinta,
California, and I expect to be there till the first of May.
        Please don't imagine that I didn't appreciate your offer to
come and see me here. To begin with, I was no treat; besides,
the doc wouldn't permit visitors for quite a while, though God
knows you would have done me good, whereas some of the boys and
girls who crashed the gate set me back weeks in half an hour,
finally forcing me to take advice and arrange the impending
hegira. When I return I will remind you of your promise or pay
you a visit I don't owe.
                    Yours,
                    R.L.
After February 4 - La Quinta, Calif.

        Elder quotes from a letter sent the same day to
Lardner's sister Lena in Niles, Michigan:

_____

[1]William Lengel was associate editor of COSMOPOLITAN at that
time.

[31 January 1933]

The doctors think it is necessary for me to get out of this climate and into the desert. So Ellis and I are leaving next Saturday by boat, via the Panama Canal, for California (on borrowed money) and will stay for three months . . . in a dry quiet place, hoping my condition will improve enough to permit me to work again. It is hard to leave John and not to see the other boys occasionally, but I think it will be best in the long run.

The next letter, the last he ever wrote to Max Perkins, is particularly significant for its varying tone. Ring's depressed state of mind over his bad health and declining creative power is evident, but so is his ability to retain his sense of humor.

Doctors Hospital
East End Ave. At 87th St.
New York
February 3, 1933.

Dear Max:-
Some day I will probably realize that there is a depression. I wouldn't have asked you for any advance if I hadn't got into a sudden jam. The doctor and I decided that my place was the desert for a while, and not having done any real work since June, I was obliged to borrow money. I borrowed less than I needed, figuring I would sell a story to the Post. Once I wrote a complete story, "Alibi Ike," between 2 P.M. and midnight, with an hour off for dinner. This last one was begun in July and finished ten days ago, and the Post turned it down just as promptly as it had accepted "Ike." Since then, Bill Lengel has said it was great (but he ain't the boss), Collier's has rejected it as too long and tenuous (It runs 7,500 words) and Mencken has told me it was too much of a domestica symphonica or something for the Mercury. Mr. Graeve[1] (Delineator), suggested, perhaps sarcastically, by Mencken, now has it as a week-end guest and I have asked him to return it to my brother on the Times, who will give it to some poor author's agent to peddle. I have always scoffed at agents, but I am leaving tomorrow morning for La Quinta, California, to be gone till the money has disappeared. I have promised the doctor that I won't work on anything but a play which George Kaufman has been waiting for me to start for three years; of course, I will have to cheat a little, but I can't cheat much.
What I started to say is that the fiction story (really not bad, and just as really not a Pulitzer prize winner) has a great many local stops to make, and if I were to stay here and wait till the last possible purchaser had said no, I would die of

---

[1]Oscar Graeve, editor-in-chief of DELINEATOR.

jitters. Your loan has made it possible for me to get out of here before I am committed to Bellevue, and I am truly grateful. I won't need the "other" two hundred, and if the sale of "Lose With a Smile" never totals the amount you have advanced me, I will see to it that you don't lose. The agent can make the rounds much quicker than I could from 3,500 miles away.

This letter doesn't seem to be properly constructed or quite clear. That is a symptom of my state of mind, but the fact that I can laugh at the succession of turn-downs of a story which everybody but the Post has had a kind word for but no inclination to buy, makes me hopeful for the future. Maybe someday I can write a piece about the story's Cook's Tour--it is the first one I ever wrote that wasn't accepted by the first or second publication to which it was offered, and that either means go west old man or quit writing fiction or both.

Thanks again, and honestly I want you to forget the "balance" because I can easily get along without it.

Will you send me a couple of copies of "Lose With a Smile" when it is published?

Yours, RL

The widely-traveled "Poodle" finally appeared in the January 1934 DELINEATOR. Perkins wrote immediately to Ring's brother Rex offering to publish it in SCRIBNER'S MAGAZINE, but it had already been accepted by DELINEATOR.

Ring's doctors had advised strongly that Ring try the desert climate of La Quinta, California, a resort near Palm Springs. After arriving there Ring wrote another letter to Mencken, which is particularly interesting because of its criticism of New York HERALD-TRIBUNE columnist Lewis Gannett's enthusiastic review of Sinclair Lewis's ANN VICKERS, published a month earlier. Ring recognized the inferiority of this novel to Lewis's best work.

La Quinta
February 28, 1933.

Dear H.- You ought to be a literary agent and I a designer of gowns. I followed your advice about Mr. Graeve of Delineator - in sheer desperation, I must admit, and not with any idea that you were right - and he accepted the story with the comment that it was so unsuitable to his publication that he just couldn't resist it. Thanks.

Inasmuch as I always write on subjects familiar to me and am not at all with either fornication or treachery, I don't see how I can crash the Mercury. But when the Post rejects the next one, I'll at least ask you where to find a sucker.

Listen, Mr. Gannett: In five or ten years, when your judgment is more mature, please re-read "Elmer Gantry" and

"Babbitt," not from the standpoint of a debunker, but from that of a critic of literature and with an eye and ear to faithfulness in characterization, fidelity in dialogue and truth in this, that and the other, and then review both books in a special $1.00 issue, and I'll subscribe for at least six copies.

Yours,

RL.

Mencken agreed: "I begin to have an uneasy feeling that you may be right about the Lewis books. Lewis has made a big success with his last,[1] but it seems to me to be dreadful stuff."

Then Ring wrote to his sons and nephew, Richard Lardner Tobin (who was was then sharing an apartment with John in New York), describing the boat trip from New York to Los Angeles:

February 28, 1933.

Bill, John (and Dickie), David, James:-
This is a circular canary. A what, Baron?[2] An orbicular crow, a spherical sparrow. Baron, are you sure you don't mean a round robin? Why, yes, of course, Charlie! What did you _think_ I meant?

I adopt this method of writing to you little ones because I won't have time to write you separately; besides, I should hate to say something comical to one of you and forget to say it to the others. The order indicated in the salutation is probably the best from a standpoint of speed in transmission. When Bill has read and, perhaps, memorized these words, he is supposed to send them on to John, who, after mumbling them to Dickie, will forward them to David, and the last-named (in every way) will mail them to Jim or, as some call him, the dead letter office. If this proceedure is agreeable to you, I will write once a month, possibly oftener. If it isn't, you can take the consequences. I trust that Bill, John and David will vindicate my judgment in routing by being prompt to re-address and re-mail.

Well, let me tell you that boat-ride was okeh after a storm had laid Mrs. Lardner low the second day out, and would have been more okeh if my feet, unshod since last April, had not swole to elephantine proportions. All the girls on the ship dubbed them the Giant Redwood Trees of California. Yes, the boat-ride was okeh, but don't ever take it just to have a look at the Canal. It is little more than a glorified Sault Ste. Marie, and

---

[1] ANN VICKERS

[2] The Baron/Charlie dialogues in this letter are a take-off on the Baron Munchausen character that Jack Pearl was then doing on the radio.

when you have seen one lock, you have seen two locks, or my hair.
        One afternoon I sat on the prowl pack--Pardon me, Baron; the
what? The sauntering fifty-two cards. Why, Baron, I believe you
are trying to say the promenade deck. That's it, Charlie! The
promenade deck--and I was reading Van Loon's Geography and the
deck steward remarked that it was a great book.   Being a
democratic fellow, I replied to him and observed that one of my
sons had given it to me at Christmas. "Isn't that queer, Mr.
Lardner?" he said. "Because I was planning to give it to one of
my sons for his birthday. That's a paradox." So now you know
what a paradox is. Personally, I had always thought it meant two
physicians in consultation, or just two physicians.
        Warner Baxter[1] was a shipmate and walked twelve or fourteen
laps around the deck each evening before dinner. This is called
the Baxter Mile. Mrs. L. pretended she didn't know who he was,
but she followed him with her eyes every time we turned our
Baxter.   Another mate was Mr. Collins, treasurer of the Curtis
Publishing Company. He introduced himself to me and I tactfully
said, "Oh, have they still got a treasurer?" This may result in
the S. E. Post's rejecting a new story I mailed last Thursday.
I recall telling some of you chaps that the story before this one
was rejected by the Post, Cosmopolitan, Collier's and the
Mercury, the two middle ones saying it was too long, as it
certainly was, and Mencken saying it was not his style. But he
suggested that I try Delineator, adding that women's magazines
were the only ones making money. I didn't know whether
Delineator was a weekly or a college year book, but I followed
Mencken's advice and tried it, and it accepted the story, the
editor remarking that it was so unsuitable for his magazine that
he couldn't bear to turn it down. He paid, or is going to pay,
one-fourth of the Post's price and, according to him, four or
three times as much as Mencken would have paid. So, fellows, we
have crashed Delineator and there are no more worlds to conquer.
        The boat landed at San Diego at noon of Friday the 17th and
stayed there long enough to permit the madam and myself to go to
the races at Aqua Caliente. At that dismal joint the finishing
touches were put to my feet by a half-mile walk almost straight
up hill. We would have quit even on the day but for the presence
in the seventh race of a horse named June Moon. Golden Prize or
something was favorite and I would have played him but for the
June Moon hunch, as favorites were doing pretty well.   Little
Ellis, always timid, wanted me to play June Moon for show, she
urging that June Moon had been a show. I urged right back that
it had also been a straight play. For one instant I had a flash
to bet on Golden Prize to win and June Moon to show, and that is
exactly what they did, but I neglected Golden Prize and played
June Moon across the board, and the show money barely paid for
itself.

_____

[1]The movie star

If I could afford the trip, I would go in to Los Angeles, now that Vidmer's[1] here, and shoot him. They would never suspect me, because I would have to go barefooted and they would think I was a Hollywood boy. Don't get chesty, John, for winning arguments from your sports department, unless you win one from George Daley,[2] who Sees Everything, Knows Everything, Is Everything. I done tol' your ol' mammy that you had written most of Bill Macbeth's Corbett stuff. Jim was really a good old soul who made good in vaudeville because he had sense enough to act as straight man instead of trying to be the comic; the team of him and Billy Van was actually worth seeing. His eating habits, such as two helpings of coffee, doughnuts and wheatcakes in the Lambs at one or two in the morning, were not conducive to longevity.

I am sorry (still addressing John) that Gannett appeared to like your book.[3] I was hoping he would pannett. But you can bet that F. Adams wouldn't have said it was funny if he hadn't thought so, and he is anything but a bad judge. However, I will do my own judging when, if ever, I see the book. I presume, and hope, I'll get most of the reviews in my clippings. Remember my advice and don't give first refusal rights to any of those publishers, unless they pay you for them, and even then, don't tie up for more than one or two books with a decent firm, such as Farrar and Rinehart or Simon and Schuster.

I had a letter yesterday from your ma, Dickie, who said, among other important things, "D. S. Schoffern is dear and Oh, the difference to me!" Having known her for forty-seven years, man and boy scout, I am aware that when she writes "dear" she means "dead." We are all a-flitter to see the "Peter Stuyvesant Review," or whatever the name of it is.

Bill, how about finishing in Group 1 or Group 2 this semester? They tell me it's almost impossible not to at Princeton.

Dave, for my sake and dear old Andover (sometimes they call her Nancy) get a new picture taken so I can destroy the one of the noseless Jap which now makes our parlor table a living Bedlam on horseback.

Jim, we received one, not two, cables from you and what we'd like to receive is a letter stating what marks you got in each

---

[1] Richards Vidmar was a sportswriter and columnist on the HERALD-TRIBUNE. Whatever dispute Ring or John Lardner may have had with him is unknown.

[2] George Dailey had become sports editor of the HERALD-TRIBUNE in 1931. He introduced the all-star football game to New York.

[3] John's book was THE CROWNING OF TECHNOCRACY, by John Lardner and Thomas Sugrue.

and every subject. Soon I shall write to Tom Shaw or Jack Doyle[1]
and ascertain the pre-season odds on the clubs in each league
(some of them, I mean) and possible parlays such as the
Yankees-Pittsburgh, the Yankees-Cubs. I wish some one would tell
me whom Brooklyn got in exchange for Vance.[2] Brooklyn, my lads,
is not out of the race yet. It came pretty close last year
without much help from the Doozzler.

We are expecting a visit soon from Claudette and Norman,[3] and
possibly one from Jean Dixon.

Meanwhile, the play's[4] the thing
Which is worrying the life out of your
Shoeless Uncle Ring.

The National League race, I say, is between Pittsburgh and
Brooklyn, which the acquisition of Joe Judge will strengthen. In
the other league, watch the Red Sox so Cocky Collins won't have
to do it alone.

Ring also wrote at this time to Jean Dixon, in
Hollywood:

La Quinta
March seventh.

Dear Jean:-
The vague address on this envelope was given me by a Mr.
Kaufman of the Pulitzer Prize Kaufmans. I have no doubt it is
wrong because his mind, at the time, was occupied with what he
thinks of as the London Horror, which consists in the fact that
it takes <u>six minutes</u> longer to play a performance of "Dinner at
Eight" over there than in New York. I tried to comfort him with
the suggestion that it was owing to the difference in longitude,
but he continued to mope.

My earnest wish is that when a few of my ailments show signs
of improvement under the desert sun, as promised, you will be
nice enough to pay me and Madame X a visit. We have no
inducements excepting decent food and absolute quiet, so much of

----

[1]Sports promoters. Doyle was founder of the famous Vernon
Arena frequented by motion picture stars, sports figures, and
celebrities for many years.

[2]After winning twelve and losing eleven games for Brooklyn
in 1932, the popular Clarence "Dazzy" Vance had been traded to
the St. Louis Cardinals.

[3]Claudette Colbert and Norman Foster had been close friends
with Ring since Foster had played the lead in JUNE MOON. Colbert
was on the eve of a distinguished film career.

[4]A new effort with George Kaufman.

the latter, in fact, that I am afraid the joint won't stay open as long as I want it to. No doubt you have been at Palm Springs; we are eighteen miles east of it. Some people drive here from Los Angeles in five hours. For myself, I prefer the ease and luxury of railroad travel, and the Southern Pacific has a convenient train (quaintly termed "The Apache") which leaves Los Angeles at 12:15 and arrives at Indio (our nearest railway station) at 4:29. Are you still good-hearted enough to make such a trip when I am in better condition to act as genial host?

I pass my sitting-up hours at the typewriter, working on the first act of a future Pulitzer winner. George has promised that if I can complete an act and a half that are worth tearing to bits, he will come out here to do the tearing. I have a secret hunch that he wants to come anyway, so perhaps the act and 1/2 need not be as good as normally.

Ring

The play on which Ring was working was, interestingly enough, about a reformed alcoholic who falls off the wagon as an act of revolt against a lack of human sympathy and understanding on the part of his fiancee's family. Ring had written one act of this play and a fragment of a second act before he died.

March 29, 1933

Bill, John, Dickie, David and James:- Would you like to know what I have been doing lately? (Oh, goodness, what has father dad unk popsie wopsie been doing lately?) Well, occasionally working on the first draft of the first act of a play, and now I am on the 23rd page of rewriting, which is just about one-third of the way through. For this first act, my burdens, is nearly an hour and a half long in its present plight, which will give Mr. Kaufman the opportunity he lacked in "June Moon" of masticating and spitting out five and six pages at a time. I would have been in the midst of Act 2, the comical act, if hell had't popped loose a fortnight ago. Possibly as an aftermath of the temblors (if you think you're pronouncing that word right, look it up) things began happening in La Quinta and as they are things that might happen to anybody named Mr. and Mrs. Ring Lardner who came to the place called La Quinta in search of absolute La Quieta, I will outline them by way of warning (via Warneke):

Vincent Lawrence, former playwright, now Hollywood scenarist, and Dorothy Speare, novelist, entered our hut uninvited and wanted to know whether I had an idea for Harold Lloyd. Mr. Lawrence wrote his last picture, "Movie Crazy" or something; it was a flop, so Harold came back to him for more. I said I had no idea, but would try to think of one. I did think of one and it was a good one; so I thought and so Mr. Lawrence thought. However, it is well-known (to me, at least) that I can't tell things in synopsis form, or any other form--I have to write them out at length.

Well, a week ago Sunday came. The Rices were visiting us, I think. So was Phillips Holmes. So, suddenly, were Mr. Lawrence, Miss Speare, Harold Lloyd, Sam Harris,[1] some anonymous girl, and Louella O. Parsons and her latest husband, one Dr. Martin, who says he knew me in Chicago, which he did not if I am any judge. Louella also said that when she was working on the Chicago Tribune, she and I used to go on lots of parties together, which we did not if I am any judge.

Harold was all steamed up over my having an idea, and I was all steamed up over the same miracle, but when he and I managed to get a moment alone, it developed that all he wanted was the bare idea, told in two paragraphs (as he phrased it) and his scenarists and gag men would attend to the rest. Well, to be modest, this was like sending Babe Ruth to bat and letting him stand there till the umpire had called one ball, then taking him out and substituting a good hitter. Harold and I both steamed down as quickly as he had up--and I had wasted two or three days of thinking and writing. Unless, as Mr. Lawrence suggests, Buster Keaton can be caught sober and interested in the same idea, which remains, yours sincerely, a good idea, reeking with gags that Harold and his gag men wouldn't think of in a month of Sundays, and if there were a month of Sundays, you could all call yourselves Little Orphan Annie.

Now Louella's interview with G. B. Shaw at the Hearst ranch may have been printed in papers to which you have access. If not, you are much obliged to me for the following excerpt from it, to appreciate which you must know that if Louella is fifty-five years old, she's fifty-six: "'Mr. Shaw,' I said, 'is it true that Gene Tunney was the original of Cashel Byron?'[2] 'Young woman,' he replied, 'Cashel Byron was superannuated before you and Tunney were born.'"

Bill--Does this projected publication promise you or anyone else a living wage? Would you room and board at the Swopes'?

John--What's this I hear about you and one Sorghum having written a tune or a book called "The Crooning of Telegraphy"? If there is such a product, who is hoarding it?

Dickie--I imagine that Mr. Daley did Mr. Vidmer an injustice. The latter probably wrote a story about a ball game and it sounded like a story about an earthquake. All your baseball writers are tricky.

David--Please rush me a photograph of yourself. Ellis is mad and I am glad because I tore up a caricature of a noseless Jap which she was telling the waiters was sa jungest kind.

---

[1]Sam Harris was a Broadway producer who won three Pulitzer Prizes for ICEBOUND (1923), OF THEE I SING (1932), and YOU CAN'T TAKE IT WITH YOU (1937).

[2]Cashel Byron was the protagonist in George Bernard Shaw's novel of the same name.

James--If you get a bronze medal for defaulting to a Swiss in a consolation bout, why not stay away from the meets and win a Cecil Pulitzer scholarship?

Anxious

"Myrt," to whom the following letter is addressed, was Lizabeth Vereen, the sister of Kate Rice.

La Quinta, Calif.
Saturday, April first.
[1933]

Dear Myrt:-

The enclosed is not just a cash prize for you, but the Lardners will be much obliged if you will turn it over to your sister Kate. It is a debt we owe her and please tell her not to send it back again - That would simply mean returning it to her, and so on ad infinitum.

Today the thermometer registered 100 in the shade (I don't know where they found the shade) and everybody was saying how wonderful! a temperature like that and you don't feel it! Well, Mrs. Vereen, this one felt it and longed for the refreshing breezes of an August afternoon in Macon. I must admit, though, that when the sun has disappeared behind our mountain, the weather is invariably perfect, as advertised.

With the slump in picture production, most of Hollywood can be found in La Quinta. Our next door neighbors all week have been Lilya Tashman and Edmund Lowe,[1] who, I presume, are married. Mr. Lowe had grown fat - a terrible blow, Ellis says, to the waitresses at the hotel. Miss Tashman, when she whispers, can be heard in Seattle and today she lost her diamond and emerald broach, which was no whispering matter. I am told she is supposed to be the best-dressed of all the picture people. She would look better to me in a soiled old Mother Hubbard than the beautifully pressed trousers she always wears.

We were expecting Floncey this week-end, but haven't heard from her. Norman and Claudette (Colbert or Foster) are coming tomorrow to spend the day with us. It will be an excuse for me not to work. Poor Norman had an automobile accident two weeks ago and knocked out a couple of front teeth. He is to start work Monday on a new picture and had put in a pleasant week at the dentist's - a secret from his producers.

_____

[1]Lilyan Tashman came out of the Follies in 1917 to appear in several Broadway musicals before she went to Hollywood. She met and married Edmund Lowe while they were both making PORTS OF CALL. He was already established as a leading man in films. She died in 1934.

The other enclosure[1] (the one without Lincoln's picture) will tell you the latest news of me - and to me. The writer is evidently a fellow from whom you simply can't keep a secret. But I do resent being called police dog, or dog of any kind.

I hope all the Hollises are well and that Mr. Crisp is much better. Love to everybody, including Mrs. Vereen.

A Born Hater.

La Quinta, California.
Sunday, April 9.

Dear James:-

I think I promised to tell you the official odds on the pennant races as soon as they were told to me. Here, then, they are:

Yankees, 1 to 3; Washington, 3± to 1; Athletics, 4 to 1.

----

[1]Enclosed with the above letter was the following newspaper clipping:

Hate Is Back of Ring Lardner's Fun; He Hates His Characters, Says Writer

Ring Lardner, who is said to do his writing from a sick-bed somewhere in the west, is popularly regarded as a funny man. But hear Clifton Fadiman's opinion in this week's The Nation. Fadiman says:-

The special force of Ring Lardner's work springs from a single fact; he just doesn't like people. Except Swift, no writer had gone farther on hatred alone. I believe he hates himself; more certainly he hates his characters; and most clearly of all, his characters hate each other. There is no mitigating soft streak in him as there is in the half-affectionate portraitures of Sinclair Lewis; and none of the amused complacency of H. L. Mencken.

He has found nothing whatsoever in American life to which to cling. Other writers who reveal this masochist pattern in a less pure form are George S. Kaufman and F. Scott Fitzgerald. But neither of these is cursed with Lardner's intuitive knowledge of the great American swine . . . .

Read beneath the lines and you will see that everything he meets or touches drives him into a cold frenzy, leaving him without faith, hope or charity.

What Lardner, even in his simplest magazine stories, is interested in getting at is the core of egotism from which even our apparently most impeccable virtues spring.

Somewhere Lardner had a remark about "this special police dog" which "was like the most of them and hated everybody." Lardner himself is the police dog of American fiction, except that his hatred is not the product of mere crabbedness but of an eye that sees too deep for comfort.

Pittsburgh, 2 to 1; Cubs the same; St. Louis, 3 to 1; Brooklyn, 6 to 1; Giants, 4 to 1.

Parlays: Yankees with Pittsburgh or Chicago, 3 to 1; Yankees with St. Louis, 4± to 1; Yankees with Brooklyn, 8 to 1.

The price on the Yankees makes things tough. Yet, counting them as safe, I could make bets that would insure me an even break (if the Cubs or Pittsburgh won) or a profit (if St. Louis or Brooklyn won). There's no fun to that, however, so I'm playing the Yankees straight and parlaying them besides with Pittsburgh and Brooklyn. If the Yankees lose, you will find my body in a sour apple tree. If they win and my National League selections lose, I'll be ahead a trifle. If they win and Pittsburgh wins, it will be quite nice. And if they win and Brooklyn wins, it will be lovely.[1]

We are starting for home the end of this week and after making brief stop-overs in Niles and Detroit, will reach New York on or about the 24th. I will probably hang around the metropolis a week, to see Dr. Gerber, Dr. Tyson and Dr. Kaufman, but your mother will go to East Hampton and that is where you had better address future letters, of which I hope there will be a great many.

I'd like to know how you are getting along with your strenuous course.

Popsy.

When Ring and Ellis returned to New York, Ring did indeed see his dentist ("Dr. Gerber"), his physician ("Dr. Tyson"), and George Kaufman (about the new play on which they were working). A passage from an unlocated letter "to a friend," quoted by Donald Elder,[2] was probably written at this time, and exhibits Ring's desire professionally and personally to "keep on going":

Ellis is in East Hampton and I am staying in town for two reasons--one is a long-delayed session with the dentist, which will last at least two weeks, and the other to play with George the first two acts of our next collaboration. I am fortunate, I guess, to be one of the chosen to work with him. There are flocks of more experienced playwrights seeking his partnership and the only thing that wins consideration for me is the fact that he keeps promises and as soon as we had finished "June Moon," we agreed to do another one on a subject I had in mind--as

---

[1] Unfortunately, the Washington Senators beat out the second place Yankees by seven games in the American League, and the New York Giants finished five games ahead of Pittsburgh in the National League. Brooklyn finished sixth, twenty-six and a half games back. The Giants won the Series, four games to one.

[2] Elder, pp. 282-83.

soon as I got around to it, which has been a long, long time.   I
only   hope   I   can stay well enough to work.   If I can, I promise
you and the rest of the world one thing: that never again will I
take a vacation when I am through with a job.   I think it is   the
biggest   mistake   a   person   can   make--not to keep on going.   I
never felt better in my life than when I was working twenty hours
a day, trying to get "June Moon" into shape, and never felt worse
than afterwards, when it was in shape and I treated myself   to   a
"layoff," which was mostly spent in the lovely atmosphere of
hospitals.

        In June Ring returned to East Hampton, where, since
it was the beginning of summer vacation, the boys had
gathered too, except for John, who was in nearby New
York. Ring was quite weak, and was mostly confined   to
his workroom and sleeping porch, overlooking the ocean.

        Of   the   following letter Richard Lardner Tobin
writes:

            This letter . . . was written from East
        Hampton in either the late spring or early summer
        of 1933, just before Mr.   Lardner died.   As   he
        indicated in the letter, he has just left Doctors
        Hospital for East Hampton, where he died September
        25, 1933.   I find it fascinating, (and I remember
        it to be true), that Ring Lardner was writing
        lyrics for Jerome Kern, but I don't for a moment
        doubt it because he was, obviously, intensely
        musical. The quote 'Jim' mentioned in the first
        paragraph is Ring's second son, James, who was
        later killed in the International Brigade in Spain
        and, about this time, an unhappy student at Harvard
        -- unhappy because he knew more about literature
        than the people who were teaching him.

                            [East Hampton
                            Late spring or early summer of 1933]
                            Solomon Gr--dy.

Dear Dickie:-
    Attached are two or three documents[1] of value to you and   me.
The envelope is sent in the hope you will see it to its way via
the New York PO. I don't dare send it from here or   Jerome   Kern
would have to put the lyrics enclosed into his farewell opus and
while Jim is home for the week-end giving it to him is like
sending it to the dead letter office.

----

    [1]The "documents" were some lyrics Jerome Kern apparently did
not use, and a check for Richard Lardner Tobin.

Sherwood Anders-n and Rabbit Maranville paid calls before I left No Visitors, N. Y., for this bed o' pain. Anders-n and I got to talking why we'd ever left our small towns. Maranville says the Yankees are a cinch so he isn't putting up anything on them. I've got what the boys call a yard and a half unless Doyle wiggles out, and he's trying.

Claudette Colbert was in town before I left and came up to say hello. I never knew they was so many interns in Doctors' Hospital. Every five seconds a new one would come in and say, "Can't I get you some icewater, Mr. Lardner?" or "I'm going out, would you like anything from the drug store?" Her hair is now pink but she's cute, anyway.

Your aberrated mother hasn't send me any of your clippings but I caught one Sunday under a by-line. Good stuff, congratulations. When you see my son John tell him we now have mail delivery in East Hampton.

Ring.

Ring Lardner
East Hampton, Long Island
Thursday, July twentieth.
[1933]

[To Mildred Luthy]
Dear Millie:-

The young man who said "Hello, Sweetheart" to you on the telephone doubtless knew whom he was addressing and wanted a little encouragement. When you replied to him so cruelly, he had to think of an explanation that would salve his wounded pride.

Your child is really beautiful and has the Hollis charm, which means that hundreds of members of my poor sex will suffer. If I didn't know how bored and uncomfortable it would make her, I would insist on her visiting me at least once a day, just so I could hear her talk and see her close up. I have refrained from demanding her presence (except once) because I don't want her to think of me as an old pest, but lots of times I watch and admire her from my cell without interfering with her normal activities. I offered to answer all the letters she got from Americus if she would let me read them all. She accepted the offer but evidently changed her mind.

This is a gala night in East Hampton, with Floncey opening in the local stock company's play. Enough people to fill the theater are going from the Rice and Lardner houses. As usual, the undersigned will have to be satisfied with hearing about it. Floncey has a much bigger part than in "June Moon" and I presume Kate is quite nervous, probably more so than the artiste herself.

John's vacation begins next Monday and on Thursday, Albert[1] and all the Lardners excepting the old man are leaving by

---

[1] Albert Mayer, the Lardners' chauffeur for more than twenty years.

automobile for Chicago and the Fair. They intend to see how cheaply they can make the trip, for two reasons - the "fun" of the experiment and the fact that they won't have anything to spend. Two Scandinavians and I will have the house to ourselves for a couple of weeks, and I'll bet you can't guess my plans for the first two or three days and nights. After that I may accept the hospitality of the Rices for one meal (they haven't invited me yet), but I am terrified while I am there because, as you know, they are never safe from invasion by people I used to like, but who, in my old age, make me jittery. There is simply no sense in a person's reaching the anti-social state I seem to have attained and if I had any will power, I would snap out of it.

Which subject naturally leads to the Boswell Sisters.[1] Did you know they were in London, singing in a night club? That is, they were till Connie got the mumps. I imagine it improved her looks, but interfered with her singing and, worst of all, with her interesting conversations on the Life and Loves of Connie Boswell.

Lizabeth,[2] who does not make me jittery, has been kind enough to obey my positive orders to call. I think she looks very well, infinitely better than last time she was here. The other night, Ellis went to Kate's to play backgammon, and I made Liz come here and play contract with Bill, Him and me. Before the game she protested that she knew nothing about it, and then proceded to show up the Lardners. She and I gave my little ones a good beating, and I assure you it was her doings, not mine.

Please give my love to your mother and tell her I think of her often and particularly when there is a beautiful moon, such as we had earlier in the month. One of you told me she was a moon lover and it makes me proud to know we have that taste in common - as well as a few others.

Try to get well and strong for your trip up here, and arrange to stay a long, long time.

                                        R.

The next letter is explicitly a reply to a letter from Dorothy Dudley Harvey, whose book DREISER AND THE LAND OF THE FREE, published in 1932, contained this statement: "Ring Lardner, asked by a producer to serve with Dreiser and Robert Frost as one of three founders of an American theatre for only American plays, refused

---

[1]Connee, Vet (Helvetia), and Martha Boswell, an internationally-known singing trio, were among the first to introduce swing. Connee, the trio's soloist and arranger, overcame a childhood paralysis to be the motivating force in the trio.

[2]Lizabeth Vereen, Kate Rice's sister

on the ground that Dreiser was both ridiculous and immoral."[1]

East Hampton, Long Island
July 21, 1933.

Dear Mrs. Harvey:-
    Honestly I have a dozen real alibis for not having answered your letter before, but I won't bore you with them. I do hope, though, that you haven't taken my silence as consent to the report in your book of my attitude toward Mr. Dreiser. I am telling you the truth when I say that I can't recall ever having heard of the Art Theater you mention, and the true explanation of your sister's story must be either that some one was impersonating me or I was under an anaesthetic. Never consciously did I speak of Mr. Dreiser's work as repellent to me in any way. I have never met him, but have had some very pleasant (to me) correspondence with him. I have undoubtedly expressed the opinion, in private conversations, that I thought his style awkward. Otherwise I admire him intensely for the drama of his writing and its wealth of detail. I am sorry to add that your book never reached me and probably was held up somewhere along the route taken by your letter.
                            Sincerely,
                                Ring Lardner

        A few days later Ring sent a telegram to Mrs. Hollis:

EASTHAMPTON NY   1933 JUL 31 PM 4 20
MRS FLORENCE D HOLLIS=
    AMERICUS GA=
AN ASTRONOMER IS GOING TO TELL US ALL ABOUT THE MOON THURSDAY NIGHT OVER NEWYORK STATION WJZ NINE FIFTEEN YOUR TIME STOP THE MOON WILL BE NEARLY FULL THAT NIGHT STOP IF HE SAYS ANYTHING YOU DONT LIKE LET ME KNOW AND I WILL ECLIPSE HIM STOP LOVE=
    RING.

        In the June 1933 AMERICAN MERCURY, Mencken had praised Ring's LOSE WITH A SMILE, arguing mainly that Ring would eventually be acknowledged by literary critics as a major American writer. One month and a day before Ring died, he wrote to thank Mencken:

----

    [1]Dorothy Dudley, DREISER AND THE LAND OF THE FREE (New York: Smith and Haas, 1932), p. 470.

                                        East Hampton, Long Island
                                        August 24, 1933

Dear H.-
     It is almost time I thanked you for that piece about the
baseball book, which you know perfectly well did not deserve any
of the space you gave it. Believe it or not, I appreciated it
more than the checks it brought from Brother Lorimer
                                        Yours,
                                             R. L.

          The same day Ring wrote what may have been his last
     letter. It is addressed to a Miss Wilma Seavey, who
     later became Mrs. Paul Ogden. She had written to Ring
     as a result of a friendly argument with her future
     husband over Ring's attitude toward his characters.
     His response is of particular importance, because it
     constitutes his only direct comment on Clifton
     Fadiman's interpretation of Ring's work.

                                        East Hampton, Long Island
                                        August 24, 1933

Dear Miss Seavey:-
     I must apologize for delaying so long in answering your
letter, but my health has prevented me from attending to my
correspondence for the last few months.
     I don't suppose any author either hates or loves all his
characters. I try to write about people as real as possible, and
some of them are naturally more likeable than others. In regard
to your argument, I think the decision should be awarded to you,
because I cannot remember ever having felt any bitterness or
hatred toward the characters I have written about. I am grateful
to you for your defense of me.
                              Yours Sincerely,
                              Ring Lardner

          Though Ring had seemed better at first after the
     stay in La Quinta, he now began to decline repidly.
     Miss Feldmann, who was a trained nurse, returned late
     in the summer to care for him. His last written
     communication was probably the following telegram
     congratulating John for a front-page story John had
     written for the HERALD-TRIBUNE:

                              EASTHAMPTON NY AUG 31-518 P
JOHN LARDNER:
          HERALD TRIBUNE NYK
     Very proud of my sons eclipse of suns eclipse on page one.
          STOOPNAGLE.

On the evening of 24 September, after Jim and David had departed for their fall terms at Harvard and Andover, Ring played some bridge with Ellis, Ring, Jr., and Kate Rice. The next morning he suffered a heart attack and, later that day, he died. He was forty-eight.

INDEX

LT: Letters To

LF: Letters From

Williams, Churchill, 160.
  LT 160, 162
Williams, James, 18
Wills, Harry, 224
Wilson, Edmund, 177, 182, 228
Wilson, Harry Leon, 160n
Winchell, Walter, 241
Wood, Barry, 261
Woollcott, Alexander, 178, 218
Woodford, Louise, 11
Woodruff, Harry, 179
Wright, Harold Bell, 180
Wylie, Elinor, 238

Wynn, Ed, 204
Yost, Fielding, 260, 262-63
Yost, Walter, 199
YOU KNOW ME AL, 140, 156, 188,
  195, 269n
Youmans, Vincent, 210, 243-46,
  256
YOUNG IMMIGRUNTS, THE, 152, 154,
  156, 166, 188, 190, 195
YOUNG VISITERS, THE, 153, 195
Ziegfeld, Florenz, 203-04, 210,
  219, 223, 225, 243-45, 250